HOMOSEXUALITY

A Cross Cultural Approach

Donald Webster Cory
is the author of
The Homosexual in America

HOMOSEXUALITY

A CROSS CULTURAL APPROACH

DONALD WEBSTER CORY

THE JULIAN PRESS, INC., PUBLISHERS
New York

Published by The Julian Press Inc.
80 East 11th Street, New York 3

Copyright 1956 by The Julian Press Inc.

Printed in the United States of America

CONTENTS

Introduction   vii
    Donald Webster Cory

A Problem in Modern Ethics   3
    John Addington Symonds

Homosexual Love   101
    Edward Westermarck

The Intermediate Sex   139
A Study of Some Transitional Types of Men and Women
    Edward Carpenter

Terminal Essay   207
The Book of the Thousand Nights and a Night
    Richard Burton

The Perversions of Love   248
    Paolo Mantegazza

Male Homosexuality in Ancient Greece   267
    Hans Licht

The Love Called "Socrates"   350
    Voltaire

Defensive Homosexuality   354
Homosexuality as a Defense Against Incest
    Gilbert Van Tassel Hamilton, M.D.

Criteria for a Hormonal Explanation   370
    Alfred C. Kinsey

Pastoral Counseling for Homosexuals   384
    George W. Henry, M.D.

Homosexuality, Sodomy and Crimes Against Nature   394
    Morris Ploscowe

Are Homosexuals Necessarily Neurotic?   407
    Albert Ellis

The Influence of Heterosexual Culture   415
    Albert Ellis

Homosexual Attitudes and Heterosexual Prejudices   420
    Donald Webster Cory

Changing Attitudes Toward Homosexuals   427
    Donald Webster Cory

INTRODUCTION

When Clellan S. Ford and Frank A. Beach collaborated on *Patterns of Sexual Behavior,* they used what they called a "cross cultural approach." In other words, they studied the behavior of human beings (and of other species as well) so far as sexual activities and attitudes are concerned, as these patterns were manifested in primitive tribes of Africa, the South Sea Islanders, Eskimoes, and in other groups or societies whose cultures interest anthropologists.

In the collection presented in this book, there is a cross cultural approach to one particular aspect of sexual behavior. This approach is quite different from the approach of Ford and Beach. For the attitude of various cultures toward any phenomenon is not merely a matter of investigating the aboriginal societies of Peru or some isolated group of bushmen in Australia, but it is of equal interest to study the attitudes (as shown in the writings) of French libertarians, Eighteenth Century scientists, mid-Victorian moralists, or Twentieth Century theologians. Such a cross section of thinking is presented in this volume.

The selections found in any anthology are personal, and the words of the collector can only serve as an apologia, even if they are not so intended. Let the few who read an introductory note be patient, as I explain the purpose of the collection and the choice. I sought, in this anthology, first to resurrect from the past the most important gems of writing on homosexuality; those that have been buried in books long out-of-print, sometimes forgotten, sometimes difficult to obtain, frequently expurgated—which gems, as I saw them, best expressed the thinking and the attitudes of a given cultural pattern. Let us, for example, cite Edward Carpenter, whose little book, *The Intermediate Sex,* is reprinted fully in this volume. If Carpenter is interpreted as being one of the first to make an outspoken, though outmoded, plea for homosexuals, his book may be interesting, but its significance is lost. For above all else, Carpenter was the high priest of Puritanism within the realm of an innately anti-Puritanical group. He expresses the result of mid-Victorian culture, and this is apparent in all he writes. And if Carpenter is read as the spokesman for that culture, one can gain a broader understanding of the changing attitude toward (and of) homosexuals over the centuries. It is the same with Burton and his historical essay; with Mantegazza and the first scientific investigations; with Voltaire and his philosophical dictionary; with Symonds and his daring inquiry.

So much for the past. What of the few modern, shorter pieces? It was my hope to continue the approach of the various cultural groups, by bringing forth the viewpoints of psychoanalysts, psychologists, jurists, and others. They, too, in a professional sense, are mirrors of cultural attitudes.

The pieces collected here seem to me to be of more than passing interest. In some cases I have included material of my own since I felt the need for reviewing some of my own ideas. In other cases materials were included because of the intrinsic merit of the viewpoints, or because of the historical importance of the men who expressed them. With some of the items, particularly the older ones, and with a few of the modern writings, I have made some brief comments as editor's notes.

Donald Webster Cory

New York
December 1955

HOMOSEXUALITY

A Cross Cultural Approach

A PROBLEM
IN
MODERN ETHICS

John Addington Symonds

FROM THE ORIGINAL PIRATED ISSUE (LIMITED PRINTING, 1896, LONDON) SUPPRESSED BY H. F. BROWN. THIS EDITION WAS PRINTED WITHOUT SYMONDS NAME ON TITLE PAGE.

1. INTRODUCTION

There is a passion, or a perversion of appetite, which, like all human passions, has played a considerable part in the world's history for good or evil; but which has hardly yet received the philosophical attention and the scientific investigation it deserves. The reason for this may be that in all Christian societies the passion under consideration has been condemned to pariahdom. Consequently, philosophy and science have not considered it dignified to make it the subject of special enquiry.

Only the Greek race, to whom we owe the inheritance of our ideas, succeeded in raising it to the level of chivalrous enthusiasm. Nevertheless, we find it present everywhere and in all periods of history. We cannot take up the religious books, the legal codes, the annals, the descriptions of the manners of any

3

nation, whether large or small, powerful or feeble, civilized or savage, without finding it in one form or other. Sometimes it assumes the calm and dignified attitude of conscious merit, as in Sparta, Athens, Thebes. Sometimes it skulks in holes and corners, hiding an abashed head and shrinking from the light of day, as in the capitals of modern Europe. It confronts us on the steppes of Asia, where hordes of nomads drink the milk of mares; in the bivouac of Keltish warriors lying wrapped in wolves' skins round their camp-fires; upon the sands of Arabia where the Bedoiun raise desert dust in flying squadrons. We discern it among the palm groves of the South Sea Islands; in the card houses and temple gardens of Japan; under Eskimos' snow-huts; beneath the sultry vegetation of Peru; beside the streams of Shiraz and the waters of the Ganges; in the cold clear air of Scandinavian winters. It throbs in our huge cities. The pulse of it can be felt in London, Paris, Berlin, Vienna, no less than in Constantinople, Naples, Teheran, and Moscow. It finds a home in Alpine valleys, Albanian ravines, Californian canyons, and gorges of Caucasian mountains. It once sat, clothed in imperial purple, on the throne of the Roman Cæsars, crowned with the tiara on the chair of St. Peter. It has flaunted the heraldries of France and England, in coronation ceremonies at Rheims and Westminster. The royal palaces of Madrid and Aranjuez could tell their tales of it. So do the ruined courtyards of Granada and the castle-keep of Avignon. It shone with clear radiance in the gymnasium of Hellas, and nerved the dying heroes of Greek freedom for their last forlorn hope upon the plains of Chæronea. Endowed with inextinguishable life, in spite of all that has been done to suppress it, this passion survives at large and penetrates society, makes itself felt in every quarter of the globe where men are brought into communion with men.

Yet no one dares to speak of it; or if they do, they bate their breath, and preface their remarks with maledictions.

Those who read these lines will hardly doubt what passion

it is that I am hinting at. *Quod semper ubique et ab omnibus* —surely it deserves a name. Yet I can hardly find a name which will not seem to soil this paper. The accomplished languages of Europe in the nineteenth century supply no term for this persistent feature of human psychology, without importing some implication of disgust, disgrace, vituperation. Science, however, has recently—within the last twenty years in fact— invented a convenient phrase, which does not prejudice the matter under consideration. It is called "inverted sexual instinct;" and with this neutral nomenclature this investigator has good reason to be satisfied.

Inverted sexuality, the sexual instinct diverted from its normal channel, directed (in the case of males) to males, forms the topic of the following discourse. The study will be confined to modern times, and to those nations which regard the phenomenon with religious detestation. This renders the enquiry peculiarly difficult, and exposes the enquirer, unless he be a professed expert in diseases of the mind and nervous centres, to almost certain misconstruction. Still, there is no valid reason why the task of statement and analysis should not be undertaken. Indeed, one might rather wonder why candid and curious observers of humanity have not attempted to fathom a problem which faces them at every turn in their historical researches and in daily life. Doubtless, their neglect is due to natural or acquired repugnance, to feelings of disgust and hatred, derived from immemorial tradition, and destructive of the sympathies which animate a really zealous pioneer. Nevertheless, what is human is alien to no human being. What the law punishes, but what, in spite of law, persists and energizes, ought to arrest attention. We are, all of us, responsible to some extent for the maintenance and enforcement of our laws. We are as evolutionary science teaches, interested in the facts of anthropology, however repellant some of these may be to our own feelings. We cannot evade the conditions of atavism and heredity. Every family runs the risk of producing a boy or a girl, whose life will be embittered by inverted sexuality, but who in all other respects will be no worse or better than the normal members of the home. Surely, then, it is our duty and our interest to learn what we can about its nature, and to arrive through comprehension at some rational method of dealing with it.

2. CHRISTIAN OPINION

Since this enquiry is limited to actual conditions of contemporary life, we need not discuss the various ways in which sexual inversion has been practically treated by races whose habits and religions are unlike our own.

On the other hand, it is important to obtain a correct conception of the steps whereby the Christian nations, separating themselves from ancient paganism, introduced a new and stringent morality into their opinion on this topic, and enforced their ethical views by very formidable legal prohibitions.

Without prejudging or prejudicing this new morality, now almost universally regarded as a great advance upon the ethics of the earlier pagan world, we must observe that it arose when science was nonexistent, when the study of humanity had not emerged from the cradle, and when theology was in the ascendant. Therefore, we can not expect any delicate distinctions, anthropological investigations, psychological analysis, or spirit of toleration. It simply decreed that what hitherto had been viewed as immorality at worst should henceforth be classed among crimes against God, nature, humanity, and the state.

Opening the Bible, we find severe penalties attached to sexual inversion by the Mosaic law, in the interests of population and in harmony with the Jewish theory of abominations. The lesson is driven home by the legend of Sodom and Gomorrah, overwhelmed with fire because of the population's addiction to abnormal sexual indulgence. Here the *vindices flammæ* of the Roman code appear for the first time—the stake and the flames, which mediæval legislation appointed for offenders of this sort.

St. Paul, penetrated with Hebrew ethics, denounced the corruption of the Gentiles in these words: "For this cause God gave them up into vile affections: for even their women did change the natural use into that which is against nature; and likewise also the men, leaving the natural use of the woman, burned in their lust one toward another; men with men working that which is unseemly, and receiving in themselves that recompence of their error which was meet."

Christ uttered no opinion upon what we now call sexual inversion. Neither light nor leading comes from Him, except such as may be indirectly derived from his treatment of the woman taken in adultery.

When the Empire adopted Christianity, it had therefore the traditions of the Mosaic law and the first chapter of the Epistle to the Romans to guide its legislators on this topic. The Emperors felt obscurely that the main pulses of human energy were slackening; population tended to dwindle; the territory of the empire shrank slowly year by year before their eyes. As the depositaries of a higher religion and a nobler morality, they felt it their duty to stamp out pagan customs, and to unfurl the banner of social purity. The corruption of the Roman cities had become abominable. The laziness and cowardice of Roman citizens threatened the commonwealth with ruin. To repress sexual appetites was not the ruler's object. It was only too apparent that these natural desires no longer prompted the people to sufficient procreation or fertility. The brood begotten upon Roman soil was inadequate to cope with the inrushing tide of barbarians. Wisdom lay in attempting to rehabilitate marriage, the family domestic life. Meanwhile a certain vice ran riot through society, a vice for which Jehovah had rained fire and brimstone upon Sodom, a vice which the Mosaic code punished with death, a vice threatened by St. Paul with "that recompence of their error which was meet."

Justinian, in 538 A.D., seems to have been terrified by famines, earthquakes and pestilences. He saw, or professed to see, in these visitations the avenging hand of Jehovah, the "recompence which was meet" mysteriously prophesied by St. Paul. Thereupon he fulminated his edict against unnatural sinners, whereby they were condemned to torments and the supreme penalty of death. The preamble to his famous Novella 77 sets forth the principles on which it has been framed: "Lest, as the result of these impious acts, whole cities should perish together with their inhabitants; for we are taught by Holy Scripture, to know that through these acts cities have perished with the men in them. . . . It is on account of such crimes that famines and earthquakes take place, and also pestilences."

Before Justinian, both Constantine and Theodosius passed laws against sexual inversion, committing the offenders to "avenging flames." But these statutes were not rigidly enforced, and modern opinion on the subject may be said to flow from Justinian's legislation. Opinion, in matters of custom and manners, always follows law. Though Imperial edicts could not eradicate a passion which is inherent in human nature, they had the effect of stereotyping extreme punishments in all the codes of Christian nations, and of creating a permanent social antipathy.

3. VULGAR ERRORS

Gibbon's remarks (upon the legislation of Constantine, Theodosius, and Justinian) supply a fair example of the way in which men of learning and open mind have hitherto regarded what, after all, is a phenomenon worthy of cold and calm consideration. "I touch," he says, "with reluctance, and despatch with impatience, a more odious vice, of which modesty rejects the name, and nature abominates the idea." After briefly alluding to the morals of Etruria, Greece, and Rome, he proceeds to the enactments of Constantine: "Adultery was first declared to be a capital offence . . . . the same penalties were inflicted on the passive and active guilt of pederasty; and all criminals, of free or servile condition, were either drowned, or beheaded, or cast alive into the avenging flames." Then, without further comment, he observes: "The adulterers were spared by the common sympathy of mankind; but the lovers of their own sex were pursued by general and pious indignation." "Justinian relaxed the punishment at least of female infidelity: the guilty spouse was only condemned to solitude and penance, and at the end of two years she might be recalled to the arms of a forgiving husband. But the same Emperor declared himself the implacable enemy of unmanly lust, and the cruelty of his persecution can scarcely be excused by the purity of his motives. In defiance of every principle of justice, he stretched to past as well as future offences the operations of his edicts, with the previous allowance of a short respite for confession and pardon. A painful death was inflicted by the amputation of the sinful instrument, or the insertion of sharp reeds into the pores and tubes of most exquisite sensibility." One consequence of such legislation may be easily foreseen. "A sentence of death and infamy was often founded on the slight and suspicious evidence of a child or a servant: the guilt of the green faction, of the rich, and of the enemies of Theodora, was presumed by the judges, and pederasty became the crime of those to whom no crime could be imputed."

This state of things has prevailed wherever the edicts of Justinian have been adopted into the laws of nations. The Cathari, the Paterini, the heretics of Provence, the Templars, the Fraticelli were all accused of unnatural crimes, tortured into confession, and put to death. Where nothing else could be adduced against an unpopular sect, a political antagonist, a wealthy corporation, a rival in literature, a powerful party-leader, unnatural crime was insinuated, and a cry of "Down with the pests of society" prepared the populace for a crusade.

It is the common belief that all subjects of sexual inversion have originally loved women, but that, through monstrous debauchery and superfluity of naughtiness, tiring of normal pleasure, they have wilfully turned their appetites into other channels. This is true about a certain number. But the sequel of this essay will prove that it does not mean by far the larger proportion of cases, in whom such instincts are inborn, and a considerable percentage in whom they are also inconvertible. Medical jurists and physicists have recently agreed to accept this as a fact.

It is the common belief that a male who loves his own sex must be despicable, degraded, depraved, vicious, and incapable of humane or generous sentiments. If Greek history did not contradict this supposition, a little patient enquiry into contemporary manners would suffice to remove it. But people will not take this trouble about a matter, which, like Gibbon, they "touch with reluctance and despatch with impatience." Those who are obliged to do so find to their surprise that "among the men who are subject to this deplorable vice, there are even quite intelligent, talented, and highly-placed persons, of excellent and even noble character." The vulgar expect to discover the objects of their outraged animosity in the scum of humanity. But these may be met with every day in drawing-rooms, law-courts, banks, universities, mess-rooms; on the bench, the throne, the chair of the professor; under the blouse of the workman, the cassock of the priest, the epaulettes of the officer, the smock-frock of the ploughman, the wig of the barrister, the mantle of the peer, the costume of the actor, the tights of the athlete, the gown of the academician.

It is the common belief that one, and only one, unmentionable act is what the lovers seek as the source of their unnatural gratification, and that this produces spinal disease, epilepsy, consumption, dropsy, and the like. Nothing can be more mistaken, as the scientifically reported cases of avowed and adult sinners amply demonstrate. Neither do they invariably or even usually prefer the *aversa Venus;* nor, when this happens, do they exhibit peculiar signs of suffering in health. Excess in any venereal pleasure will produce diseases of nervous exhaustion and imperfect nutrition. But the indulgence of inverted sexual instincts within due limits, cannot be proved to be especially pernicious. Were it so, the Dorians and Athenians, including Sophocles, Pindar, Æschines, Epaminondas, all the Spartan kings and generals, the Theban legion, Pheidias, Plato, would have been one nation of rickety, phthisical, dropsical paralytics. The grain of truth contained in this vulgar error is that, under the prevalent laws and hostilities of modern society, the inverted passion has to be indulged furtively, spasmodically, hysterically; that the repression of it through fear and shame frequently leads to habits of self-abuse; and that its unconquerable solicitations sometimes convert it from a healthy outlet of the sexual nature into a morbid monomania. It is also true that professional male prostitutes, like their female counterparts, suffer from local and constitutional disorders.

It is common belief that boys under age are specially liable to corruption. This error need not be confuted here. Anyone who chooses to read the cases recorded by Casper-Liman, Casper in his *Novellen*, Krafft-Ebing, and Ulrichs, or to follow the developments of the present treatise, or to watch the manners of London after dark, will be convicted of its absurdity. Young boys are less exposed to dangers from the abnormal than young girls from normal voluptuaries.

It is common belief that all subjects from inverted instinct carry their lusts written in their faces; that they are pale, languid, scented, effeminate, painted, timid, and oblique in expression. This vulgar error rests upon imperfect observation. A certain class of such people are undoubtedly feminine. From their earliest youth they have shown marked inclination for the habits and the dress of women; and when they are adult, they do everything in their power to obliterate their manhood. It is equally true that such unsexed males possess a strong attraction for some abnormal individuals. But it is a gross mistake to suppose that all the tribe betray these attributes. The majority differ in no detail of their outward appearance, physique, or dress, from normal men. They are athletic, masculine in habits, frank in manner, passing through society year after year without arousing a suspicion of their inner temperament. Were it not so, society would long ago have had its eyes opened to the amount of perverted sexuality it harbours.

The upshot of this discourse on vulgar errors is that popular opinion is made up of a number of contradictory misconceptions and confusions. Moreover, it has been taken for granted that "to investigate the depraved instincts of humanity is unprofitable and disgusting." Consequently the subject has been imperfectly studied; and individuals belonging to radically different species are confounded in one vague sentiment of reprobation. Assuming that they are all abominable, society is contented to punish them indiscriminately. The depraved debauchee who abuses boys receives the same treatment as the young man who loves a comrade. The male prostitute who earns his money by extortion is scarcely more condemned than a man of birth and breeding who has been seen walking with soldiers.

4. LITERATURE—DESCRIPTIVE

Sexual inversion can boast a voluminous modern literature, little known to general readers. A considerable part of this is pornographic, and need not arrest our attention. But a good deal is descriptive, scientific, historic, anthropologic, apologetic, and polemic. With a few books of each of these, I propose to deal now.

The first is written by a French official, who was formerly Chief of the Police Department for Morals in Paris. M. Carlier, for ten years, had excellent opportunities for studying the habits of professional male prostitutes and those who frequented them. He has condensed the results of his experience in seven chapters, which offer a revolting picture of vice and systematized extortion in a great metropolis.

"In the numerous books," says M. Carlier, "which treat of prostitution, the antiphysical passions hitherto have been always deliberately omitted. Officially, public opinion does not recognise them, the legislature will take no notice of them. The police are left alone to react against them; and the unequal combat may some day cease, since it is supported by no text of the code and no regulation of the state. When that happens, pederasty will become a calamity far more dangerous, more scandalous, than female prostitution, the organization of which it shares in full. A magistrate once declared that "in Paris it is the school where the cleverest and boldest criminals are formed;" and, as a matter of fact, it produces associations of special scoundrels, who use it as the means of theft and *chantage*, not stopping short of murder in the execution of their plots."

It will be seen from this exordium that M. Carlier regards the subject wholly from the point of view of prostitution. He has proved abundantly that male prostitution is organized in Paris upon the same system as its female counterpart, and he has demonstrated that this system is attended with the same dangers to society.

A violent animus against antiphysical passions makes him exaggerate these dangers, for it is clear that normal vice is no less free from sordid demoralisation and crimes of violence than its abnormal twin-brother. Both are fornication; and everywhere, in Corinth as in Sodom, the prostitute goes hand in hand with the bully, the robber, and the cutthroat.

With reference to the legal position of these passions in France, he says: "Pederasty is not punished by our laws. It can only come within the reach of the code by virtue of circumstances under which it may be practised. If the facts take place in the presence of witnesses, or in a place open to public observation, there will be an outrage to decency. If minors are seduced, there may be proof of the habitual incitement of minors to debauch, corrupt, or even rape. But the passion itself is not subject to penalty; it is only a vice arising from one of the seven deadly sins. We have no intention of analysing this perverted instinct. Since the law does not regard it, we will do like the law. We will pass in silence all its private details, occupying ourselves only with what meets the eye, with what may be called a veritable prostitution."

M. Carlier describes the two main classes, which in France are known as *tantes* and *amateurs*. The former are subdivided into minor branches, under the names of *jésus, petits jésus, corvettes* (naval), soldiers. The latter, called also *rivettes*, are distinguished by their tastes for different sorts of *tantes*.

Those who are interested in such matters may turn to M. Carlier's pages for minute information regarding the habits, coteries, houses of debauch, bullies, earnings, methods of extortion, dwellings, balls, banquets, and even wedding-parties of these people. A peculiar world of clandestine vice in a great city is revealed; and the authentic documents, abundantly presented, render the picture vivid in its details. From the official papers which passed through M. Carlier's bureau during ten years (1860-70), he compiles a list of 6342 pederasts who came within the cognizance of the police: 2049 Parisians, 3709 provincials, 484 foreigners. Of these 2532, or more than the half, could not be convicted of illegal acts.

While devoting most of his attention to professionals who dress like women, and have become exactly similar to the effeminated youth described in *Monsieur Vénus*, Carlier gives some curious details about the French army. Soldiers are no less sought after in France than in England or in Germany, and special houses exist for military prostitution both in Paris and the garrison towns. Upon this point it should be remarked that Carlier expresses a very strong opinion regarding the contagiousness of antiphysical passion. And certainly many facts known about the French army go to prove that these habits have been contracted in Algeria, and have spread to a formidable extent through whole regiments.

In conclusion, M. Carlier, though he so strongly deplores the impunity extended by French law to sexual inversion, admits that this has not augmented the evil. Speaking about England, where legal penalties are heavy enough, he says: "Though they call it the *nameless crime* there, it has in England at least as many votaries as in France, and they are quite as depraved."

5. LITERATURE—MEDICO-FORENSIC

Carlier's book deals with the external aspects of inverted sexuality, as this exists in Paris under the special form of prostitution. The author professes to know nothing more about the subject than what came to his notice in the daily practice of his trade as a policeman. He writes with excusable animosity. We see at once that he is neither a philosopher by nature, nor a man of science, but only a citizen, endowed with the normal citizen's antipathy for passions alien to his own. Placed at the head of the Bureau of Morals, Carlier was brought into collision with a tribe of people whom he could not legally arrest, but whom he cordially hated. They were patently vicious; and (what was peculiarly odious to the normal man) these degraded beings were all males. He saw that the public intolerance of "antiphysical passions," which he warmly shared, encouraged an organized system of *chantage*. Without entertaining the question whether public opinion might be modified, he denounced the noxious gang as pests of society. The fact that England, with her legal prohibitions, suffered to the same extent as France from the curse of "pederasty," did not make him pause. Consequently, the light which he has thrown upon the subject of this treatise only illuminates the dark dens of male vice in a big city. He leaves us where we were about the psychological and ethical problem. He shows what deep roots the passion strikes in the centres of modern civilization, and how it thrives under conditions at once painful to its victims and embarrassing to an agent of the police.

Writers on forensic medicine take the next place in the row of literary witnesses. It is not their business to investigate the psychological condition of persons submitted to the action of the laws. They are concerned with the law itself, and with those physical circumstances which may bring the accused within its operation, or may dismiss him free from punishment.

Yet their function, by importing the quality of the physician into the sphere of jurisprudence, renders them more apprehensive of the underlying problem than a mere agent of police. We expect impartial scientific scrutiny in such authorities, and to some extent we find it.

The leading writers on forensic medicine at the present time in Europe are Casper (edited by Liman) for Germany, Tardieu for France, and Taylor for England. Taylor is so reticent upon the subject of unnatural crime that his handbook on *The principles and practice of medical jurisprudence* does not demand minute examination. However, it may be remarked that he believes false accusations to be even commoner in this matter than in the case of rape, since they are only too frequently made the means of blackmailing. For this reason he leaves the investigation of such crimes to the lawyers.

Both Casper and Tardieu discuss the topic of sexual inversion with antipathy. But there are notable points of difference in the method and in the conclusions of the two authors. Tardieu, perhaps because he is a Frenchman, educated in the school of Paris, which we have learned to know from Carlier, assumes that all subjects of the passion are criminal or vicious. He draws no psychological distinction between pederast and pederast. He finds no other name for them, and looks upon the whole class as voluntarily degraded beings, who, for the gratification of monstrous desires, have unsexed themselves. A large part of his work is devoted to describing what he believes to be the signs of active and passive immorality in the bodies of persons addicted to these habits. It is evident that imagination has acted powerfully in the formation of his theories. But this is not the place to discuss their details.

Casper and Liman approach the subject with almost equal disgust, but with more regard for scientific truth than Tardieu. They point out that the term pederast is wholly inadequate to describe the several classes of male persons afflicted with sexual inversion. They clearly expect, in course of time, a general mitigation of the penalties in force against such individuals. According to them, the penal laws of North Germany on the occasion of their last revision, would probably have been altered, had not the jurists felt that the popular belief in the criminality of pederasts ought to be considered. Consequently, a large number of irresponsible persons, in the opinion of experts like Casper and Liman, are still exposed to punishment by laws enacted under the influence of vulgar errors.

These writers are not concerned with the framing of codes, nor again with the psychological diagnosis of accused persons. It is their business to lay down rules whereby a medical authority, consulted in a doubtful case, may form his own view as to the guilt or innocence of the accused. Their attention is therefore mainly directed to the detection of signs upon the bodies of incriminated individuals.

This question of physical diagnosis leads them into a severe critique of Tardieu. Their polemic attacks each of the points which he attempted to establish. I must content myself by referring to the passage of their work which deals with this important topic. Suffice it here to say that they reject all signs as worse than doubtful, except a certain deformation of one part of the body, which may possibly be taken as the proof of habitual prostitution, when it occurs in quite young persons. Of course they admit that wounds, violent abrasions of the skin, in certain places, and some syphilitic affections strongly favour the presumption of a criminal act. Finally, after insisting on the insecurity of Tardieu's alleged signs, and pointing out the responsibility assumed by physicians who base a judgment on them, the two Germans sum up their conclusions in the following words: "It is extremely remarkable that while Tardieu mentions 206 cases, and communicates a select list of 19, which to him exhibit these peculiar conformations of the organs, he can only produce one single instance where the formation seemed indubitable. Let any one peruse his 19 cases, and he will be horrified at the unhesitating condemnations pronounced by Tardieu." The two notes of exclamation which close this sentence in the original are fully justified. It is indeed horrifying to think that a person, implicated in some foul accusation, may have his doom fixed by a doctrinaire like Tardieu. Antipathy and ignorance in judges and the public, combined with erroneous canons of evidence in the expert, cannot fail to lead in such cases to some serious miscarriage of justice.

Passing from the problem of diagnosis and the polemic against Tardieu, it must be remarked that Casper was the first writer of this class to lay down the distinction between inborn and acquired perversion of the sexual instinct. The law does not recognize this distinction. If a criminal act be proved, the psychological condition of the agent is legally indifferent— unless it can be shown that he was clearly mad and irresponsible, in which case he may be consigned to a lunatic asylum instead of the jail. But Casper and Liman, having studied the question of sexual maladies in general, and given due weight to the works of Ulrichs, call attention to the broad differences which exist between persons in whom abnormal appetites are innate and those in whom they are acquired. Their companion sketches of the two types deserve to be translated and presented in a somewhat condensed form.

"In the majority of persons who are subject to this vice, it is congenital; or at any rate the sexual inclination can be followed back into the years of childhood, like a kind of physical hermaphroditism. Sexual contact with a woman inspires them with real disgust. Their imagination delights in handsome young men, and statues or pictures of the same. In the case of this numerous class of pederasts, there is no depraved fancy at work, no demoralization through satiety of natural sexual appetite. Their congenital impulse explains the fact, moreover, that very many pederasts are addicted to what may be termed a Platonic voluptuousness, and feel themselves drawn towards the object of their desire with a warmth of passion more fervent than is common in the relations of the opposed sexes; that, in other cases again, they are satisfied with embracements, from which they derive a mutual pleasure. Westphal maintains that this anomalous direction of the sexual appetite is more often the symptom of a psychopathic, neuropathic condition than people commonly suppose."

"In the case of another class of men, upon the contrary, the taste for this vice has been acquired in life, and is the result of oversatiety with natural pleasures. People of this stamp sometimes indulge their gross appetites alternately with either sex. I once observed a man, after contracting a venereal disease with women, adopt pederasty out of fear of another infection; but he was, it must be admitted, a weak-minded individual. In all the great towns of Europe the vice goes creeping around, unobserved by the uninitiated. It appears that there is no inhabited spot of the globe where it may not be discovered. I said, unobserved by the uninitiated, advisedly. In antiquity, the members of the sect had their own means of mutual recognition. And at the present time, these men know each other at first sight; moreover, they are found everywhere, in every station of society, without a single exception. 'We recognize each other at once,' says the writer of a report which I shall communicate below: 'A mere glance at the eye suffices; and I have never been deceived. On the Rigi, at Palermo, in the Louvre, in the Highlands of Scotland, in Petersburg, at the port of Barcelona, I have found people, never seen by me before, and whom I discriminated in a second.' Several men of this sort whom I have known (continues Casper) are certainly accustomed to dress and adorn themselves in a rather feminine way. Nevertheless, there are indisputable pederasts, who present an entirely different aspect, some of them elderly and negligent in their attire, and people of the lower classes, distinguished by absolutely nothing in their exterior from other persons of the same rank."

Medicojuristic science made a considerable step when Casper adopted this distinction of two types of sexual inversion. But, as is always the case in the analysis of hitherto neglected phenomena, his classification falls far short of the necessities of the problem. While treating of acquired sexual inversion, he only thinks of debauchees. He does not seem to have considered a deeper question—deeper in its bearing upon the way in which society will have to deal with the whole problem—the question of how far these instincts are capable of being communicated by contagion to persons in their fullest exercise of sexual vigour. Taste, fashion, preference, as factors in the dissemination of anomalous passions, he has left out of his account. It is also, but this is a minor matter, singular that he should have restricted his observations on the freemasonry among pederasts to those in whom the instinct is acquired. That exists quite as much or even more among those in whom it is congenital.

However, the upshot of the whole matter is that the best book on medical jurisprudence now extant repudiates the enormities of Tardieu's method, and lays it down for proved that "the majority of persons who are subject" to sexual inversion come into the world, or issue from the cradle, with their inclination clearly marked.

6. LITERATURE—MEDICINE

Medical writers upon this subject are comparatively numerous in French and German literature, and they have been multiplying rapidly lately. The phenomenon of sexual inversion is usually regarded in these books from the point of view of psychopathic or neuropathic derangement, inherited from morbid ancestors, and developed in the patient by early habits of self-abuse.

What is the exact distinction between "psychopathic" and "neuropathic" I do not know. The former term seems intelligible in the theologian's mouth, the latter in a physician's. But I cannot understand both being used together to indicate different kinds of pathologic diathesis. What is the soul, what are the nerves? We have probably to take the two terms as indicating two ways of considering the same phenomenon; the one subjective, the other objective; "psychopathic" pointing to the derangement as observed in the mind emotions of its subject; "neuropathic" to the derangement as observed in anomalies of the nervous system.

It would be impossible, in an essay of this kind, to review the whole mass of medical observation, inference, and speculation which we have at our command. Nor is a layman, perhaps, well qualified for the task of criticism and comparison in a matter of delicacy where doctors differ as to details. I shall therefore content myself with giving an account of four of the most recent, most authoritative, and, as it seems to me, most sensible studies. Moreau, Tarnowsky, Krafft-Ebing, and Lombroso take nearly similar views of the phenomenon; between them they are gradually forming a theory which is likely to become widely accepted.

Des aberrations du sens génésique, par le Dr. Paul Moreau,
4th edition, 1887.

Moreau starts with the proposition that there is a sixth sense, "le sens génital," which, like other senses, can be injured psychically and physically without the mental functions, whether affective or intellectual, suffering thereby. His book is therefore a treatise on the diseases of the sexual sense. These diseases are by no means of recent origin, he says. They have always and everywhere existed.

He begins with a historical survey, which, so far as antiquity is concerned, is very defective. Having quoted with approval the following passage about Greek society:

"La sodomie se répand dans toute la Grèce; les écoles des philosophes deviennent des maisons de débauche, et les grands exemples d'amitié légués par le paganisme ne sont, pour la plupart, qu'une infâme turpitude voilée par une sainte apparence:" having quoted these words of Dr. Descuret, Moreau leaves Greece alone, and goes on to Rome. The state of morals in Rome under the empire he describes as *"une dépravation maladive, devenue par la force des choses héréditaire, endémique, épidémique."* Then follows a short account of the emperors and their female relatives. *"Cet éréthisme génésique qui, pendant près de deux siècles, régna à l'état épidémique dans Rome"* he ascribes mainly to heridity. Of Julia, the daughter of August, he says, *"Peut-on lutter contre un état morbide héréditaire?"* The union of unrestrained debauchery and ferocity with great mental gifts strikes him as a note of disease; and he winds up with this sentence:*"Parmi les causes les plus fréquentes des aberrations du sens génital, l'hérédité tient la première place."*

Then he passes to the middle ages, and dwells upon the popular belief in *incubi* and *succubi*. It is curious to find him placing Leo X, François I, Henri IV, Louis XIV, among the neuropathics. When it comes to this, everybody with strong sexual instincts, and the opportunity of indulging them, is a nervous invalid. Modern times are illustrated by the debaucheries of the Regency, the reign of Louis XV, Russian ladies, and the Marquis de Sade. The House of Orleans seems in truth to have been tainted with hereditary impudicity of a morbid kind. But if it was so at the end of the last century, it has since the revolution remarkably recovered health—by what miracle?

Moreau now formulates the thesis he wishes to prove: *"L'aberration pathologique des sentiments génésiques doit être assimilée complètement à une névrose, et, comme telle, son existence est compatible avec les plus hautes intelligences.*" He discovers hereditary taint universally present in these cases. "*Hérédité directe, hérédité indirecte, hérédité transformée, se trouve chez les génésiaques.*"

Passing to etiology, he rests mainly upon an organism predisposed by ancestry, and placed in a milieu favourable to its morbid development. Provocative causes are not sufficient to awake the aberration in healthy organisms, but the least thing will set a predisposed organism on the track. This I may observe seems to preclude simple imitation, upon which Moreau afterwards lays considerable stress; for if none but the already tainted can be influenced by their milieu, none but the tainted will imitate.

What he calls "general physical causes" are (1) extreme poverty, (2) age, (3) constitution, (4) temperament, (5) seasons of the year, (6) climate, (7) food.

Extreme poverty leads to indiscriminate vice, incest, sodomy, etc. That is true, and we know that our city poor and the peasants of some countries are habitually immoral. Yet Moreau proves too much here. For according to his principles, hereditary neurosis ought by this time to have become chronic, epidemic, endemic, in all the city poor and in all the peasants of all countries; which is notably not the fact. Puberty and the approach of senility are pointed out as times when genesiac symptoms manifest themselves. His observations upon the other points are commonplace enough; and he repeats the current notion that inhabitants of hot climates are more lascivious than those of the North.

Among "individual physical causes," Moreau treats of malformation of the sexual organs, diseases of those organs, injuries to the organism by wounds, blows, poisons, masturbation, excessive indulgence in venery, and exaggerated continence.

When we come to "general moral causes," heredity plays the first part. This may be direct; *i.e.,* the son of a genesiac will have the same tastes as his father: or transformed; what is phthisis in one generation assuming the form of sexual aberration in another. Bad education and exposure to bad examples, together with imitation, are insisted on more vaguely.

The "individual moral causes" include impressions received in early youth, on which I think perhaps Moreau does not lay sufficient stress, and certain tendencies to subjective preoccupations with ideal ideas, certain abnormal physical conditions which disturb the whole moral sensibility.

Passing to pathologic anatomy, Moreau declares that it is, as yet, impossible to localize the sexual sense. The brain, the cerebellum, the spinal marrow? We do not know. He seems to incline toward the cerebellum.

It is not necessary to follow Moreau in his otherwise interesting account of the various manifestations of sexual disease. The greater part of these have no relation to the subject of my work. But what he says in passing about "pederasts, sodomites, sapphists," has to be resumed. He reckons them among "a class of individuals who cannot and ought not to be confounded either with men enjoying the fullness of their intellectual faculties, or yet with madmen properly so called. They form an intermediate class, a mixed class, constituting a real link of union between reason and madness, the nature and existence of which can most frequently be explained only by one word: heredity." It is surprising, after this announcement, to discover that what he has to say about sexual inversion is limited to Europe and its moral system, "having nothing to do with the morals of other countries where pederasty is accepted and admitted." Literally, then, he regards sexual inversion in modern Christian Europe as a form of hereditary neuropathy, a link between reason and madness; but in ancient Greece, in modern Persia and Turkey, he regards the same psychological anomaly from the point of view, not of disease, but of custom. In other words, an Englishman or a Frenchman who loves the male sex must be diagnosed as tainted with disease; while

Sophocles, Pindar, Phedias, Epaminondas, Plato are credited with yielding to an instinct with was healthy in their times because society accepted it. The inefficiency of this distinction in a treatise of analytical science ought to be indicated. The bare fact that ancient Greece tolerated, and that modern Europe refuses to tolerate sexual inversion, can have nothing to do with the etiology, the pathology, the psychological definition of the phenomenon in its essence. What has to be faced is that a certain type of passion flourished under the light of day and bore good fruits for society in Hellas; that the same type of passion flourishes in the shade and is the source of misery and shame in Europe. The passion has not altered; but the way of regarding it morally and legally is changed. A scientific investigator ought not to take changes of public opinion into account when he is analysing a psychological peculiarity.

This point on which I am insisting—namely that it is illogical to treat sexual inversion among the modern European races as a malady, when you refer its prevalence among Oriental peoples and the ancient Hellenes to custom—is so important that I shall illustrate it by a passage from one of Dr. W. R. Huggard's *Essays*. "It may be said that the difference between the delusion of the overpowering impulse in the Fijian and in the insane Englishman is that, in the savage, the mental characters are caused by education and surroundings; while, in the lunatic, they are the result of disease. In a twofold manner, however, would this explanation fail?

On the one hand, even if in the Fijian there were disease, the question of insanity could not arise in regard to a matter considered by his society to be one of indifference. It would be absurd to talk of homicidal mania, of nymphomania, and of kleptomania, as forms of insanity, where murder, promiscuous intercourse, and stealing are not condemned.

"On the other hand, the assumption that insanity is always the result of disease is not merely an unproved, but an improbable supposition. There must, of course, be some defect of organism; but there is every reason to think that, in many cases, the defect is of the nature of a congenital lack of balance between healthy structures; and that many cases of insanity might properly be regarded as a kind of 'throw-back' to a type of organization now common only among the lower races of mankind." Substitute any term to indicate sexual inversion for "nymphomania" in this paragraph; and the reasoning precisely suits my argument. It is interesting, by the way, to find this writer agreeing with Ulrichs in his suggestion of a "congenital lack of balance between healthy structures," and with Lombroso in his supposition of atavistic reversion to savagery. Lombroso, we shall see, ultimately identifies congenital criminality (one form of which is sexual aberration in this theory) with moral insanity; and here Dr. Huggard is, unconsciously perhaps, in agreement with him: for he defines insanity to be "any mental defect that renders a person unable (and not capable of being made able by punishment) to conform to the requirements of society"—a definition which is no less applicable to the born criminal than to the madman.

How little Dr. Moreau has weighed the importance of ancient Greece in his discussion of this topic, appears from the omission of all facts supplied by Greek literature and history in the introduction to his essay. He dilates upon the legends recorded by the Roman emperors, because these seem to support his theory of hereditary malady. He uses Juvenal, Tacitus, Suetonius, and the Augustan Histories to support his position, although they form part of the annals of a people among whom "pederasty was accepted and admitted." He ignores the biographies of the Spartan kings, the institutions of Crete, the Theban Sacred Band, the dialogues of Plato, the anecdotes related about Pheidias, Sophocles, Pindar, Demosthenes, Alcibiades, etc. Does he perhaps do so because they cannot in any way be made to square with his theory of morbidity? The truth is that ancient Greece offers insuperable difficulties to theorists who treat sexual inversion exclusively from the points of view of neuropathy, tainted heredity, and masturbation. And how incompetent Dr. Moreau is to deal with Greek matters may be seen in the grotesque synonym he has invented for pederasty-*philopodie*. Properly, the word is compounded of *philein* and *poup*; but I suppose it is meant to suggest *philein* and *podech*.

In a chapter on legal medicine, Moreau starts by observing that "the facts are so monstrous, so tainted with aberration, and yet their agents offer so strong an appearance of sound reason; occupy such respectable positions in the world; are reputed to enjoy such probity; such honourable sentiments, etc., that one hesitates to utter an opinion." Proceeding further, he considers it sufficiently established that: "Not unfrequently, under the influence of some vice of organism, generally of heredity, the moral faculties may undergo alterations, which, if they do not actually destroy the social relations of the individual, as happens in cases of declared insanity, modify them to a remarkable degree, and certainly demand to be taken into account, when we have to estimate the morality of these acts." His conclusion therefore is that the aberrations of the sexual sense, including its inversion, are matters for the physician rather than the judge, for therapeutics rather than punishment, and that representatives of the medical faculty ought to sit upon the bench as advisers or assessors when persons accused of outrages against decency come to trial. "While we blame and stigmatize these crimes with reason, the horrified intellect seeks an explanation and a moral excuse (nothing more) for such odious acts. It insists on asking what can have brought a man honourably known in society, enjoying (apparently at least) the fullness of his mental faculties, to these base and shameful self-indulgences. We answer: Such men for the most part have abnormal intelligences; are veritable candidates for lunacy, and, what is more, they are subjects of hereditary maladies. But let us cast a veil over a subject so humiliating to the honour of humanity!"

As the final result of this analysis, Moreau classifies sexual inversion with erotomania, nymphomania, satyriasis, bestiality, rape, profanation of corpses, etc., as the symptom of a grave lesion of the procreative sense. He seeks to save its victims from the prison by delivering them over to the asylum. His moral sentiments are so revolted that he does not even entertain the question whether their instincts are natural and healthy though abnormal. Lastly, he refuses to face the aspects of this psychological anomaly which are forced upon the student of ancient Hellas. He does not even take into account the fact, patent to experienced observers, that simple folk not unfrequently display no greater disgust for the abnormalities of sexual appetite than they do for its normal manifestations.

Die krankhaften Erscheinungen des Geschlechtssinnes. B. Tarnowsky. Berlin, Hirschwald, 1886.

This is avowedly an attempt to distinguish the morbid kinds of sexual perversion from the merely vicious, and to enforce the necessity of treating the former not as criminal but as pathologic. "The forensic physician discerns corruption, over-satiated sensuality, deep-rooted vice, perverse will, etc., where the clinical observer recognizes with certainty a morbid condition of the patient marked by typical steps of development and termination. Where the one wishes to punish immorality, the other pleads for the necessity of methodical therapeutic treatment."

The author is a Russian, whose practice in St. Petersburg has brought him into close professional relations with the male prostitutes and habitual pederasts of that capital.

Therefore he is able to speak with authority, on the ground of a quite exceptional knowledge of the moral and physical disturbances connected with sodomy. I cannot but think that the very peculiarities of his experience have led him to form incomplete theories. He is too familiar with venal pathics, pedicators, and effeminates who prostitute their bodies in the grossest way, to be able to appreciate the subtler bearings of the problem.

Tarnowsky makes two broad divisions of sexual inversion. The first kind is inborn, dependent upon hereditary taint and neuropathic diathesis. He distinguishes three sorts of inborn perversity. In the most marked of its forms, it is chronic and persistent, appearing with the earliest dawn of puberty, unmodified by education, attaining to its maximum of intensity in manhood, manifesting in fact all the signs of ordinary sexual inclination. In a second form, it is not chronic and persistent, but periodical. The patient is subject to occasional disturbances of the nervous centres, which express themselves in violent and irresistible attacks of the perverted instinct. The third form is epileptical.

With regard to acquired sexual inversion, he dwells upon the influence of bad example, the power of imitation, fashion, corrupt literature, curiosity in persons jaded with normal excesses. Extraordinary details are given concerning the state of schools in Russia; and a particular case is mentioned, in which Tarnowsky himself identified twenty-nine passive pederasts, between the ages of nine and fifteen, in a single school. He had been called in to pronounce upon the causes of an outbreak of syphilis among the pupils. Interesting information is also communicated regarding the prevalence of abnormal vice in St. Petersburg, where it appears that bath men, cab drivers, caretakers of houses, and artisans are particularly in request. The Russian people show no repugnance for what they call "gentlemen's tricks." Tarnowsky calls attention to ships, garrisons, prisons, as milieux well calculated for the development of this vice, when it had once been introduced by some one tainted with it. His view about nations like the Greeks, the Persians, and the Afghans is that, through imitation, fashion, and social toleration, it has become endemic. But all the sorts of abnormality included under the title of acquired Tarnowsky

regards as criminal. The individual ought, he thinks, to be
punished by the law. He naturally includes under this category
of acquired perversion the vices of old debauchees. At this
point, however, his classification becomes confused; for he
shows how senile tendencies to sodomitic passion are frequently
the symptom of approaching brain disease, to which the reason
and the constitution of the patient will succumb. French physi-
sians call this "*la pédérastie des ramollis.*"

Returning to what Tarnowsky says about the inborn species
of sexual inversion, I may call attention to an admirable
description of the type in general. However, I think that he
lays too great stress upon the passivity of the emotions in these
persons, their effeminacy of dress, habits, inclinations. He is
clearly speaking from large experience. So it must be supposed
that he has not come across frequent instances of men who
feel, look, and act like men, the only difference between them
and normal males being that they love their own sex. In
describing a second degree of the aberration, he still accen-
tuates effeminacy in dress and habits beyond the point which
general observation would justify. Careful study of the cases
adduced in Krafft-Ebing's *Psychopathia* supplies a just measure
for the criticism of Tarnowsky upon this head. From them we
learn that effeminacy of physique and habit is by no means a
distinctive mark of the born pederast. Next it may be noticed
that Tarnowsky believes even innate and hereditary tendencies
can be modified and overcome by proper moral, and physical
discipline in youth, and that the subjects of them will even
be brought to marry in some cases.

It would not serve any purpose of utility here to follow
Tarnowsky into further details regarding the particular forms
assumed by perverted appetite. But attention must be directed
to his definition of hereditary predisposition. This is extraordinarily wide. He regards every disturbance of the nervous system in an ancestor as sufficient: epilepsy, brain-disease, hysteria,
insanity. He includes alcoholism, syphilitic affections, pneu-

monia, typhus, physical exhaustion, excessive anemia, debauchery, "anything in short which is sufficient to enfeeble the nervous system and the sexual potency of the parent." At this point, he remarks that long residence at high altitudes tends to weaken the sexual activity and to develop perversity, adducing an old belief of the Persians that paiderastia originated in the high pleateau of Armenia. It need hardly, I think, be said that these theories are contradicted to the fullest extent by the experience of those who have lived with the mountaineers of Central Europe. They are indeed capable of continence to a remarkable degree, but they are also vigorously procreative and remarkably free from sexual inversion.

Finally, it must be observed that Tarnowsky discusses the physical signs of active and passive sodomy at some length. His opportunities of special observation in medical practice, as the trusted physician of the St. Petersburg pederasts, give him the right to speak with authority. The most decisive thing he says is that Casper, through want of familiarity with the phenomena, is too contemptuous toward one point in Tardieu's theory. In short, Tarnowsky feels sure that a habitually passive pederast will show something like the sign in question, if examined by an expert in the proper position. But that is the only deformation of the body on which he relies.

Psychopathia Sexualis, mit besonderer Berücksichtigung der Conträren Sexualempfindung. Von Dr. R. v. Krafft-Ebing. Stuttgart, Enke, 1889.

Krafft-Ebing took the problem of sexual inversion up, when it had been already investigated by a number of pioneers and predecessors. They mapped the ground out, and established a kind of psychical chart. We have seen the medical system growing in the works of Moreau and Tarnowsky. If anything, Krafft-Ebing's treatment suffers from too much subdivision and parade of classification. However, it is only by following the author in his differentiation of the several species that we can form a conception of his general theory, and of the extent of the observations upon which this is based. He starts with (A) Sexual inversion as an acquired morbid phenomenon. Then he reviews (B) Sexual inversion as an inborn morbid phenomenon.

(A). "Sexual feeling and sexual instinct," he begins, "remain latent, except in obscure foreshadowings and impulses, until the time when the organs of procreation come to be developed. During this period of latency, when sex has not arrived at consciousness, is only potentially existent, and has no powerful organic bias, influences may operate, injurious to its normal and natural evolution. In that case the germinating sexual sensibility runs a risk of being both qualitatively and quantitatively impaired, and under certain circumstances may even be perverted into a false channel. Tarnowsky has already published this experience. I can thoroughly confirm it, and I am prepared to define the conditions of this acquired, or in other words this cultivated perversion of the sexual instinct in the following terms. The fundamental or ground predisposition is a neuropathic hereditary bias. The exciting or efficient cause is sexual abuse, and more particularly onanism. The etiological centre of gravity has to be sought in hereditary disease; *and I think it questionable whether an untainted individual is capable of homosexual feelings at all.*"

Krafft-Ebing's theory seems then to be that all cases of acquired sexual inversion may be ascribed in the first place to morbid predispositions inherited by the patient (*Belastung*), and in the second place to onanism as the exciting cause of the latent neuropathic ailment.

He excludes the hypothesis of a physiological and healthy deflection from the normal rule of sex. "I think it questionable," he says, "whether the untainted individual (*das unbelastete Individuum*) is capable of homosexual feelings at all." The importance of this sentence will be apparent when we come to deal with Krafft-Ebing's account of congenital sexual inversion, which he establishes upon a large induction of cases observed in his own practice.

For the present, we have the right to assume that Krafft-Ebing regards sexual inversion, whether "acquired" or "congenital," as a form of inherited neuropathy (*Belastung*). In cases where it seems to be "acquired," he lays stress upon the habit of self-pollution.

This is how he states his theory of onanism as an exciting cause of inherited neuropathy, resulting in sexual inversion. The habit of self-abuse prepares the patient for abnormal appetites by weakening his nervous force, degrading his sexual imagination, and inducing hypersensibility in his sexual apparatus. Partial impotence is not unfrequently exhibited. In consequence of this sophistication of his nature, the victim of inherited neuropathy and onanism feels shy with women, and finds its convenient to frequent persons of his own sex. In other words, it is supposed to be easier for an individual thus broken down at the centres of his nervous life to defy the law and to demand sexual gratification from men than to consort with venal women in a brothel.

Krafft-Ebing assumes that males who have been born with neuropathic ailments of an indefinite kind will masturbate, destroy their virility, and then embark upon a course of vice which offers incalculable dangers, inconceivable difficulties, and inexpressible repugnances. That is the theory. But whence, if not from some overwhelming appetite, do the demoralized victims of self-abuse derive courage for facing the obstacles which a career of sexual inversion carries with it in our civilization? One would have thought that such people, if they could not approach a prostitute in a brothel, would have been unable to solicit a healthy man upon the streets. The theory seems to be constructed in order to elude the fact that the persons designated are driven by a natural impulse into paths far more beset with difficulties than those of normal libertines.

Krafft-Ebing gives the details of five cases of "acquired" sexual inversion. Three of these were the children of afflicted parents. One had no morbid strain in his ancestry, except pulmonary consumption. The fifth sprang from a strong father and a healthy mother. Masturbation entered into the history of all.

It must be observed, in criticizing Krafft-Ebing's theory, that it is so constructed as to render controversy almost impossible. If we point out that a large percentage of males who practise onanism in their adolescence do not acquire sexual inversion, he will answer that these were not tainted with hereditary disease. The autobiographies of onanists and passionate woman-lovers (J. J. Rousseau, for example, who evinced a perfect horror of homosexual indulgence, and J. J. Bouchard, whose disgusting eccentricities were directed toward females even in the period of his total impotence) will be dismissed with the remark that the ancestors of these writers must have shown a clean record.

It is difficult to square Krafft-Ebing's theory with the phenomena presented by schools both public and private in all parts of Europe. In these institutions, not only is masturbation practised to a formidable extent, but is is also everywhere connected with some form of sexual inversion, either passionately Platonic or grossly sensual. Nevertheless we know that few of the boys addicted to these practices remain abnormal after they have begun to frequent women. The same may be said about convict establishments, military prisons, and the like. With such a body of facts staring us in the face, it cannot be contended that "only tainted individuals are capable of homosexual feelings." Where females are absent or forbidden, males turn for sexual gratification to males. And in certain conditions of society sexual inversion may become permanently established, recognized, all but universal. It would be absurd to maintain that all the boy-lovers of ancient Greece owed their instincts to hereditary neuropathy complicated with onanism.

The invocation of heredity in problems of this kind is always hazardous. We only throw the difficulty of explanation further back. At what point of the world's history was the morbid taste acquired? If none but tainted individuals are capable of homosexual feelings, how did these feelings first come into existence? On the supposition that neuropathy forms a necessary condition of abnormal instinct, is it generic neuropathy or a specific type of that disorder? If generic, can valid reasons be adduced for regarding nervous malady in any of its aspects (hysteria in the mother, insanity in the father) as the cause of so peculiarly differentiated an affection of the sexual appetite? If specific, that is if the ancestors of the patient must have been afflicted with sexual inversion, in what way did they acquire it, supposing all untainted individuals to be incapable of the feeling?

At this moment of history there is probably no individual in Europe who has not inherited some portion of a neuropathic strain. If that be granted, everybody is liable to sexual inversion, and the principle of heredity becomes purely theoretical.

That sexual inversion may be and actually is transmitted, like any other quality, appears to be proved by the history of well-known families both in England and in Germany. That it is not unfrequently exhibited by persons who have a bad ancestral record, may be taken for demonstrated. In certain cases we are justified then in regarding it as the sign or concomitant of nervous maladies. But the evidence of ancient Greece and Rome, of what Burton calls the "sotadic races" at the present time, of European schools and prisons, ought to make us hesitate before we commit ourselves to Krafft-Ebing's theory that hereditary affliction is a necessary predisposing cause.

In like manner, masturbation may be credited with certain cases of acquired homosexual feeling. Undoubtedly the instinct is occasionally evoked in some obscure way by the depraved habit of inordinate self-abuse. Yet the autobiographies of avowed Urnings do not corroborate the view that they were originally more addicted to onanism than normal males. Ulrichs has successfully combated the theory advanced by Tarnowsky, Prager, and Krafft-Ebing, if considered as a complete explanation of the problem. On the other hand, common experience shows beyond all doubt, that young men between 16 and 20 give themselves up to daily self-abuse without weakening their appetite for women. They love boys and practice mutual self-abuse with persons of their own sex; yet they crave all the while for women. Of the many who live thus during the years of adolescence, some have undoubtedly as bad a family record as the worst of Krafft-Ebing's cases show. Finally, as regards the onanism which is a marked characteristic of some adult Urnings, this must be ascribed in most cases to the repression of their abnormal instincts. They adopt the habit, as Krafft-Ebing himself says, *faute de mieux.*

In justice to the theory I am criticizing, it ought to be remarked that Krafft-Ebing does not contend that wherever hereditary taint and onanism concur, the result will be sexual inversion; but rather that wherever we have diagnosed an acquired form of sexual inversion, we shall discover hereditary taint and onanism. Considering the frequency of both hereditary taint and onanism in our civilization, this is not risking much. Those factors are discoverable in a large percentage of male persons. What seems unwarranted by facts is the suggestion that inherited neuropathy is an indispensable condition and the fundamental cause of homosexual instincts. The evidence of ancient Greece, schools, prisons, and sotadic races, compels us to believe that normally healthy people are often born with these instincts or else acquire them by the way of custom. Again, his insinuation that onanism, regarded as the main exciting cause, is more frequent among young people of abnormal inclinations than among their normal brethren, will not bear the test of common observation and of facts communicated in the autobiographies of professed onanists and confessed Urnings.

The problem is too delicate, too complicated, also too natural and simple, to be solved by hereditary disease and self-abuse. When we shift the ground of argument from acquired to inborn sexual inversion, its puzzling character will become still more apparent. We shall hardly be able to resist the conclusion that theories of disease are incompetent to explain the phenomenon in modern Europe. Medical writers abandon the phenomenon in savage races, in classical antiquity, and in the sotadic zone. They strive to isolate it as an abnormal and specifically morbid exception in our civilization. But facts tend to show that it is a recurring impulse of humanity, natural to some people, adopted by others, and in the majority of cases compatible with an otherwise normal and healthy temperament.

Krafft-Ebing calls attention to the phenomenon of permanent *effeminatio*, in males unsexed by constant riding and the exhaustion of their virility by friction of the genitals—a phenomenon observed by Herodotus among Scythians, and prevalent among some nomadic races of the Caucasus at the present day. He claims this in support of his theory of masturbation; and within due limits, he has the right to do so. The destruction of the male apparatus for reproduction, whether it be by castration after puberty, or by an accident to the parts, or by a lesion of the spine, or by excessive equitation, as appears proved from the history of nomadic tribes, causes men to approximate physically to the female type, and to affect feminine occupations and habits. In proportion, as the masculine functions are interfered with, masculine characteristics tend to disappear; it is curious to notice that the same result is reached upon so many diverse ways.

Next, he discusses a few cases in which it seems that sexual inversion displays itself episodically under the conditions of a psychopathic disturbance. That is to say, three persons, two women and one man, have been observed by him, under con-

ditions approaching mental alienation, to exchange their normal sexual inclination for abnormal appetite. In the analysis
of the problem these cases cannot be regarded as wholly insignificant. The details show that the subjects were clearly morbid. Therefore they have their value for the building up of a
theory of sexual inversion upon the basis of inherited and
active disease.

(B). Ultimately, Krafft-Ebing attacks the problems of what
he calls "the innate morbid phenomenon" of sexual inversion.
While giving a general description of the subjects of this class,
he remarks that the males display a pronounced sexual antipathy for women, and a strongly accentuated sympathy for men.
Their reproductive organs are perfectly differentiated on the
masculine type; but they desire men instinctively, and are inclined to express their bias by assuming characters of femininity.
Women, affected by a like inversion, exhibit corresponding
anomalies.

Casper, continues Krafft-Ebing, thoroughly diagnosed the
phenomenon. Griesinger referred it to hereditary affliction.
Westphal defined it as "a congenital inversion of the sexual
feeling, together with a consciousness of its morbidity." Ulrichs
explained it by the presence of a feminine soul in a male body,
and gave the name *Urning* to its subjects. Gley suggested that
a female brain was combined with masculine glands of sex.
Magnan hypothesized a woman's brain in a man's body.

Krafft-Ebing asserts that hardly any of these Urnings are
conscious of morbidity. They look upon themselves as unfortunate mainly because law and social prejudice stand in the
way of their natural indulgence. He also takes for proof, together with all the authorities he cites, that the abnormal
sexual appetite is constitutional and inborn.

Krafft-Ebing, as might have been expected, refers the phenomenon to functional degeneration dependent upon neuropathic conditions in the patient, which are mainly derived
from hereditary affliction.

He confirms the account reported above from Casper as to
the platonic or semiplatonic relations of the Urning with the
men he likes, his abhorrence of coition, and his sexual gratification through acts of mutual embracement. The number of
Urnings in the world, he says, is far greater than we can form
the least conception of from present means of calculation.

At this point, he begins to subdivide the subjects of congenital inversion. The first class he constitutes are called by
him "physical hermaphrodites."' Born with a predominant
inclination toward persons of their own sex, they possess rudimentary feelings of a semisexual nature for the opposite. These
people not unfrequently marry; and Krafft-Ebing supposes
that many cases of frigidity in matrimony, unhappy unions,
and so forth, are attributable to the peculiar diathesis of the
male—or it may be, of the female—in these marriages. They
are distinguished from his previous class of "acquired" inversion by the fact that the latter start with instincts for the other
sex, which are gradually obliterated; whereas the psychical
hermaphrodites commence life with an attraction toward their
own sex, which they attempt to overcome by making demands
upon their rudimentary normal instincts. Five cases are given
of such persons.

In the next place he comes to true homosexual individuals,
or Urnings in the strict sense of that phrase. With them there
is no rudimentary appetite for the other sex apparent. They
present a "grotesque" parallel to normal men and women,
inverting or caricaturing natural appetites. The male of this
class shrinks from the female, and the female from the male.
Each is vehemently attracted from earliest childhood to persons of the same sex. But they, in their turn, have to be subdivided into two subspecies. In the first of these, the sexual life
alone is implicate: the persons who compose it, do not differ
in any marked or external characteristics from the type of their
own sex; their habits and outward appearance remain unchanged. With the second subspecies the case is different. Here

the character, the mental constitution, the habits, and the occupations of the subject have been altered by his or her
predominant sexual inversion; so that a male addicts himself
to a woman's work, assumes female clothes, acquires a shriller
key of voice, and expresses the inversion of his sexual instinct
in every act and gesture of his daily life.

It appears from Krafft-Ebing's recorded cases that the first
of these subspecies yields nearly the largest number of individuals. He presents eleven detailed autobiographies of male
Urnings, in whom the *vita sexualis* alone is abnormal, and who
are differentiated to common observation from normal men
by nothing but the nature of their amorous proclivities. The
class includes powerfully developed masculine beings, who are
unsexed in no particular except that they possess an inordinate
appetite for males, and will not look at females.

In regard to the family history of the eleven selected cases,
five could show a clear bill of health; some were decidedly bad;
a small minority were uncertain.

One of these Urnings, a physician, informed Krafft-Ebing
that he had consorted with at least six hundred men of his own
stamp; many of them in high positions of respectability. In
none had he observed an abnormal formation of the sexual
organs; but frequently some approximation to the feminine
type of body—hair sparingly distributed, tender complexion,
and high tone of voice. About ten per cent eventually adopted
love for women. Not ten per cent exhibited any sign of the
habitus muliebris in their occupations, dress, and so forth. A
large majority felt like men in their relations to men, and were
even inclined toward active pederasty. From the unmentionable act they were deterred by æsthetical repulsion and fear
of the law.

The second of these subspecies embraces the individuals
with whom the reader of Carlier is familiar, and whom Ulrichs
calls Weiblinge. In their boyhood they exhibited a marked
disinclination for the games of their school-fellows, and pre-

ferred to consort with girls. They helped their mothers in the household, learned to sew and knit, caught at every opportunity of dressing up in female clothes. Later on, they began to call themselves by names of women, avoided the society of normal comrades, hated sport and physical exercise, were averse to smoking and drinking, could not whistle. Whether they refrained from swearing, is not recorded. Many of them developed a taste for music, and prided themselves upon their culture. Eventually, when they became unclassed, they occupied themselves with toilette, scandal, tea, and talk about their lovers—dressed as far as possible in female clothes, painted, perfumed, and curled their hair—addressed each other in the feminine gender, adopted pseudonyms of Countess or of Princess, and lived the life of women of a dubious demimonde.

Yet they remained males in their physical configuration. Unlike the preceeding subspecies, they did not feel as men feel toward their sweethearts, but on the contrary like women. They had no impulse toward active pederasty, no inclination for blooming adolescents. What they wanted was a robust adult; and to him they submitted themselves with self-abandonment. Like all Urnings, they shrank from the act of coition for the most part, and preferred embracements which produced a brief and pleasurable orgasm. But some developed a peculiar liking for the passive act of sodomy or the anomalous act of fellatio.

In this characterization I have overpassed the limits of the fifteen cases presented by Krafft-Ebing. In order to constitute the type, I have drawn upon one reliable, because sympathetic, source in Ulrichs, and on another reliable, because antipathetic, source in Carlier.

Sexual inversion, in persons of the third main-species, has reached its final development. Descending, if we follow Krafft-Ebing's categories, from acquired to innate inversion, dividing the latter into psychopathic hermaphrodites and Urnings, then subdividing Urnings into those who retain their masculine habit and those who develop a habit analogous to that of females, we come in this last class to the most striking phenomenon of inverted sex. Here the soul which is doomed to love a man, and is nevertheless imprisoned in a male body, strives to convert that body to feminine uses so entirely that the marks of sex, except in the determined organs of sex, shall be obliterated. And sometimes it appears that the singular operation of nature, with which we are occupied in this Essay, goes even further. The inverted bias given to the sexual appetite, as part of the spiritual nature of the man, can never quite transmute male organs into female organs of procreation. But it modifies the bony structure of the body, the form of face, the fleshly and muscular integuments, to such an obvious extent that Krafft-Ebing thinks himself justified in placing a separate class of androgynous being (with their gynandrous correspondents) at the end of the extraordinary process.

At this point it will be well to present a scheme of his analysis under the form of a table.

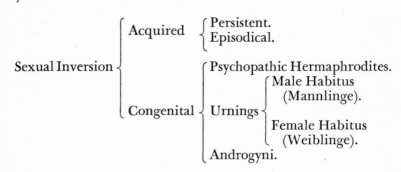

Sexual Inversion
- Acquired
  - Persistent.
  - Episodical.
- Congenital
  - Psychopathic Hermaphrodites.
  - Urnings
    - Male Habitus (Mannlinge).
    - Female Habitus (Weiblinge).
  - Androgyni.

What is the rational explanation of the facts presented to us by the analysis which I have formulated in this table, cannot as yet be thoroughly determined. We do not know enough about the law of sex in human beings to advance a theory. Krafft-Ebing and writers of his school are at present inclined to refer them all to diseases of the nervous centres, inherited, congenital, excited by early habits of self-abuse. The inadequacy of this method I have already attempted to set forth; and I have also called attention to the fact that it does not sufficiently account for phenomena known to us through history and through every-day experience.

Presently we shall be introduced to a theory (that of Ulrichs) which is based upon a somewhat grotesque and metaphysical conception of nature, and which dispenses with the hypothesis of hereditary disease. I am not sure whether this theory, unsound as it may seem to medical specialists, does not square better with ascertained facts than that of inherited disorder in the nervous centres.

However that may be, the physicians, as represented by Krafft-Ebing, absolve all subjects of inverted sexuality from crime. They represent them to us as the subjects of ancestral malady. And this alters their position face to face with vulgar error, theological rancour, and the stringent indifference of legislators. A strong claim has been advanced for their treatment henceforth, not as delinquents, but as subjects of congenital depravity in the brain-centres, over which they have no adequate control.

The fourth medical author, with whom we are about to be occupied, includes sexual inversion in his general survey of human crime, and connects it less with anomalies of the nervous centres than with atavistic reversion to the state of nature and savagery. In the end, it will be seen, he accepts a concordat with the hypothesis of "moral insanity."

Cesare Lombroso. "Der Verbrecher in Anthropologischer, Aerztlicher und Juristischer Beziehung."

This famous book, which has contributed so much to a revolution of opinion regarding crime and its punishment in Italy, contains a searching inquiry into the psychological nature, physical peculiarities, habits, and previous history of criminals. It is, in fact, a study of the criminal temperament. Lombroso deals in the main, as is natural, with murder, theft, rape, cruelty, and their allied species. But he includes sexual inversion in the category of crimes, and regards the abnormal appetites as signs of that morbid condition into which he eventually resolves the criminal impulse.

Wishing to base his doctrine on a sound foundation, Lombroso begins with what may be termed the embryology of crime. He finds unnatural vices frequent among horses, donkeys, cattle, insects, fowls, dogs, ants. The phenomenon, he says, is usually observable in cases where the male animal has been excluded from intercourse with females. Having established his general position that what we call crimes of violence, robbery, murder, cruelty, bloodthirstiness, cannibalism, unnatural lust, etc., exist among the brutes—in fact that most of these crimes form the rule and not the exception in their lives —he passes on to the consideration of the savage man. In following his analysis, I shall confine myself to what he says about abnormal sexual passion.

He points out that in New Caledonia the male savages meet together at night in huts for the purpose of promiscuous intercourse. The same occurs in Tahiti, where the practice is placed under the protection of a god. Next he alludes to the ancient Mexicans; and then proceeds to Hellas and Rome, where this phase of savage immorality survived and became a recognized factor in social life. At Rome, he says, the Venus of the sodomites received the title of Castina.

Lombroso's treatment of sexual inversion regarded as a survival from prehistoric times is by no means exhaustive. It might be supplemented and confirmed by what we know about the manners of the Kelts, as reported by Aristotle—Tartars, Persians, Afghans, North American Indians, etc. Diodorus Siculus, writing upon the morals of the Gauls, deserves attention in this respect. It is also singular to find that the Norman marauders of the tenth century carried unnatural vices wherever they appeared in Europe. The Abbot of Clairvaux, as quoted by Lombroso, accused them of spreading their brutal habits through society. People accustomed to look upon these vices as a form of corruption in great cities will perhaps be surprised to find them prevalent among nomadic and warlike tribes. But, in addition to survival from half-savage periods of social life, the necessities of warriors thrown together with an insufficiency of women must be considered. I have already suggested that Greek love grew into a custom during the Dorian migration and the conquest of Crete and Peloponnesus by bands of soldiers.

Cannibalism, Lombroso points out, originated in necessity, became consecrated by religion, and finally remained as custom and a form of gluttony. The same process of reasoning, when applied to sexual aberrations, helps us to understand how a nonethical habit, based on scarcity of women, survived as a social and chivalrous institution among the civilized Hellenes.

Lombroso traces the growth of justice in criminal affairs, and the establishment of pains and penalties, up to the instinct of revenge and the despotic selfishness of chiefs, in whom the whole property of savage tribes, including women, was vested. This section of his work concludes with the following remarkable sentence: "The universal diffusion of crime which we have demonstrated at a certain remote epoch, and its gradual disappearance as a consequence of new crimes springing up, traces of which are still discoverable in our penal codes (he means revenge, the egotism of princes, and ecclesiastical rapacity), are calculated even more than the criminality of brutes to make us doubt of what metaphysicians call eternal justice, and indicate the real cause of the perpetual reappearance of crime among civilized races, namely atavism."

Having established this principle, Lombroso proceeds to trace the atavism of criminality in children. He shows that just as the human embryo passes through all forms of lower lives, so men and women in their infancy exactly reproduce the moral type of savages. Ungovernable rage, revengeful instincts, jealousy, envy, lying, stealing, cruelty, laziness, vanity, sexual proclivities, imperfect family affections, a general blunt- ness of the ethical sense, are common qualities of children, which the parent and the teacher strive to control or to eradi- cate by training. "The child, considered as a human being devoid of moral sense, presents a perfect picture of what mad doctors call moral insanity, and I prefer to classify as inborn crime." "All species of anomalous sexual appetite, with the exception of those dependent upon senile decadence, make their appearance in childhood, together with the other crim- inal tendencies."

Lombroso arrives then at the conclusion that what civilized humanity punishes as a crime, is the law of nature in brutes, and persists as a normal condition among savages, and displays itself in the habits and instincts of children. The moral instinct is therefore slowly elaborated out of crime in the course of generations by whole races, and in the course of infancy and adolescence in the individual. The habitual criminal, who remains a criminal in his maturity, in whom crime is inborn and ineradicable, who cannot develop a moral sense, he ex- plains at first by atavism. A large section of his volume is devoted to anthropometrical observations upon the physical structure, the cranial and cerebral development, and the phy- siognomy of such criminals. Into this part of his work we need not enter. Nor is it necessary to follow his interesting researches into the biology and psychology of "born criminals"—chapters on tattooing, ways of thinking and feeling, passions, tendencies to suicide, religious sentiment, intelligence and culture, capa- city of self-control, liability to relapse, and so forth. Many curious facts relating to sexual inversion are treated in the course of these enquiries; and one passage describing the gen- eral characteristics of pederasts ought to be alluded to. Con- sidering this subject solely as a phase of crime, Lombroso reveals a superficial conception of its perplexity.

It is more important to reflect upon his theory of crime in

general. Having started with the hypothesis of atavism, and adopted the term "born criminal," he later on identifies "innate crime" with "moral insanity," and illustrates both by the phenomena of epilepsy. This introduces a certain confusion and incoherence into his speculative system; for he frankly admits that he has only gradually and tardily been led to recognise the identity of what is called crime and what is called moral insanity. Criminal atavism might be defined as the sporadic reversion to savagery in certain individuals. It has nothing logically to connect it with distortion or disease— unless we assume that all our savage ancestors were malformed or diseased, and that the Greeks, in whom one form of Lombroso's criminal atavism became established, were as a nation morally insane. The appearance of structural defects in habitual criminals points less to atavistic reversion than to radical divergence from the normal type of humanity. In like manner the invocation of heredity as a principle involves a similar confusion. Hereditary taint is a thing differing not in degree but in kind from savage atavism prolonged from childhood into manhood.

Be this as it may, whether we regard offenders against law and ethic as "born criminals," or as "morally insane," or whether we transcend the distinction implied in these two terms, Lombroso maintains that there is no good in trying to deal with them by punishment. They ought to be treated by life-long sequestration in asylums and rigidly forbidden to perpetuate the species. That is the conclusion to which the whole of his long argument is carried. He contends that the prevalent juristic conception of crime rests upon ignorance of nature, brute life, savagery, and the gradual emergence of morality. So radical a revolution in ideas, which gives new meaning to the words sin and conscience, which removes moral responsibility, and which substitutes the anthropologist and the physician for the judge and jury, cannot be carried out even by its fervent apostle, without some want of severe logic.

Thus we find Lombroso frequently drawing distinctions between "habitual" or "born" criminals and what he calls "occasional" criminals, without explaining the phenomenon of "occasional crime" and saying how he thinks this ought to be regarded by society. Moreover, he almost wholly ignores the possibility of correcting criminal tendencies by appeal to reason, by establishing habits of self-restraint, and by the employment of such means as hypnotic suggestion. Yet experience and the common practice of the world prove that these remedies are not wholly inefficacious; and indeed the passage from childish savagery to moralized manhood, on which he lays so great a stress, is daily effected by the employment of such measures in combination with the fear of punishment and the desire to win esteem.

The final word upon Lombroso's book is this: Having started with the natural history of crime, as a prime constituent in nature and humanity, which only becomes crime through the development of social morality, and which survives atavistically in persons ill adapted to their civilized environment, he suddenly turns round and identifies the crime thus analysed with morbid nerve-conditions, malformations, and moral insanity. Logically, it is impossible to effect this coalition of two radically different conceptions. If crime was not crime but nature in the earlier stages, and only appeared as crime under the conditions of advancing culture, its manifestation as a survival in certain individuals ought to be referred to nature, and cannot be relegated to the category of physical or mental disease. Savages are savages, but not lunatics or epileptics.

At the close of this enquiry into medical theories of sexual inversion, for all of us who assume that the phenomenon is morbid, it may not be superfluous to append the protest of an Urning against that solution of the problem. I translate it from the original document published by Krafft-Ebing. He says that the writer is "a man of high position in London;" but whether the communication was made in German or in English, does not appear.

"You have no conception what sustained and difficult struggles we, all of us, (the thoughtful and refined among us most of all) have to carry on, and how terribly we are forced to suffer under the false opinions which still prevail regarding us and our so-called immorality.

"Your view that, in most cases, the phenomenon in question has to be ascribed to congenital morbidity, offers perhaps the easiest way of overcoming popular prejudices, and awakening sympathy instead of horror and contempt for us poor 'afflicted' creatures.

"Still, while I believe that this view is the most favourable for us in the present state of things, I am unable in the interest of science to accept the term *morbid* without qualification, and venture to suggest some further distinctions bearing on the central difficulties of the problem.

"The phenomenon is certainly anomalous; but the term *morbid* carries a meaning which seems to me inapplicable to the subject, or at all events to very many cases which have come within my cognizance. I will concede *a priori* that a far larger proportion of mental disturbance, nervous hypersensibility, etc., can be proved in Urnings than in normal men. But ought this excess of nervous erethism be referred to necessarily as the peculiar nature of the Urning? Is not this the true explanation, in a vast majority of cases, that the Urning, owing to present laws and social prejudices, cannot like other men obtain a simple and easy satisfaction of his inborn sexual desires?

"To begin with the years of boyhood: an Urning, when he first becomes aware of sexual stirrings in his nature and innocently speaks about them to his comrades, soon finds that he is unintelligible. So he wraps himself within his own thoughts. Or should he attempt to tell a teacher or his parents about these feelings, the inclination, which for him is as natural as swim-

ming to a fish, will be treated by them as corrupt and sinful;
he is exhorted at any cost to overcome and trample on it. Then
there begins in him a hidden conflict, a forcible suppression of
the sexual impulse; and in proportion as the natural satisfaction of his craving is denied, fancy works with still more lively
efforts, conjuring up those seductive pictures which he would
fain expel from his imagination. The more energetic is the
youth who has to fight this inner battle, the more seriously
must his whole nervous system suffer from it. It is this forcible
suppression of an instinct so deeply rooted in our nature, it is
this, in my opinion, which first originates the morbid symptoms, that may often be observed in Urnings. But such consequences have nothing in themselves to do with the sexual inversion of the Urning.

"Well then: some persons prolong this never-ending inner
conflict, and ruin their constitutions in course of time; others
arrive eventually at the conviction that an inborn impulse,
which exists in them so powerfully, cannot possibly be sinful—
so they abandon the impossible task of suppressing it. But just
at this point begins in real earnest the Iliad of their sufferings
and constant nervous excitations. The normal man, if he looks
for means to satisfy his sexual inclinations, knows always where
to find that without trouble. Not so the Urning. He sees the
men who attract him; but he dares not utter, no, dares not
even let it be perceived, what stirs him. He imagines that he
alone of all the people in the world is the subject of emotions,
so eccentric. Naturally, he cultivates the society of young men,
but does not venture to confide in them. So at last, he is driven
to seek some relief in himself, some makeshift for the satisfaction he cannot obtain. This results in masturbation, probably
excessive, with its usual pernicious consequences to health.
When, after the lapse of a certain time, his nervous system is
gravely compromised, this morbid phenomenon ought not to
be ascribed to sexual inversion in itself; far rather we have to
regard it as the logical issue of the Urning's position, driven

as he is by dominant opinion to forego the gratification which *for him* is natural and normal, and to betake himself to onanism.

"But let us now suppose that the Urning has enjoyed the exceptional good-fortune of finding upon his path in life, a soul who feels the same as he does, or else that he has been early introduced by some initiated friend into the circles of the Urning-world. In this case, it is possible that he will have escaped many painful conflicts; yet a long series of exciting cares and anxieties attend on every step he takes. He knows indeed now that he is by no means the only individual in the world who harbours these abnormal emotions; he opens his eyes, and marvels to discover how numerous are his comrades in all social spheres and every class of industry; he also soon perceives that Urnings, no less than normal men and women, have developed prostitution, and that male strumpets can be bought for money just as easily as females. Accordingly, there is no longer any difficulty for him in gratifying his sexual impulse. But how differently do things develop themselves in his case! How far less fortunate is he than the normal man!

"Let us assume the luckiest case that can befall him. The sympathetic friend, for whom he has been sighing all his life, is found. Yet he cannot openly give himself up to this connection, as a young fellow does with the girl he loves. Both of the comrades are continually forced to hide their *liaison;* their anxiety on this point is incessant; anything like an excessive intimacy, which could arouse suspicion (especially when they are not of the same age, or do not belong to the same class in society), has to be concealed from the external world. In this way, the very commencement of the relation sets a whole chain of exciting incidents in motion; and the dread lest the secret should be betrayed or divined, prevents the unfortunate lover from ever arriving at a simple happiness. Trifling circumstances, which would have no importance for another sort of man, make him tremble: lest suspicion should awake, his secret be discovered, and he become a social outcast, lose his official appointment, be excluded from his profession. Is it conceivable that this incessant anxiety and care should pass over him without a trace, and not react upon his nervous system?

"Another individual, less lucky, has not found a sympathetic comrade, but has fallen into the hands of some pretty fellow, who at the outset readily responded to his wishes, till he drew the very deepest secret of his nature forth. At that point the subtlest methods of blackmailing begin to be employed. The miserable persecuted wretch, placed between the alternative of paying money down or of becoming socially impossible, losing a valued position, seeing dishonour bursting upon himself and family, pays and still the more he pays, the greedier becomes the vampire who sucks his life-blood, until at last there lies nothing else before him except total financial ruin or disgrace. Who will be astonished if the nerves of an individual in this position are not equal to the horrid strain?

"In some cases, the nerves give way altogether: mental alienation sets in; at last the wretch finds in a madhouse that repose which life would not afford him. Others terminate their unendurable situation by the desperate act of suicide. How many unexplained cases of suicide in young men ought to be ascribed to this cause!

"I do not think I am far wrong when I maintain that at least half of the suicides of young men are caused by this one circumstance. Even in cases where no merciless blackmailer persecutes the Urning, but a connection has existed which lasted satisfactorily on both sides, still in these cases even discovery, or the dread of discovery, leads only too often to suicide. How many officers, who have had connection with their subordinates, how many soldiers, who have lived in such relation with a comrade, when they thought they were about to be discovered, have put a bullet through their brains to avoid the coming disgrace! And the same thing might be said about all the other callings in life.

"In consequence of all this, it seems clear that if, as a matter of fact, mental abnormalities and real disturbances of the intellect are commoner with Urnings than in the case of other men, this does not establish an inevitable connection between the mental eccentricity and the Urning's specific temperament, or prove that the latter causes the former. According to my firm conviction, mental disturbances and morbid symptoms which may be observed in Urnings ought in the large majority of instances not to be referred to their sexual anomaly; the real fact is that they are educed in them by the prevalent false theory of sexual inversion, together with the legislation in force against Urnings and the reigning tone of public opinion. It is only one who has some approximate notion of the mental and moral sufferings, of the anxieties and perturbations, to which an Urning is exposed, who knows the never-ending hypocrisies and concealments he must practise in order to cloak his indwelling inclination, who comprehends the infinite difficulties which oppose the natural satisfaction of his sexual desire—it is only such a one, I say, who is able properly to wonder at the comparative rarity of mental aberrations and nervous ailments in the class of Urnings. The larger proportion of these morbid circumstances would certainly not be developed if the Urning, like the normal man, could obtain a simple and facile gratification of his sexual appetite, and if he were not everlastingly exposed to the torturing anxieties I have attempted to describe."

This is powerfully yet temperately written. It confirms what I have attempted to establish while criticizing the medical hypothesis; and raises the further question whether the phenomenon of sexual inversion ought not to be approached from the point of view of embryology rather than of psychical pathology. In other words, is not the true Urning to be regarded as a person born with sexual instincts improperly correlated to his sexual organs? This he can be without any inherited or latent morbidity; and the nervous anomalies discovered in him when he falls at last beneath the observation of physicians, may be not the evidence of an originally tainted constitution, but the consequence of unnatural conditions to which he has been exposed from the age of puberty.

7. LITERATURE—HISTORICAL, ANTHROPOLOGICAL

No one has yet attempted a complete history of inverted sexuality in all ages and in all races. This would be well worth doing. Materials, though not extremely plentiful, lie to hand in the religious books and codes of ancient nations, in mythology and poetry and literature, in narratives of travel, and the reports of observant explorers.

Gibbon once suggested that: "A curious dissertation might be formed on the introduction of pederasty after the time of Homer, its progress among the Greeks of Asia and Europe, the vehemence of their passions, and the thin device of virtue and friendship which amused the philosophers of Athens. But," adds the prurient prude, *"scelera ostendi oportet dum puniunter, abscondi flagitia."*

Two scholars responded to this call. The result is that the chapter on Greek love has been very fairly written by equally impartial, equally learned, and independent authors, who approached the subject from somewhat different points of view, but who arrived in the main at similar conclusions.

The first of these histories is M.H.E. Meier's article on *Pederastie* in Ersch and Gruber's *Allgemeine Encyklopädie*; Leipzig, Brockhaus, 1837.

The second is a treatise entitled *A Problem in Greek Ethics* composed by an Englishman in English. The anonymous author was not acquainted with Meier's article before he wrote, and only came across it long after he had printed his own essay. This work is extremely rare, ten copies only having been impressed for private use.

Enquirers into the psychology and morality of sexual inversion should not fail to study one or other of these treatises. It will surprise many a well-read scholar, when he sees the whole list of Greek authorities and passages collected and coordinated, to find how thoroughly the manners and the literature of that great people were penetrated with paiderastia. The myths and heroic legends of prehistoric Hellas, the educational institutions of the Dorian state, the dialogues of Plato, the history of the Theban army, the biographies of innumerable eminent citizens—lawgivers and thinkers, governors and generals, founders of colonies and philosophers, poets and sculptors—render it impossible to maintain that this passion was either a degraded vice or a form of inherited neuropathy in the race to whom we owe so much of our intellectual heritage. Having surveyed the picture, we may turn aside to wonder whether modern European nations, imbued with the opinions I have described above in the section on Vulgar Errors, are wise in making Greek literature a staple of the higher education. Their motto is *Érasez l'infâme!* Here the infamous thing clothes itself like an angel of light, and raises its forehead unabashed to heaven among the marble peristyles and olive-groves of an unrivalled civilization.

Another book, written from a medical point of view, is valuable upon the pathology of sexual inversion and cognate aberrations among the nations of antiquity. It bears the title *Geschichte der Lustseuche im Alterhume,* and is composed by Dr. Julius Rosenbaum. Rosenbaum attempts to solve the problem of the existence of syphilis and other venereal diseases in the remote past. This enquiry leads him to investigate the whole of Greek and Latin literature in its bearing upon sexual vice. Students will therefore expect from his pages no profound psychological speculations and no idealistic presentation of an eminently repulsive subject. One of the most interesting chapters of this work is devoted to what Herodotus called *Nousos pheleia* among the Scythians, a wide-spread effemination prevailing in a wild warlike and nomadic race. We have already alluded to Krafft-Ebing's remarks on this disease, which has curious points of resemblance with some of the facts of male prostitution in modern cities.

Professed anthropologists have dealt with the subject, collecting evidence from many quarters, and in some cases attempting to draw general conclusions. Bastian's *Der Mensch in der Geschichte* and Herbert Spencer's *Tables* deserve special mention for their encyclopedic fullness of information regarding the distribution of abnormal sexuality and the customs of savage tribes.

In England an essay appended to the last volume of Sir Richard Burton's *Arabian Nights* made a considerable stir upon its first appearance. The author endeavoured to coordinate a large amount of miscellaneous matter, and to frame a general theory regarding the origin and prevalence of homosexual passions. However, his erudition is incomplete; and though he possesses a copious store of anthropological details, he is not at the proper point of view for discussing the topic philosophically. For example, he takes for granted that "Pederasty," as he calls it, is everywhere and always what the vulgar think it. He seems to have no notion of the complicated psychology of Urnings, revealed to us by their recently published confessions in French and German medical and legal works. Still his views deserve consideration.

Burton regards the phenomenon as "geographical and climatic, not racial." He summarizes the result of his investigations in the following conclusions.

"There exists what I shall call a 'Sotadic Zone,' bounded westwards by the northern shores of the Mediterranean (N. lat. 43°) and by the southern (N. lat. 30°). Thus the depth would be 780 to 800 miles, including meridional France, the Iberian Peninsula, Italy and Greece, with the coast regions of Africa from Morocco to Egypt.

"Running eastward the Sotadic Zone narrows, embracing Asia

Minor, Mesopotamia and Chaldea, Afghanistan, Sind, the Punjaub, and Kashmir.

"In Indo-China, the belt begins to broaden, enfolding China, Japan, and Turkistan.

"It then embraces the South Sea Islands and the New World, where at the time of its discovery, Sotadic love was, with some exceptions, an established racial institution.

"Within the Sotadic Zone, the vice is popular and endemic, held at the worst to be a mere peccadillo, whilst the races to the North and South of the limits here defined practise it only sporadically, amid the opprobrium of their fellows, who, as a rule, are physically incapable of performing the operation, and look upon it with the liveliest disgust."

This is a curious and interesting generalization, though it does not account for what history has transmitted regarding the customs of the Kelts, Scythians, Bulgars, Tartars, Normans, and for the acknowledged leniency of modern Slavs to this form of vice.

Burton advances an explanation of its origin. "The only physical cause for the practice which suggests itself to me, and that must be owned to be purely conjectural, is that within the Sotadic Zone there is a blending of the masculine and feminine temperament, a crasis which elsewhere occurs only sporadically." So far as it goes, this suggestion rests upon ground admitted to be empirically sound by the medical writers we have already examined, and vehemently declared to be indisputable as a fact of physiology by Ulrichs, whom I shall presently introduce to my readers. But Burton makes no effort to account for the occurrence of this combination of masculine and feminine temperaments in the Sotadic Zone at large, and for its sporadic appearance in other regions. Would it not be more philosophical to conjecture that the temperament, if that exists at all, takes place universally; but that the consequences are only tolerated in certain parts of the globe, which he defines as the Sotadic Zone? Ancient Greece and Rome permitted them.

Modern Greece and Italy have excluded them to the same extent as Northern European nations. North and South America, before the Conquest, saw no harm in them. Since its colonization by Europeans, they have been discountenanced. The phenomenon cannot therefore be regarded as specifically geographical climatic. Besides, there is one fact mentioned by Burton which ought to make him doubt his geographical theory. He says that, after the conquest of Algiers, the French troops were infected to an enormous extent by the habits they had acquired there, and from them it spread so far and wide into civilian society that "the vice may be said to have been democratized in cities and large towns." This surely proves that north of the Sotadic Zone males are neither physically incapable of the acts involved in abnormal passion, nor gifted with an insuperable disgust for them. Law, and the public opinion generated by law and religious teaching, have been deterrent causes in those regions. The problem is therefore not geographical and climatic, but social. Again, may it not be suggested that the absence of "the vice" among the Negroes and Negroid races of South Africa, noticed by Burton, is the result of their excellent customs of sexual initiation and education at the age of puberty—customs which it is the shame of modern civilization to have left unimitated?

However this may be, Burton regards the instinct as natural, not *contre nature,* and says that its patients "deserve, not prosecution but the pitiful care of the physician and the study of the psychologist."

Another distinguished anthropologist, Paolo Mantegazza, has devoted special attention to the physiology and psychology of what he calls *"I pervertimenti dell'amore,"* starting with the vulgar error that all sexual inversion implies the unmentionable act of coition (for which by the way he is severely rebuked by Krafft-Ebing), he explains anomalous passions by supposing that the nerves of pleasurable sensation, which ought to be carried to the genital organs, are in some cases carried to the rectum. This malformation makes its subject desire *coitum per anum*. That an intimate connection exists between the nerves of the reproductive organs and the nerves of the rectum, is known to anatomists and is felt by everybody. Probably some *cinedi* are excited voluptuously in the mode suggested. Seneca, in his Epistles, records such cases; and it is difficult in any other way to account for the transports felt by male prostitutes of the Weibling type. Finally, writers upon female prostitution mention women who are incapable of deriving pleasure from any sexual act except *aversa venus*.

Mantegazza's observation deserves to be remembered, and ought to be tested by investigation. But, it is obvious, he pushes the corollary he draws from it, as to the prevalence of sexual inversion, too far.

He distinguishes three classes of sodomy: 1 Peripheric or anatomical, caused by an unusual distribution of the nerves passing from the spine to the reproductive organs and the rectum. 2 Psychical, which he describes as "specific to intelligent men, cultivated, and frequently neurotic," but which he does not attempt to elucidate, though he calls it "not a vice, but a passion." 3 Luxurious or lustful, when the *aversa venus* is deliberately chosen on account of what Mantegazza terms "*la desolante larghezza*" of the female.

Mantegazza winds up, like Burton, by observing that "sodomy, studied with the pitying and indulgent eye of the physician and the physiologist, is consequently a disease, which claims to be cured, and can in many cases be cured."

After perusing what physicians, historians, and anthropologists have to say about sexual inversion, there is good reason for us to feel uneasy as to the present condition of our laws. And yet it might be argued that anomalous desires are not always maladies, not always congenital, not always psychical passions. In some cases they must surely be vices deliberately adopted out of lustfulness, wanton curiosity, and seeking after sensual refinements. The difficult question still remains then—

how to repress vice, without acting unjustly toward the naturally abnormal, the unfortunate, and the irresponsible.

I pass now to the polemic writings of a man who maintains that homosexual passions, even in their vicious aspects, ought not to be punished except in the same degree and under the same conditions as the normal passions of the majority.

8. LITERATURE—POLEMIC

It can hardly be said that inverted sexuality received a serious and sympathetic treatment until a German jurist, named Karl Heinrich Ulrichs. He began his long warfare against what he considered to be prejudice and ignorance upon a topic of the greatest moment to himself. A native of Hanover, and writing at first under the assumed name of Numa Numantius, he kept pouring out a series of polemic, analytic, theoretic, and apologetic pamphlets between the years 1864 and 1870. The most important of these works is a lengthy and comprehensive essay entitled *Memnon. Die Geschlechtsnatur des mannliebenden Urnings. Eine naturwissenschaftliche Darstellung.* Schleiz, 1868. *Memnon* may be used as the textbook of its author's theories; but it is also necessary to study earlier and later treatises—*Inclusa, Formatrix, Vindex, Ara Spei, Gladius Furens, Incubus, Argonauticus, Prometheus, Araxes, Kritische Pfeile*—in order to obtain a complete knowledge of his opinions, and to master the whole mass of information he has brought together.

The object of Ulrichs in these miscellaneous writings is twofold. He seeks to establish a theory of sexual inversion upon the basis of natural science, proving that abnormal instincts are inborn and healthy in a considerable percentage of human beings; that they do not owe their origin to bad habits of any kind, to hereditary disease, or to wilful depravity; that they are incapable in the majority of cases of being extirpated or converted into normal channels; and that the men subject to them are neither physically, intellectually, nor morally inferior to normally constituted individuals. Having demonstrated these points to his own satisfaction, and supported his views with a large induction of instances and a respectable show of erudition, he proceeds to argue that the present state of the law in many states of Europe is flagrantly unjust to a class of innocent persons, who may indeed be regarded as unfortunate and inconvenient, but who are guilty of nothing which deserves reprobation and punishment. In this second and polemic branch of his exposition, Ulrichs assumes, for his juristic starting-point, that each human being is born with natural rights which legislation ought not to infringe but to protect. He does not attempt to confute the utilitarian theory of jurisprudence, which regards laws as regulations made by the majority in the supposed interests of society. Yet a large amount of his reasoning is designed to invalidate utilitarian arguments in favour of repression, by showing that no social evil ensues in those countries which have placed abnormal sexuality upon the same footing as the normal, and that the toleration of inverted passion threatens no danger to the well-being of nations.

After this prelude, an abstract of Ulrichs' theory and his pleading may be given, deduced from the comparative study of his numerous essays.

The right key to the solution of the problem is to be found in physiology, in that obscure department of natural science which deals with the evolution of sex. The embryo, as we are now aware, contains an undetermined element of sex during the first months of pregnancy. This is gradually worked up into male and female organs of procreation; and these, when the age of puberty arrives, are generally accompanied by corresponding male and female appetites. That is to say, the man in an immense majority of cases desires the woman, and the woman desires the man. Nature, so to speak, aims at differentiating the undecided fetus into a human being of one or the

other sex, the propagation of the species being the main object
of life. Still, as Aristotle puts it, and as we observe in many of
her operations, "Nature wishes, but has not always the power":
the phusis bouletai men all'ou dunatai. Consequently, in respect of physical structure, there come to light imperfect individuals, so-called hermaphrodites, whose sexual apparatus is so
far undetermined that many a real male has passed a portion
of his life under a mistake, has worn female clothes, and has
cohabited by preference with men. Likewise, in respect of
spiritual nature, there appear males who, notwithstanding
their marked masculine organization, feel from the earliest
childhood a sexual proclivity toward men, with a corresponding indifference for women. In some of these abnormal but
natural beings, the appetite for men resembles the normal
appetite of men for women; in others it resembles the normal
appetite of women for men. That is to say, some prefer effeminate males, dressed in feminine clothes and addicted to female
occupations. Others prefer powerful adults of an ultramascu-
line stamp. A third class manifest their predilection for healthy
young men in the bloom of adolescence, between nineteen and
twenty. The attitude of such persons toward women also varies.
In genuine cases of inborn sexual inversion a positive horror
is felt when the woman has to be carnally known; and this
horror is of the same sort as that which normal men experience
when they think of cohabitation with a male. In others, the
disinclination does not amount to repugnance; but the abnormal man finds considerable difficulty in stimulating himself to
the sexual act with females, and derives a very imperfect satisfaction from the same. A certain type of man, in the last place,
seems to be indifferent, desiring males at one time and females
at another.

In order to gain clearness in his exposition, Ulrichs has
invented names for these several species. The so-called hermaphrodite he dismisses with the German designation of *Zwitter.*

Imperfect individuals of this type are not to be considered, because it is well known that the male and female organs are never developed in one and the same body. It is also, as we shall presently discover, an essential part of his theory to regard the problem of inversion psychologically.

The normal man he calls *Dioning,* the abnormal man *Urning.* Among Urnings, those who prefer effeminate males are christened by the name of *Mannling;* those who prefer powerful and masculine adults receive the name of *Weibling;* the Urning who cares for adolescents is styled a *Zwischen-Urning.* Men who seem to be indifferently attracted by both sexes, he calls *Uranodioninge.* A genuine Dioning, who, from lack of women, or under the influence of special circumstances, consorts with persons of his own sex, is denominated *Uranias-ter.* A genuine Urning, who has put restraint upon his inborn impulse, who has forced himself to cohabit with women, or has perhaps contracted marriage, is said to be *Virilisirt*—a virilized Urning.

These outlandish names, though seemingly pedantic and superfluous, have their technical value, and are necessary to the proper understanding of Ulrichs' system. He is dealing exclusively with individuals classified by common parlance as males without distinction. Ulrichs believes that he can establish a real natural division between men proper whom he calls *Dioninge,* and males of an anomalous sexual development whom he calls *Urninge.* Having proceeded so far, he finds the necessity of distinguishing three broad types of the Urning, and of making out the crosses between Urning and Dioning, of which he also finds three species. It will appear in the sequel that, whatever may be thought about his psychological hypothesis, the nomenclature he has adopted is useful in discussion, and corresponds to well-defined phenomena, of which we have abundant information. The following table will make his analysis sufficiently plain.

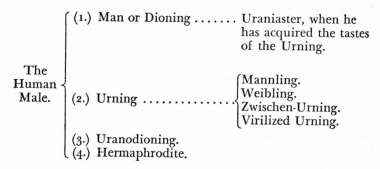

The
Human
Male.

(1.) Man or Dioning .... Uraniaster, when he has acquired the tastes of the Urning.

(2.) Urning .... Mannling. Weibling. Zwischen-Urning. Virilized Urning.

(3.) Uranodioning.
(4.) Hermaphrodite.

Broadly speaking, the male includes two main species: Dioning and Urning, men with normal, and men with abnormal instincts. What then constitutes the distinction between them? How are we justified in regarding them as radically divergent?

Ulrichs replies that the phenomenon of sexual inversion is to be explained by physiology, and particularly by the evolution of the embryo. Nature fails to complete her work regularly and in every instance. Having succeeded in differentiating a male with full formed sexual organs from the undecided fetus, she does not always effect the proper differentiation of that portion of the psychical being in which resides the sexual appetite. There remains a female soul in a male body. *Anima muliebris virili corpore inclusa,* is the formula adopted by Ulrichs; and he quotes a passage from the "Vestiges of Creation," which suggests that the male is a more advanced product of sexual evolution than the female. The male instinct of sex is a more advanced product than the female instinct. Consequently, men appear whose bodies have been differentiated as masculine, but whose sexual instincts have not progressed beyond the feminine stage.

Ulrichs' own words ought to be cited upon this fundamental part of his hypothesis, since he does not adopt the opinion that the Urning is a Dioning arrested at a certain point of development; but rather that there is an element of uncertainty attending the simultaneous evolution of physical and psychical factors from the indeterminate ground stuff. "Sex," says he, "is only an affair of development. Up to a certain stage of embryonic existence all living mammals are hermaphroditic. A certain number of them advance to the condition of what I call man (Dioning), others to what I call woman (Dioningin), a third class become what I call *Urning* (including *Urningin*). It ensues therefrom that between these three sexes there are no primary, but only secondary differences. And yet true differences, constituting sexual species, exist as facts." Man, woman, and Urning—the third being either a male or a female in whom we observe a real and inborn, not an acquired or a spurious inversion of appetite—are consequently regarded by him as the three main divisions of humanity viewed from the point of view of sex. The embryonic ground stuff in the case of each was homologous; but while the two former, man and woman, have been normally differentiated, the Urning's sexual instinct, owing to some imperfection in the process of development, does not correspond to his or her sexual organs.

The line of division between the sexes, even in adult life, is a subtle one; and the physical structure of men and women yields indubitable signs of their emergence from a common ground stuff. Perfect men have rudimentary breasts. Perfect women carry a rudimentary penis in their clitoris. The raphé of the scrotum shows where the aperture, common at first to masculine and feminine beings, but afterwards only retained in the female vulva, was closed up to form a male. Other anatomical details of the same sort might be adduced. But these will suffice to make thinking persons reflect upon the mysterious dubiety of what we call sex. That gradual development, which ends in normal differentiation, goes on very slowly. It is only at the age of puberty that a boy distinguishes himself abruptly from a girl, by changing his voice and growing hair on parts of the body where it is not usually found in women. This being so, it is surely not surprising that the sexual appetite should sometimes fail to be normally determined, or in other words should be inverted.

Ulrichs maintains that the body of an Urning is masculine, his soul feminine, so far as sex is concerned. Accordingly, though physically unfitted for coition with men, he is imperatively drawn towards them by a natural impulse. Opponents meet him with this objection: "Your position is untenable. Body and soul constitute one inseparable entity." So they do, replies Ulrichs; but the way in which these factors of the person are combined in human beings differs extremely, as I can prove by indisputable facts. The body of a male is visible to the eyes, is mensurable and ponderable, is clearly marked in its specific organs. But what we call his soul—his passions, inclinations, sensibilities, emotional characteristics, sexual desires —eludes the observation of the senses. This second factor, like the first, existed in the undetermined stages of the fetus. And when I find that the soul, this element of instinct and emotion and desire existing in a male, has been directed in its sexual appetite from earliest boyhood towards persons of the male sex, I have no right to qualify it with the attribute of femininity. You assume that soul-sex is indissolubly connected and inevitably derived from body-sex. The facts contradict you, as I can prove by referring to the veracious autobiographies of Urnings and to known phenomena regarding them.

Such is the theory of Ulrichs; and though we may not incline to his peculiar mode of explaining the want of harmony between sexual organs and sexual appetite in Urnings, there can be no doubt that in some way or other their eccentric diathesis must be referred to the obscure process of sexual differentiation. Perhaps he antedates the moment at which the aberration sometimes takes its origin, not accounting sufficiently for imperative impressions made on the imagination or the senses of boys during the years which precede puberty.

However this may be, the tendency to such inversion is certainly inborn in an extremely large percentage of cases. That can be demonstrated from the reports of persons whose instincts were directed to the male before they knew what sex meant. It is worth extracting passages from these confessions. "As a schoolboy of eight years, I sat near a comrade rather older than myself; and how happy was I, when he touched me. That was the first indefinite perception of an inclination which remained a secret for me till my nineteenth year."

"Going back to my seventh year, I had a lively feeling for a schoolfellow, two years older than myself; I was happy when I could be as close as possible to him, and in our games could place my head near to his private parts."

"At ten years of age, he had a romantic attachment for a comrade; and the passion for people of his own sex became always more and more marked."

Another confessed that "already at the age of four he used to dream of handsome grooms."

A fifth said: "My passion for people of my own sex awoke at the age of eight. I used to enjoy seeing my brother's nakedness; while bathing with other children, I took no interest at all in girls, but felt the liveliest attraction toward boys."

A sixth dates his experience from his sixth or seventh year.

A seventh remembers that "while yet a boy, before the age of puberty, sleeping in the company of a male agitated him to such an extent that he lay awake for hours."

An eighth relates that "while three years old, I got possession of a fashion book, cut out the pictures of men, and kissed them to tatters. The pictures of women I did not care to look at."

A ninth goes back to his thirteenth year, and a schoolfriendship.

A tenth records the same about his seventh year.

An eleventh says that his inverted instincts awoke in early childhood, and that from his ninth year onward he fell over and over again in love with adult men.

A twelfth spoke as follows: "So far back as I can remember, I was always subject to this passion. Quite as a child, young men made a deeper impression on me than women or girls. The earliest sensual perturbation of which I have any recollection was excited by a tutor, when I was nine or ten, and my greatest pleasure was to be allowed to ride astride upon his leg."

A thirteenth: "From the earliest childhood I have been haunted by visions of men, and only of men; never has a woman exercised the least influence over me. At school I kept these instincts to myself, and lived quite retired."

A fourteenth can recollect "receiving a distinctly sensual impression at the age of four, when the man-servants caressed him."

A fifteenth says that at the age of thirteen, together with puberty, the inversion of appetite awoke in him.

A sixteenth confesses that he felt an unconquerable desire for soldiers in his thirteenth year.

A seventeenth remembers having always dreamed only of men; and at school, he says, "when my comrades looked at pretty girls and criticized them during our daily promenades, I could not comprehend how they found anything to admire in such creatures." On the other hand, the sight and touch of soldiers and strong fellows excited him enormously.

An eighteenth dates the awakening of passion in him at the age of eleven, when he saw a handsome man in church; and from that time forward his instinct never altered.

A nineteenth fell in love with an officer at the age of thirteen, and since then always desired vigorous adult males.

A twentieth confessed to have begun to love boys of his own age, sensually, while only eight years of age.

A twenty-first records that, when he was eight, he began to crave after the sight of naked men.

In addition to these cases, a great many others might be culled from the writings of Ulrichs, who has published a full account from his own early experience. "I was fifteen years and ten and a half months old," he says, "when the first erotic dream announced the arrival of puberty. Never before that period had I known sexual gratification of any kind whatever. The occurrence was therefore wholly normal. However, from a much earlier time I had been subject to emotions, partly romantic, partly sensual, without any definite desire, and never for one and the same young man. These aimless yearnings of the senses plagued me in my solitary hours, and I could not overcome them. During my fifteenth year, while at school at Detmold, the vague longing took a twofold shape. First, I came across Norman's *Säulenordnungen,* and there I was vehemently attracted by the figure of a Greek god or hero, standing in naked beauty. Secondly, while studying in my little room, or before going to sleep, the thought used suddenly and irresistibly to rise up in my mind—if only a soldier would clamber through the window and come into my room! I then painted in my fancy the picture of a splendid soldier of twenty to twenty-two years old. And yet I had no definite idea of why I wanted him; nor had I ever come in contact with soldiers. About two years after this, I happened to sit next a soldier in a postcarriage. The contact with his thigh excited me to the highest degree." Ulrichs also relates that in his tenth year he conceived an enthusiastic and romantic friendship for a boy two years his senior.

That experiences of the kind are very common, every one who has at all conversed with Urnings knows well. From private sources of unquestionable veracity, these may be added. A relates that, before he was eight years old, reveries occurred to him during the day, and dreams at night, of naked sailors. When he began to study Latin and Greek, he dreamed of young gods, and at the age of fourteen, became deeply enamoured of the photograph of the Praxitelian Erôs in the Vatican. He had a great dislike for physical contact with girls; and with boys was shy and reserved, indulging in no acts of sense. B says that during his tenderest boyhood, long before the age of puberty, he fell in love with a young shepherd on one of his father's farms, for whom he was so enthusiastic that the man had to be sent to a distant moor. C at the same early age, conceived a violent affection for a footman; D for an officer, who came to stay at his home; E for the bridegroom of his eldest sister.

In nearly all the cases here cited, the inverted sexual instinct sprang up spontaneously. Only a few of the autobiographies record seduction by an elder male as the origin of the affection. In none of them was it ever wholly overcome. Only five out of the twenty-seven men married. Twenty declare that, tortured by the sense of their dissimilarity to other males, haunted by shame and fear, they forced themselves to frequent public women soon after the age of puberty. Some found themselves impotent. Others succeeded in accomplishing their object with difficulty, or by means of evoking the images of men on whom their affections were set. All, except one, concur in emphatically asserting the superior attraction which men have always exercised for them over women. Women leave them, if not altogether disgusted, yet cold and indifferent. Men rouse their strongest sympathies and instincts. The one exception just alluded to is what Ulrichs would call an Uranodioning. The others are capable of friendship with women, some even of esthetic admiration, and the tenderest regard for them, but not of genuine sexual desire. Their case is literally an inversion of the ordinary.

Some observations may be made on Ulrichs' theory. It is now recognized by the leading authorities, medical and medicojuristic, in Germany, by writers like Casper-Liman and Krafft-Ebing, that sexual inversion is more often than not innate. So far, without discussing the physiological or metaphysical explanations of this phenomenon, without considering whether Ulrichs is right in his theory of *anima muliebris inclusa in corpore virili,* or whether heredity, insanity, and similar general conditions are to be held responsible for the fact, it may be taken as admitted on all sides that the sexual diathesis in question is in a very large number of instances congenital. But Ulrichs seems to claim too much for the position he has won. He ignores the frequency of acquired habits. He shuts his eyes to the force of fashion and depravity. He reckons men like Horace and Ovid and Catullus, among the ancients, who were clearly indifferent in their tastes (as indifferent as the modern Turks) to the account of Uranodionings. In one word, he is so enthusiastic for his physiological theory that he over-looks all other aspects of the question. Nevertheless, he has acquired the right to an impartial hearing, while pleading in defence of those who are acknowledged by all investigators of the problem to be the subjects of an inborn misplacement of the sexual appetite.

Let us turn then to the consideration of his arguments in favour of freeing Urnings from the terrible legal penalties to which they are at present subject, and, if this were possible, from the no less terrible social condemnation to which they are exposed by the repugnance they engender in the normally constituted majority. Dealing with these exceptions to the kindly race of men and women, these unfortunates who have no family ties knotted by bonds of mutual love, no children to expect, no reciprocity of passion to enjoy, mankind, says Ulrichs, has hitherto acted just in the same way as a herd of deer acts when it drives the sickly and the weakly out to die in solitude, burdened with contumely, and cut off from common sympathy.

From the point of view of morality and law, he argues, it does not signify whether we regard the sexual inversion of an Urning as morbid or as natural. He has become what he is, in the dawn and first emergence of emotional existence. You may contend that he derives perverted instincts from his ancestry, that he is the subject of a psychical disorder, that from the cradle he is predestined by atavism or disease to misery. I maintain that he is one of nature's sports, a creature healthy and well organized, evolved in her superb indifference to aberrations from the normal type. We need not quarrel over our solutions of the problem. The fact that he is there, among us, and that he constitutes an ever present factor in our social system, has to be faced. How are we to deal with him? Has society the right to punish individuals sent into the world with homosexual instincts? Putting the question at its lowest point, admitting that these persons are the victims of congenital morbidity, ought they to be treated as criminals? It is established that their appetites, being innate, are *to them* at least natural and undepraved; the common appetites, being excluded from their sexual scheme, are *to them* unnatural and abhorrent. Ought not such beings, instead of being hunted down and persecuted by legal bloodhounds, to be regarded with pitying solicitude as among the most unfortunate of human beings, doomed as they are to inextinguishable longings and life-long deprivation of that which is the chief prize of man's existence on this planet, a reciprocated love? As your laws at present stand, you include all cases of sexual inversion under the one denomination of crime. You make exceptions in some special instances, and treat the men involved as lunatics. But the Urning is neither criminal nor insane. He is only less fortunate than you are, through an accident of birth, which is at present obscure to our imperfect science of sexual determination.

So far Ulrichs is justified in his pleading. When it has been admitted, that sexual inversion is usually a fact of congenital diathesis, the criminal law stands in no logical relation to the phenomenon. It is monstrous to punish people as wilfully wicked because, having been born with the same organs and the same appetites as their neighbours, they are doomed to suffer under the frightful disability of not being able to use their organs or to gratify their appetites in the ordinary way.

But here arises a difficulty, which cannot be ignored, since upon it is based the only valid excuse for the position taken up by society in dealing with this matter. Not all men and women possessed by abnormal sexual desires can claim that these are innate. It is certain that the habits of sodomy are frequently acquired under conditions of exclusion from the company of persons of the other sex—as in public schools, barracks, prisons, convents, ships. In some cases, they are deliberately adopted by natures tired of normal sexual pleasure. They may even become fashionable and epidemic. Lastly, it is probable that curiosity and imitation communicate them to otherwise normal individuals at a susceptible moment of development. Therefore, society has the right to say: those who are the unfortunate subjects of inborn sexual inversion shall not be allowed to indulge their passions, lest the mischief should spread, and a vicious habit should contaminate our youth. From the utilitarian point of view, society is justified in protecting itself against a minority of exceptional beings whom it regards as pernicious to the general welfare. From any point of view, the majority is strong enough to coerce to inborn instincts and to trample on the anguish of a few unfortunates. But, asks Ulrichs, is this consistent with humanity, is it consistent with the august ideal of impartial equity? Are people, sound in body, vigorous in mind, wholesome in habit, capable of generous affections, good servants of the state, trustworthy in all the ordinary relations of life, to be condemned at law as criminals because they cannot feel sexually as the majority feel, because they find some satisfaction for their inborn want in ways which the majority dislike?

Seeking a solution of this difficulty, Ulrichs finds it in fact and history. His answer is that if society leaves nature to take her course, with the abnormal as well as with the normal subjects of sexual inclination, society will not suffer. In countries where legal penalties have been removed from inverted sexuality, where this is placed upon the same footing as the normal— in France, and perhaps also Bavaria and the Netherlands—no inconvenience has hitherto arisen. There has ensued no sudden and flagrant outburst of a depraved habit, no dissemination of a spreading moral poison. On the other hand, in countries where these penalties exist and are enforced—England, for example, in London—inverted sexuality runs riot, despite legal prohibitions, despite threats of prison, dread of exposure, and the intolerable pest of organized *chantage*. In the eyes of Ulrichs, society is engaged in sitting on a safety-valve, which if nature were allowed to operate unhindered, would do society no harm, but good. The majority, he thinks, are not going to become Urnings, for the simple reason that they have not the unhappy constitution of the Urning. Cease to persecute Urnings, accept them as inconsiderable yet real factors in the social commonwealth, leave them to themselves; and you will not be the worse for it, and will also not carry on your conscience the burden of intolerant vindictiveness.

Substantiating this position, Ulrichs demonstrates that acquired habits of sexual inversion are almost invariably thrown off by normal natures. Your boys at public schools, he says, behave as though they were Urnings. In the lack of women, at the time when their passions are predominant, they yield themselves up together to mutual indulgences which would bring your laws down with terrible effect upon adults. You are aware of this. You send your sons to Eton and to Harrow, and you know very well what goes on there. Yet you remain untroubled in your minds. And why? Because you feel convinced that they will return to their congenital instincts.

When the school, the barrack, the prison, the ship has been abandoned, the male reverts to the female. This is the truth about Dionings. The large majority of men and women remain normal, simply because they were made normal. They cannot find the satisfaction of their nature in those inverted practices, to which they yielded for a time through want of normal outlet. Society risks little by the occasional caprice of the school, the barrack, the prison, and the ship. Some genuine Urnings may indeed discover their inborn inclinations by means of the process to which you subject them. But you are quite right in supposing that a Dioning, though you have forced him to become for a time an Uraniaster, will never in the long run appear as an Urning. The extensive experience which English people possess regarding such matters, owing to the notorious condition of their public schools, goes to confirm Ulrichs' position. Headmasters know how many Uraniasters they have dealt with, what excellent Dionings they become, and how comparatively rare, and yet how incorrigibly steadfast, are the genuine Urnings in their flock.

The upshot of this matter is that we are continually forcing our young men into conditions under which, if sexual inversion were an acquired attribute, it would become stereotyped in their natures. Yet it does not do so. Provisionally, because they are shut off from girls, because they find no other outlet for their sex at the moment of its most imperious claims, they turn toward males, and treat their younger school fellows in ways which would consign an adult to penal servitude. They are Uraniasters by necessity and *faute de mieux*. But no sooner are they let loose upon the world than the majority revert to normal channels. They pick up women in the streets, and form connections, as the phrase goes. Some undoubtedly, in this fiery furnace through which they have been passed, discover their inborn sexual inversion. Then, when they cannot resist the ply of their proclivity, you condemn them as criminals in their later years. Is that just? Would it not be better to revert from our civilization to the manners of the savage man—to initiate youths into the mysteries of sex, and to give each in his turn the chance of developing a normal instinct by putting him during his time of puberty freely and frankly to the female? If you abhor Urnings, as you surely do, you are at least responsible for their mishap by the extraordinary way in which you bring them up. At all events, when they develop into the eccentric beings which they are, you are the last people in the world who have any right to punish them with legal penalties and social obloquy.

Considering the present state of the law in most countries

to be inequitable toward a respectable minority of citizens, Ulrichs proposes that Urnings should be placed upon the same footing as other men. That is to say, sexual relations between males and males should not be treated as criminal, unless they be attended with violence (as in the case of rape), or be carried on in such a way as to offend the public sense of decency (in places of general resort or on the open street), or thirdly be entertained between an adult and a boy under age (the protected age to be decided as in the case of girls). What he demands is that when an adult male, freely and of his own consent, complies with the proposals of an adult person of his own sex, and their intercourse takes place with due regard for public decency, neither party shall be liable to prosecution and punishment at law. In fact he would be satisfied with the same conditions as those prevalent in France, and since June 1889 in Italy.

If so much were conceded by the majority of normal people to the abnormal minority, continues Ulrichs, an immense amount of misery and furtive vice would be abolished at once. And it is difficult to conceive what evil results would follow. A defender of the present laws of England, Prussia, etc., might indeed reply: "This is opening a free way to the seduction and corruption of young men." But young men are surely at least as capable of defending themselves against seduction and corruption as young women are. Nay, they are far more able, not merely because they are stronger, but because they are not usually weakened by an overpowering sexual instinct on which the seducer plays. Yet the seduction and corruption of young women is tolerated, in spite of the attendant consequences of illegitimate childbirth, and all which that involves. This toleration of the seduction of women by men springs from the assumption that only the normal sexual appetite is natural. The seduction of a man by a male passes for criminal, because the inverted sexual instinct is regarded as unnatural, depraved, and wilfully perverse. On the hypothesis that individuals sub-

ject to perverted instincts can suppress them at pleasure or
convert them into normal appetite, it is argued that they must
be punished. But when the real facts come to be studied, it will
be found: 1 that these instincts are inborn in Urnings, and are
therefore in their case natural; 2 that the suppression of them
is tantamount to life-long abstinence under the constant torture of sexual solicitation; 3 that the conversion of them into
normal channels is in a large percentage of cases totally impossible, in nearly all where it has been attempted is only
partially successful, and where marriage ensues has generally
ended in misery for both parties.

Ulrichs, it will be noticed, does not distinguish between
Urnings, in whom the inversion is admitted to be congenital,
and Urianasters, in whom it has been acquired or deliberately
adopted. And it would be very difficult to frame laws which
should take separate cognizance of these two classes. The Code
Napoleon legalizes the position of both, theoretically, at any
rate. The English code treats both as criminal, therefore, it
must be admitted, marked injustice to recognized Urnings,
who at the worst are morbid or insane, or sexually deformed,
through no fault of their own.

In the present state of things, adds Ulrichs, the men who
yield their bodies to abnormal lovers, do not merely do so out
of compliance, sympathy, or the desire for reasonable reward.
Too often, they speculate upon the illegality of the connection,
and have their main object in the extortion of money by
threats of exposure. Thus, the very basest of all trades, that of
chantage, is encouraged by the law. Alter the law, and instead
of increasing vice, you will diminish it; for a man who should
then meet the advances of an Urning, would do so out of compliance, or, as is the case with female prostitutes, upon the
expectation of a reasonable gain. The temptation to ply a
disgraceful profession with the object of extorting money
would be removed. Moreover, in regard to individuals abnormally alike, voluntary and mutually satisfying relations, free

from degrading risks, and possibly permanent, might be formed between responsible agents. Finally, if it be feared that the removal of legal disabilities would turn the whole male population into Urnings, consider whether London is now so much purer in this respect than Paris?

One serious objection to recognizing and tolerating sexual inversion has always been that it tends to check the population. This was a sound political and social argument in the time of Moses, when a small and militant tribe needed to multiply to the full extent of its procreative capacity. It is by no means so valid in our age, when the habitable portions of the globe are rapidly becoming overcrowded. Moreover, we must bear in mind, that society, under the existing order, sanctions female prostitution, whereby men and women, the normally procreative, are sterilized to an indefinite extent. Logic, in these circumstances, renders it inequitable and ridiculous to deny a sterile exercise of sex to abnormal men and women, who are by instinct and congenital diathesis non-procreative.

As the result of these considerations, Ulrichs concludes that there is no real ground for the persecution of Urnings except such as may be found in the repugnance felt by the vast numerical majority for an insignificant minority. The majority encourages matrimony, condones seduction, sanctions prostitution, legalizes divorce, in the interest of its own sexual proclivities. It makes temporary or permanent unions illegal for the minority whose inversion of instinct it abhors. And this persecution, in the popular mind at any rate, is justified, like many other inequitable acts of prejudice or ignorance, by theological assumptions and the so called mandates of revelation.

In the next place it is objected that inverted sexuality is demoralizing to the manhood of a nation, that it degrades the dignity of man, and that it is incapable of moral elevation. Each of these points may be taken separately. They are all of them at once and together contradicted by the history of ancient Greece. There the most warlike sections of the race, the

Dorians of Crete and Sparta, and the Thebans, organized the love of male for male because of the social and military advantages they found in it. Their annals abound in eminent instances of heroic enthusiasm, patriotic devotion, and high living, inspired by homosexual passion. The fighting peoples of the world, Kelts in ancient story, Normans, Turks, Afghans, Albanians, Tartars, have been distinguished by the frequency among them of what popular prejudice regards as an effeminate vice.

With regard to the dignity of man, is there, asks Ulrichs, anything more degrading to humanity in sexual acts performed between male and male than in similar acts performed betwen male and female? In a certain sense, all sex has an element of grossness which inspires repugnance. The gods, says Swinburne,

> have strewed one marriage-bed with tears and fire,
> For extreme loathing and supreme desire.

It would not be easy to maintain that a curate begetting his fourteenth baby on the body of a worn-out wife is a more elevating object of mental contemplation than Harmodius in the embrace of Aristogeiton, or that a young man sleeping with a prostitute picked up in the Haymarket is cleaner than his brother sleeping with a soldier picked up in the Park. Much of this talk about the dignity of man, says Ulrichs, proceeds from a vulgar misconception as to the nature of inverted sexual desire. People assume that Urnings seek their pleasure only or mainly in an act of unmentionable indecency. The exact opposite, he assures them, is the truth. The act in question is no commoner between men and men than it is between men and women. Ulrichs, upon this point, may be suspected, perhaps, as an untrustworthy witness. However, his testimony is confirmed by Krafft-Ebing, who, as we have seen, has studied sexual inversion long and minutely from the point of view of psychical pathology. "As regards the nature of their sexual

gratification," he writes, "it must be established at the outset
that the majority of them are contented with reciprocal embraces; the act commonly ascribed to them they generally
abhor as much as normal men do; and, inasmuch as they
always prefer adults, they are in no sense specially dangerous
to boys." This author proceeds to draw a distinction between
Urnings, in whom sexual inversion is congenital, and old
debauchees or half-idiotic individuals, who are in the habit of
misusing boys. The vulgar have confounded two different
classes; and everybody who studies the psychology of Urnings
is aware that this involves a grave injustice to the latter.

"But, after all," continues the objector, "you cannot show
that inverted sexuality is capable of any moral elevation."
Without appealing to antiquity, the records of which confute
this objection overwhelmingly, one might refer to the numerous passages in Ulrichs' writings where he relates the fidelity,
loyalty, self-sacrifice, and romantic enthusiasm which frequently
accompany such loves, and raise them above baseness. But,
since here again he may be considered a suspicious witness, it
will suffice, as before, to translate a brief passage from Krafft-
Ebing. "The Urning loves, idolizes his friend, quite as much
as the normal man loves and idolizes his girl. He is capable of
making the greatest sacrifices for him. He suffers the pangs of
unhappy, often unreturned affection; feels jealousy, mourns
under the fear of his friend's infidelity." When the time comes
for speaking about Walt Whitman's treatment of this topic,
it will appear that the passion of a man for his comrade has
been idealized in fact and deed, as well as in poetry. For the
present it is enough to remark that a kind of love, however
spontaneous and powerful, which is scouted, despised, tabooed,
banned, punished, relegated to holes and corners, cannot be
expected to show its best side to the world. The sense of sin
and crime and danger, the humiliation and repression and
distress, to which the unfortunate pariahs of inverted sexuality
are daily and hourly exposed, must inevitably deteriorate the

nobler elements in their emotion. Give abnormal love the same chance as normal love, subject it to the wholesome control of public opinion, allow it to be self-respecting, draw it from dark slums into the light of day, strike off its chains and set it free—and I am confident, says Ulrichs, that it will exhibit analogous virtues, checkered of course by analogous vices, to those with which you are familiar in the mutual love of male and female. The slave has of necessity a slavish soul. The way to elevate is to emancipate him.

"All that may be true," replies the objector: "it is even possible that society will take the hard case of your Urnings into consideration, and listen to their bitter cry. But, in the meanwhile, supposing these inverted instincts to be inborn, supposing them to be irrepressible and inconvertible, supposing them to be less dirty and nasty than they are commonly considered, is it not the plain duty of the individual to suppress them, so long as the law of his country condemns them?" No, rejoins Ulrichs, a thousand times no! It is only the ignorant antipathy of the majority which renders such law as you speak of possible. Go to the best books of medical jurisprudence, go to the best authorities on physical deviations from the normal type. You will find that these support me in my main contention. These, though hostile in their sentiments and chilled by natural repugnance, have a respect for science, and they agree with me in saying that the Urning came into this world an Urning, and must remain till the end of his life an Urning still. To deal with him according to your code is no less monstrous than if you were to punish the colour-blind, or the deaf and dumb, or albinoes, or crooked-back cripples. "Very well," answers the objector: "But I will quote the words of an eloquent living writer, and appeal to your generous instincts and your patriotism. Professor Dowden observes that 'self-surrender is at times sternly enjoined, and if the egoistic desires are brought into conflict with social duties, the individual life and joy within us, at whatever cost of personal suffering, must be sacrificed to the just claims of our fellows.' What have you to say to that?" In the first place, replies Ulrichs, I demur in this case to the phrases *egoistic desires, social duties, just claims of our fellows.* I maintain that in trying to rehabilitate men of my own stamp and to justify their natural right to toleration, I am not egoistic. It is begging the question to stigmatize their inborn desire as selfish. The social duties of which you speak are not duties, but compliances to law framed in blindness and prejudice. The claims of our fellows, to which you appeal, are not just, but cruelly inequitous. My insurgence against all these things makes me act indeed as an innovator; and I may be condemned, as a consequence of my rashness, to persecution, exile, defamation, proscription. But let me remind you that Christ was crucified, and that he is now regarded as a benefactor. "Stop," breaks in the objector: "We need not bring most sacred names into this discussion. I admit that innovators have done the greatest service to society. But you have not proved that you are working for the salvation of humanity at large. Would it not be better to remain quiet, and to sacrifice your life and joy, the life and joy of an avowed minority, for the sake of the immense majority who cannot tolerate you, and who dread your innovation? The Catholic priesthood is vowed to celibacy; and unquestionably there are some adult men in that order who have trampled out the imperious appetite of the male for the female. What they do for the sake of their vow will not you accomplish, when you have so much of good to gain, of evil to escape?" What good, what evil? rejoins Ulrichs. You are again begging the question; and now you are making appeals to my selfishness, my personal desire for tranquillity, my wish to avoid persecution and shame. I have taken no vow of celibacy. If I have taken any vow at all, it is to fight for the right of an innocent, harmless, down-trodden group of outraged personalities. The cross of a Crusade is sewn upon the sleeve of my right arm. To expect from me and from my fellows the renouncement voluntarily undertaken by a Catholic priest is an absurdity, when we join no order, have no faith to uphold, no ecclesiastical system to support. We maintain that we have the right to exist after the fashion in which nature made us. And if we cannot alter your laws, we shall go on breaking them. You may condemn us to infamy, exile, prison—as you formerly burned witches. You may degrade our emotional instincts and drive us into vice and misery. But you will not eradicate inverted sexuality. Expel nature with a fork, and you know what happens. "That is enough," says the objector: "We had better close this conversation. I am sorry for you, sorry that you will not yield to sense and force. The Urning must be punished."

9. LITERATURE—IDEALISTIC

To speak of Walt Whitman at all in connection with Ulrichs and sexual inversion seems paradoxical. At the outset it must be definitely stated that he has nothing to do with anomalous, abnormal, vicious, or diseased forms of the emotion which males entertain for males. Yet no man in the modern world has expressed so strong a conviction that "manly attachment," "athletic love," "the high towering love of comrades," is a main factor in human life, a virtue upon which society will have to rest, and a passion equal in its permanence and intensity to sexual affection.

He assumes, without raising the question, that the love of man for man coexists with the love of man for woman in one and the same individual. The relation of the two modes of feeling is clearly stated in this poem:

Fast-anchored, eternal, O love! O woman I love;
O bride! O wife! More resistless than I can tell you, the thought of you!
Then separate, as disembodied, or another born,
Ethereal, the last athletic reality, my consolation;
I ascend—I float in the regions of your love, O man,
O sharer of my roving life.

Neuropathic Urnings are not hinted at in any passage of his works. As his friend and commentator Mr. Burroughs puts it: "The sentiment is primitive, athletic, taking form in all manner of large and homely out-of-door images, and springs, as anyone may see, directly from the heart and experience of the poet."

This being so, Whitman never suggests that comradeship may occasion the development of physical desires. But then he does not in set terms condemn these desires, or warn his disciples against them. To a Western boy he says:

"If you be not silently selected by lovers, and do not silently
        select lovers,
Of what use is it that you seek to become eleve of mine?"

Like Plato, in the Phedrus, Whitman describes an enthusiastic type of masculine emotion, leaving its private details to the moral sense and special inclination of the person concerned.

The language of "Calamus" (that section of *Leaves of Grass* which is devoted to the gospel of comradeship) has a passionate glow, a warmth of emotional tone, beyond anything to which the modern world is used in the celebration of the love of friends. It recalls to our mind the early Greek enthusiasm— that fellowship in arms which flourished among Dorian tribes, and made a chivalry for prehistoric Hellas. Nor does the poet himself appear to be unconscious that there are dangers and difficulties involved in the highly-pitched emotions he is praising. The whole tenor of two mysterious compositions, entitled "Whoever you are, Holding me now in Hand," and "Trickle, Drops," suggests an underlying sense of spiritual conflict. The following poem, again, is sufficiently significant and typical to call for literal transcription:

Earth, my likeness!
Though you look so impressive, ample and spheric here,
I now suspect that is not all;

I now suspect there is something fierce in you, eligible to burst
    forth;
For an athletic is enamoured of me—and I of him,
But toward him there is something fierce and terrible in me,
    eligible to burst forth,
I dare not tell it in words—not even in these songs.

The reality of Whitman's feeling, the intense delight which
he derives from the personal presence and physical contact of a
beloved man, find expression in "A Glimpse," "Recorders ages
hence," "When I heard at the Close of Day," "I saw in Louisiana a Live-Oak growing," "Long I thought that Knowledge
alone would content me," "O Tan-faced Prairie-Boy," and
"Vigil Strange I kept on the Field one Night."

It is clear then that, in his treatment of comradeship, or the
impassioned love of man for man, Whitman has struck a key-
note, to the emotional intensity of which the modern world
is unaccustomed. It therefore becomes of much importance to
discover the poet-prophet's *Stimmung*—his radical instinct
with regard to the moral quality of the feeling he encourages.
Studying his works by their own light, and by the light of their
author's character, interpreting each part by reference to the
whole and in the spirit of the whole, an impartial critic will, I
think, be drawn to the conclusion that what he calls the "adhesiveness" of comradeship is meant to have no interblending
with the "amativeness" of sexual love. Personally, it is undeniable that Whitman possesses a specially keen sense of the
fine restraint and continence, the cleanliness and chastity, that
are inseparable from the perfectly virile and physically complete nature of healthy manhood. Still we may predicate the
same ground-qualities in the early Dorians, those martial founders of the institution of Greek Love; and it is notorious to
students of Greek civilization that the lofty sentiment of their
chivalry was intertwined with singular anomalies in its historical development.

To remove all doubt about Whitman's own intentions when

he composed "Calamus," and promulgated his doctrine of impassioned comradeship, I wrote to him, frankly posing the questions which perplexed my mind. The answer I received, dated Camden, New Jersey, U.S.A., August 19, 1890, and which he permits me to make use of, puts the matter beyond all debate, and confirms the conclusions to which I had been led by criticism. He writes as follows: "About the questions on 'Calamus,' etc., they quite daze me. *Leaves of Grass* is only to be rightly construed by and within its own atmosphere and essential character—all its pages and pieces so coming strictly under. That the Calamus part has ever allowed the possibility of such construction as mentioned is terrible. I am fain to hope the pages themselves are not to be even mentioned for such gratuitous and quite at the time undreamed and unwished possibility of morbid inferences—which are disavowed by me and seem damnable."

No one who knows anything about Walt Whitman will for a moment doubt his candour and sincerity. Therefore the man who wrote "Calamus" and preached the gospel of comradeship, entertains feelings at least as hostile to sexual inversion as any law abiding humdrum Anglo-Saxon could desire. It is obvious that he has not even taken the phenomena of abnormal instinct into account. Else he must have foreseen that, human nature being what it is, we cannot expect to eliminate all sensual alloy from emotions raised to a high pitch of passionate intensity, and that permanent elements within the midst of our society will imperil the absolute purity of the ideal he attempts to establish.

However, these considerations do not affect the spiritual nature of that ideal. After acknowledging, what Whitman has omitted to perceive, that there are inevitable points of contact between sexual inversion and his doctrine of comradeship, the question now remains whether he has not suggested the way whereby abnormal instincts may be moralized and raised to higher value. In other words, are those instincts provided in

"Calamus" with the means of their salvation from the filth and mire of brutal appetite? It is difficult to answer this question; for the issue involved is nothing less momentous than the possibility of evoking a new chivalrous enthusiasm, analogous to that of primitive Hellenic society, from emotions which are at present classified among the turpitudes of human nature.

Let us look a little closer at the expression which Whitman has given to his own feelings about friendship. The first thing that strikes us is the mystic emblem he has chosen for masculine love. That is the water-plant, or scented rush, called Calamus, which springs in wild places, "in paths untrodden, in the growth by margins of pond-waters." He has chosen these "emblematic and capricious blades" because of their shyness, their aromatic perfume, their aloofness from the patent life of the world. He calls them "sweet leaves, pink-tongued roots, timid leaves," "scented herbage of my breast." Finally, he says:

Here my last words, and the most baffling,
Here the frailest leaves of me, and yet my strongest-lasting,
Here I shade down and hide my thoughts—I do not expose them,
And yet they expose me more than all my other poems.

The manliness of the emotion, which is thus so shyly, mystically indicated, appears in the magnificent address to soldiers at the close of the great war: "Over the Carnage rose Prophetic a Voice." Its tenderness emerges in the elegy on a slain comrade:

Vigil for boy of responding kisses, (never again on earth responding:)
Vigil for comrade swiftly slain—vigil I never forget, how as day brightened,
I rose from the chill ground, and folded my soldier well in his blanket,
And buried him where he fell.

Its pathos and clinging intensity transpire through the last lines of the following piece, which may have been suggested by the legends of David and Jonathan, Achilles and Patroclus, Orestes and Pylades:

> When I peruse the conquered fame of heroes, and the victories of
>   mighty generals,
> I do not envy the generals,
> Nor the president in his Presidency, nor the rich in his great
>   house;
> But when I read of the brotherhood of lovers, how it was with
>   them,
> How through life, through dangers, odium, unchanging, long
>   and long,
> Through youth, and through middle and old age, how unfalter-
>   ing, how affectionate and faithful they were,
> Then I am pensive—I hastily put down the book, and walk away,
>   filled with the bitterest envy.

But Whitman does not conceive of comradeship as a merely personal possession, delightful to the friends it links in bonds of amity. He regards it essentially as a social and political virtue. This human emotion is destined to cement society and to render commonwealths inviolable. Reading some of his poems, we are carried back to ancient Greece—to Plato's Symposium, to Philip gazing on the Sacred Band of Thebans after the fight at Chaeronea.

> I dream'd in a dream, I saw a city invincible to the attacks of the
>   whole of the rest of the earth:
> I dream'd that was the new City of Friends;
> Nothing was greater there than the quality of robust love—it led
>   the rest;
> It was seen every hour in the actions of the men of that city,
> And in all their looks and words.

And again:

> I believe the main purport of these States is to found a superb friend-
>   ship, exalté, previously unknown,
> Because I perceive it waits, and has been always waiting, latent in
>   all men.

And once again:

> Come, I will make the continent indissoluble;
> I will make the most splendid race the sun ever yet shone upon;
> I will make divine magnetic lands,
>> With the love of comrades,
>> With the life-long love of comrades.
> I will plant companionship thick as trees all along the shores of America, and along the shores of the great lakes, and all over the prairies;
> I will make inseparable cities, with their arms about each other's necks;
>> By the love of comrades,
>> By the manly love of comrades.
> For you these from me, O Democracy, to serve you ma femme!
> For you, for you I am thrilling these songs.

In the company of Walt Whitman we are very far away from Gibbon and Carlier, from Tardieux and Casper-Liman, from Krafft-Ebing and Ulrichs. What indeed has this "superb friendship, exalté, previously unknown," which "waits, and has been always waiting, latent in all men," that "something fierce in me, eligible to burst forth," "ethereal comradeship," "the last athletic reality"—what has all this in common with the painful topic of the preceding sections of my essay?

It has this in common with it. Whitman recognises among the sacred emotions and social virtues, destined to regenerate political life and to cement nations, an intense, jealous, throbbing, sensitive, expectant love of man for man: a love which yearns in absence, droops under the sense of neglect, revives at the return of the beloved: a love that finds honest delight in hand touching, meeting lips, hours of privacy, close personal contact. He proclaims this love to be not only a daily fact in the present, but also a saving and ennobling aspiration. While he expressly repudiates, disowns, and brands as "damnable" all "morbid inferences" which may be drawn by malevolence or vicious cunning from this doctrine, he is prepared to extend the gospel of comradeship to the whole human race. He expects democracy, the new social and political medium, the new religious ideal of mankind, to develop and extend "that fervid comradeship," and by its means to counterbalance and to spiritualize what is vulgar and materialistic in the modern world. "Democracy,'" he maintains, "infers such loving comradeship, as its most inevitable twin or counterpart, without which it will be incomplete, in vain, and incapable of perpetuating itself."

It this be not a dream, if he is right in believing that "threads of manly friendship, fond and loving, pure and sweet, strong and life-long, carried to degrees hitherto unknown," will penetrate the organism of society, "not only giving tone to individual character, and making it unprecedentedly emotional, muscular, heroic, and refined, but having deepest relations to general politics"—then are we perhaps justified in foreseeing here the advent of an enthusiasm which shall rehabilitate those outcast instincts, by giving them a spiritual atmosphere, an environment of recognized and healthy emotions, wherein to expand at liberty and purge away the grossness and the madness of their pariahdom?

This prospect, like all ideals, until they are realized in experience, may seem fantastically visionary. Moreover, the substance of human nature is so mixed that it would perhaps be fanatical to expect from Whitman's chivalry of "adhesiveness" a more immaculate purity than was attained by the medieval chivalry of "amativeness." Still that medieval chivalry, the great emotional product of feudalism, though it fell short of its own aspiration, bequeathed incalculable good to modern society by refining and clarifying the crudest of male appetites. In like manner, the democratic chivalry, announced by Whitman, may be destined to absorb, control, and elevate those darker, more mysterious, apparently abnormal appetites, which we have seen to be widely diffused and ineradicable in the ground-work of human nature.

Returning from the dream, the vision of a future possibility, it will at any rate be conceded that Whitman has founded comradeship, the enthusiasm which binds man to man in

fervent love, upon a natural basis. Eliminating classical associations of corruption, ignoring the perplexed questions of a
guilty passion doomed by law and popular antipathy to failure,
he begins anew with sound and primitive humanity. There he
discovers "a superb friendship, exalté, previously unknown."
He perceives that "it waits, and has been always waiting, latent
in all men." His method of treatment, fearless and uncowed by
any thought of evil, his touch upon the matter, chaste and
wholesome and aspiring, reveal the possibility of restoring in
all innocence to human life a portion of its alienated or un-
claimed moral birthright. The aberrations we have been discussing in this treatise are perhaps the morbid symptoms of
suppression, of hypertrophy, of ignorant misregulation, in a
genuine emotion capable of being raised to good by sympathetic treatment.

It were well to close upon this note. The half, as the Greeks
said, is more than the whole; and the time has not yet come to
raise the question whether the love of man for man shall be
elevated through a hitherto unapprehended chivalry to nobler
powers, even as the barbarous love of man for woman once
was. This question at the present moment is deficient in actuality. The world cannot be invited to entertain it.

10. EPILOGUE

The conclusions to which I am led by this enquiry into
sexual inversion are that its several manifestations may be
classified under the following categories: 1 Forced abstinence
from intercourse with females, or *faute de mieux;* 2 Wantonness and curious seeking after novel pleasure; 3 Pronounced
morbidity; 4 Inborn instinctive preference for the male and
indifference to the female sex; 5 Epochs of history when the
habit has become established and endemic in whole nations.

Under the first category, we group the phenomena presented
by schools, prisons, convents, ships, garrisons in solitary sta-

tions, nomadic tribes of marauding conquerors. Under the second belong those individuals who amuse themselves with experiments in sensual pleasure, men jaded with ordinary sexual indulgence, and indifferent voluptuaries. It is possible that something morbid or abnormal usually marks this class.

Under the third we assign clear cases of hereditary malady, in which a want of self control is prominent, together with sufferers from nervous lesion, wounds, epilepsy, senile brain softening, in so far as these physical disturbances are complicated with abnormal passions.

The fourth includes the whole class of Urnings, who have been hitherto ignored by medical investigators, and on whose numerical importance Ulrichs has perhaps laid exaggerated stress. These individuals behave precisely like persons of normal sexual proclivities, display no signs of insanity, and have no morbid constitutional diathesis to account for their peculiarity.

Under the existing conditions of European society, these four categories exist sporadically. That is to say, the members of them are found scattered through all communities, but are nowhere recognized except by the penal code and the medical profession. In the fifth category, we are brought face to face with the problem offered by ancient Hellas, by Persia, by Afghan, by the peoples of what Burton calls the Sotadic Zone. However we may account for the origin of sexual inversion, the instinct has through usage, tradition, and social toleration, passed here into the nature of the race; so that the four previous categories are confounded, or, if distinguished, are only separable in the same way as the vicious and morbid affections of the ordinary sexual appetite may be differentiated from its healthier manifestations.

Returning to the first four categories, which alone have any importance for a modern European, we perceive that only one of them, the third, (pronounced morbidity) is positively morbid, and only one, the second, (wantonness and curious seeking after novel pleasure) is, *ipso facto*, vicious. The first is immoral in the same sense as all incontinence (forced abstinence from intercourse with females), including self-abuse, fornication, and so forth, practised *faute de mieux,* is immoral; but it cannot be called either morbid or positively vicious, because the habit in question springs up under extrasocial circumstances. The members of the fourth category are abnormal through their constitution. Whether we refer that abnormality to atavism, or to some hitherto unapprehended deviation from the rule in their sexual conformation, there is no proof that they are the subjects of disease. At the same time it is certain that they are not deliberately vicious.

The treatment of sexual inversion by society and legislation follows the view taken of its origin and nature. Ever since the age of Justinian, it has been regarded as an unqualified crime against God, the order of the world, and the state. This opinion, which has been incorporated in the codes of all the Occidental races, sprang originally from the conviction that sterile passions are injurious to the tribe by checking propagation. Religion adopted this view, and, through the legend of Sodom and Gomorrha, taught that God was ready to punish whole nations with violent destruction if they practised "the unmentionable vice." Advancing civilization, at the same time, sought in every way to limit and regulate the sexual appetite; and while doing so, it naturally excluded those forms which were not agreeable to the majority, which possessed no obvious utility, and which *prima facie* seemed to violate the cardinal laws of human nature.

Social feeling, moulded by religion, by legislation, by civility, and by the persistent antipathies of the majority, regards sexual inversion with immitigable abhorrence. It does not distinguish between the categories I have indicated, but includes all species under the common condemnation of crime.

Meanwhile, of late years, we have come to perceive that the phenomena presented by sexual inversion cannot be so roughly dealt with. Two great nations, the French and the

Italians, by the "Code Napoleon" and the "Codice Penale" of 1889, remove these phenomena from the category of crime into that of immorality at worst. That is to say, they place the intercourse of males with males upon the same legal ground as the normal sex relation. They punish violence, protect minors, and provide for the maintenance of public decency. Within these limitations, they recognize the right of adults to deal as they choose with their persons.

The new school of anthropologists and psychological physicians study sexual inversion partly on the lines of historical evolution, and partly from the point of view of disease. Mixing up atavism and heredity with nervous malady in the individual, they wish to substitute medical treatment for punishment, lifelong sequestration in asylums for terms of imprisonment differing in duration according to the offence.

Neither society nor science entertains the notion that those instincts which the laws of France and Italy tolerate, under certain restrictions, can be simply natural in a certain percentage of male persons. Up to the present time the Urning has not been considered as a sport of nature in her attempt to differentiate the sexes. Ulrichs is the only European who has maintained this view in a long series of polemical and imperfectly scientific works. Yet facts brought daily beneath the notice of open-eyed observers prove that Ulrichs is justified in his main contention. Society lies under the spell of ancient terrorism and coagulated errors. Science is either wilfully hypocritical or radically misinformed.

Walt Whitman, in America, regards what he calls "manly love" as destined to be a leading virtue of democratic nations, and the source of a new chivalry. But he does not define what he means by "manly love." And he emphatically disavows any "morbid inferences" from his doctrine as "damnable."

This is how the matter stands now. The one thing which seems clear is that sexual inversion is no subject for legislation, and that the example of France and Italy might well be followed by other nations. The problem ought to be left to the physician, the moralist, the educator, and finally to the operation of social opinion.

11. SUGGESTIONS ON THE SUBJECT OF SEXUAL INVERSION IN RELATION TO LAW AND EDUCATION

I

§ The laws in force against what are called unnatural offences derive from an edict of Justinian, A.D. 538. The Emperor treated these offences as criminal, on the ground that they brought plagues, famines, earthquakes, and the destruction of whole cities, together with their inhabitants, upon the nations who tolerated them.

II

§ A belief that sexual inversion is a crime against God, nature, and the state pervades all subsequent legislation on the subject. This belief rests on (1) theological conceptions derived from the Scriptures; (2) a dread of decreasing the population; (3) the antipathy of the majority for the tastes of the minority; (4) the vulgar error that antiphysical desires are invariably voluntary, and the result either of inordinate lust or of satiated appetites.

III

§ Scientific investigation has proved in recent years that a very large porportion of persons in whom abnormal sexual inclinations are manifested, possess them from their earliest childhood, that they cannot divert them into normal channels, and that they are powerless to get rid of them. In these cases then, legislation is interfering with the liberty of individuals, under a certain misconception regarding the nature of their offence.

IV

§ Those who support the present laws are therefore bound to prove that the coercion, punishment, and defamation of such persons are justified either (1) by any injury which these persons suffer in health of body or mind, or (2) by any serious danger arising from them to the social organism.

V

§ Experience, confirmed by scientific observation, proves that the temperate indulgence of abnormal sexuality is no more injurious to the individual than a similar indulgence of normal sexuality.

VI

§ In the present state of overpopulation, it is not to be apprehended that a small minority of men exercising sterile and abnormal sexual inclinations should seriously injure society by limiting the increase of the human race.

VII

§ Legislation does not interfere with various forms of sterile intercourse between men and women: (1) prostitution, (2) cohabitation in marriage during the period of pregnancy, (3) artificial precautions against impregnation, and (4) some abnormal modes of congress with the consent of the female. It is therefore in an illogical position, when it interferes with the action of those who are naturally sterile, on the ground of maintaining the numerical standard of the population.

VIII

§ The danger that unnatural vices, if tolerated by the law, would increase until whole nations acquired them, does not seem to be formidable. The position of women in our civilization renders sexual relations among us occidentals different from those of any country—ancient Greece and Rome, modern Turkey and Persia—where antiphysical habits have hitherto become endemic.

IX

§ In modern France, since the promulgation of the Code Napoleon, sexual inversion has been tolerated under the same restrictions as normal sexuality. That is to say, violence and outrages to public decency are punished, and minors are protected, but adults are allowed to dispose as they like of their own persons. The experience of nearly a century shows that in France, where sexual inversion is not criminal *per se,* there has been no extension of it through society. Competent observers, like agents of police, declare that London, in spite of our penal legislation, is no less notorious for abnormal vice than Paris.

X

§ Italy, by the Penal Code of 1889, adopted the principles of the Code Napoleon on this point. It would be interesting to know what led to this alteration of the Italian law. But it cannot be supposed that the results of the Code Napoleon in France were not fully considered.

XI

§ The severity of the English statutes render them almost incapable of being put in force. In consequence of this, the law is not unfrequently evaded, and crimes are winked at.

XII

§ At the same time our laws encourage blackmailing upon false accusation; and the presumed evasion of their execution places from time to time a vile weapon in the hands of unscrupulous politicians, to attack the Government in office. Examples: the Dublin Castle Scandals of 1884, the Cleveland Street Scandals of 1889.

XIII

§ Those who hold that our penal laws are required by the interests of society, must turn their attention to the higher education. This still rests on the study of the Greek and Latin classics, a literature impregnated with paiderastia. It is carried on at public schools, where young men are kept apart from females, and where homosexual vices are frequent. The best minds of our youth are therefore exposed to the influences of a paiderastic literature, at the same time that they acquire the knowledge and experience of unnatural practices. Nor is any trouble taken to correct these adverse influences by physiological instruction in the laws of sex.

XIV

§ The points suggested for consideration are whether England is still justified in restricting the freedom of adult persons, and rendering certain abnormal forms of sexuality criminal, by any real dangers to society: after it has been shown 1 that abnormal inclinations are congenital, natural, and ineradicable in a large percentage of individuals; 2 that we tolerate sterile intercourse of various types between the two sexes; 3 that our legislation has not suppressed the immorality in question; 4 that the operation of the Code Napoleon for nearly a century has not increased this immorality in France; 5 that Italy, with the experience of the Code Napoleon to guide her, adopted its principles in 1889; 6 that the English penalties are rarely inflicted to their full extent; 7 that their existence encourages blackmailing, and their nonenforcement gives occasion for base political agitation; 8 that our higher education is in open contradiction to the spirit of our laws.

[EDITOR'S NOTES]

It is acknowledged almost universally that *A Problem In Modern Ethics* is the work of John Addington Symonds, poet, critic, biographer, and scholar. Symonds, assuming he was the author, gave what was, for the turn of the century, an up-to-date summary of the thinking on homosexuality. His brilliant introductory remarks constitute, to this very day, the most eloquent argument against silence, on the one hand, and prejudicial diatribe, on the other.

Nevertheless, the main value of the Symonds work for the reader of today, is that it places in its period and in its cultural milieu the thinking of those who were among the first in modern times to put pen to paper and mention the hitherto unmentionable. Here is a summary of Lombroso, Krafft-Ebing, and others; here is an analysis of the Calamus poems of Whitman.

On the eve of the Freudian era, it is not surprising, then, that among the many theories on the etiology of homosexuality, there shouldn't be a hint of those later to emerge from Freud and the neo-Freudians.

Let us read the repeated remarks, not only from Symonds but from those whom he quotes, on congenital inversion with this in mind—that such theory was indicative of the thinking of this era, even among those (unlike Symonds) whom he quotes and paraphrases. Other than such comment, Symonds' theories require no refutation, for they could be taken seriously today only as the warp and woof of an historical period.

Of the many interesting passages in this document, the writer would like to call special attention to the remarks about the lack of homosexuality among certain African tribes. This, Symonds points out, is not a geographical condition but a social one, and suggests that this may be due to "the excellent customs" of these tribes "of sexual initiation and education at the age of puberty—customs which it is the shame of modern civilization to have left unimitated."

Thus, if in the field of psychology and psychopathology Symonds was not much in advance of his contemporaries, in the socio-sexual area he was truly a pioneer. At the end of a Victorian era, his was a voice being raised (with many reservations, it is true) against Mrs. Grundy. His was a voice for sexual education, for outspoken discussion, and even for initiation into sexual customs (heterosexual customs, that is) at the age of puberty. For this reason alone, *A Problem In Modern Ethics* is a remarkable document, particularly when placed alongside of the work, contemporaneous with Symonds, of Carpenter and Burton.

D. W. C.

HOMOSEXUAL LOVE

Edward Westermarck

FROM THE ORIGIN AND DEVELOPMENT OF (THE) MORAL IDEAS,
1ST ED., LONDON, MACMILLAN, 1906.

Our review of the moral ideas concerning sexual relations
has not yet come to an end. The gratification of the sexual
instinct assumes forms which fall outside the ordinary pale
of nature. Of these there is one which, on account of the *rôle*
which it has played in the moral history of mankind, cannot
be passed over in silence, namely, intercourse between individuals of the same sex, what is nowadays commonly called
homosexual love.

It is frequently met with among the lower animals.[1] It
probably occurs, at least sporadically, among every race of
mankind.[2] And among some peoples it has assumed such proportions as to form a true national habit.

In America, homosexual customs have been observed among
a great number of native tribes. In nearly every part of the
continent there seem to have been, since ancient times, men
dressing themselves in the clothes and performing the functions of women, and living with other men as their concubines
or wives.[3] Moreover, between young men who are comrades

in arms there are *liaisons d'amitié,* which, according to Lafitau, "*ne lassent aucun soupçon de vice apparent, quoiqu'il y ait, ou qu'il puisse y avoir, beaucoup de vice réel.*"[4]

Homosexual practices are, or have been, very prominent among the peoples in the neighborhood of the Behring Sea.[5] In Kadiak, it was the custom of the parent who had a girl-like son to try to dress and rear him as a girl, teaching him only domestic duties, keeping him at woman's work, and letting him associate only with women and girls. Arriving at the age of ten or fifteen years, he was married to some wealthy man and was then called an *achnuchik* or *shoopan.*[6] Dr. Bogoras gives the following account of a similar practice prevalent among the Chukchi: "It happens frequently that, under the supernatural influence of one of their shamans, or priests, a Chukchi lad at sixteen years of age will suddenly relinquish his sex and imagine himself to be a woman. He adopts a woman's attire, lets his hair grow, and devotes himself altogether to female occupation. Furthermore, this disowner of his sex takes a husband into the *Yurt* and does all the work which is usually incumbent on the wife in most unnatural and voluntary subjection. Thus it frequently happens in a *Yurt* that the husband is a woman, while the wife is a man! These abnormal changes of sex imply the most abject immorality in the community, and appear to be strongly encouraged by the shamans who interpret such cases as an injunction of their individual deity."

The change of sex was usually accompanied by future shamanship; indeed, nearly all the shamans were former delinquents of their sex.[7] Among the Chukchi male shamans who are clothed in woman's attire and are believed to be transformed physically into woman are still quite common; and traces of the change of a shaman's sex into that of a woman may be found among many other Siberian tribes.[8] In some cases at least, there can be no doubt that these transformations were connected with homosexual practices. In his description of the Koriaks, Krasheninnikoff makes mention of the *ke'yev,* that is, men occupying the position of concubines; and he compares them with the Kamchadale *koe'kčuč,* as he calls them, that is, men transformed into women. Every *koe'kčuč,* he says is regarded as a magician and interpreter of dreams; but from his confused description Mr. Jochelson thinks it may be inferred that the most important feature of the institution of the *koe'kčuč* lay, not in their shamanistic power, but in their position with regard to the satisfaction of the unnatural inclinations of the Kamchadales. The *koe'kčuč* wore women's clothes, did women's work, and were in the position of wives or concubines.[9]

In the Malay Archipelago, homosexual love is common,[10] thought not in all of the islands.[11] It is widely spread among the Bataks of Sumatra.[12] In Bali, it is practiced openly, and there are persons who make it a profession. The *basir* of the Dyaks are men who make their living by witchcraft and debauchery. They "are dressed as women, they are made use of at idolatrous feasts and for sodomitic abominations, and many of them are formally married to other men."[13] Dr. Haddon says that he never heard of any unnatural offenses in Torres Straits;[14] but in the Rigo district of British New Guinea, several instances of pederasty have been found,[15] and at Mowat in Daudai, it is regularly indulged in.[16] Homosexual love is reported as common among the Marshall Islanders[17] and in Hawaii.[18] From Tahiti, we hear of a set of men called by the natives *mahoos,* who "assume the dress, attitude, and manners, of women, and affect all the fantastic oddities and coquetries of the vainest of females. They mostly associate with the women, who court their acquaintance. With the manners of the women, they adopt their peculiar employments. . . . The encouragement of this abomination is almost solely confined to the chiefs."[19] Of the New Caledonians, M. Foley writes: "*La plus grande fraternité n'est pas chez eux la fraternité utérine, mais la fraternité des armes. Il en est ainsi surtout au village de*

*poepo. Il est vrai que cette fraternité des armes est compli-
quée de pédérastie."*[20]

Among the natives of the Kimberley District in West Australia, if a young man on reaching a marriageable age can find
no wife, he is presented with a boy-wife, known as *chookadoo*.
In this case, also, the ordinary exogamic rules are observed,
and the "husband" has to avoid his "mother-in-law" just as
if he were married to a woman. The *chookadoo* is a boy of five
to ten years, when he is initiated. "The relations which exist
between him and his protecting *billalu*," says Mr. Hardman,
"are somewhat doubtful. There is no doubt they have connection, but the natives repudiate with horror and disgust the
idea of sodomy."[21] Such marriages are evidently exceedingly
common. As the women are generally monopolized by the
older and more influential men of the tribe, it is rare to find
a man under thirty or forty who has a wife; hence it is the
rule that, when a boy becomes five years old, he is given as a
boy-wife to one of the young men.[22] According to Mr. Purcell's
description of the natives of the same district, "every useless
member of the tribe" gets a boy about five or seven years old;
and these boys, who are called *mullawongahs,* are used for
sexual purposes.[23] Among the Chingalee of South Australia,
Northern Territory, old men are often noticed with no wives
but accompanied by one or two boys, whom they jealously
guard and with whom they have sodomitic intercourse.[24]

That homosexual practices are not unknown among other
Australian tribes may be inferred from Mr. Howitt's statement
relating to Southeastern natives, that unnatural offenses are
forbidden to the novices by the old men and guardians after
leaving the initiation camp.[25]

In Madagascar there are certain boys who live like women
and have intercourse with men, paying those men who please
them.[26] In an old account of that island, dating from the seventeenth century, it is said: *"Il y a quelques hommes qu'ils appel-
lent Tsecats, qui sont hommes effeminez et impuissans, qui*

recherchent les garçons, et font mine d'en estre amoureux, en contrefaisons les filles et se vestans ainsi qu'elles leurs font des présents pour dormir avec eux, et mesmes se donnent des noms de filles, en faisant les honteuses et les modestes. . . . Ils haïssent les femmes et ne les veulent point hanter."[27] Men behaving like women have also been observed among the Ondonga in German Southwest Africa [28] and the Diakité-Sarracolese in the French Soudan,[29] but in regard to their sexual habits, details are wanting. Homosexual practices are common among the Banaka and Bapuku in the Cameroons.[30] But among the natives of Africa generally such practices seem to be comparatively rare,[31] except among Arabic-speaking peoples and in countries like Zanzibar,[32] where there has been a strong Arab influence.

In North Africa they are not restricted to the inhabitants of towns; they are frequently among the peasants of Egypt[33] and universal among the Jbâla inhabiting the Northern mountains of Morocco. On the other hand, they are much less common or even rare among the Berbers and the nomadic Bedouins,[34] and it is reported that the Bedouins of Arabia are quite exempt from them.[35]

Homosexual love is spread over Asia Minor and Mesopotamia.[36] It is very prevalent among the Tartars and Karatchai of the Caucasus,[37] the Persians,[38] Sikhs,[39] and Afghans; in Kaubul a bazaar or street is set apart for it.[40] Old travelers make reference to its enormous frequency among the Mohammedans of India,[41] and in this respect time seems to have produced no change.[42] In China, where it is also extremely common, there are special houses devoted to male prostitution, and boys are sold by their parents about the age of four, to be trained for this occupation.[43] In Japan, pederasty is said by some to have prevailed from the most ancient times, whereas others are of opinion that it was introduced by Buddhism about the sixth century of our era. The monks used to live with handsome youths, to whom they were often passionately devoted; and in feudal times nearly every knight had as his favorite a young man with whom he entertained relations of the most intimate kind, and on behalf of whom he was always ready to fight a duel when occasion occurred. Tea-houses with male *gheishas* were found in Japan till the middle of the nineteenth century. Nowadays, pederasty seems to be more prevalent in the Southern than in the Northern provinces of the country, but there are also districts where it is hardly known.[44]

No reference is made to pederasty either in the Homeric poems or by Hesiod, but later on we meet with it almost as a national institution in Greece. It was known in Rome and other parts of Italy at an early period;[45] but here also it became much more frequent in the course of time. At the close of the sixth century, Polybius tells us, many Romans paid a talent for the possession of a beautiful youth.[46] During the Empire, *"il était d'usage, dans les familles patriciennes, de donner au jeune homme pubère un esclave du même âge comme compagnon de lit, afin qu'il pût satisfaire . . . 'ses premiers élans' génésiques";*[47] and formal marriages between men were introduced with all the solemnities of ordinary nuptials.[48] Homosexual practices occurred among the Celts,[49] and were by no means unknown to the ancient Scandinavians, who had a whole nomenclature on the subject.[50]

Of late years, a voluminous and constantly increasing literature on homosexuality has revealed its frequency in modern Europe. No country and no class of society is free from it. In certain parts of Albania it even exists as a popular custom, the young men from the age of sixteen upwards regularly having boy favorites of between twelve and seventeen.[51]

These statements chiefly refer to homosexual practices between men, but similar practices also occur between women.[52] Among the American aborigines there are not only men who behave like women, but women who behave like men. Thus, in certain Brazilian tribes, women are found who abstain from every womanly occupation and imitate the men in everything,

who wear their hair in masculine fashion, who go to war with
a bow and arrows, who hunt together with the men, and who
would rather allow themselves to be killed than have sexual
intercourse with a man. "Each of these women has a woman
who serves her and with whom she says she is married; they
live together as husband and wife."[53] So also there are among
the Eastern Eskimoes some women who refuse to accept husbands, preferring to adopt masculine manners, following the
deer on the mountains, trapping and fishing for themselves.[54]
Homosexual practices are said to be common among Hotten-
tot[55] and Herero[56] women. In Zanzibar there are women who
wear men's clothes in private, show a preference for masculine
occupations, and seek sexual satisfaction among women who
have the same inclination, or else among normal women who
are won over by presents or other means.[57] In Egyptian harems,
every woman is said to have a "friend."[58] In Bali, homosexuality is almost as common among women as among men, though
it is exercised more secretly;[59] and the same seems to be the
case in India.[60] From Greek antiquity we hear of "Lesbian"
love. The fact that homosexuality has been much more frequently noticed in men than in women does not imply that the
latter are less addicted to it. For various reasons the sexual
abnormalities of women have attracted much less attention,[61]
and moral opinion has generally taken little notice of them.

Homosexual practices are sometimes the result of instinctive
preference, sometimes caused by external conditions unfavorable to normal intercourse.[62] A frequent cause is congenital
sexual inversion, that is, "sexual instinct turned by inborn
constitutional abnormality toward persons of the same sex."[63]
It seems likely that the feminine men and the masculine
women referred to here are, at least in many instances, sexual
inverts; though, in the case of shamans, the change of sex may
also result from the belief that such transformed shamans, like
their female colleagues, are particularly powerful.[64] Dr. Holder
affirms the existence of congenital inversion among the North-

western tribes of the United States,[65] Dr. Baumann among the people of Zanzibar;[66] and in Morocco, also, I believe it is common enough. But in regard to its prevalence among non-European people, we have mostly to resort to mere conjectures; our real knowledge of congenital inversion is derived from the voluntary confessions of inverts. The large majority of travelers are totally ignorant of the psychological side of the subject, and even to an expert it must very often be impossible to decide whether a certain case of inversion is congenital or acquired. Indeed, acquired inversion itself presupposes an innate disposition which under certain circumstances develops into actual inversion.[67] Even between inversion and normal sexuality there seems to be all shades of variation. Professor James thinks that inversion is "a kind of sexual appetite, of which very likely most men possess the germinal possibility."[68] This is certainly the case in early puberty.[69]

A very important cause of homosexual practices is absence of the other sex. There are many instances of this among the lower animals.[70] Buffon long ago observed that, if male or female birds of various species were shut up together, they would soon begin to have sexual relations among themselves, the males sooner than the females.[71] The West Australian boy-marriage is a substitute for ordinary marriage in cases when women are not obtainable. Among the Bororo of Brazil homosexual intercourse is said to occur in their men-houses only when the scarcity of accessible girls is unusually great.[72] Its prevalence in Tahiti may perhaps be connected with the fact that there was only one woman to four or five men, owing to the habit of female infanticide.[73] Among the Chinese in certain regions, for instance Java, the lack of accessible women is the principal cause of homosexual practices.[74] According to some writers, such practices are the results of polygamy.[75] In Muhammedan countries they are no doubt largely due to the seclusion of women, preventing free intercourse between the sexes and compelling the unmarried people to associate almost exclu-

sively with members of their own sex. Among the mountaineers of northern Morocco, the excessive indulgence in
pederasty thus goes hand in hand with great isolation of the
women and a very high standard of female chastity, whereas
among the Arabs of the plains, who are little addicted to boy-
love, the unmarried girls enjoy considerable freedom. Both in
Asia[76] and Europe[77] the obligatory celibacy of the monks and
priests has been a cause of homosexual practices, though it
must not be forgotten that a profession which imposes abstinence from marriage is likely to attract a comparatively large
number of congenital inverts. The temporary separation of the
sexes involved in a military mode of life no doubt accounts for
the extreme prevalence of homosexual love among warlike
races,[78] like the Sikhs, Afghans, Dorians, and Normans.[79] In
Persia[80] and Morocco it is particularly common among soldiers.
In Japan, it was an incident of knighthood, in New Caledonia
and North America of brotherhood in arms. At least in some
of the North American tribes men who were dressed as women
accompanied the other men as servants in war and the chase.[81]
Among the Banaka and Bapuku in the Cameroons pederasty is
practiced especially by men who are long absent from their
wives.[82] In Morocco, I have heard it advocated on account of
the convenience it affords to persons who are traveling.

Dr. Havelock Ellis justly observes that when homosexual
attraction is due simply to the absence of the other sex we are
not concerned with sexual inversion, but merely with the
accidental turning of the sexual instinct into an abnormal
channel, the instinct being called out by an approximate substitute, or even by diffused emotional excitement, in the absence of the normal object.[83] But it seems to me probable that
in such cases the homosexual attraction in the course of time
quite easily develops into genuine inversion. I cannot but
think that our chief authorities on homosexuality have under-
estimated the modifying influence which habit may exercise on
the sexual instinct. Professor Krafft-Ebing[84] and Dr. Moll[85]

deny the existence of acquired inversion except in occasional instances; Dr. Havelock Ellis takes a similar view, if putting aside those cases of a more or less morbid character in which old men with failing sexual powers, or younger men exhausted by heterosexual debauchery, are attracted to members of their own sex.[86] But how is it that in some parts of Morocco such a very large proportion of the men are distinctly sexual inverts, in the sense in which this word is used by Dr. Havelock Ellis,[87] that is, persons who for the gratification of their sexual desire prefer their own sex to the opposite one? It may be that in Morocco and in Oriental countries generally, where almost every individual marries, congenital inversion, through the influence of heredity, is more frequent than in Europe, where inverts so commonly abstain from marrying. But that this could not be an adequate explanation of the fact in question becomes at once apparent when we consider the extremely unequal distribution of inverts among different neighboring tribes of the same stock, some of which are very little or hardly at all addicted to pederasty. I take the case to be, that homosexual practices in early youth have had a lasting effect on the sexual instinct, which at its first appearance, being somewhat indefinite, is easily turned into a homosexual direction.[88] In Morocco inversion is most prevalent among the scribes, who from childhood have lived in very close association with their fellow-students. Of course, influences of this kind "require a favorable organic predisposition to act on";[89] but this predisposition is probably no abnormality at all, only a feature in the ordinary sexual constitution of man.[90] It should be noticed that the most common form of inversion, at least in Mohammedan countries, is love of boys or youths not yet in the age of puberty, that is, of male individuals who are physically very like girls. Voltaire observes: *"Souvent un jeune garçon, par la fraîcheur de son teint, par l'éclat de ses couleurs, et par la douceur de ses yeux, ressemble pendant deux ou trois ans à une belle fille; si on l'aime c'est parce que la nature se méprend."*[91]

Moreover, in normal cases, sexual attraction depends not only on sex, but on a youthful appearance as well; and there are persons so constituted that to them the latter factor is of chief importance, whilst the question of sex is almost a matter of indifference.

In ancient Greece, also, not only homosexual intercourse, but actual inversion, seems to have been very common; and although this, like every form of love, must have contained a congenital element, there can be little doubt, I think, that it was largely due to external circumstances of a social character. It may, in the first place, be traced to the methods of training the youth. In Sparta it seems to have been the practice for every youth of good character to have his lover, or "inspirator,"[92] and for every well-educated man to be the lover of some youth.[93] The relations between the "inspirator" and the "listener" were extremely intimate: at home the youth was constantly under the eyes of his lover, who was supposed to be to him a model and pattern of life,[94] in battle, they stood near one another and their fidelity and affection were often shown till death;[95] if his relatives were absent, the youth might be represented in the public assembly by his lover;[96] and for many faults, particularly want of ambition, the lover could be punished instead of the "listener."[97] This ancient custom prevailed with still greater force in Crete, which island was hence by many persons considered to be the place of its birth.[98] Whatever may have been the case originally, there can be no doubt that in later times the relations between the youth and his lover implied unchaste intercourse.[99] And in other Greek states the education of the youth was accompanied by similar consequences. At an early age, the boy was taken away from his mother, and spent thenceforth all his time in the company of men, until he reached the age when marriage became for him a civic duty.[100] According to Plato, the gymnasia and common meals among the youth "seem always to have had a tendency to degrade the ancient and natural custom of love below the level, not only of man, but of the beasts."[101] Plato also mentions the effect which these habits had on the sexual instincts of the men: "When they reached manhood they were lovers of youths and not naturally inclined to marry or beget children, but, if at all, they did so only in obedience to the law."[102] Is not this, in all probability, an instance of acquired inversion? But besides the influence of education there was another factor which, coöperating with it, favored the development of homosexual tendencies, namely, the great gulf which mentally separated the sexes. Nowhere else has the difference in culture between men and women been so immense as in the fully developed Greek civilization. The lot of a wife in Greece was retirement and ignorance. She lived in almost absolute seclusion, in a separate part of the house, together with her female slaves, deprived of all the educating influence of male society, and having no place at those public spectacles which were the chief means of culture.[103] In such circumstances, it is not difficult to understand that men so highly intellectual as those of Athens regarded the love of women as the offspring of the common Aphrodite, who "is of the body rather than of the soul."[104] They had reached a stage of mental culture at which the sexual instinct normally has a craving for refinement, at which the gratification of mere physical lust appears brutal. In the eyes of the most refined, among them those who were inspired by the heavenly Aphrodite loved neither women nor boys, but intelligent beings whose reason was beginning to be developed, much about the time at which the beards began to grow.[105] In present China we meet with a parallel case. Dr. Matignon observes: *"Il y a tout lieu de supposer que ce tains Chinois, raffinés au point de vue intellectuel, recherchent dans le pédérastie la satisfaction des sens et de l'esprit. La femme chinoise est peu cultivée, ignorante même, quelle soit sa condition, honnête femme ou prostituée. Or le Chinois a souvent l'âme poétique: il aime les vers, la musique, les belles sentences des philosophes, autant de choses qu'il ne peut trouver chez le beau sexe de l'Empire du Milieu."*[106] So also it seems that the ignorance and dullness of Mohammedan women, which is a result of their total lack of education and their secluded life, is a cause of homosexual practices; Moors are sometimes heard to defend pederasty on the plea that the company of boys, who have always news to tell, is so much more entertaining than the company of women.

We have hitherto dealt with homosexual love as a fact; we shall now pass to the moral valuation to which it is subject. Where it occurs as a national habit we may assume that no censure, or no severe censure, is passed on it. Among the Bataks of Sumatra there is no punishment for it.[107] Of the *bazirs* among the Ngajus of Pula Patak, in Borneo, Dr. Schwaner says that "in spite of their loathsome calling they escape well-merited contempt."[108] The Society Islanders had for their homosexual practices "not only the sanction of their priests, but direct example of their respective deities."[109] The *tsekats* of Madagascar maintained that they were serving the deity by leading a feminine life;[110] but we are told that at Ankisimane and in Nossi-Bé, opposite to it, pederasts are objects of public contempt.[111] Father Veniaminoff says of the Atkha Aleuts that "sodomy and too early cohabitation with a betrothed or intended wife are called among them grave sins";[112] but apart from the fact that his account of these natives in general gives the impression of being somewhat eulogistic, the details stated by him only show that the acts in question were considered to require a simple ceremony of purification.[113] There is no indication that the North American aborigines attached any opprobrium to men who had intercourse with those members of their own sex who had assumed the dress and habits of women. In Kadiak such a companion was on the contrary regarded as a great acquisition; and the effeminate men themselves, far from being despised, were held in repute by the people, most of them being wizards.[114] We have previously noticed the connection between homosexual practices and shamanism among the various Siberian peoples; and it is said that such shamans as had changed their sex were greatly feared by the people, being regarded as very powerful.[115] Among the Illinois and Neudowessies, the effeminate men assist in all the Juggleries and the solemn dance in honor of the *calumet,* or sacred tobacco pipe, for which the Indians have such a deference that one may call it "the god of peace and war, and the arbiter of life and death"; but they are not permitted either to dance or sing. They are called into the councils of the Indians, and nothing can be decided upon without their advice; for because of their extraordinary manner of living they are looked upon as *manitous,* or supernatural beings, and persons of consequence.[116] The Sioux, Sacs, and Fox Indians give once a year, or oftener if they choose, a feast to the *Berdashe,* or *I-coo-coo-a,* who is a man dressed in woman's clothes, as he has been all his life. "For extraordinary privileges which he is known to possess, he is driven to the most servile and degrading duties, which he is not allowed to escape; and he being the only one of the tribe submitting to this disgraceful degradation, is looked upon as 'medicine' and sacred, and a feast is given to him annually; and initiatory to it, a dance by those few young men of the tribe who can . . . dance forward and publicly make their boast (without the denial of the Berdashe). . . . Such, and such only, are allowed to enter the dance and partake of the feast."[117] Among some American tribes, however, these effeminate men are said to be despised, especially by the women.[118] In ancient Peru, also, homosexual practices seem to have entered in the religious cult. In some particular places, says Cieza de Leon, boys were kept as priests in the temples, with whom it was rumored that the lords joined in company on days of festivity. They did not meditate, he adds, the committing of such sin, but only the offering of sacrifice to the demon. If the Incas by chance had some knowledge of such proceedings in the temple, they might have ignored them out of religious tolerance.[119] But the Incas themselves were not only free from such practices in their own persons, they would not even permit any one who was guilty of them to remain in the royal houses or palaces. And Cieza heard it related that, if it came to their knowledge that somebody had committed an offense of that kind, they punished it with such a severity that it was known to all.[120] Las Casas tells us that in several of the more remote provinces of Mexico, sodomy was tolerated, if not actually permitted, because the people believed that their gods were addicted to it; and it is not improbable that in earlier times the same was the case in the entire empire.[121] But in a later age, severe measures were adopted by legislators in order to suppress the practice. In Mexico, people found guilty of it were killed.[122] In Nicaragua, it was punished capitally by stoning,[123] and none of the Maya nations was without strict laws against it.[124] Among the Chibchas of Bogota the punishment for it was the infliction of a painful death.[125] However, it should be remembered that the ancient culture nations of America were generally extravagant in their punishments, and that their penal codes in the first place expressed rather the will of their rulers than the feelings of the people at large.[126]

Homosexual practices are said to be taken little notice of even by some uncivilized peoples who are not addicted to them. In the Pelew Islands, where such practices occur only sporadically, they are not punished, although, if I understand Herr Kubary rightly, the persons committing them may be put to shame.[127] The Ossetes of the Caucasus, among whom pederasty is very rare, do not generally prosecute persons for committing it, but ignore the act.[128] The East African Masai do not punish sodomy.[129] But we also meet with statements of a contrary nature. In a Kafir tribe, Mr. Warner heard of a case of it—the only one during a residence of twenty-five years—which was punished with a fine of some cattle claimed by the chief.[130] Among the Ondonga, pederasts are hated, and the men who behave like women are detested, most of them being wizards.[131] The Washambala consider pederasty a grave moral aberration and subject it to severe punishment.[132] Among the Waganda homosexual practices, which have been introduced by the Arabs and are of rare occurrence, "are intensely abhorred," the stake being the punishment.[133] The Negroes of Accra, who are not addicted to such practices, are said to detest them.[134] In Nubia, pederasty is held in abhorrence, except by the Kashefs and their relations, who endeavor to imitate the Mamelukes in everything.[135]

Mohammed forbade sodomy,[136] and the general opinion of his followers is that it should be punished like fornication— for which the punishment is, theoretically, severe enough[137]— unless the offenders make a public act of penitence. In order to convict, however, the law requires that four reliable persons shall swear to have been eye-witnesses,[138] and this alone would make the law a dead letter, even if it had the support of pop- ular feelings; but such support is certainly wanting. In Mo- rocco, active pederasty is regarded with almost complete indif- ference, whilst the passive sodomite, if a grown-up individual, is spoken of with scorn. Dr. Polak says the same of the Per- sians.[139] In Zanzibar, a clear distinction is made between male congenital inverts and male prostitutes; the latter are looked upon with contempt, whereas the former, as being what they are "by the will of God," are tolerated.[140] The Mohammedans of India and other Asiatic countries regard pederasty, at most, as a mere peccadillo.[141] Among the Hindus, it is said to be held in abhorrence,[142] but their sacred books deal with it leniently. According to the "Laws of Manu," "a twice-born man who commits an unnatural offense with a male, or has intercourse with a female in a cart drawn by oxen, in water, or in the day time shall bathe, dressed in his clothes"; and all these are reckoned as minor offenses.[143]

Chinese law makes little distinction between unnatural and other sexual offenses. An unnatural offense is variously con- sidered according to the age of the patient, and whether or not consent was given. If the patient be an adult, or a boy over the age of twelve, and consent, the case is treated as a slightly aggravated form of fornication, both parties being punished with a hundred blows and one month's cangue, whilst ordinary fornication is punished with eighty blows. If the adult or boy over twelve resist, the offense is considered as rape; and if the boy be under twelve, the offense is rape irrespective of consent or resistance, unless the boy has previously gone astray.[144] But, as a matter of fact, unnatural offenses are regarded as less hurtful to the community than ordinary immorality,[145] and pederasty is not looked down upon. *"L'opinion publique reste tout à fait indifférente à ce genre de distraction et la morale ne s'en émeut en rien: puisque cela plaît à l'opératéur et que l'opere est consentant, tout est pour le mieux; la loi chinoise n'aime guère à s'occuper des affaires trop intimes. La pédérastie est même considérée comme une chose de bon ton, une fantasie dispendieuse et partout un plaisir élégant. . . . La pédérastie a une consécration officielle en Chine. Il existe, en effet, des pédérés pour l'Empereur."*[146] Indeed, the only objection which Dr. Matignon has heard to be raised to pederasty by public opinion in China is that it has a bad influence on the eyesight.[147] In Japan there was no law against homosexual intercourse till the revolution of 1868.[148] In the period of Japanese chivalry it was considered more heroic if a man loved a person of his own sex than if he loved a woman; and nowadays people are heard to say that in those provinces of the country where pederasty is widely spread the men are more manly and robust than in those where it does not prevail.[149]

The laws of the ancient Scandinavians ignore homosexual practices; but passive pederasts were much despised by them. They were identified with cowards and regarded as sorcerers. The epithets applied to them—*argr, ragr, blandr,* and others— assumed the meaning of "poltroon" in general, and there are instances of the word *arg* being used in the sense of "practicing witchcraft." This connection between pederasty and sorcery, as a Norwegian scholar justly points out, helps us to understand Tacitus' statement that among the ancient Teutons individuals whom he describes as *corpore infames* were buried alive in a morass.[150] Considering that drowning was a common penalty for sorcery, it seems probable that this punishment was inflicted upon them not, in the first place, on account of their sexual practices, but in their capacity of wizards. It is certain that the opprobrium which the pagan Scandinavians attached to homosexual love was chiefly restricted to him who played the woman's part. In one of the poems the hero even boasts of being the father of offspring borne by another man.[151]

In Greece pederasty in its baser forms was censured, though generally, it seems, with not any great severity, and in some states it was legally prohibited.[152] According to an Athenian law, a youth who prostituted himself for money lost his rights as a free citizen and was liable to the punishment of death if he took part in a public feast or entered the *agora*.[153] In Sparta it was necessary that the "listener" should accept the "inspirator" from real affection; he who did so out of pecuniary consideration was punished by the ephors.[154] We are even told that among the Spartans the relations between the lover and his friend were truly innocent, and that if anything unlawful happened both must forsake either their country or their lives.[155] But the universal rule in Greece seems to have been that when decorum was observed in the friendship between a man and a youth, no inquiries were made into the details of the relationship.[156] And this attachment was not only regarded as permissible, but was praised as the highest and purest form of love, as the offspring of the heavenly Aphrodite, as a path leading to virtue, as a weapon against tyranny, as a safeguard of civic liberty, as a source of national greatness and glory. Phedrus said that he knew no greater blessing to a young man who is beginning life than a virtuous lover, or to the lover than a beloved youth; for the principle which ought to be the guide of men who would lead a noble life cannot be implanted by any other motive so well as by love.[157] The Platonic Pausanis argued that if love of youths is held in ill repute it is so only because it is inimical to tyranny; "the interests of rulers require that their subjects should be poor in spirit, and that there should be no strong bond of friendship or society among them, which love, above all other motives, is likely to inspire."[158] The power of the Athenian tyrants was broken by the love of Aristogeiton and the constancy of Harmodius; at Agrigentum in Sicily the mutual love of Chariton and Melanippus produced a similar result; and the greatness of Thebes was due to the Sacred Band established by Epaminondas. For "in the presence of his favorite, a man would choose to do anything rather than to get the character of a coward."[159] It was pointed out that the greatest heroes and the most warlike nations were those who were most addicted to the love of youths;[160] and it was said that an army consisting of lovers and their beloved ones, fighting at each other's side, although a mere handful, would overcome the whole world.[161]

Herodotus asserts that the love of boys was introduced from Greece into Persia.[162] Whether his statement be correct or not, such love could certainly not have been a habit of the Mazda worshipers.[163] In the Zoroastrian books "unnatural sin" is treated with a severity to which there is a parallel only in Hebrewism and Christianity. According to the Vendîdâd, there is no atonement for it.[164] It is punished with torments in the other world, and is capital here below.[165] Even he who committed it involuntarily, by force, is subject to corporal punishment.[166] Indeed, it is a more heinous sin than the slaying of a righteous man.[167] "There is no worse sin than this in the good religion, and it is proper to call those who commit it worthy of death in reality. If any one comes forth to them, and shall see them in the act, and is working with an ax, it is requisite for him to cut off the heads or to rip up the bellies of both, and it is no sin for him. But it is not proper to kill any person without the authority of high-priests and kings, except on account of committing or permitting unnatural intercourse."[168]

Nor are unnatural sins allowed to defile the land of the

Lord. Whosoever shall commit such abominations, be he Israelite or stranger dwelling among the Israelites, shall be put to death, the souls that do them shall be cut off from their people. By unnatural sins of lust the Canaanites polluted their land, so that God visited their guilt, and the land spued out its inhabitants.[169]

This horror of homosexual practices was shared by Christianity. According to St. Paul, they form the climax of the moral corruption to which God gave over the heathen because of their apostasy from him.[170] Tertullian says that they are banished "not only from the threshold, but from all shelter of the church, because they are not sins, but monstrosities."[171] St. Basil maintains that they deserve the same punishment as murder, idolatry, and witchcraft.[172] According to a decree of the Council of Elvira, those who abuse boys to satisfy their lusts are denied communion even at their last hour.[173] In no other point of morals was the contrast between the teachings of Christianity and the habits and opinions of the world over which it spread more radical than in this. In Rome there was an old law of unknown date, called Lex Scantinia (or Scatinia), which imposed a mulct on him who committed pederasty with a free person;[174] but this law, of which very little is known, had lain dormant for ages, and the subject of ordinary homosexual intercourse had never afterwards attracted the attetntion of the pagan legislators.[175] But when Christianity became the religion of the Roman Empire, a veritable crusade was opened against it. Constantius and Constans made it a capital crime, punishable with the sword.[176] Valentinian went further still and ordered that those who were found guilty of it should be burned alive in the presence of all the people.[177] Justinian, terrified by certain famines, earthquakes, and pestilences, issued an edict which again condemned persons guilty of unnatural offenses to the sword, "lest, as the result of these impious acts, whole cities should perish together with their inhabitants," as we are taught by Holy Scripture that through such acts cities have perished with the men in them.[178] "A sentence of death and infamy," says Gibbon, "was often founded on the slight and suspicious evidence of a child or a servant, . . . and pederasty became the crime of those to whom no crime could be imputed."[179]

This attitude towards homosexual practices had a profound and lasting influence on European legislation. Throughout the Middle Ages and later, Christian lawgivers thought that nothing but a painful death in the flames could atone for the sinful act.[180] In England Fleta speaks of the offender being buried alive;[181] but we are elsewhere told that burning was the due punishment.[182] As unnatural intercourse, however, was a subject for ecclesiastic cognizance, capital punishment could not be inflicted on the criminal unless the Church relinquished him to the secular arm; and it seems very doubtful whether she did relinquish him. Sir Frederick Pollack and Professor Maitland consider that the statute of 1533, which makes sodomy a felony, affords an almost sufficient proof that the temporal courts had not punished it, and that no one had been put to death for it for a very long time past.[183] It was said that the punishment for this crime—which the English law, in its very indictments, treats as a crime not fit to be named[184]—was determined to be capital by "the voice of nature and of reason, and the express law of God";[185] and it remained so till 1861,[186] although in practice the extreme punishment was not inflicted.[187] In France, persons were actually burned for this crime in the middle and latter part of the eighteenth century.[188] But in this, as in so many other respects, the rationalistic movement of that age brought about a change.[189] To punish sodomy with death, it was said, is atrocious; when unconnected with violence, the law ought to take no notice of it at all. It does not violate any other person's right, its influence on society is merely indirect, like that of drunkenness and free love; it is a disgusting vice, but its only proper punishment is contempt.[190] This view was adopted by the French "Code pénal," according to which homosexual practices in private, between two consenting adult parties, whether men or women, are absolutely unpunished. The homosexual act is treated as a crime only when it implies an outrage on public decency, or when there is violence or absence of consent, or when one of the parties is under age or unable to give valid consent.[191] This method of dealing with homosexuality has been followed by the legislators of various European countries,[192] and in those where the law still treats the act in question per se as a penal offense, notably in Germany, a propaganda in favor of its alteration is carried on with the support of many men of scientific eminence. This changed attitude of the law towards homosexual intercourse undoubtedly indicates a change of moral opinions. Though it is impossible to measure exactly the degree of moral condemnation, I suppose that few persons nowadays attach to it the same enormity of guilt as did our forefathers. And the question has even been put whether morality has anything at all to do with a sexual act, committed by the mutual consent of two adult individuals, which is productive of no offspring, and which on the whole concerns the welfare of nobody but the parties themselves.[193]

From this review of the moral ideas on the subject, incomplete though it be, it appears that homosexual practices are very frequently subject to some degree of censure, though the degree varies extremely. This censure is no doubt, in the first place, due to that feeling of aversion or disgust which the idea of homosexual intercourse tends to call forth in normally constituted adult individuals whose sexual instincts have developed under normal conditions. I presume that nobody will deny the general prevalence of such a tendency. It corresponds to that instinctive repugnance to sexual connections with women which is so frequently found in congenital inverts; whilst that particular form of it with which legislators have chiefly busied themselves evokes, in addition, a physical disgust of its own. And in a society where the large majority of people are endowed with normal sexual desires their aversion to homosexuality easily develops into moral censure and finds a lasting expression in custom, law, or religious tenets. On the other hand, where special circumstances have given rise to widely spread homosexual practices, there will be no general feeling of disgust even in the adults, and the moral opinion of the society will be modified accordingly. The act may still be condemned, in consequence of a moral doctrine formed under different conditions, or of the vain attempts of legislators to check sexual irregularities, or out of utilitarian considerations; but such a condemnation would in most people be rather theoretical than genuine. At the same time the baser forms of homosexual love may be strongly disapproved of for the same reasons as the baser forms of intercourse between men and women; and the passive pederast may be an object of contempt on account of the feminine practices to which he lends himself, as also an object of hatred on account of his reputation for sorcery. We have seen that the effeminate men are frequently believed to be versed in magic;[194] their abnormalities readily suggest that they are endowed with supernatural power, and they may resort to witchcraft as a substitute for their lack of manliness and physical strength. But the supernatural qualities or skill in magic ascribed to men who behave like women may also, instead of causing hatred, make them honored or reverenced.

It has been suggested that the popular attitude towards homosexuality was originally an aspect of economics, a question of under or over population, and that it was forbidden or allowed accordingly. Dr. Havelock Ellis thinks it probable that there is a certain relationship between the social reaction against homosexuality and against infanticide: "Where the one is regarded leniently and favorably, there generally the other is also; where the one is stamped out, the other is usually stamped out."[195] But our defective knowledge of the opinions of the various savage races concerning homosexuality hardly warrants such a conclusion; and if a connection really does exist between homosexual practices and infanticide it may be simply due to the numerical disproportion between the sexes resulting from the destruction of a multitude of female infants.[196] On the other hand, we are acquainted with several facts which are quite at variance with Dr. Ellis's suggestion. Among many Hindu castes female infanticide has for ages been a genuine custom,[197] and yet pederasty is remarkably rare among the Hindus. The ancient Arabs were addicted to infanticide,[198] but not to homosexual love,[199] whereas among modern Arabs the case is exactly the reverse. And if the early Christianity deemed infanticide and pederasty equally heinous sins, they did so certainly not because they were anxious that the population should increase; if this had been their motive, they would hardly have glorified celibacy. It is true that in a few cases, the unproductiveness of homosexual love has been given by indigenous writers as a reason for its encouragement or condemnation. It was said that the Cretan law on the subject had in view to check the growth of population; but, like Dollinger,[200] I do not believe that this assertion touches the real root of the matter. More importance may be attached to the following passage in Pahlavi texts: "He who is wasting seed makes a practice of causing the death of progeny; when the custom is completely continuous, which produces an evil stoppage of the progress of the race, the creatures have become annihilated; and certainly, that action, from which, when it is universally proceeding, the depopulation of the world must arise, has become and furthered the greatest wish of Aharman."[201] I am, however, of opinion that considerations of this kind have generally played only a subordinate, if any, part in the formation of the moral opinions concerning homosexual practices. And it can certainly not be admitted that the severe Jewish law against sodomy was simply due to the fact that the enlargement of the population was a strongly felt social need among the Jews.[202] However much they condemned celibacy, they did not put it on a par with the abominations of Sodom.

The excessive sinfulness which was attached to homosexual love by Zoroastrianism, Hebrewism, and Christianity, had quite a special foundation. It cannot be sufficiently accounted for either by utilitarian considerations or instinctive disgust. The abhorrence of incest is generally a much stronger feeling than the aversion to homosexuality. Yet in the very same chapter of Genesis which describes the destruction of Sodom and Gomorrah we read of the incest committed by the daughters of Lot with their father;[203] and according to the Roman Catholic doctrine, unnatural intercourse is an even more heinous sin than incest and adultery.[204] The fact is that homosexual practices were intimately associated with the gravest of all sins: unbelief, idolatry, or heresy.

According to Zoroastrianism, unnatural sin had been created by Angra Mainyu.[205] "Aharman, the wicked, miscreated the demons and fiends, and also the remaining corrupted ones, by his own unnatural intercourse."[206] Such intercourse is on a par with Afrasiyab, a Turanian king who conquered the Iranians for twelve years;[207] with Dahak, a king or dynasty who is said to have conquered Yim and reigned for a thousand years;[208] with Tur-i Bradar-vakhsh, a heterodox wizard by whom the best men were put to death.[209] He who commits unnatural sin is "in his whole being a Daeva";[210] and a Daeva worshiper is not a bad Zoroastrian, but a man who does not belong to the Zoroastrian system, a foreigner, a non-Aryan.[211] In the Vendî-dâd, after the statement that the voluntary commission of un-natural sin is a trespass for which there is no atonement for ever and ever, the question is put, When is it so? And the answer given is: If the sinner be a professor of the religion of Mazda, or one who has been taught in it. If not, his sin is taken from him, in case he makes confession of the religion of Mazda and resolves never to commit again such forbidden deeds.[212] This is to say, the sin is inexpiable if it involves a downright defiance of the true religion, it is forgiven if it is committed in ignorance of it and is followed by submission. From all this it appears that Zoroastrianism stigmatized unnatural intercourse as a practice of infidels, as a sign of unbelief. And I think that certain facts referred to previously help us to understand why it did so. Not only have homosexual practices been commonly associated with sorcery, but such an association has formed, and partly still forms, an incident of the shamanistic system prevalent among the Asiatic peoples of Turanian stock, and that it did so already in remote antiquity is made extremely probable by statements which I have just quoted from Zoroastrian texts. To this system Zoroastrianism was naturally furiously opposed, and the "change of sex" therefore appeared to the Mazda worshiper as a devilish abomination.

So also the Hebrews' abhorrence of sodomy was largely due to their hatred of a foreign cult. According to Genesis, unnatural vice was the sin of a people who were not the Lord's people, and the Levitical legislation represents Canaanitish abominations as the chief reason why the Canaanites were exterminated.[213] Now we know that sodomy entered as an element in their religion. Besides *kedeshoth,* or female prostitutes, there were *kedeshim,* or male prostitutes, attached to their temples.[214] The word *kadesh,* translated "sodomite," properly denotes a man dedicated to a deity;[215] and it appears that such men were consecrated to the mother of the gods, the famous Dea Syria, whose priests or devotees they were considered to be.[216] The male devotees of this and other goddesses were probably in a position analogous to that occupied by the female devotees of certain gods, who also, as we have seen, have developed into libertines;[217] and the sodomitic acts committed with these temple prostitutes may, like the connections with priestesses, have had in view to transfer blessings to the worshipers.[218] In Morocco, supernatural benefits are expected not only from heterosexual, but also from homosexual intercourse with a holy person. The *kedeshim* are frequently alluded to in the Old Testament, especially in the period of the monarchy, when rites of foreign origin made their way into both Israel and

Judah.[219] And it is natural that the Yahveh worshiper should regard their practices with the utmost horror as forming part of an idolatrous cult.

The Hebrew conception of homosexual love to some extent affected Mohammedanism, and passed into Christianity. The notion that it is a form of sacrilege was here strengthened by the habits of the gentiles. St. Paul found the abominations of Sodom prevalent among nations who had "changed the truth of God into a lie, and worshiped and served the creature more than the Creator."[220] During the Middle Ages heretics were accused of unnatural vice as a matter of course.[221] Indeed, so closely was sodomy associated with heresy that the same name was applied to both. In "La Coutume de Touraine-Anjou" the word *herite,* which is the ancient form of *heretique,*[222] seems to be used in the sense of "sodomite";[223] and the French *bougre* (from the Latin *Bulgarus,* Bulgarian), as also its English synonym, was originally a name given to a sect of heretics who came from Bulgaria in the eleventh century and was afterwards applied to other heretics, but at the same time it became the regular expression for a person guilty of unnatural intercourse.[224] In medieval laws sodomy was also repeatedly mentioned together with heresy, and the punishment was the same for both.[225] It thus remained a religious offense of the first order. It was not only a *"victim nefandum et super omnia detestandum,"*[226] but it was one of the four *"clamantia peccata,"* or "crying sins,"[227] a *crime de Majestie, vers le Roy celestre."*[228] Very naturally, therefore, it has come to be regarded with somewhat greater leniency by law and public opinion in proportion as they have emancipated themselves from theological doctrines. And the fresh light which the scientific study of the sexual impulse has lately thrown upon the subject of homosexuality must also necessarily influence the moral ideas relating to it, in so far as no scrutinizing judge can fail to take into account the pressure which a powerful nonvolitional desire exercises upon an agent's will.

REFERENCES

[1] Karsch, "Päderastie und Tribadie bei den Tieren," in *Jahrbuch für sexuelle Zwischenstufen*, II, p. 126, Havelock Ellis, *Studies in the Psychology of Sex*, "Sexual Inversion," p. 2.

[2] Ives, *Classification of Crimes*, p. 49. The statement that it is unknown among a certain people cannot reasonably mean that it may not be practiced in secret.

[3] Von Spix and von Martius, *Travels in Brazil*, ii, p. 246; von Martius, *Von dem Rechtszustande unter den Ureinwohnern Brasiliens*, p. 27; Lomonaco, "Sulle razze indigene del Brasile," in *Archivio per l'antropologia e la etnologia*, xix, p. 46; Burton, *Arabian Nights*, x, p. 246 (Brazilian Indians); Garcilasso de la Vega, *First Part of the Royal Commentaries of the Yncas*, ii, p. 441; Cieza de Leon, "La crónica del Perú (primera parte)," ch. 49, in *Biblioteca de autores españoles*, xxvi, p. 403 (Peruvian Indians at the time of the Spanish conquest). Oviedo Valdés, "Sumario de la natural historia de las Indias," ch. 81, in *Biblioteca de autores españoles*, xxii, p. 508 (Isthmians).
Bancroft, *Native Races of the Pacific States*, i, p. 585 (Indians of New Mexico); ii, p. 497 (Ancient Mexicans).
Diaz del Castillo, "Conquista de Nueva-España," ch. 208, in *Biblioteca de autores españoles*, xxvi, p. 309 (Ancient Mexicans).
Landa, *Relacion de las cosas de Yucatan*, p. 178 (Ancient Yucatans).
Nuñez Cabeza de Vaca, "Naufragios y relacion de la jornada que hizo a la Florida," ch. 26, in *Biblioteca de autores españoles*, xxii, p. 538; Coreal, *Voyages aux Indes Occidentales*, i, p. 33 (Indians of Florida).
Perrin du Lac, *Voyage dans les deux Louisianes et chez les nations sauvages du Missouri*, p. 352; Bossu, *Travels Through Louisiana*, i, p. 303.
Hennepin, *Nouvelle Découverte d'un très Grand Pays Situé dans L'Amérique*, p. 219; "La Salle's Last Expedition and Discoveries in North America," in *Collections of the New York Historical Society*, ii, p. 237 *sq.;* de Lahontan, *Mémories de l'Amérique septentrionale*, p. 142 (Illinois).
Marquette, *Recit des Voyages*, p. 52 (Illinois and Naudowessies).
Wied-Neuwied, *Travels in the Interior of North America*, p. 351 (Manitaries, Mandans, etc.).
McCoy, *History of Baptist Indian Missions*, p. 360 (Osages).
Heriot, *Travels Through the Canadas*, p. 278; Catlin, *North American Indians*, ii, p. 214 (Sioux).
Dorsey, "Omaha Sociology," in *Ann. Rep. Bur. Ethn.*, iii, p. 365; James, *Expedition from Pittsburgh to the Rocky Mountains*, i, p. 267 (Omahas).
Loskiel, *History of the Mission of the United Brethren Among the Indians*, i, p. 14 (Iroquois).
Richardson, *Artic Searching Expedition*, iii, p. 42 (Cretes).
Oswald, quoted by Bastian, *Der Mensch in der Geschichte*, iii, p. 314 (Indians of California).
Holder, in *New York Medical Journal*, December 7, 1889, quoted by Havelock Ellis, p. 9 (Indians of Washington and other tribes in the Northwestern United States). See also Karsch, "Uranismus oder Päderastie und Tribadie bei den Naturvölkern," in *Jahrbuch für sexuelle Zwischenstufen*, iii, p. 122.
[4] Lafitau, *Mœrs des sauvages amériquains*, i. pp. 603, 697, *sqq.*

HOMOSEXUAL LOVE 129

5 Dall, *Alaska*, p. 402; Bancroft, i, p. 92; Waitz, *Anthropologie der Naturvölker*, v, p. 314 (Aleuts); von Langsdorf, *Voyages and Travels*, ii, p. 48 (Natives of Oonalaska); Steller, *Kamtschatka*, p. 289; Georgi, *Russia*, iii, p. 132 (Kamchadales).

6 Davydow, quoted by Holmberg, "Ethnographische Skizzen über die völker des russischen Amerika," in *Acta So. Scientiarum Fennicæ*, iv, p. 400. Lisiansky, *Voyage Round the World*, p. 109. Von Langsdorf, ii, p. 64. Sauer, *Billing's Expedition to the Northern Parts of Russia*, p. 176. Sarytschew, "Voyage of Discovery to the North-East of Siberia," in *Collection of Modern and Contemporary Voyages*, vi, p. 16.

7 Bogoras, quoted by Demidoff, *Shooting Trip to Kamchatka*, p. 74.

8 Jochelson, *Koryak Religion and Myth*, pp. 52, 53, n. 3.

9 *Ibid., op. cit.*, p. 52 sq.

10 Wilken, "Plechtigheden en gebruiken bij verlovingen en haweliiken bij de volken van den Indischen Archipel," in *Bijdragen tot de taalland- en volkenkunde van Nederlandsch-Indie*, 33 (series v, vol. iv), p. 457.

11 Crawford, *History of the Indian Archipelago*, iii, p. 139. Marsden, *History of Sumatra*, p. 261.

12 Junghuhn, *Die Battalander auf Sumatra*, ii, p. 157.

13 Hardeland, *Dajacksch-deutsches Wörterbuch*, p. 53, Schwaner, *Borneo*, p. 186. Perelaer, *Ethnographische beschrijving der Dajaks*, p. 32.

14 Haddon, "Ethnography of the Western Tribe of Torres Straits," in *Jour. Anthr. Inst.*, xix, p. 315.

15 Seligmann, "Sexual Inversion Among Primitive Races," in *The Alienist and Neurologist*, xxiii, p. 3.

16 Beardmore, "Natives of Mowat, Daudai, New Guinea," in *Jour. Anthr. Inst.*, xix, p. 464. Haddon, *ibid.*, xix, p. 315.

17 Hernsheim, *Beitrag zur Sprache der Marshall-Inseln*, p. 40. A different opinion is expressed by Senft, in Steinmetz, *Rechtsverhältnisse von eingeborenen Völkern in Afrika und Ozeanien*, p. 437.

18 Remy, *Ka Moolelo Hawaii*, p. 43.

19 Turnbull, *Voyage Round the World*, p. 382. See: Wilson, *Missionary Voyage to the S. Pacific*, pp. 333, 361; Ellis, *Polynesian Researches*, pp. 246, 258.

20 Foley, "Sur les habitations et les mœurs des Néo-Calédoniens," in *Bull. Soc. d'Anthrop. Paris*, ser. iii, vol. ii, p. 606. See: de Rochas, *Nouvelle Calédonie*, p. 235.

21 Hardman, "Notes on Some Habits and Customs of the Natives of the Kimberley District," in *Proceed. Roy. Irish Academy*, ser. iii, vol. i, p. 74.

22 *Ibid.*, pp. 71, 73.

23 Purcell, "Rites and Customs of Australian Aborigines," in *Verhandl. Berliner Gesellsch. Anthrop.*, 1893, p. 287.

24 Ravenscroft, "Some Habits and Customs of the Chingalee Tribe," in *Trans. Roy. Soc. South Australia*, xv, p. 122. I am indebted to Mr. N. W. Thomas for drawing my attention to these statements.

25 Howitt, "Some Australian Ceremonies of Initiation," in *Jour. Anthr. Inst.*, xii, p. 450.

26 Lasnet, in *Annales d'hygiène et de médicine coloniales*, 1899, p. 494, quoted by Havelock Ellis, *op. cit.*, p. 10. Cf. Rencurel, in *Annales d'hygiène*, 1900, p. 562, quoted *ibid.*, p. 11. See: Leguével de Lacombe, *Voyage à Madagaskar*, i, p. 97 sq. Pederasty prevails to some extent in the island of Nossi-Bé, close to

Madagaskar, and is very common at Ankisimane, opposite to it, on Jassandava Bay (Walter, in Steinmetz, *Rechtsverhältnisse*, p. 376).

27 De Flacourt, *Histoire de la grande isle Madagascar*, p. 86.

28 Rautanen, in Steinmetz, *Rechtsverhältnisse*, p. 333.

29 Nicole, *ibid.*, p. 3.

30 *Ibid.*, p. 38.

31 Munzinger, *Ostafrikanische Studien*, p. 525 (Barea and Kunáma). Baumann, "Conträre Sexual-Erscheinungen bei der Neger-Bevölkerung Zanzibars," in *Verhandl. der Berliner Gesellsch. für Anthropologie*, 1899, p. 668. Felkin, "Notes on the Waganda Tribe of Central Africa," in *Proceed. Roy Soc. Edinburgh*, xiii, p. 723. Johnston, *British Central Africa*, p. 404 (Bakongo). Monrad, *Skildring of Guinea-Kysten*, p. 57 (Negroes of Accra). Torday and Joyce, "Ethnography of the Ba-Mbala," in *Jour. Anthr. Inst.*, xxxv, p. 410. Nicole, in Steinmetz, *Rechtsverhältnisse*, p. 3 (Muhammedan Negroes). Tellier, *ibid.*, p. 159 (Kreis Kita in the French Soudan). Beverley, *ibid.*, p. 210 (Wagogo). Kraft, *ibid.*, p. 288 (Wapokomo).

32 Baumann, in *Verhandl. Berliner Gesellsch. Anthrop.*, 1899, p. 668.

33 Burckhardt, *Travels in Nubia*, p. 135.

34 D'Escayrac de Lautre, *Afrikanische Wüste*, p. 93.

35 Burckhardt, *Travels in Arabia*, i, p. 364. See also Von Kremer, *Culturgeschichte des Orients*, ii, p. 269.

36 Burton, *Arabian Nights*, x, p. 232.

37 Kovalewsky, *Coutume contemporaire*, p. 340.

38 Polak, "Die Prostitution in Persien," in *Wiener Medizinische Wochenschrift*, xi, p. 627. *Idem, Persien*, i, p. 237. Burton, *Arabian Nights*, x, p. 233. Wilson, *Persian Life and Customs*, p. 229.

39 Malcolm, *Sketch of the Sighs*, p. 140. Havelock Ellis, *op. cit.*, p. 5, *n.* 2. Burton, *Arabian Nights*, x, p. 236.

40 Wilson, *Abode of Snow*, p. 420. Burton, *Arabian Nights*, x, p. 236.

41 Stavorinus, *Voyages to the East-Indies*, i, p. 456. Fryer, *New Account of East-India*, p. 97. Chevers, *Manual of Medical Jurisprudence for India*, p. 705.

42 Chevers, p. 708.

43 *Indo-Chinese Gleaner*, iii, p. 193. Wells Williams, *The Middle Kingdom*, p. 836. Matignon, "Deux mots sur la pédérastie en Chine," in *Archives d'anthropologie criminelle*, xiv, p. 38. Karsch, *Das gleichgeschlechtliche Leben der Ostasiaten*, p. 6.

44 Jways, "Nan sho k," in *Jahrbuch für sexuelle Zwischenstufen*, pp. 266, 268, 270. Karsch, p. 71.

45 Dionysius of Halicarnassus, *Antiquitates Romane*, vii, p. 2. *Atheneus, Deipnosophistæ*, xii, p. 518 (Etruscans). Rein, *Criminalrecht der Römer*, p. 863.

46 Polybius, *Historiæ*, xxxii, ii, p. 5.

47 Buret, *La syphilis aujourd'hui et chez les anciens*, p. 197. Catullus, *Carmina*, lxi ("In Nuptias, Juliæ et Manlii"), p. 128. Martial, *Epigrammata*, viii, 44, p. 16.

48 Juvenal, *Satiræ*, ii, p. 117. Martial, xii, p. 42.

49 Diodorus Siculus, *Bibliotheca historica*, xxxii, p. 7. Aristotle, *Politica*, ii, 9, p. 1269.

50 "Spuren von Konträrsexualität bei den alten Skandinaviern," in *Jahrbuch für sexuelle Zwischenstufen*, iv, p. 244.

51 Hahn, *Albanesische, Studien*, ii, p. 168.

52 Karsch, in *Jahrbuch für sexuelle Zwischenstufen*, iii, p. 85. Ploss-Bartels, *Das Weib*, p. 517. Von Krafft-Ebing, *Psychopathia sexualis*, p. 278. Moll, *Die Conträre Sexualempfindung*, p. 247, Havelock Ellis, p. 118.

53 Magalhanes de Gandavo, *Histoire de la Province de Sancta-Cruz*, p. 116.

54 Dall, p. 139.

55 Fritsch, quoted by Karsh, in *Jahrbuch für sexuelle Zwischenstufen*, iii, p. 87.

56 Fritsch, *Die Eingeborenen Süd-Africa's*, p. 227. Cf. Schinz, *Deutsch Südwest-Afrika*, pp. 173, 177.

57 Baumann, in *Verhandl. Berliner Gesellsch. Anthrop.*, 1889, p. 668.

58 Havelock Ellis, *op. cit.*, p. 123.

59 Jacobs, *Eenigen tijd onder de Baliërs*, p. 134.

60 Havelock Ellis, *op. cit.*, p. 124.

61 See *ibid.*, p. 121.

62 Another reason for such practices is given by Mr. Beardmore (in *Jour. Anthrop. Inst.*, xix, p. 464), with reference to the Papuans of Mowat. He says that they indulge in sodomy because too great increase of population is undesired amongst the younger portion of the married people. Cf. *infra*, p. 484.

63 Havelock Ellis, *op. cit.*, p. 1.

64 Jochelson, *op. cit.*, p. 52.

65 Holder, quoted by Havelock Ellis, *op. cit.*, p. 9.

66 Baumann, in *Verhandl. Berliner Gesellsch. Anthrop.*, 1899, p. 668.

67 Cf. Féré, *L'instinct sexuel*, quoted by Havelock Ellis, *op. cit.*, p. 41.

68 James, *Principles of Psychology*, ii, p. 439. See also Ives, *op. cit.*, p. 56.

69 Dr. Dessoir ("Zur Psychologie der Vita sexualis," in *Allgemeine Zeitschrift für Psychiatrie*, i, p. 942) even goes so far as to conclude that "an undifferentiated sexual feeling is normal, on the average, during the first years of puberty." But this is certainly an exaggeration (cf. Havelock Ellis, *op. cit.*, p. 47).

70 Karsch, in *Jahrbuch für sexuelle Zwischenstufen*, ii, p. 126. Havelock Ellis, *op. cit.*, p. 2.

71 Havelock Ellis, *op. cit.*, p. 2.

72 Von den Steinen, *Unter den Naturvölkern Zenral-Brasiliens*, p. 502.

73 Ellis, *Polynesian Researches*, i, p. 257.

74 Matignon, in *Archives d'anthropologie criminelle*, xiv, p. 42. Karsch, *op. cit.*, p. 32.

75 Waitz, *Anthropologie der Naturvölker*, iii, p. 113. Bastian, *Der Mensch in der Geschichte*, iii, p. 305 (Dohomans).

76 *Supra*, ii, p. 462. Karsch, *op. cit.*, pp. 6 (China), 76 (Japan), 132 (Corea).

77 See Voltaire, *Dictionnaire philosophique*, "Amour Socratique" (Œuvres, vii, p. 82); Buret, *Syphilis in the Middle Ages and in Modern Times*, p. 88.

78 Cf. Havelock Ellis, *op. cit.*, p. 5.

79 Freeman, *Reign of William Rufus*, i, p. 159.

80 Polak, in *Wiener Medizinische Wochenschrift*, xi, p. 628.

81 Marquette, *op. cit.*, p. 53 (Illinois). Perrin du Lac, *Voyage dans les deux Louisianes et chez les nations sauvages du Missouri*, p. 352. Cf. Nuñez Cabeza de Vaca, *loc. cit.*, p. 538 (concerning the Indians of Florida):—". . . tiran arco y llevan muy gran carga."

82 Steinmetz, *Rechtsverhältnisse*, p. 38.

83 Havelock Ellis, *op. cit.*, p. 3.

84 Krafft-Ebing, *op. cit.*, p. 211.

85 Moll, *op. cit.*, p. 157.
86 Havelock Ellis, *op. cit.*, p. 50. Cf. *ibid.*, p. 181.
87 *Ibid.*, p. 3.
88 Cf. Norman, "Sexual Perversion," in Tuke's *Dictionary of Psychological Medicine*, ii, p. 1156.
89 Havelock Ellis, *op. cit.*, p. 191.
90 Dr. Havelock Ellis also admits (*op. cit.*, p. 190) that if in early life the sexual instincts are less definitely determined than when adolescence is complete, "it is conceivable, though unproved, that a very strong impression, acting even on a normal organism, may cause arrest of sexual development on the psychic side. It is a question," he adds, "I am not in a position to settle."
91 Voltaire, *Dictionnaire Philosophique*, art. "Amour Socratique," (Œuvres, vii, p. 81). Cf. Ovid, *Metamorphoses*, x, p. 84.
92 Servius, *In Vergilii Æneidos*, x, p. 325. For the whole subject of pederasty among the Dorians see Mueller, *History and Antiquities of the Doric Race*, ii, p. 307.
93 Elian, *Varia historia*, iii, p. 10.
94 Mueller, *op. cit.*, ii, p. 308.
95 Xenophon, *Historia Graca*, iv, p. 8.
96 Plutarch, *Lycurgus*, xxv, p. 1.
97 *Ibid.*, xviii, p. 8. Ælian, *op. cit.*, iii, p. 10.
98 Ælian, *op. cit.*, iii, p. 9. Athenæus, *Deipnosophistæ*, xiii, 77, p. 601.
99 Cf. Symonds, "Die Homosexualität in Griechenland," in Havelock Ellis and Symonds, *Das Konträre Geschlechtsgefühl*, p. 55.
100 *Ibid.*, p. 116. Döllinger, *The Gentile and the Jew*, ii, p. 244.
101 Plato, *Leges*, i, p. 636. Cf. Plutarch, *Amatorius*, v, p. 9.
102 Plato, *Symposium*, p. 192.
103 "State of Female Society in Greece," in *Quarterly Review*, xxii, p. 172. Lecky, *History of European Morals*, ii, p. 287. Döllinger, *op. cit.*, ii, p. 234.
104 Plato, *Symposium*, p. 181. That the low state of the Greek women was instrumental to pederasty has been pointed out by Döllinger (*op. cit.*, ii, p. 244) and Symonds (*loc. cit.*, pp. 77, 100, 101, 116).
105 Plato, *Symposium*, p. 181.
106 Matignon, in *Archives d'anthropologie criminelle*, xiv, p. 41.
107 Junghuhn, *op. cit.*, ii, p. 157, *n.*
108 Schwaner, *op. cit.*, i, p. 186.
109 Ellis, *Polynesian Researches*, i, p. 258. Cf. Moerenhout, *Voyages aux iles du Grand Océan*, ii, p. 167.
110 De Flacourt, *op. cit.*, p. 86.
111 Walter, in Steinmetz, *Rechtsverhältnisse*, p. 376.
112 Veniaminoff, quoted by Petroff, *Report on Alaska*, p. 158.
113 *Ibid.*, p. 158:—"The offender desirous of unburdening himself selected a time when the sun was clear and unobscured; he picked up certain weeds and carried them about his person; then deposited them and threw his sin upon them, calling the sun as a witness, and, when he had eased his heart of all that had weighed upon it, he threw the grass or weeds into the fire, and after that considered himself cleansed of his sin."
114 Davydow, quoted by Holmberg, *loc. cit.*, p. 400. Lisianski, *op. cit.*, p. 199.
115 Bogoras, quoted by Demidoff, *op. cit.*, p. 75. Jochelson, *op. cit.*, p. 52 *sq.*
116 Marquette, *op. cit.*, p. 53.

117 Catlin, *North American Indians*, ii, p. 214.

118 "La Salle's Last Expedition in North America," in *Collections of the New York Historical Society*, ii, p. 238 (Illinois). Perrin du Lac, *Voyage dans les deux Louisianes et chez les nations sauvages du Missouri*, p. 352. Bossu, *op. cit.*, i, p. 303 (Choctaws). Oviedo y Valdés, *loc. cit.*, p. 508 (Isthmians). Von Martius, *Von dem Rechtszustande unter d. Urein-wohnern Brasiliens*, p. 28 (Guayeurius).

119 Cieza de Leon, *Segunda parte de la Crónica del Perú*, ch. 25, p. 99. See also *idem, Crónica del Perú (primera parte)*, ch. 64. *Biblioteca de autores españoles*, xxvi, p. 416.

120 *Idem, Segunda parte de la Crónica del Perú*, ch. 25, p. 98. See also Garcilasso de la Vega, *op. cit.*, ii, p. 132.

121 Las Casas, quoted by Bancroft, *op. cit.*, ii, p. 467. Cf. *ibid.*, ii, p. 677.

122 Clavigero, *History of Mexico*, i, p. 357.

123 Squier, "Archæology and Ethnology of Nicaragua," in *Trans. American Ethn. Soc.*, iii, pt. i, p. 128.

124 Bancroft, *op. cit.*, ii, p. 677.

125 Piedrahita, *Historia general de las conquistas del nuevo reyno de Granada*, p. 46.

126 See *supra*, i, pp. 186, 195.

127 Kubary, "Die Verbrechen und das Strafverfahren auf den Pelau-Inseln," in *Original-Mittheilungen aus der ethnologischen Abtheilung der königlichen Museen zu Berlin*, i, p. 84.

128 Kovalewsky, *Coutume contemporaine*, p. 340.

129 Merker, *Die Masai*, p. 208. The Masai, however, slaughter at once any bullock or he-goat which is noticed to practice unnatural intercourse for fear lest otherwise their herds be visited by a plague as a divine punishment (*ibid.*, p. 159).

130 Warner, in Maclean, *Compendium of Kafir Laws*, p. 62.

131 Rautanen, in Steinmetz, *Rechtsverhältnisse*, p. 333.

132 Lang, *ibid.*, p. 232.

133 Felkin, in *Proceed. Roy. Soc. Edinburgh*, p. 723.

134 Monrad, *op. cit.*, p. 57.

135 Burckhardt, *Travels in Nubia*, p. 135.

136 *Koran*, iv, p. 20.

137 Sachau, *Muhammendanisches Recht nach Schafitischer Lehre*, pp. 809, 818:—"Sodomita si muhsan (that is, a married person in possession of full civic rights) est punitur lapidatione, si non est *muhsan* punitur et flagellatione et exsilio."

138 Burton, *Arabian Nights*, x, p. 224.

139 Polak, in *Wiener Medizinische Wochenschrift*, xi, p. 628.

140 Baumann, in *Verhandl. Berliner Gesellsch. Anthrop.*, 1899, p. 669.

141 Chevers, *op. cit.*, p. 708. Burton, *Arabian Nights*, x, p. 237.

142 Burton, *Arabian Nights*, x, p. 222.

143 *Laws of Manu*, xi, p. 175. Cf. *Institutes of Vishnu*, liii, p. 4; *Apastamba*, i, 9, 26, p. 7; *Gautama*, xxv, p. 7.

144 Alabaster, *Notes and Commentaries on Chinese Criminal Law*, p. 367 *sqq.* To *Tsing Leu Lee*, Appendix, no. xxxii, p. 570.

145 Alabaster, *op. cit.*, p. 369.

146 Matignon, in *Archives d'anthropologie criminelle*, xiv, pp. 42, 43, 52.

147 *Ibid.*, p. 44.

148 Karsch, *op. cit.*, p. 99.

149 Jwaya, in *Jahrbuch für sexuelle Zwischenstufen*, iv, pp. 266, 270.

150 Tacitus, *Germania*, p. 12.

151 "Spuren von Konträrsexualität, bei den alten Skandinaviern—Mitteilungen eines norwegischen Gelehrnten," in *Jahrbuch für sexuelle Zwischenstufen*, iv, pp. 245, 256.

152 Xenophon, *Lacedæmoniorum respublica*, ii, p. 13. Maximus Tyrius, *Dissertationes*, xxv, p. 4; xxvi, p. 9.

153 Æschines, *Contra Timarchum*, p. 21.

154 Ælian, *Varia historia*, iii, p. 10. Cf. Plato, *Leges*, viii, p. 910.

155 Ælian, *op. cit.*, iii, p. 12. Cf. Maximus Tyrius, *op. cit.*, xxvi, p. 8.

156 Cf. Symonds, *loc. cit.*, p. 92 *sqq.*

157 Plato, *Symposium*, p. 178.

158 *Ibid.*, p. 182.

159 Hieronymus, the Peripatetic, referred to by Athenæus, *op. cit.*, xiii, 78, p. 602. See also Maximus Tyrius, *op. cit.*, xxiv, p. 2.

160 Plutarch, *Amatorius*, xvii, p. 14.

161 Plato, *Symposium*, p. 178.

162 Herodotus, i, p. 135.

163 Ammanianus Marcellinus says (xxiii, p. 76) that the inhabitants of Persia were free from pederasty. But see also Sextus Empiricus, *Pyrrhoniæ hypotyposes*, i, p. 152.

164 *Vendîdâd*, i, p. 12; vii, p. 27.

165 Darmesteter, in *Sacred Books of the East*, lv, p. 86.

166 *Vendîdâd*, vii, p. 26.

167 *Dîna-i-Maînôg-i Khirad*, xxxvi, p. 1.

168 *Sad Dar*, ix, p. 2.

169 *Leviticus*, xviii:22, 24; xx:13.

170 *Romans*, i:26.

171 Tertullian, *De pudicitia*, p. 4 (Migne, *Patrologiæ cursus*, ii, p. 987).

172 St. Basil, quoted by Bingham, *Works*, vi, p. 432.

173 *Concilium Elibertianum*, ch. 71 (Labbe-Mansi, *Sacrorum Conciliorum collectio*, ii, p. 17).

174 Juvenal, *Satiræ*, ii, p. 43. Valerius Maximus, *Facta dictaque memorabilia*, vi, 1, p. 7. Quintilian, *Institutio oratoria*, iv, 2, p. 69:—"Decem milia, quæ pœna stupratori constituta est, dabit." Christ, *Hist. Legis Scatiniæ*, quoted by Döllinger, *op. cit.*, ii, p. 274. Rein, *Criminalrecht der Römer*, p. 865. Bingham, *op. cit.*, vi, p. 433. Mommsen, *Römisches Strafrecht*, p. 793.

175 Mommsen, *op. cit.*, p. 704. Rein, *op. cit.*, p. 866. The passage in *Digesta*, xlviii, 5, 35, p. 1, refers to *stuprum* independently of the sex of the victim.

176 *Codex Theodosianus*, ix, pp. 7, 3. *Codex Justinianus*, ix, pp. 9, 30.

177 *Codex Theodosianus*, ix, pp. 7, 6.

178 *Novellæ*, p. 77. See also *ibid.*, p. 141, and *Institutiones*, iv, pp. 18, 4.

179 Gibbon, *History of the Decline and Fall of the Roman Empire*, v, p. 323.

180 Du Boys, *Histoire du droit criminel de l'Espagne*, pp. 93, 403. *Les Establissements de Saint Louis*, i, p. 90; ii, p. 147. Beaumanoir, *Coutumes du beauvoisis*, xxx, II; vol. I, p. 413. Montesquieu, *De l'esprit des lois*, xii, p. 6 (*Œuvres*, p. 283). Hume, *Commentaries on the Law of Scotland*, ii, p. 335; Pitcairn, *Criminal Trials in Scotland*, ii, p. 491, *n.* 2. Clarus, *Practica criminalis*, book v. . . .
In the beginning of the nineteenth century sodomy was still nominally subject

to capital punishment by burning in Bavaria (von Feuerbach, *Kritik des Klein-schrodischen Eutwurf's zu einem peinlichen Gesetzbuche für die Chur-Pfalz-Bayrischen Stäaten*, ii, p. 13), and in Spain as late as 1843 (Du Boys, p. 721).

181 Fleta, i, 37; iii, p. 84.

182 Britton, i, p. 10; i, p. 42.

183 Pollock and Maitland, *History of English Law Before the Time of Edward I*, ii, p. 556.

184 Coke, *Third Part of the Institutes of the Laws of England*, p. 58. Blackstone, *Commentaries on the Laws of England*, iv, p. 218.

185 Blackstone, *op. cit.*, iv, p. 218.

186 Stephen, *History of the Criminal Law of England*, i, p. 475.

187 Blackstone, *op. cit.*, iv, p. 218.

188 Desmaze, *Pénalités anciennes*, p. 211. Havelock Ellis, *op. cit.*, p. 207.

189 Numa Prætorius, p. 121.

190 Note of the editors of Kehl's edition of Voltaire's *Prix de la justice et de l'humanité*, in *Œuvres complètes*, v, 437, *n.* 2.

191 Code Pénal, 330, Chevalier, *L'inversion sexuelle*, p. 431. Havelock Ellis, p. 207.

192 Numa Prætorius, *loc. cit.*, pp. 131-133, 143.

193 See, *e.g.* Bax, *Ethics of Socialism*, p. 126.

194 See also Bastian, in *Ztschr. f. Ethnol.* i, 88. Speaking of the witches of Fez, Leo Africanus says (*History and Description of Africa*, ii, p. 458) that "they have a damnable custome to commit unlawful Venerie among themselves." Among the Patagonians, according to Falkner (*Description of Patagonia*, p. 117), the male wizards are chosen for their office when they are children, and "a preference is always shown to those who at that early time of life discover an effeminate disposition." They are obliged, as it were, to leave their sex, and to dress themselves in female apparel.

195 Havelock Ellis, *op. cit.*, p. 206.

196 Cf. *supra*, ii, p. 466 (Society Islanders).

197 *Supra*, i, p. 307.

198 *Supra*, i, p. 406.

199 Von Kremer, *Culturgeschichte des Orients*, ii, p. 129.

200 Döllinger, *op cit.*, p. 239

201 *Dadistan-i Dinik*, lxxii, 2.

202 Havelock Ellis, *op. cit.*, p. 206.

203 *Genesis*, xix, p. 31.

204 Thomas Aquinas, *Summa theologica*, ii, iii. 154, 12. Katz, *Grundriss des kanonischen Strafrechts*, pp. 104, 118, 120. Clarus, *Practica criminalis*, book v. #Sodomia, Additiones, i (*Opera omnia*, ii, p. 152): "Hoc vitium est majus, quam si quis propriam matrem cognosceret."

205 *Vendîdâd*, i, p. 12.

206 *Dîna-î Maînôg-î Khirad*, viii, p. 10.

207 *Sad Dar* ix, p. 5. West's note to *Dîna-î Maînôg-î Khirad*, viii, p. 29 (*Sacred Books of the East*, xxiv, p. 35, *n.* 4).

208 *Sad Dar* ix, p. 5. West's note to *Dîna-î Maînôg-î Khirad*, viii, p. 29 (*Sacred Books of the East*, xxiv, p. 35, *n.* 3).

209 *Sad Dar* ix, p. 5. West's note to *Dadistan-i Dinik*, lxxii, p. 8 (*Sacred Books of the East*, xviii, p. 218).

210 *Vendidad*, viii, p. 82.

211 Darmesteter, in *Sacred Books of the East*, i, p. 2.

212 *Vendidad*, viii, p. 27.

213 *Leviticus*, xx, 23.

214 *Deuteronomy*. xxiii, 17. Driver, *Commentary on Deuteronomy*, p. 264.

215 Driver, *op. cit.*, p. 264. Selbie, "Sodomite," in Hastings, *Dictionary of the Bible*, iv, p. 559.

216 St. Jerome, *In Osee*, i, pp. 4, 14 (Migne, *op. cit.*, xxv, 851). Cook's note to I *Kings*, xiv, 24, in his edition of *The Holy Bible*, i, p. 571.

217 *Supra*, ii, p. 444.

218 Rosenbaum suggests (*Geschichte der Lustseuche im Alterhume*, p. 120) that the eunuch priest connected with the cult of the Ephesian Artemis and the Phrygian worship of Cybele likewise were sodomites.

219 I *Kings*, xiv, 24; xv. 12; xxii, 46. II *Kings*, xxiii 7. *Job*, xxvi, 14. Driver, *op. cit.*, p. 265.

220 *Romans*, i, 25.

221 Littre, *Dictionnaire de la langue française*, i, p. 386. "Bougre." Haynes, *Religious Persecution*, p. 54.

222 Littre, *op. cit.*, i, p. 2010, "Heretique."

223 *Les Establissements de Saint Louis*, i, p. 90; ii, p. 147. Viollet, in his Introduction to the same work, i, p. 254.

224 Littre, *op. cit.*, i, p. 386, "Bougre." Murray, *New English Dictionary*, i, p. 1160, "Bugger." Lea, *History of the Inquisition of the Middle Ages*, i, p. 115, note.

225 Beaumanoir, *Coutumes du Beauvoisis*, xxx, II, vol. i, p. 413: "Qui erre contre le foi, comme en méscreance, de le quele il ne veut venir a voie de verité, ou qui fet sodomiterie, il droit estre ars, et forfet tout le sien en le manière dessus." Britton, i, p. 10, vol. i, p. 42. Montesquieu, *De l'esprit des lois*, xii, 6 (*Œuvres*, p. 283). Du Boys, *Histoire du droit criminel de l'Espagne*, pp. 486, 721.

226 Clarus, *Practica criminalis*, book v. #Sodomia, I (*Opera omnia*, ii, p. 151).

227 Coke, *Third Part of the Institutes of the Laws of England*, p. 59.

228 *Mirror*, quoted *ibid.*, p. 58.

[EDITOR'S NOTES]

One of the outstanding thinkers of the early 20th century, Edward Westermarck, weaved anthropology and sociology into his histories of marriage, ethics, and moral ideas. This chapter, which significantly enough obtained its title from the original author, appeared in *The Origin and Development of Moral Ideas.*

Although Westermarck was a contemporary of Freud, his work reflects the influence of Havelock Ellis and J. A. Symonds to a greater degree. Without question, he accepted the concept of congenital inversion: "Homosexual practices are due sometimes to instinctive preference, sometimes to external conditions unfavorable to normal intercourse," he writes, and then goes on to state that as a matter of fact, a frequent cause is congenital sexual inversion; the authority for this statement is Havelock Ellis. But there must have been some doubt about this in the mind of Westermarck, for he returns again and again to the thought that indulgence in pederasty "goes hand in hand with great isolation of the women," and even suggests that the tendency can be avoided by a freer relationship between the sexes: "Among the Arabs of the plains, who are little addicted to boy-love, the unmarried girls enjoy considerable freedom."

Thus, out of Westermarck's exhaustive anthropologic study, certainly the best of its kind, what arises? An acceptance of congenital inversion as the only seeming method of explanation of effeminacy; an inkling of a realization that homosexuality becomes less frequent in areas where there is a better opportunity for the development of frequent early heterosexual relations; and a documented report on the attitude of the various tribes, in different ages and different cultures, toward such practices.

It is in this latter respect that Westermarck gathered the greatest information, yet displayed the least originality; for nowhere does he seek to delve into the *origin* of these moral ideas, but only in their development. He details information on cultures that attached no opprobrium to these practices, and others that called for stoning or death. Is one to assume that these attitudes arose spontaneously? Did the condemnation come out of the need for growth of population, as is usually contended by the historian of the Judeo-Christian morality?

Westermarck envisaged a more liberal attitude by society toward homosexuals, but he probably did not quite understand what difficulties modern society would encounter in its attempts to put such liberal concepts into its codes. In this respect, he pointed out that sodomy was often linked with heresy, and he concluded that as modern culture becomes further "emancipated from theological doctrines," public opinion would show greater leniency. In addition to failing to foresee the hold that theological doctrines would continue to have over society for many years to come, Westermarck did not see that, regardless of the source of hostility, the attitude toward homosexuality becomes an independent moral force in and of itself. It may have been linked with heresy in its origins and developments, but the impact of such an attitude becomes independent and opens far beyond the theology from which it arose. In the same way, even though in its origins homosexuality was condemned by cultures that found a great need for encouraging the growth of population, the moral ideas developed because such origin takes on an independent, dynamic form, and continues to exert pressures and influence long after the need for greater population has ceased.

It is in Westermarck's conclusions that one must look for greatest foresight, even though it is in his gathering of data that one finds the greatest erudition. For Westermarck found in the then nascent scientific studies on homosexuality, the hope for change in social and legal attitudes, and his conclusion can be quoted today as one of the most simple, most objective and yet most significant statements on this subject that has been made to date: "The fresh light which the scientific study of the sexual impulse has lately thrown upon the subject of homosexuality must also necessarily influence the moral ideas relating to it, insofar as no scrutinizing judge can fail to take into account the pressure which a powerful nonvolitional desire exercises upon an agent's will."

D. W. C.

THE
INTERMEDIATE SEX

A Study of Some Transitional Types
of Men and Women

Edward Carpenter

FIRST EDITION PUBLISHED BY GEORGE ALLEN & UNWIN, LTD.,
LONDON, 1908.

1. INTRODUCTORY

The subject dealt with in this book is one of great, and growing, importance. Whether it is that the present period is one of
large increase in the numbers of men and women of an intermediate or mixed temperament, or it merely is a period in
which more than usual attention happens to be accorded to
them, the fact certainly remains that the subject has great
actuality and is pressing upon us from all sides. It is recognised
that anyhow the number of persons occupying an intermediate
position between the two sexes is very great, that they play a
considerable part in general society, and that they necessarily
present and embody many problems which, both for their own
sakes and that of society, demand solution. The literature of
the question has in consequence already grown to be very

extensive, especially on the continent, and includes a great quantity of scientific works, medical treatises, literary essays, romances, historical novels, poetry, etc. And it is now generally admitted that some knowledge and enlightened understanding of the subject is greatly needed for the use of certain classes—as, for instance, medical men, teachers, parents, magistrates, judges, and the like.

That there are distinctions and gradations of soul-material in relation to sex—that the inner psychical affections and affinities shade off and graduate, in a vast number of instances, most subtly from male to female, and not always in obvious correspondence with the outer bodily sex—is a thing evident enough to anyone who considers the subject; nor could any good purpose well be served by ignoring this fact—even if it were possible to do so. It is easy of course (as some do) to classify all these mixed or intermediate types as *bad*. It is also easy (as some do) to argue that just because they combine opposite qualities they are likely to be *good* and valuable. But the subtleties and complexities of nature cannot be despatched in this off-hand manner. The great probability is that, as in any other class of human beings, there will be among these too, good and bad, high and low, worthy and unworthy—some perhaps exhibiting through their double temperament a rare and beautiful flower of humanity, others a perverse and tangled ruin.

Before the facts of nature, we have to preserve a certain humility and reverence; and not rush in with our preconceived and obstinate assumptions. Though these gradations of human type have always, and among all peoples, been more or less known and recognised, yet their frequency today, or even the concentration of attention on them, may be the indication of some important change actually in progress. We do not know, in fact, what possible evolutions are to come, or what new forms, of permanent place and value, are being already slowly differentiated from the surrounding mass of humanity. It may be that as at some past period of evolution, the worker bee was differentiated from the two ordinary bee sexes, so at the present time, certain new types of human kind may be emerging, which will have an important part to play in the societies of the future, even though for the moment, their appearance is attended by a good deal of confusion and misapprehension. We do not know; the best attitude we can adopt is one of sincere and dispassionate observation of facts.

Of course, wherever this subject touches on the domain of love, we may expect difficult queries to arise. Yet probably it is here that the noblest work of the intermediate sex or sexes will be accomplished, as well as the greatest errors committed. It seems almost a law of nature that new and important movements should be misunderstood and vilified, though afterwards they may be widely approved or admitted to honour.

Such movements are always envisaged first from whatever aspect they may present, ludicrous or contemptible. The early Christians, in the eyes of Romans, were chiefly known as the perpetrators of obscure rites and crimes in the darkness of the catacombs.

Modern socialism was for a long time supposed to be an affair of daggers and dynamite; and even now there are thousands of good people, ignorant enough to believe that it simply means "divide up all round, and each take his threepenny bit."

Vegetarians were supposed to be a feeble and brainless set of cabbage-eaters.

The women's movement, so vast in its scope and importance, was once thought to be nothing but an absurd attempt to make women "the apes of men."

And so on without end; the accusation in each case being some tag or last fag-end of fact, caught up by ignorance, and coloured by prejudice. So commonplace is it to misunderstand, so easy is it to misrepresent.

The Uranian temperament, especially in regard to its affectional side, is not without faults; but that it has been grossly and absurdly misunderstood is certain. With a good deal of experience in the matter, I think one may safely say that the defect of the male Uranian, or Urning, is *not* sensuality—but rather sentimentality. The lower, more ordinary types of Urning are often terribly sentimental; the superior types strangely, almost incredibly emotional; but neither as a rule (though of course there must be exceptions) are as sensual as the average normal man.

This immense capacity of emotional love represents a great driving force. Whether in the individual or in society, love is eminently creative. It is their great genius for attachment which gives to the best Uranian types their penetrating influence and activity, and which often makes them beloved and accepted far and wide even by those who know nothing of their inner mind. How many so-called philanthropists of the best kind have been inspired by the Uranian temperament, the world will probably never know. And in all walks of life the great number and influence of folks of this disposition, and the distinguished place they already occupy, is only realised by those who are more or less behind the scenes. It is probable also that it is this genius for emotional love which gives to the Uranians their remarkable youthfulness.

Anyhow, with their extraordinary gift for, and experience in affairs of the heart—from the double point of view, both of the man and of the woman—it is not difficult to see that these people have a special work to do as reconcilers and interpreters of each sex to the other. I will write of this at more length later. It is probable that the superior Urnings will become, in affairs of the heart, to a large extent the teachers of future society; and if so their influence will tend to the realisation and expression of an attachment less exclusively sensual than the average of today, and to the diffusion of this in all directions.

While at any rate not presuming to speak with authority on so difficult a subject, I plead for the necessity of a patient consideration of it, and for the due recognition of the types of character concerned, and for some endeavour to give them their fitting place and sphere of usefulness in the general scheme of society.

One thing more by way of introductory explanation. The word love is commonly used in so general and almost indiscriminate a fashion as to denote sometimes physical instincts and acts, and sometimes the most intimate and profound feelings; and in this way, a good deal of misunderstanding is caused. In this book, the word is used to denote the inner devotion of one person to another; and when anything else is meant—as, for instance, sexual relations and actions—this is clearly stated and expressed.

2. THE INTERMEDIATE SEX

In late years (and since the arrival of the New Woman amongst us) many things in the relation of men and women to each other have altered, or at any rate become clearer. The growing sense of equality in habits and customs—university studies, art, music, politics, the bicycle, etc.—all these things have brought about a *rapprochement* between the sexes. If the modern woman is a little more masculine in some ways than her predecessor, the modern man (it is to be hoped), while by no means effeminate, is a little more sensitive in temperament and artistic in feeling than the original John Bull. Society is beginning to recognise that the sexes do not or should not normally form two groups hopelessly isolated in habit and feeling from each other, but that they rather represent the two poles of *one* group—which is the human race; so that while certainly the extreme specimens at either pole are vastly divergent, there are great numbers in the middle region who (though differing corporeally as men and women) are by emotion and temperament very near to each other. We all know women with a strong dash of the masculine temperament, and we all know men whose almost feminine sensibility and intuition seem to belie their bodily form. Nature, it might appear, in mixing the elements which go to compose each individual, does not always keep her two groups of ingredients—which represent the two sexes—properly apart, but often throws them crosswise in a somewhat baffling manner, now this way and now that; yet wisely, we must think—for if a severe distinction of elements were always maintained the two sexes would soon drift into far latitudes and absolutely cease to understand each other. As it is, there are some remarkable and (we think) indispensable types of character in whom there is such a union or balance of the feminine and masculine qualities, that these people become to a great extent, the interpreters of men and women to each other.

There is another point which has become clearer of late. For as people are beginning to see that the sexes form in a certain sense a continuous group, so they are beginning to see that love and friendship—which have been so often set apart from each other as things distinct—are in reality closely related and shade imperceptibly into each other. Women are beginning to demand that marriage will mean friendship as well as passion; that a comrade-like equality shall be included in the word love; and it is recognised that from the one extreme of a "Platonic" friendship (generally between persons of the same sex) up to the other extreme of passionate love (generally between persons of opposite sex) no hard and fast line can at any point be drawn effectively separating the different kinds of attachment. We know, in fact, of friendships so romantic in sentiment that they verge into love; we know of loves so intellectual and spiritual that they hardly dwell in the sphere of passion.

A moment's thought will show that the general conceptions indicated above, if anywhere near the truth, point to an immense diversity of human temperament and character in matters relating to sex and love; but though such diversity has probably always existed, it has only in comparatively recent times become a subject of study.

More than thirty years ago, however, an Austrian writer, K. H. Ulrichs, drew attention in a series of pamphlets (*Memnon, Ara Spei, Inclusa,* etc.) to the existence of a class of people who strongly illustrate the above remarks, and with whom especially this work is concerned. He pointed out that there were people born in such a position—as it were on the dividing line between the sexes—that while belonging distinctly to one sex as far as their bodies are concerned they may be said to belong mentally and emotionally to the other; that there were men, for instance, who might be described as of feminine soul enclosed in a male body (*anima muliebris in corpore virili inclusa*), or in other cases, women whose definition would be just the reverse. And he maintained that this doubleness of nature was to a great extent proved by the special direction of their love-sentiment. In such cases, as might be expected, the (apparently) masculine person, instead of forming a love-union with a female, tended to contract romantic friendships with one of his own sex; while the apparently feminine would, instead of marrying in the usual way, devote herself to the love of another feminine.

People of this kind (i.e., having this special variation of the love-sentiment) he called Urnings; and though we are not obliged to accept his theory about the crosswise connexion between "soul" and "body," since at best these words are somewhat vague and indefinite; yet his work was important because it was one of the first attempts, in modern times, to recognise the existence of what might be called an intermediate sex, and to give at any rate some explanation of it.

Since then the subject has been widely studied and written about by scientific men and others on the continent (in England it is still comparatively unknown), and by means of an extended observation of present-day cases, and indirect testimony of the history and literature of past times, a body of general conclusions has been arrived at. I propose in the following to give some slight account.

Contrary to the general impression, one of the first points that emerges from this study is that 'Urnings,' or Uranians, are by no means so very rare; but they form, beneath the surface of society, a large class. However, it remains difficult to get an exact statement of their numbers. This is because of the want of any general understanding of their case; these folk tend to conceal their true feelings from all but their own kind, and indeed often deliberately act in such a manner as to lead the world astray (whence it arises that a normal man living in a certain society will often refuse to believe that there is a single Urning in the circle of his acquaintance, while one of the latter, or one that understands the nature, living in the same society, can count perhaps a score or more). Another reason is because it is indubitable that the numbers do vary very greatly, not only in different countries but also in different classes in the same country. The consequence of all this is that we have estimates differing very widely from each other. Dr. Grabowsky, a well known writer in Germany, quotes figures (which we think must be exaggerated) as high as one man in every 22, while Dr. Albert Moll (*Die Conträre Sexualempfindung*) gives estimates varying from 1 in every 50 to as low as 1 in every 500. These figures apply to such as are exclusively of the said nature, i.e., to those whose deepest feelings of love and friendship go out only to persons of their own sex. If, in addition, those double-natured people (of whom there is a great number) are included, who experience the normal attachment, with the homogenic tendency in less or greater degree added, the estimates must be higher.

In the second place, it emerges (also contrary to the general impression) that men and women of the exclusively Uranian type are by no means necessarily morbid in any way, unless their peculiar temperament be pronounced morbid in itself. Formerly, it was assumed as a matter of course, that the type was merely a result of disease and degeneration; but now with the examination of the actual facts, it appears that on the contrary, many are fine, healthy specimens of their sex, muscular and well-developed in body, powerful in brain, high in standard of conduct, and with nothing abnormal or morbid of any kind observable in their physical structure or constitution.

Of course, this is not true of all, and there still remains a certain number of cases of weakly type to support the neuropathic view. Yet it is very noticeable that this view is much less insisted on by the later writers than by the earlier. It is also worth noticing that it is now acknowledged that even in the most healthy cases the special affectional temperament of the "intermediate" is, as a rule, ineradicable; so much so that when frequently such men and women, from social or other considerations, have forced themselves to marry and even have children, they have still not been able to overcome their own bias, or the leaning after all of their life attachment to some friend of their own sex.

This subject, though obviously one of considerable interest and importance, has been hitherto, as I have pointed out, but little discusssed in this country, partly owing to a certain amount of doubt and distrust which has, naturally, surrounded it. And certainly if the men and women born with the tendency in question were only rare, though it would not be fair on that account to ignore them, yet it would hardly be necessary to dwell at great length on their case. But as the class is really, on any computation, numerous, it becomes a duty for society not only to understand them but also to help them understand themselves.

There is no doubt that in many cases people of this kind suffer a great deal from their own temperament, and after all, it is possible that they may have an important part to play in the evolution of the race. Anyone who realises what love is, the dedication of the heart, so profound, so absorbing, so mysterious, so imperative, and always just in the noblest natures so strong, cannot fail to see how difficult, how tragic even, must often be the fate of those whose deepest feelings are destined from the earliest days to be a riddle and a stumbling-block, unexplained to themselves, passed over in silence by others. To call people of such temperament "morbid," etc., is of no use. Such a term is absurdly inapplicable to many, who are among the most active, the most amiable and accepted members of society; besides, it forms no solution of the problem in question, and only amounts to marking down for disparagement a fellow creature who has already considerable difficulties to contend with. Says Dr. Moll, "Anyone who has seen many Urnings will probably admit that they form, by no means an enervated human group; on the contrary, one finds powerful, healthy-looking folk among them;" but in the very next sentence he says that they "suffer severely" from the way they are regarded; and in the manifesto of a considerable community of such people in Germany occur these words, "The rays of sunshine in the night of our existence are so rare, that we are responsive and deeply grateful for the least movement, for every single voice that speaks in our favour in the forum of mankind."

In dealing with this class of folk, while I do not deny that they present a difficult problem, I think that just for that very reason their case needs discussion. It would be a great mistake to suppose that their attachments are necessarily sexual, or connected with sexual acts. On the contrary (as abundant evidence shows), they are often purely emotional in their character; and to confuse Uranians (as is so often done) with libertines having no law but curiosity in self-indulgence is to do them a great wrong. At the same time, it is evident that their special temperament may sometimes cause them difficulty in regard to their sexual relations. Into this subject we need not just now enter. But we may point out how hard it is, especially for the young among them, that a veil of complete silence should be drawn over the subject, leading to the most painful misunderstandings, perversions and confusions of mind; and that there should be no hint of guidance; nor any recognition of the solitary and really serious inner struggles they may have to face. If the problem is a difficult one, as it undoubtedly is, the fate of those people is already hard who have to meet it in their own persons, without their suffering in addition from the refusal of society to give them any help. It is partly for these reasons, and to throw a little light where it may be needed, that I have thought it might be advisable in this paper simply to give a few general characteristics of the intermediate types.

As indicated then already, in bodily structure there is, as a rule, nothing to distinguish the subjects of our discussion from ordinary men and women; but if we take the general mental characteristics it appears from almost universal testimony that the male tends to be of a rather gentle, emotional disposition— with defects, if such exist, in the direction of subtlety, evasiveness, timidity, vanity, etc.; while the female is just the opposite, fiery, active, bold and truthful, with defects running to brusqueness and coarseness. Moreover, the mind of the former is generally intuitive and instinctive in its perceptions, with more or less of artistic feeling; while the mind of the latter is more logical, scientific, and precise than usual with the normal woman. So marked indeed are these general characteristics that sometimes by means of them (though not an infallible guide) the nature of the boy or girl can be detected in childhood, before full development has taken place; and needless to say it may often be very important to be able to do this.

It was no doubt in consequence of the observation of these signs that K. H. Ulrichs proposed his theory; and though the theory, as we have said, does not by any means meet all the facts, still it is perhaps not without merit, and may be worth bearing in mind.

In the case, for instance, of a woman of this temperament (defined we suppose as "a male soul in a female body") the theory helps us to understand how it might be possible for her to fall *bona fide* in love with another woman. Krafft-Ebing gives the case of a lady (A.), 28 years of age, who fell deeply in love with a younger one (B.). "I loved her divinely," she said. They lived together, and the union lasted four years, but was then broken by the marriage of B. A. suffered in consequence from frightful depression; but in the end—though without real love—got married herself. Her depression however only increased and deepened into illness. The doctors, when consulted, said that all would be well if she could only have a child. The husband, who loved his wife sincerely, could not understand her enigmatic behaviour. She was friendly to him, suffered his caresses, but for days afterwards remained "dull, exhausted, plagued with irritation of the spine, and nervous." Presently a journey of the married pair led to another meeting with the female friend—who had now been wedded (but also unhappily) for three years. "Both ladies trembled with joy and excitement as they fell into each other's arms, and were thenceforth inseparable. The man found that this friendship relation was a singular one, and hastened the departure. When the opportunity occurred, he convinced himself from the correspondence between his wife and her 'friend' that their letters were exactly like those of two lovers."

It appears that the loves of such women are often very intense, and (as also in the case of male Urnings) life-long. Both classes feel themselves blessed when they love happily. Nevertheless, to many of them it is a painful fact that in consequence of their peculiar temperament, they are, though fond of children, not in the position to found a family.

We have so far limited ourselves to some very general characteristics of the intermediate race. It may help to clear and fix our ideas if we now describe more in detail, first, what may be called the extreme and exaggerated types of the race, and then the more normal and perfect types. By doing so, we shall get a more definite and concrete view of our subject.

In the first place, then, the extreme specimens, as in most cases of extremes, are not particularly attractive, sometimes quite the reverse. In the male of this kind we have a distinctly effeminate type, sentimental, lackadaisical, mincing in gait and manners, something of a chatterbox, skillful in woman's work, sometimes taking pleasure in dressing in woman's clothes; his figure not unfrequently betraying a tendency towards the feminine, large at the hips, supple, not muscular, the face wanting in hair, the voice inclining to be high-pitched, etc.; while his dwelling-room is orderly in the extreme, even natty, and choice of decoration and perfume. His affection, too, is often feminine in character, clinging, dependent and jealous, as of one desiring to be loved almost more than to love.

On the other hand, as the extreme type of the homogenic female, we have a rather markedly aggressive person, of strong passions, masculine manners and movements, practical in the conduct of life, sensuous rather than sentimental in love, often untidy, and *outré* in attire; her figure muscular, her voice rather low in pitch; her dwelling-room decorated with sporting scenes, pistols, etc., and not without a suspicion of the fragrant weed in the atmosphere; while her love (generally to rather soft and feminine specimens of her own sex) is often a sort of furor, similar to the ordinary masculine love, and at times almost uncontrollable.

These are types which, on account of their salience, everyone will recognize more or less. Naturally, when they occur they excite a good deal of attention, and it is not an uncommon impression that most persons of the homogenic nature belong to either one or other of these classes. But in reality, of course, these extreme developments are rare, and for the most part the temperament in question is embodied in men and women of quite normal and unsensational exterior. Speaking of this subject and the connection between effeminateness and the homogenic nature in men, Dr. Moll says: "It is, however, as well to point out at the outset that effeminacy does not by any means show itself in all Urnings. Though one may find this or that indication in a great number of cases, yet it cannot be denied that a very large percentage, perhaps by far the majority of them, do not exhibit pronounced effeminacy."

And it may be supposed that we may draw the same conclusion with regard to women of this class—namely, that the majority of them do not exhibit pronounced masculine habits. In fact, while these extreme cases are of the greatest value from a scientific point of view as marking tendencies and limits of development in certain directions, it would be a serious mistake to look upon them as representative cases of the whole phases of human evolution concerned.

If now we come to what may be called the more normal type of the Uranian man, we find a man who, while possessing thoroughly masculine powers of mind and body, combines with them the tenderer and more emotional soul-nature of the woman—and sometimes to a remarkable degree. Such men, as said, are often muscular and well built, and not distinguishable in exterior structure and the carriage of body from others of their own sex, but emotionally they are extremely complex, tender, sensitive, pitiful and loving, "full of storm and stress, of ferment and fluctuation" of the heart; the logical faculty may or may not, in their case, be well developed, but intuition is always strong; like women, they read characters at a glance, and know, without knowing how, what is passing in the minds of others; for nursing and waiting on the needs of others they have often a peculiar gift; at the bottom lies the artist nature, with the artist's sensibility and perception. Such a one is often a dreamer, of brooding, reserved habits, often a musician, or a man of culture, courted in society, which nevertheless does not understand him though sometimes a child of the people, without any culture, but almost always with a peculiar inborn refinement.

De Joux, who speaks on the whole favourably of Uranian men and women, says of the former: "They are enthusiastic for poetry and music, are often eminently skillful in the fine arts, and are overcome with emotion and sympathy at the least sad occurrence. Their sensitiveness, their endless tenderness for children, their love of flowers, their great pity for beggars and crippled folk are truly womanly."

And in another passage he indicates the artist nature, when he says: "The nerve system of many an Urning is the finest and the most complicated musical instrument in the service of the interior personality that can be imagined."

It would seem probable that the attachment of such a one is of a tender and profound character; indeed, it is possible that in this class of men we have the love sentiment in one of its most perfect forms—a form in which from the necessities of the situation the sensuous element, though present, is exquisitely subordinated to the spiritual.

Says one writer on this subject, a Swiss, "Happy indeed is that man who has won a real Urning for his friend—he walks on roses, without ever having to fear the thorns"; and he adds, "Can there ever be a more perfect sick nurse than an Urning?" And though these are *ex parte* utterances, we may believe that there is an appreciable grain of truth in them. Another writer, quoted by De Joux, speaks to somewhat the same effect, and may perhaps be received in a similar spirit. "We form," he says, "a peculiar aristocracy of modest spirits, of good and refined habit, and in many masculine circles are the representatives of the higher mental and artistic element. In us dreamers and enthusiasts lies the continual counterpoise to the sheer masculine portion of society, inclining, as it always does, to mere restless greed of gain and material sensual pleasures."

That men of this kind despise women, though a not uncommon belief, is one which hardly appears to be justified. Indeed, though naturally not inclined to "fall in love" in this direction, such men are by their nature drawn rather near to women, and it would seem that they often feel a singular appreciation and understanding of the emotional needs and destinies of the other sex, leading in many cases to a genuine though what is called 'Platonic' friendship. There is little doubt that they are often instinctively sought after by women, who, without suspecting the real cause, are conscious of a sympathetic chord in the homogenic which they miss in the normal man. To quote De Joux once more: "It would be a mistake to suppose that all Urnings must be woman-haters. Quite the contrary. They are not seldom the faithfulest friends, the truest allies, and most convinced defenders of women."

To come now to the more normal and perfect specimens of the homogenic woman, we find a type in which the body is thoroughly feminine and gracious, with the rondure and fullness of the female form, and the continence and aptness of its movements, but in which the inner nature is to a great extent masculine; a temperament active, brave, originative, somewhat decisive, not too emotional; fond of outdoor life, of games and sports, of science, politics, or even business; good at organisation, and well pleased with positions of responsibility, sometimes indeed making an excellent and generous leader. Such a woman, it is easily seen, from her special combination of qualities, is often fitted for remarkable work, in professional life, or as a manageress of institutions, or even as a ruler of a country. Her love goes out to younger and more feminine natures than her own; it is a powerful passion, almost of heroic type, and capable of inspiring great deeds; and when held duly in leash may sometimes become an invaluable force in the teaching and training of girlhood, or in the creation of a school of thought or action among women. Many a Santa Clara, or abbess founder of religious houses, has probably been a woman of this type; and in all times such women, not being bound to men by the ordinary ties, have been able to work more freely for the interests of their sex, a cause to which their own temperament impels them to devote themselves *con amore*.

I have now sketched—very briefly and inadequately it is true, both the extreme types and the more healthy types of the "intermediate" man and woman: types which can be verified from history and literature, though more certainly and satisfactorily perhaps from actual life around us. Unfamiliar though the subject is, it begins to appear that it is one which modern thought and science will have to face. Of the latter and more normal types it may be said that they exist, and have always existed, in considerable abundance, and from that circumstance alone there is a strong probability that they have their place and purpose. As pointed out there is no particular indication of morbidity about them, unless the special nature of their love sentiment be itself accounted morbid; and in the alienation of the sexes from each other, of which complaint is so often made today, it must be admitted that they do much to fill the gap.

The instinctive artistic nature of the male of this class, his sensitive spirit, his wavelike emotional temperament, combined with hardihood of intellect and body; and the frank, free nature of the female, her masculine independence and strength wedded to thoroughly feminine grace of form and manner; may be said to give them both, through their double nature, command of life in all its phases, and a certain freemasonry of the secrets of the two sexes which may well favour their function as reconcilers and interpreters. Certainly it is remarkable that some of the world's greatest leaders and artists have been dowered either wholly or in part with the Uranian temperament—as in the cases of Michel Angelo, Shakespeare, Marlowe, Alexander the Great, Julius Cæsar, or, among women, Christine of Sweden, Sappho the poetess, and others.

3. THE HOMOGENIC ATTACHMENT

In its various forms, so far as we know them, love seems always to have a deep significance and a most practical importance to us little mortals. In one form, as the mere semiconscious sex-love, which runs through creation and is common to the lowest animals and plants, it appears as a kind of organic basis for the unity of all creatures; in another, as the love of the mother for her offspring, which may also be termed a passion, it seems to pledge itself to the care and guardianship of the future race; in another, as the marriage of man and woman, it becomes the very foundation of human society. And so we can hardly believe that in its homogenic form, with which we are here concerned, it has not also a deep significance, and social uses and functions which will become clearer to us, the more we study it.

To some perhaps, it may appear a little strained to place this last-mentioned form of attachment on a level of importance with the others, and such persons may be inclined to deny to the homogenic or homosexual love that intense, that penetrating, and at times overmastering character which would entitle it to rank as a great human passion. But in truth this view, when entertained, arises from a want of acquaintance with the actual facts; and it may not be amiss here, in the briefest possible way, to indicate what the world's history, literature, and art has to say to us on this aspect of the subject, before going on to further considerations. Certainly, if the confronting of danger and the endurance of pain and distress for the sake of the loved one, if sacrifice, unswerving devotion and life long union, constitute proofs of the reality and intensity (and let us say healthiness) of an affection, then these proofs have been given in numberless cases of such attachment, not only as existing between men, but between women, since the world began. The records of chivalric love, the feats of enamoured knights for their ladies' sakes, the stories of Hero and Leander, etc., are easily paralleled, if not surpassed, by the stories of the Greek comrades-in-arms and tyrannicides, of Cratinus and Aristodemus, who offered themselves together as a voluntary sacrifice for the purification of Athens; of Chariton and Melanippus, who attempted to assassinate Phalaris, the tyrant of Agrigentum; or of Cleomachus who in like manner, in a battle between the Chalkidians and Eretrians, being entreated to charge the latter, "asked the youth he loved, who was standing by, whether he would be a spectator of the fight; and when he said he

would, and affectionately kissed Cleomachus and put his helmet on his head, Cleomachus with a proud joy placed himself
in the front of the bravest of the Thessalians and charged the
enemy's cavalry with such impetuosity that he threw them into
disorder and routed them; and the Eretrian cavalry fleeing in
consequence, the Chalkidians won a splendid victory."

The annals of all nations contain similar records, though
probably among none has the ideal of this love been quite so
enthusiastic and heroic as among the post-Homeric Greeks. It
is well known that among the Polynesian Islanders, for the
most part a very gentle and affectionate people, probably inher-
iting the traditions of a higher culture than they now possess,
the most romantic male friendships are (or were) in vogue.

Says Herman Melville in *Omoo*: "The really curious way in
which all Polynesians are in the habit of making bosom friends
is deserving of remark. . . . In the annals of the island (Tahiti)
are examples of extravagant friendships, unsurpassed by the
story of Damon and Pythias, in truth much more wonderful;
for notwithstanding the devotion, even of life in some cases,
to which they led, they were frequently entertained at first
sight for some stranger from another island."

So thoroughly recognised indeed were these unions that
Melville explains (in *Typee*) that if two men of hostile tribes
or islands became thus pledged to each other, then each could
pass through the enemy's territory without fear of molestation
or injury; and the passionate nature of these attachments is
indicated by the following passage from *Omoo*:

"Though little inclined to jealousy in ordinary love matters,
the Tahitian will hear of no rivals in his friendship."

Even among savage races lower down than these in the scale
of evolution, and who are generally accused of being governed
in their love-relations only by the most animal desires, we find
a genuine sentiment of comradeship beginning to assert itself
—as among the Balonda and other African tribes, where regular ceremonies of the betrothal of comrades take place, by the

transfusion of a few drops of blood into each other's drinking bowls, by the exchange of names, and the mutual gift of their most precious possessions; but unfortunately, owing to the obtuseness of current European opinion on this subject, these and other such customs have been but little investigated and have by no means received the attention that they ought.

When we turn to the poetic and literary utterances of the more civilised nations on this subject, we cannot but be struck by the range and intensity of the emotions expressed, from the beautiful threnody of David over his friend whose love was passing the love of women, through the vast panorama of the Homeric Iliad, of which the heroic friendship of Achilles and his dear Patroclus forms really the basic theme, down to the works of the great Greek age, the splendid odes of Pindar burning with clear fire of passion, the lofty elegies of Theognis, full of wise precepts to his beloved Kurnus, the sweet pastorals of Theocritus, the passionate lyrics of Sappho, or the more sensual raptures of Anacreon. Some of the dramas of Eschylus and Sophocles—as the *Myrmidones* of the former and the *Lovers of Achilles* of the latter, appear to have had this subject for their motive; and many of the prose-poem dialogues of Plato were certainly inspired by it.

Then coming to the literature of the Roman age, whose materialistic spirit could only with difficulty seize the finer inspiration of the homogenic love, and which in such writers as Catullus and Martial could only for the most part give expression to its grosser side, we still find in Vergil, a noble and notable instance. His second *Eclogue* bears the marks of a genuine passion; and, according to some, he, under the name of Alexis, immortalises his own love for the youthful Alexander. Nor is it possible to pass over in this connection the great mass of Persian literature, and the poets Sadi, Hafiz, Jami, and many others, whose names and works are for all time, and whose marvellous love songs ("Bitter and sweet is the parting kiss on the lips of a friend") are to a large extent, if not mostly, addressed to those of their own sex.

Of the medieval period in Europe we have of course but few literary monuments. Towards its close we come upon the interesting story of Amis and Amile (thirteenth century), unearthed by W. Pater from the Bibliotheca Elzeviriana. Though there is historic evidence of the prevalence of the passion, we may say of this period that its ideal was undoubtedly rather the chivalric love than the love of comrades. But with the Renaissance in Italy and the Elizabethan period in England, the latter once more comes to evidence in a burst of poetic utterance, which culminates perhaps in the magnificent sonnets of Michel Angelo and of Shakespeare; of Michel Angelo whose pure beauty of expression lifts the enthusiasm into the highest region as the direct perception of the divine in mortal form; and of Shakespeare—whose passionate words and amorous spirituality of friendship have for long enough been a perplexity to hidebound commentators. Thence through minor writers (not overlooking Winckelmann in Germany) we pass to quite modern times—in which, notwithstanding the fact that the passion has been much misunderstood and misinterpreted, two names stand conspicuously forth—those of Tennyson, whose "In Memoriam" is perhaps his finest work, and of Walt Whitman, the enthusiasm of whose poems on comradeship is only paralleled by the devotedness of his labors for his wounded brothers in the American Civil War.

It will be noticed that here we have some of the very greatest names in all literature concerned; and that their utterances on this subject equal if they do not surpass, in beauty, intensity and humanity of sentiment, whatever has been written in praise of the other more ordinarily recognised love.

And when again we turn to the records of art, and compare the way in which man's sense of love and beauty has expressed itself in the portrayal of the male form and the female form respectively we find exactly the same thing. The whole vista of Greek statuary shows the male passion of beauty in high degree. Yet though the statues of men and youths (by men sculptors) preponderate probably considerably, both in actual number and in devotedness of execution, over the statues of female figures, it is, as J. A. Symonds says in his *Life of Michel Angelo*, remarkable that in all the range of the former there are hardly two or three that show a base or licentious expression, such as is not so very uncommon in the female statues. Knowing as we do the strength of the male physical passion in the life of the Greeks, this one fact speaks strongly for the sense of proportion which must have characterized this passion—at any rate in the most productive age of their art.

In the case of Michel Angelo, we have an artist who with brush and chisel portrayed literally thousands of human forms; but with this peculiarity, that while scores and scores of his male figures are obviously suffused and inspired by a romantic sentiment, there is hardly one of his female figures that is so,— the latter being mostly representative of woman in her part as mother, or sufferer, or prophetess or poetess, or in old age, or in any aspect of strength or tenderness, except that which associates itself especially with romantic love. Yet the cleanliness and dignity of Michel Angelo's male figures are incontestable, and bear striking witness to that nobility of the sentiment in him, which we have already seen illustrated in his sonnets.

This brief sketch may suffice to give the reader some idea of the place and position in the world of the particular sentiment which we are discussing; nor can it fail to impress him, if any reference is made to the authorities quoted, with a sense of the dignity and solidity of the sentiment, at any rate as handled by some of the world's greatest men. At the same time it would be affectation to ignore the fact that side by side with this view of the subject there has been another current of opinion leading people, especially in quite modern times in Europe, to look upon attachments of the kind in question with much suspicion and disfavour. And it may be necessary here to say a few words on this latter view.

The origin of it is not far to seek. Those who have no great gift themselves for this kind of friendship, who are not in the inner circle of it, so to speak, and do not understand or appreciate its deep emotional and romantic character, have nevertheless heard of certain corruptions and excesses; for these latter leap to publicity. They have heard of the debaucheries of a Nero or a Tiberius; they have noted the scandals of the Police Courts; they have had some experience perhaps of abuses which may be found in Public Schools or Barracks; and they (naturally) infer that these things, these excesses and sensualities, are the motive of comrade attachments, and the object for which they exist; nor do they easily recognise any more profound and intimate bond. To such people physical intimacies of any kind (at any rate between males) seem inexcusable. There is no distinction in their minds between the simplest or most naive expression of feeling and the gravest abuse of human rights and decency; there is no distinction between a genuine heart attachment and a mere carnal curiosity. They see certain evils that occur or have occurred, and they think, quite candidly, that any measures are justifiable to prevent such things recurring. But they do not see the interior love feeling which when it exists, does legitimately demand some expression. Such folk, in fact, not having the key in themselves to the real situation hastily assume that the homogenic attachment has no other motive than, or is simply a veil and a cover for, sensuality, and suspect or condemn it accordingly.

Thus arises the curious discrepancy of people's views on this important subject, a discrepancy depending on the side from which they approach it.

On the one hand, we have anathemas and execrations, on the other we have the lofty enthusiasm of a man like Plato— one of the leaders of the world's thought for all time, who puts, for example, into the mouth of Phedrus (in the *Symposium*) such a passage as this:

"I know not any greater blessing to a young man beginning life than a virtuous lover, or to the lover than a beloved youth. For the principle which ought to be the guide of men who would nobly live, that principle, I say, neither kindred, nor honour, nor wealth, nor any other motive is able to implant so well as love. Of what am I speaking? Of the sense of honour and dishonour, without which neither states nor individuals ever do any good or great work. . . . For what lover would not choose rather to be seen of all mankind than by his beloved, either when abandoning his post or throwing away his arms? He would be ready to die a thousand deaths rather than endure this. Or who would desert his beloved or fail him in the hour of danger? The veriest coward would become an inspired hero, equal to the bravest, at such a time; love would inspire him. That courage which, as Homer says, the god breathes into the soul of heroes, love of his own nature inspires, into the lover."

Or again in the *Phedrus* Plato makes Socrates say:

"In like manner the followers of Apollo and of every other god, walking in the ways of their god, seek a love who is to be like their god, and when they have found him, they themselves imitate their god, and persuade their love to do the same, and bring him into harmony with the form and ways of the god as fast as they can; for they have no feelings of envy or jealousy towards their beloved, but they do their utmost to create in him the greatest likeness of themselves and the god whom they honour. Thus fair and blissful to the beloved when he is taken, is the desire of the inspired lover, and the initiation of which I speak into the mysteries of true love, if their purpose is effected."

With these few preliminary remarks, we may pass on to consider some recent scientific investigations of the matter in hand. In late times, that is, during the last thirty years or so, a group of scientific and capable men chiefly in Germany, France, and

Italy, have made a special and more or less impartial study of it. Among these may be mentioned Albert Moll of Berlin; R. von Krafft-Ebing, one of the leading medical authorities of Vienna, whose book on *Sexual Psychopathy* has passed into its tenth edition; Paul Moreau (*Des Aberrations du sens géné-sique*); Cesare Lombroso, the author of various works on anthropology; M. A. Raffalovich (*Uranisme et unisexualité*); Auguste Forel (*Die Sexuelle Frage*); Mantegazza, K. H. Ulrichs; and Havelock Ellis, whose great work on the *Psychology of Sex*, the second volume is dedicated to the subject of *Sexual Inversion*. The result of these investigations has been that a very altered complexion has been given to the subject. For whereas at first it was easily assumed that the phenomena were of morbid character, and that the leaning of the love sentiment towards one of the same sex was always associated with degeneracy, or disease, it is very noticeable that step by step with the accumulation of reliable information, this assumption has been abandoned. The point of view has changed; and the change has been most marked in the latest authors, such as A. Moll and Havelock Ellis.

It is not possible here to go into anything like a detailed account of the works of these various authors, their theories, and the immense number of interesting cases and observations which they have contributed; but some of the general conclusions which flow from their researches may be pointed out. In the first place their labors have established the fact, known hitherto only to individuals, that sexual inversion, that is the leaning of desire to one of the same sex, is in a vast number of cases quite instinctive and congenital, mentally and physically, and therefore twined in the very roots of individual life and practically ineradicable. To men or women thus affected with an innate homosexual bias, Ulrichs gave the name of Urning, since pretty widely accepted by scientists. Some details with regard to Urnings, I have given in the preceding material, but it should be said here that too much emphasis cannot be laid on the distinction between these born lovers of their own kind, and that class of persons, with whom they are so often confused, who out of mere carnal curiosity or extravagance of desire, or from the dearth of opportunities for a more normal satisfaction (as in schools, barracks, etc.) adopt some homosexual practices.

It is the latter class who become chiefly prominent in the public eye, and who excite, naturally enough, public reprobation. In their case, the attraction is felt, by themselves and all concerned, to be merely sensual and morbid. In the case of the others, however, the feeling is, as said, so deeply rooted and twined with the mental and emotional life that the person concerned has difficulty in imagining himself affected otherwise than he is; and to him at least his love appears healthy and natural, and indeed a necessary part of his individuality.

In the second place it has become clear that the number of individuals affected with "sexual inversion" in some degree or other is very great—much greater than is generally supposed to be the case. It is however very difficult or perhaps impossible to arrive at satisfactory figures on the subject, for the simple reasons that the proportions vary so greatly among different peoples and even in different sections of society and in different localities, and because of course there are all possible grades of sexual inversion to deal with, from that in which the instinct is *quite exclusively* directed towards the same sex, to the other extreme in which it is normally towards the opposite sex but capable, occasionally and under exceptional attractions, of inversion towards its own—this last condition being probably among some peoples very widespread, if not universal.

In the third place, by the tabulation and comparison of a great number of cases and "confessions," it has become pretty well established that the individuals affected with inversion in marked degree do not after all differ from the rest of mankind, or womankind, in any other physical or mental particular which can be distinctly indicated. No congenital association with any particular physical conformation or malformation has yet been discovered; nor with any distinct disease of body or mind. Nor does it appear that persons of this class are usually of a gross or specially low type, but if anything rather the opposite—being mostly of refined, sensitive nature and including, as Krafft-Ebing points out, a great number "highly gifted in the fine arts, especially music and poetry"; and, as Mantegazza says, many persons of high literary and social distinction. It is true that Krafft-Ebing insists on the generally strong sexual equipment of this class of persons (among men), but he hastens to say that their emotional love is also "enthusiastic and exalted," and that, while bodily congress is desired, the special act with which they are vulgarly credited is in most cases repugnant to them.

The only distinct characteristic which the scientific writers claim to have established is a marked tendency to nervous development in the subject, not infrequently associated with nervous maladies; but, as I shall presently have occasion to show, there is reason to think that the validity even of this characteristic has been exaggerated.

Taking the general case of men with a marked exclusive preference for persons of their own sex, Krafft-Ebing says: "The sexual life of these homosexuals is *mutatis mutandis* just the same as in the case of normal sex love. . . . The Urning loves, deifies his male beloved one, exactly as the woman-wooing man does his beloved. For him, he is capable of the greatest sacrifice, experiences the torments of unhappy, often unrequited love, of faithlessness on his beloved's part, of jealousy, etc. His attention is enchained only by the male form . . . The sight of feminine charms is indifferent to him, if not repugnant." Then he goes on to say that many such men, notwithstanding their actual aversion to intercourse with the female, do ultimately marry—either from ethical, as sometimes happens, or from social considerations. But very remarkable, as illustrating the depth and tenacity of the homogenic instinct, and pathetic too, are the records that he gives of these cases;

for in many of them, a real friendship and regard between the
married pair was still of no avail to overcome the distaste on
the part of one to sexual intercourse with the other, or to prevent the experience of actual physical distress after such intercourse, or to check the continual flow of affection to some third
person of the same sex; and thus unwillingly, so to speak, this
bias remained a cause of suffering to the end.

I have said that at the outset it was assumed that the homogenic emotion was morbid in itself, and probably always associated with distinct disease, either physical or mental, but that
the progress of the inquiry has served more and more to dissipate this view; and that it is noticeable that the latest of the
purely scientific authorities are the least disposed to insist upon
the theory of morbidity. It is true that Krafft-Ebing clings to
the opinion that there is generally some neurosis or degeneration of nerve centre, or inherited tendency in that direction,
associated with the instinct; he speaks, rather vaguely of "an
hereditary neuropathic or psychopathic tendency," *neuro-
(psycho)pathische Belastung*. But it is an obvious criticism on
this that there are few people in modern life, perhaps none,
who could be pronounced absolutely free from such a *Belastung!* And whether the Dorian Greeks or the Polynesian Islanders or the Albanian mountaineers, or any of the other
notably hardy races among whom this affection has developed,
were particularly troubled by nervous degeneration, we may
well doubt!

As to Moll, though he speaks of the instinct as morbid (feeling perhaps in duty bound to do so), it is very noticeable that
he abandons the ground of its association with other morbid
symptoms, as this association, he says, is by no means always to
be observed; and is fain to rest his judgment on the dictum
that the mere failure of the sexual instinct to propagate the
species is itself pathologic—a dictum which in its turn obviously springs from that prejudgment of scientists that generation is the sole object of love, and which if pressed would

involve the good doctor in awkward dilemmas, as for instance that every worker bee is a pathologic specimen.

Finally, we find that Havelock Ellis, one of the latest writers of weight on this subject, in his *Sexual Inversion,* combats the idea that this temperament is necessarily morbid; and suggests that the tendency should rather be called an anomaly than a disease. He says: "Thus in sexual inversion we have what may fairly be called a 'sport' or variation, one of those organic aberrations which we see throughout living nature in plants and in animals."

With regard to the nerve-degeneration theory, while it may be allowed that sexual inversion is not uncommonly found in connection with the specially nervous temperament, it must be remembered that its occasional association with nervous troubles or disease is quite another matter; since such troubles ought perhaps to be looked upon as the results rather than the causes of the inversion. Of course, it is difficult for outsiders not personally experienced in the matter, to realise the great strain and tension of nerves under which those persons grow up from boyhood to manhood, or from girl to womanhood, who find their deepest and strongest instincts under the ban of the society around them; who, before they clearly understand the drift of their own natures, discover that they are somehow cut off from the sympathy and understanding of those nearest to them; and who know that they can never give expression to their tenderest yearnings of affection without exposing themselves to the possible charge of actions stigmatised as odious crimes. That such a strain, acting on one who is perhaps already of a nervous temperament, should tend to cause nervous prostration or even mental disturbance is of course obvious; and if such disturbances are really found to be commoner among homogenic lovers than among ordinary folk we have in these social causes probably a sufficient explanation of the fact.

Then again, in this connexion it must never be forgotten that the medicoscientific enquirer is bound on the whole to meet with those cases that are of a morbid character, rather than with those that are healthy in their manifestation, since indeed it is the former that he lays himself out for. And since the field of his research is usually a great modern city, there is little wonder if disease colours his conclusions. In the case of A. Moll, who carried out his research largely under the guidance of the Berlin police (whose acquaintance with the subject would naturally be limited to its least satisfactory sides), the only marvel is that his verdict is so markedly favorable as it is. As Krafft-Ebing says in his own preface:

"It is the sad privilege of medicine, and especially of psychiatry, to look always on the reverse side of life, on the weakness and wretchedness of man."

Having regard then to the direction in which science has been steadily moving in this matter, it is not difficult to see that the epithet "morbid" will probably before long be abandoned as descriptive of the homogenic bias, that is, of the general sentiment of love towards a person of the same sex. That there are excesses of the passion—cases, as in ordinary sex love, where mere physical desire becomes a mania, we may freely admit; but as it would be unfair to judge of the purity of marriage by the evidence of the divorce courts, so it would be monstrous to measure the truth and beauty of the attachment in question by those instances which stand most prominently perhaps in the eye of the modern public; and after all deductions there remains, we contend, the vast body of cases in which the manifestation of the instinct has on the whole the character of normality and healthfulness—sufficiently so in fact to constitute this a distinct variety of the sexual passion. The question, of course, not being whether the instinct is capable of morbid and extravagant manifestation, for that can easily be proved of any instinct, but whether it is capable of a healthy and sane expression. And this, we think, it has abundantly shown itself to be.

Anyhow, the work that science has practically done has been

to destroy the dogmatic attitude of the former current opinion from which it started, and to leave the whole subject freed from a great deal of misunderstanding, and much more open than before. If, on the one hand, its results have been chiefly of a negative character, and it admits that it does not understand the exact place and foundation of this attachment; on the other hand since it recognises the deeply beneficial influences of an intimate love relation of the usual kind on those concerned, it also allows that there are some persons for whom these necessary reactions can only come from one of the same sex as themselves.

"Successful love," says Moll, "exercises a helpful influence on the Urning. His mental and bodily condition improves, and capacity of work increases—just as it happens in the case of a normal youth with his love." And further on, in a letter from a man of this kind occur these words: "The passion is, I suppose, so powerful, just because one looks for everything in the loved man—love, friendship, ideal, and sense-satisfaction. . . . As it is at present, I suffer the agonies of a deep unresponded passion, which wake me like a nightmare from sleep. And I am conscious of physical pain in the region of the heart." In such cases the love, in some degree physically expressed, of another person of the same sex, is allowed to be as much a necessity and a condition of healthy life and activity, as in more ordinary cases is the love of a person of the opposite sex.

If then, the physical element which is sometimes present in the love of which we are speaking is a difficulty and a stumbling block, it must be allowed that it is a difficulty that Nature confronts us with, and which cannot be disposed of by mere anathema and execration. The only theory, from K. H. Ulrichs to Havelock Ellis, which has at all held its ground in this matter, is that in congenital cases of sex inversion there is a mixture of male and female elements in the same person; so that for instance in the same embryo the emotional and nervous regions may develop along feminine lines while the outer body

and functions may determine themselves as distinctly masculine, or vice versa. Such cross development may take place
obviously in a great variety of ways, and thus possibly explain
the remarkable varieties of the Uranian temperament; but in
all such cases, strange as may be the problems thus arising,
these problems are of Nature's own producing and can hardly
be laid to the door of the individual who has literally to bear
their cross. For such individuals, expressions of feeling become
natural, which to others seem out of place and uncalled for;
and not only natural, but needful and inevitable. To deny to
such people all expression of their emotion, is probably in the
end to cause it to burst forth with the greater violence; and it
may be suggested that our British code of manners, by for-
bidding the lighter marks of affection between youths and
men, acts just contrary to its own purpose, and drives intimacies
down into less open and unexceptionable channels.

With regard to this physical element it must also be remembered that since the homogenic love, whether between man
and man, or between woman and woman, can from the nature
of the case never find expression on the physical side so freely
and completely as is the case with the ordinary love; it must
tend rather more than the latter to run along emotional channels, and to find its vent in sympathies of social life and companionship. If one studies carefully the expression of the Greek
statues and the lesson of the Greek literature, one sees clearly
that the ideal of Greek life was a very continent one: the trained
male, the athlete, the man temperate and restrained, even
chaste, for the sake of bettering his powers. It was round this
conception that the Greeks kindled their finer emotions. And
so of their love: a base and licentious indulgence was not in
line with it. They may not have always kept to their ideal, but
there it was. And I am inclined to think that the homogenic
instinct (for the reasons given above) would in the long run
tend to work itself out in this direction. And consonant with
this is the fact that this passion in the past (as pointed out by

J. Addington Symonds in his paper on "Dantesque and Platonic Ideals of Love") has, as a matter of fact, inspired such a vast amount of heroism and romance, only paralleled indeed by the loves of chivalry, which of course, owing to their special character, were subject to a similar transmutation.

On all these matters, the popular opinion has probably been largely influenced by the arbitrary notion that the function of love is limited to child breeding; and that any love not concerned in the propagation of the race must necessarily be of dubious character. And in enforcing this view, no doubt the Hebraic and Christian tradition has exercised a powerful influence—dating, as it almost certainly does, from far-back times when the multiplication of the tribe was one of the first duties of its members, and one of the first necessities of corporate life. But nowadays, when the need has swung round all the other way it is not unreasonable to suppose that a similar revolution will take place in people's views of the place and purpose of the nonchild-bearing love.

I have now said enough I think to show that though much in relation to the homogenic attachment is obscure, and though it may have its special pitfalls and temptations, making it quite necessary to guard against a too great latitude on the physical side; yet on its ethical and social sides it is pregnant with meaning and has received at various times in history abundant justification. It certainly does not seem impossible to suppose that as the ordinary love has a special function in the propagation of the race, so the other has its special function in social and heroic work, and in the generation—not of bodily children— but of those children of the mind, the philosophical conceptions and ideals which transform our lives and those of society. J. Addington Symonds, in his privately printed pamphlets, *A problem in Greek ethics* (now published in a German translation), endeavours to reconstruct as it were the genesis of comrade-love among the Dorians in early Greek times. Thus: "Without sufficiency of women, without the sanctities of established domestic life, inspired by the memories of Achilles and venerating their ancestor, Herakles, the Dorian warriors had special opportunity for elevating comradeship to the rank of an enthusiasm. The incidents of emigration into a foreign country, perils of the sea, passages of rivers and mountains, assaults of fortresses and cities, landings on a hostile shore, night vigils by the side of blazing beacons, foragings for food, picquet service in the front of watchful foes, involved adventures capable of shedding the lustre of romance of friendship. These circumstances, by bringing the virtues of sympathy with the weak, tenderness for the beautiful, protection for the young, together with corresponding qualities of gratitude, self-devotion, and admiring attachment into play, may have tended to cement unions between man and man no less firm than that of marriage. On such connections a wise captain would have relied for giving strength to his battalions, and for keeping alive the flames of enterprise and daring." The author then goes on to suggest that though in such relations as those indicated the physical probably had some share, yet it did not at that time over-balance the emotional and spiritual elements, or lead to the corruption and effeminacy of a later age.

At Sparta, the lover was called *Eispnêlos,* the inspirer, and the younger beloved *Aïtes,* the hearer. This, alone, would show the partly educational aspects in which comradeship was conceived; and a hundred passages from classic literature might be quoted to prove how deeply it had entered into the Greek mind that this love was the cradle of social chivalry and heroic life. Finally, it seems to have been Plato's favorite doctrine that the relation if properly conducted led up to the disclosure of true philosophy in the mind, to the divine vision or mania, and to the remembrance or rekindling within the soul of all the forms of celestial beauty. He speaks of this kind of love as causing a "generation in the beautiful" within the souls of the lovers. The image of the beloved one passing into the mind of the lover and upward through its deepest recesses reaches and unites itself to the essential forms of divine beauty there long hidden, the originals as it were of all creation, and stirring them to life excites a kind of generative descent of noble thoughts and impulses, which henceforth modify the whole cast of thought and life of the one so affected.

If there is any truth, even only a grain or two, in these speculations, it is easy to see that the love with which we are specially dealing is a very important factor in society, and that its neglect, or its repression, or its vulgar misapprehension, may be matters of considerable danger or damage to the common-weal. It is easy to see that while on the one hand marriage is of indispensable importance to the state as providing the workshop as it were for the breeding and rearing of children, another form of union is almost equally indispensable to supply the basis for social activities of other kinds. Every one is conscious that without a close affectional tie of some kind his life is not complete, his powers are crippled, and his energies are inadequately spent. Yet it is not to be expected (though it may of course happen) that the man or woman who has dedicated themselves to each other and to family life should leave the care of their children and the work they have to do at home in order to perform social duties of a remote and less obvious, though may be more arduous, character. Nor is it to be expected that a man or woman single handed, without the counsel of a helpmate in the hour of difficulty, or his or her love in the hour of need, should feel equal to these wider activities. If, to refer once more to classic story, the love of Harmodius had been for a wife and children at home, he would probably not have cared, and it would hardly have been his business, to slay the tyrant. And, unless on the other hand, each of the friends had had the love of his comrade to support him, the two could hardly have nerved themselves to this audacious and ever memorable exploit. So it is difficult to believe that anything can supply the force and liberate the energies required for social and mental activities of the most necessary kind so well as a comrade union, which yet leaves the two lovers free from the responsibilities and impediments of family life.

For if the slaughter of tyrants is not the chief social duty now-a-days, we have with us hydra-headed monsters at least as numerous as the tyrants of old, and more difficult to deal with, and requiring no little courage to encounter. And beyond the extirpation of evils we have solid work waiting to be done in the patient and life-long building up of new forms of society, new orders of thought, and new institutions of human solidarity—all of which in their genesis must meet with opposition, ridicule, hatred, and even violence. Such campaigns as these, though different in kind from those of the Dorian mountaineers described above, will call for equal hardihood and courage, and will stand in need of a comradeship as true and valiant. And it may indeed be doubted whether the higher heroic and spiritual life of a nation is ever quite possible without the sanction of this attachment in its institutions, adding a new range and scope to the possibilities of love.

Walt Whitman, the inaugurator, it may almost be said, of a new world of democratic ideals and literature, and as one of the best of our critics has remarked, the most Greek in spirit and in performance of modern writers, insists continually on this social function of "intense and loving comradeship, the personal and passionate attachment of man to man."

"I will make," he says, "the most splendid race the sun ever shone upon, I will make divine magnetic lands. . . . I will make inseparable cities with their arms about each others necks, by the love of comrades." And again, in *Democratic Vistas,* "It is to the development, identification, and general prevalence of that fervid comradeship (the adhesive love at least rivaling the amative love hitherto possessing imaginative literature, if not going beyond it), that I look for the counterbalance and offset of materialistic and vulgar American democracy, and for the spiritualisation thereof. . . . I say democracy infers such loving comradeship, as its most inevitable twin or counterpart, without which it will be incomplete, in vain, and incapable of perpetuating itself."

Yet Whitman could not have spoken, as he did, with a kind of authority on this subject, if he had not been fully aware that through the masses of the people this attachment was already alive and working, though doubtless in a somewhat suppressed and unself-conscious form, and if he had not had ample knowledge of its effects and influence in himself and others around him. Like all great artists he could but give form and light to that which already existed dim and inchoate in the heart of the people. To those, who have dived at all below the surface in this direction, it will be familiar enough that the homogenic passion ramifies widely through all modern society, and that among the masses of the people as among the classes, even below the stolid surface and reserve of British manners, letters pass and enduring attachments are formed, differing in no very obvious respect from those correspondences which persons of opposite sex knit with each other under similar circumstances; but that hitherto while this relation has occasionally, in its grosser forms and abuses, come into public notice through the police reports, etc., its more sane and spiritual manifestations, though really a moving force in the body politic, have remained unrecognised.

It is hardly needful in these days when social questions loom so large upon us to emphasise the importance of a bond which by the most passionate and lasting compulsion may draw members of the different classes together, and (as it often seems to do) none the less strongly because they are members of different classes. A moment's consideration must convince us that such a comradeship may, as Whitman says, have "deepest relations to general politics." It is noticeable, too, in this deepest relation to politics that the movement among women towards their own liberation and emancipation, which is taking place all over the civilised world, has been accompanied by a marked development of the homogenic passion among the female sex. It may be said that a certain strain in the relations between the opposite sexes which has come about owing to a growing consciousness among women that they have been oppressed and unfairly treated by men, and a growing unwillingness to ally themselves unequally in marriage, that this strain has caused the womenkind to draw more closely together and to cement alliances of their own. But whatever the cause may be it is pretty certain that such comrade-alliances, and of quite devoted kind, are becoming increasingly common, and especially perhaps among the more cultured classes of women, who are working out the great cause of their sex's liberation; nor is it difficult to see the importance of such alliances in such a campaign. In the United States where the battle of women's independence is also being fought, the tendency mentioned is as strongly marked.

A few words may here be said about the legal aspect of this important question. It has to be remarked that the present state of the law, both in Germany and Britain, arising as it does partly out of some of the misapprehensions above alluded to, and partly out of the sheer unwillingness of legislators to discuss the question, is really impracticable. While the law rightly seeks to prevent acts of violence or public scandal, it may be argued that it is going beyond its province when it attempts to regulate the private and voluntary relations of adult persons to each other. The homogenic affection is a valuable social force, and in some cases a necessary element of noble human character, yet the Act of 1885 makes almost any familiarity in such cases the possible basis of a criminal charge. The law has no doubt had substantial ground for previous statutes on this subject, dealing with a certain gross act; but in so severely condemning the least familiarity between male persons we think it has gone too far. It has undertaken a censorship over private morals (entirely apart from social results) which is beyond its province, and which, even if it were its province, it could not possibly fullfil; it has opened wider than ever before, the door to a real, most serious social evil and crime—that of blackmailing; and it has thrown a shadow over even the simplest and most ordinary expressions of an attachment which may, as we have seen, be of great value in the national life.

That the homosexual feeling, like the heterosexual, may lead to public abuses of liberty and decency; that it needs a strict self-control; and that much teaching and instruction on the subject is needed; we of course do not deny. But as, in the case of persons of opposite sex, the law limits itself on the whole to a maintenance of public order, the protection of the weak from violence and insult, and of the young from their inexperience; so we think it should be here. The much-needed teaching and the true morality on the subject must be given, as it can only be given, by the spread of proper education and ideas, and not by the clumsy bludgeon of the statute-book.

Having thus shown the importance of the homogenic or comrade attachment, in some form, in national life, it would seem high time now that the modern peoples should recognise this in their institutions, and endeavour at least in their public opinion and systems of education to understand this factor and give it its proper place. The undoubted evils which exist in relation to it, for instance in our public schools as well as in our public life, owe their existence largely to the fact that the whole subject is left in the gutter so to speak, in darkness and concealment. No one offers a clue of better things, nor to point a way out of the wilderness; and by this very nonrecognition the passion is perverted into its least satisfactory channels. All love, one would say, must have its responsibilities, else it is liable to degenerate, and to dissipate itself in mere sentiment or sensuality. The normal marriage between man and woman leads up to the foundation of the household and the family; the love between parents and children implies duties and cares on both sides. The homogenic attachment left unrecognised, easily loses some of its best quality and becomes an ephemeral or corrupt thing. Yet, as we have seen, and as I am pointing out in the following chapter, it may, when occurring between an elder and younger, prove to be an immense educational force; while, as between equals, it may be turned to social and heroic uses, such as can hardly be demanded or expected from the ordinary marriage. It would seem high time, I say, that public opinion should recognise these facts; and so give to this attachment the sanction and dignity which arise from public recognition, as well as the definite form and outline which would flow from the existence of an accepted ideal or standard in the matter. It is often said how necessary for the morality of the ordinary marriage is some public recognition of the relation, and some accepted standard of conduct in it. May not, to a lesser degree, something of the same kind be true of the homogenic attachment? It has had its place as a recognised and guarded institution in the elder and more primitive societies; and it seems quite probable that a similar place will be accorded to it in the societies of the future.

4. AFFECTION IN EDUCATION

The place of affection, and the need of it, as an educative force in school life, is a subject which is beginning to attract a good deal of attention. Hitherto education has been concentrated on intellectual (and physical) development; but the affections have been left to take care of themselves. Now it is beginning to be seen that the affections have an immense deal to say in the building up of the brain and the body. Their evolution and organisation in some degree is probably going to become an important part of school management.

School friendships of course exist; and almost every one remembers that they filled a large place in the outlook of his early years; but he remembers, too, that they were not recognised in any way, and that, in consequence, the main part of their force and value was wasted. Yet it is evident that the first unfolding of a strong attachment in boyhood or girlhood must have a profound influence; while if it occurs between an elder and a younger schoolmate, or as sometimes happens, between the young thing and its teacher, its importance in the educational sense can hardly be overrated.

That such feelings sometimes take quite intense and romantic forms, few will deny. I have before me a letter, in which the author, speaking of an attachment he experienced when a boy of sixteen for a youth somewhat older than himself, says:

"I would have died for him ten times over. My devices and planning to meet him (to come across him casually, as it were) were those of a lad for his sweetheart, and when I saw him my heart beat so violently, that it caught my breath, and I could not speak. We met in——, and for the weeks that he stayed there I thought of nothing else—thought of him night and day, and when he returned to London I used to write him weekly letters, veritable love letters of many sheets in length. Yet I never felt one particle of jealousy, though our friendship lasted for some years. The passion, violent and extravagant as it was, I believe to have been perfectly free from sex feeling and perfectly wholesome and good for me. It distinctly contributed to my growth.

Looking back upon it and analysing it as well as I can, I seem to see, as the chief element in it, an escape from the extremely narrow Puritanism in which I was reared, into a large sunny ingenuous nature which knew nothing at all of the bondage of which I was beginning to be acutely conscious."

Shelley in his fragmentary *Essay on friendship* speaks in the most glowing terms of an attachment he formed at school. And Leigh Hunt says in his *Autobiography*.

"If I had reaped no other benefit from Christ Hospital, the school would be ever dear to me from the recollection of the friendships I formed in it, and of the first heavenly taste it gave me of that most spiritual of the affections. . . . I shall never forget the impression it made on me. I loved my friend for his gentleness, his candour, his truth, his good repute, his freedom even from my own livelier manner, his calm and reasonable kindness. . . . I doubt whether he ever had a conception of a tithe of the regard and respect I entertained for him, and I smile to think of the perplexity (though he never showed it) which he probably felt sometimes at my enthusiastic expressions; for I thought him a kind of angel."

However, it is not necessary to quote authorities on such a subject as this. Any one who has had experience of schoolboys knows well enough that they are capable of forming these romantic and devoted attachments, and that their alliances are often of the kind especially referred to as having a bearing on education, i.e., between an elder and a younger. They are genuine attractions, free as a rule, and at their inception, from secondary motives. They are not formed by the elder one for any personal ends. More often, indeed, I think they are begun by the younger, who naively allows his admiration of the elder one to become visible. But they are absorbing and intense, and on either side their influence is deeply felt and long remembered.

That such attachments may be of the very greatest value is self-evident. The younger boy looks on the other as a hero, loves to be with him, thrills with pleasure at his words of praise or kindness, imitates, and makes him his pattern and standard, learns exercises and games, contracts habits, or picks up information from him. The elder one, touched, becomes protector and helper; the unselfish side of his nature is drawn out, and he develops a real affection and tenderness towards the younger. He takes all sorts of trouble to initiate his *protégé* in field sports or studies; is proud of the latter's success; and leads him on perhaps later to share his own ideals of life and thought and work.

Sometimes the alliance will begin, in a corresponding way, from the side of the elder boy. Sometimes, as said, between a boy and a master such an attachment, or the germ of it, is found; and indeed it is difficult to say what gulf, or difference of age, or culture, or class in society, is so great that affection of this kind will not on occasion overpass it. I have by me, a letter which was written by a boy of eleven or twelve to a young man of twenty-four or twenty-five. The boy was rather a wild, "naughty" boy, and had given his parents (working-class folk) a good deal of trouble. However, he attended some sort of night school or evening class and there conceived the strongest affection (evidenced by this letter) for his teacher, the young man in question, quite spontaneously, and without any attempt on the part of the latter to elicit it; and (which was equally important) without any attempt on his part to deny it. The result was most favorable; the one force which could really reach the boy had, as it were, been found; and he developed rapidly and well.

The following extract is from a letter written by an elderly man who has had large experience as a teacher. He says:

It has always seemed to me that the rapport that exists between two human beings, whether of the same or of different sexes, is a force not sufficiently recognised, and capable of producing great results. Plato fully understood its importance, and aimed at giving what to his countrymen was more or less sensual, a noble and exalted direction. . . . As one who has had much to do in instructing boys and starting them in life, I am convinced that the great secret of being a good teacher consists in the possibility of that rapport; not only of a merely intellectual nature, but involving a certain physical element, a personal affection, almost indescribable, that grows up between pupil and teacher, and through which thoughts are shared and an influence created that could exist in no other way."

And it must be evident to every one that to the expanding mind of a small boy to have a relation of real affection with some sensible and helpful elder of his own sex must be a priceless boon. At that age, love to the other sex has hardly declared itself, and indeed is not exactly what is wanted. The unformed mind requires an ideal of itself, as it were, to which it can cling or towards which it can grow. Yet it is equally evident that the relation and the success of it, will depend immensely on the character of the elder one, on the self-restraint and tenderness of which he is capable, and on the ideal of life which he has in his mind. That, possibly, is the reason why Greek custom, at least in the early days of Hellas, not only recognised friendships between elder and younger youths, as a national institution of great importance, but laid down very distinct laws or rules concerning the conduct of them, so as to be a guide and a help to the elder in what was acknowledged to be a position of responsibility.

In Crete, for instance, the friendship was entered into in quite a formal and public way, with the understanding and consent of relatives; the position of the elder was clearly defined, and it became his business to train and exercise the younger in skill of arms, the chase, etc.; while the latter could obtain redress at law, if the elder subjected him to insult or injury of any kind. At the end of a certain period of probation, if the younger desired it he could leave his comrade; if not, he became his squire or henchman, the elder being bound to furnish his military equipments, and they fought thenceforward side by side in battle, "inspired with double valor, according to the notions of the Cretans, by the gods of war and love. Similar customs prevailed in Sparta, and, in a less defined way, in other Greek states; as, indeed, they have prevailed among many semibarbaric races on the threshold of civilisation.

When, however, we turn to modern life and the actual situation, as for instance in the public schools of today, it may well be objected that we find very little of the suggested ideal, but rather an appalling descent into the most uninspiring conditions. So far from friendship being an institution whose value is recognised and understood, it is, at best, scantily acknowledged, and is often actually discountenanced and mis-

understood. And though attachments such as we have portrayed exist, they exist underground, as it were, at their peril,
and half stifled in an atmosphere which can only be described
as that of the gutter. Somehow the disease of premature sexuality seems to have got possession of our centres of education;
wretched practices and habits abound, and (what is perhaps
their worst feature) cloud and degrade the boys' conception
of what true love or friendship may be.

To those who are familiar with large public schools the
state of affairs does not need describing. A friend (who has
placed some notes at my disposal) says that in his time a certain well known public school was a mass of uncleanness, incontinence, and dirty conversation, while at the same time a
great deal of genuine affection, even to heroism, was shown
among the boys in their relations with one another. But "all
these things were treated by masters and boys alike as more
or less unholy, with the result that they were either sought
after or flung aside according to the sexual or emotional instinct of the boy. No attempt was made at discrimination. A
kiss was by comparison as unclean as the act of *fellatio,* and
no one had any gauge or principle whatever on which to guide
the cravings of boyhood." The writer then goes into details
which it is not necessary to reproduce here. He (and others)
were initiated in the mysteries of sex by the dormitory servant;
and the boys thus corrupted mishandled each other.

Naturally, in any such atmosphere as this, the chances
against the formation of a decent and healthy attachment are
very large. If the elder youth happen to be given to sensuality,
he has here his opportunity; if on the other hand he is not
given to it, the ideas current around probably have the effect
of making him suspect his own affection, and he ends by
smothering and disowning the best part of his nature. In both
ways, harm is done. The big boys in such places become either
coarse and licentious or hard and self-righteous; the small boys,
instead of being educated and strengthened by the elder ones,

become effeminate little wretches, the favorites, the petted boys, and the "spoons" of the school. As time goes on the public opinion of the school ceases to believe in the possibility of a healthy friendship; the masters begin to presume (and not without reason) that all affection means sensual practices, and end by doing their best to discourage it.

Now this state of affairs is really desperate. There is no need to be puritanical, or to look upon the lapses of boyhood as unpardonable sins; indeed, it may be allowed, as far as that goes, that a little frivolity is better than hardness and self-righteousness; yet every one feels, and must feel, who knows anything about the matter, that the state of our schools is bad.

And it is so because, after all, purity (in the sense of continence) is of the first importance to boyhood. To prolong the period of continence in a boy's life is to prolong the period of growth. This is a simple, physiological law, and a very obvious one; and whatever other things may be said in favour of purity, it remains perhaps the most weighty. To introduce sensual and sexual habits, and one of the worst of these is self-abuse, at an early age, is to arrest growth, both physical and mental.

And what is even more, it means to arrest the capacity for affection. I believe affection, attachment, whether to the one sex or the other, springs up normally in the youthful mind in a quite diffused, ideal, emotional form—a kind of longing and amazement as at something divine, with no definite thought or distinct consciousness of sex in it. The sentiment expands and fills, as it were like a rising tide, every cranny of the emotional and moral nature; and the longer (of course within reasonable limits) its definite outlet towards sex is deferred, the longer does this period of emotional growth and development continue, and the greater is the refinement and breadth and strength of character resulting. All experience shows that a too early outlet towards sex cheapens and weakens affectional capacity.

Yet this early outlet it is which is the great trouble of our public schools. And it really does not seem unlikely that the peculiar character of the middle class man of today, his undeveloped affectional nature and something of brutishness and woodenness, is largely caused by the prevalent condition of the places of his education. The Greeks, with their wonderful instinct of fitness, seem to have perceived the right path in all this matter; and, while encouraging friendship, as we have seen, made a great point of modesty in early life, the guardians and teachers of every well born boy being especially called upon to watch over the sobriety of his habits and manners.

In education generally, we have then it seems to me (both boys and girls), two great currents to deal with, which cannot be ignored, and which certainly ought to be candidly recognized and given their right direction. One of these currents is that of friendship. The other, is that of the young thing's natural curiosity about sex. The latter is or should be a perfectly legitimate interest. A boy at puberty naturally wants to know, and ought to know, what is taking place, and what the uses and functions of his body are. He does not go very deep into things; a small amount of information will probably satisfy him; but the curiosity is there, and it is pretty certain that the boy, if he is a boy of any sense or character, will in some shape or another get to satisfy it.

The process is really a mental one. Desire, except in some abnormal cases, has not manifested itself strongly; and there is often perhaps generally, an actual repugnance at first to anything like sexual practices; but the wish for information exists and is, I say, legitimate enough. In almost all human societies, except curiously, the modern nations, there have been institutions for the initiation of the youth of either sex into these matters, and these initiations have generally been associated, in the opening blossom of the young mind, with inculcation of the ideals of manhood and womanhood, courage, hardihood, and the duties of the citizen or the soldier.

But what does the modern school do? It shuts a trapdoor

down on the whole matter. There is a hush; a grim silence. Legitimate curiosity soon becomes illegitimate of its kind; and a furtive desire creeps in, where there was no desire before. The method of the gutter prevails. In the absence of any recognition of schoolboy needs, contraband information is smuggled from one to another; chaff and "smut" take the place of sensible and decent explanations; unhealthy practices follow; the sacredness of sex goes its way, never to return, and the school is filled with premature and morbid talk and thought about a subject which should, by rights, only just be rising over the mental horizon.

The meeting of these two currents, of ideal attachment and sexual desire, constitutes a rather critical period, even when it takes place in the normal way, i.e., later on, and at the matrimonial age. Under the most favorable conditions a certain conflict occurs in the mind at their first encounter. But in the modern school this conflict, precipitated far too soon, and accompanied by an artificial suppression of the nobler current and a premature hastening of the baser one, ends in simple disaster to the former. Masters wage war against incontinence, and are right to do so. But how do they wage it? As said, by grim silence and fury, by driving the abscess deeper, by covering the drain over, and by confusing when it comes before them, both in their own minds and those of the boys, a real attachment with that which they condemn.

Not long ago, the headmaster of a large public school coming suddenly out of his study chanced upon two boys embracing each other in the corridor. Possibly, and even probably, it was the simple and natural expression of an unsophisticated attachment. Certainly, it was nothing that in itself, could be said to be either right or wrong. What did he do? He haled the two boys into his study, gave them a long lecture on the nefariousness of their conduct, with copious hints that he knew what such things meant, and what they led to, and ended by punishing both condignly. Could anything be more foolish? If their friendship was clean and natural, the master was only trying to make them feel that it was unclean and unnatural, and that a lovely and honorable thing was disgraceful; if the act was, which at least is improbable, a mere signal of lust, even then the best thing would have been to assume that it was honorable, and by talking to the boys, either together or separately, to try and inspire them with a better ideal; while if, between these positions, the master really thought the affection though honorable would lead to things undesirable, then, plainly, to punish the two was only to cement their love for each other, to give them a strong reason for concealing it, and to hasten its onward course. Yet every one knows that this is the kind of way in which the subject is treated in schools. It is the method of despair. And masters (perhaps not unnaturally) finding that they have not the time which would be needed for personal dealing with each boy, nor the forces at their command by which they might hope to introduce new ideals of life and conduct into their little community, and feeling thus utterly unable to cope with the situation, allow themselves to drift into a policy of mere silence with regard to it, tempered by outbreaks of ungoverned and unreasoning severity.

I venture to think that schoolmasters will never successfully solve the difficulty until they boldly recognize the two needs in question, and proceed candidly to give them their proper satisfaction.

The need of information, the legitimate curiosity of boys and girls must be met, 1. partly by classes on physiology, 2. partly by private talks and confidences between elder and younger based on friendship. With regard to classes, of this kind they are already, happily, being carried on at a few advanced schools, and with good results. And though such classes can only go rather generally into the facts of motherhood and generation, they cannot fail if well managed, to impress the young minds, and give them a far grander and more reverent conception of the matter than they usually gain.

But although some rudimentary teaching on sex and lessons in physiology may be given in classes, it is obvious that further instruction, and indeed, real help in the conduct of life and morals can only come through very close and tender confidences between the elder and the younger, such as exist where there is a strong friendship to begin with. It is obvious that effective help can only come in this way, and that this is the only way in which it is desirable that it should come. The elder friend, in this case would naturally be, and in many instances is the parent, mother or father, who ought certainly to be able to impress on the child the sacredness of the relation. And it is to be hoped that parents will see their way to take this part more freely in the future. But for some unexplained reason, there is often a gulf of reserve between the (British) parent and child; and the boy who is much at school comes more under the influence of his elder companions than his parents. Therefore, if boys and youths cannot be trusted and encouraged to form decent and loving friendships with each other, and with their elders or juniors in which many delicate questions could be discussed and the tradition of sensible and manly conduct with regard to sex handed down we are indeed in a bad plight and involved in a vicious circle from which escape seems difficult.

And so (we think) the need of attachment must also be met by full recognition of it, and the granting of its expression within all reasonable limits; by the dissemination of a good ideal of friendship and the enlistment of it on the side of manliness and temperance. Is it too much to hope that schools will, in time, recognise comradeship as a regular institution—considerably more important, say, than "fagging"—an institution having its definite place in the school life, in the games and in the studies, with its own duties, responsibilities, privileges, etc., and serving to ramify through the little community, hold it together, and inspire its members with the two qualities of heroism and tenderness, which together form the basis of all great character?

But here it must be said that if we are hoping for any great change in the conduct of our large boys' schools, the so called public schools are not the places in which to look for it, or at any rate for its inception. In the first place these institutions are hampered by powerful traditions which naturally make them conservative; in the second place their mere size and the number of boys make them difficult to deal with or to modify. The masters are overwhelmed with work; and the (necessary) division of so many boys into separate 'houses' has this effect that a master who introduces a better tradition into his own house has always the prospect before him that his work will be effaced by the continual and perhaps contaminating contact with the boys from the other houses. No, it will be in smaller schools, say of from 50 to 100 boys, where the personal influence of the headmaster will be a real force reaching each boy, and where he will be really able to mould the tradition of the school, that we shall alone be able to look for an improved state of affairs.

No doubt, the first steps in any reform of this kind are difficult; but masters are greately hampered by the confusion in the public mind, to which we have already alluded, which so often persists in setting down any attachment between two boys, or between a boy and his teacher, to nothing but sensuality. Many masters quite understand the situation, but feel themselves helpless in the face of public opinion. Who is so fit (they sometimes feel) to enlighten a young boy and guide his growing mind as one of themselves, when the bond of attachment exists between the two? Like the writer of a letter quoted in the early part of this paper, they believe that "a personal affection, almost indescribable, grows up between pupil and teacher, through which thoughts are shared and an influence created that could exist in no other way." Yet when the pupil comes along of whom all this might be true, who shows by his pleading looks the sentiment which animates him, and the profound impression which he is longing, as it were, to receive from his teacher, the latter belies himself, denies his own instinct and the boy's great need, and treats him distantly and with coldness. And why? Simply because he dreads, even while he desires it, the boy's confidence. He fears the ingenuous and perfectly natural expression of the boy's affection in caress or embrace, because he knows how a bastard public opinion will interpret, or misinterpret it; and rather than run such a risk as this he seals the fountains of the heart, withholds the help which love alone can give, and deliberately nips the tender bud which is turning to him for light and warmth.

The panic terror which prevails in England with regard to the expression of affection of this kind has its comic aspect. The affection exists, and is known to exist, on all sides; but we must bury our heads in the sand and pretend not to see it. And if by any chance we are compelled to recognize it, we must show our vast discernment by suspecting it. And thus we fling on the dust heap one of the noblest and most precious elements in human nature. Certainly, if the denial and suspicion of all natural affection were beneficial, we should find this out in our schools; but seeing how complete is its failure there to clarify their tone it is sufficiently evident that the method itself is wrong.

The remarks in this paper have chiefly had reference to boy's schools; but they apply in the main to girls' schools, where much the same troubles prevail, with this difference, that in girls' schools friendships instead of being repressed are rather encouraged by public opinion; only unfortunately they are for the most part friendships of a weak and sentimental turn, and not very healthy either in themselves or in the habits they lead to. Also in girls' schools, the whole subject wants facing out; friendship wants setting on a more solid and less sentimental basis; and on the subject of sex, so infinitely important to women, there needs to be sensible and consistent teaching, both public and private. Possibly the coeducation of boys and girls may be of use in making boys less ashamed of their feelings, and girls more healthy in the expression of them.

At any rate, the more the matter is thought of, the clearer I believe will it appear that a healthy affection must in the end be the basis of education, and that the recognition of this will form the only way out of the modern school difficulty. It is true that such a change would revolutionise our school life; but it will have to come, all the same, and no doubt will come *pari passu* with other changes that are taking place in society at large.

5. THE PLACE OF THE URANIAN IN SOCIETY

Whatever differing views there may be on the many problems which the intermediate sexes present, and however difficult of solution may be some of the questions involved, there is one thing which appears to me incontestable: namely that a vast number of intermediates do actually perform most valuable social work, and that they do so partly on account and by reason of their special temperament.

This fact is not generally recognised as it ought to be, for the simple reason that the Uranian himself is not recognised, and indeed (as we have already said) tends to conceal his temperament from the public. There is no doubt that if it became widely known who are the Uranians, the world would be astonished to find so many of its great or leading men among them.

I have thought it might be useful to indicate some of the lines along which valuable work is being performed, or has been performed, by people of this disposition; and in doing this I do not of course mean to disguise or conceal the fact that there are numbers of merely frivolous, or feeble or even vicious homosexuals, who practically do no useful work for society at all, just as there are the same class of normal people. The existence of those who do no valuable work does not alter the fact of the existence of others whose work is of great importance. And I wish also to make it clearly understood that I use the word Uranians to indicate simply those whose lives and activities are inspired by a genuine friendship or love for their own sex, without venturing to specify their individual and particular habits or relations towards those whom they love (which relations in most cases we have no means of knowing). Some intermediates of light and leading, doubtless not a few, are physically very reserved and continent; others are sensual in some degree or other. The point is that they are all men, or women, whose most powerful motive comes from the dedication to their own kind, and is bound up with it in some way. And if it seems strange and anomalous that in such cases, work of considerable importance to society is being done by people whose affections and dispositions society itself would blame, this is after all no more than has happened a thousand times before in the history of the world.

As I have already hinted, the Uranian temperament (probably from the very fact of its dual nature and the swift and constant interaction between its masculine and feminine elements) is exceedingly sensitive and emotional; and there is no doubt that going with this, a large number of the artist class, musical, literary or pictorial, belong to this description. That delicate and subtle sympathy with every wave and phase of feeling which makes the artist possible is also very characteristic of the Uranian (the male type), and makes it easy or natural for the Uranian man to become an artist. In the "confessions" and "cases" collected by Krafft-Ebing, Havelock Ellis and others, it is remarkable what a large percentage of men of this temperament belong to the artist class.

In his volume on *Sexual inversion,* speaking of the cases collected by himself, Ellis says:

"An examination of my cases reveals the interesting fact that thirty-two of them, or sixty-eight per cent, possess artistic aptitude in varying degree. Galton found, from the investigation of nearly one thousand persons, that the general average showing artistic taste in England is only about thirty per cent. It must also be said that my figures are probably below the truth, as no special point was made of investigating the matter, and also that in many of my cases the artistic aptitudes are of high order. With regard to the special avocations of my cases, it must of course be said that no occupation furnishes a safeguard against inversion. However, there are certain occupations to which inverts are specially attracted. Acting is certainly one of these. Three of my cases belong to the dramatic profession, and others have marked dramatic ability. Again, art in its various forms, and music, exercise much attraction. However, in my experience, literature is the avocation to which inverts seem to feel chiefly called, and that moreover in which they may find the highest degree of success and reputation. At least six of my cases are successful men of letters."

Of literature in this connection, and of the great writers of the world whose work has been partly inspired by the Uranian love, I have myself already spoken.

It may further be said that those of the modern artist writers and poets who have done the greatest service in the way of interpreting and reconstructing *Greek* life and ideals, men like Winckelmann, Goethe, Addington Symonds, Walter Pater, have had a marked strain of this temperament in them. And this has been a service of great value, and one which the world could ill have afforded to lose.

The painters and sculptors, especially of the Renaissance period in Italy, yield not a few examples of men whose work has been similarly inspired, as in the cases of Michel Angelo, Leonardo, Bazzi, Cellini, and others. As to music, this is certainly the art which in its subtlety and tenderness, and perhaps in a certain inclination to indulge in emotion, lies nearest to the Urning nature. There are few in fact of this nature who have not some gift in the direction of music, though, unless we cite

Tschaikowsky, it does not appear that any thorough-going Uranian has attained the highest eminence in this art.

Another direction, along which the temperament very naturally finds an outlet, is the important social work of education. The capacity that a man has, in cases, of devoting himself to the welfare of boys or youths, is clearly a thing which ought not to go wasted, and which may be most precious and valuable. It is incontestable that a great number of men (and women) are drawn into the teaching profession by this sentiment and the work they do is, in many cases, beyond estimation. Fortunate the boy who meets with such a helper in early life! I know a man, a rising and vigorous thinker and writer who tells me that he owes almost everything mentally to such a friend of his boyhood, who took the greatest interest in him, saw him almost every day for many years, and indeed cleared up for him not only things mental but things moral, giving him the affection and guidance his young heart needed. And I have, myself, known and watched not a few such teachers, in public schools and in private schools, and seen something of the work and of the real inspiration they have been to boys under them. Hampered as they have been by the readiness of the world to misinterpret, they still have been able to do most precious service. Of course, here and there a case occurs in which privilege is abused; but even then, the judgment of the world is often unreasonably severe. A poor boy once told me with tears in his eyes of the work a man had done for him. This man had saved the boy from drunken parents, taken him from the slums, and by means of a club, helped him out into the world. He had rescued many other boys, in the same way, scores and scores of them. But on some occasion or other he got into trouble, and was accused of improper familiarities. No excuse, or record of a useful life, was of the least avail. Every trumpery slander was believed; every mean motive imputed, and he had to throw up his position and settle elsewhere, his life work shattered, never to be resumed.

The capacity for sincere affection which causes an elder man to care so deeply for the welfare of a youth or boy, is met and responded to by a similar capacity in the young thing of devotion to an elder man. This fact is not always recognised; but I have known cases of boys and even young men who would feel the most romantic attachments to quite mature men, sometimes as much as forty or fifty years of age, and only for them, passing by their own contemporaries of either sex, and caring only to win a return affection from these others. This may seem strange, but it is true. And the fact not only makes one understand what riddles there are slumbering in the breasts of our children, but how greatly important it is that we should try to read them, since here in such cases as these, the finding of an answering heart in an elder man would probably be the younger one's salvation.

How much of the enormous amount of philanthropic work done in the present day, by women among needy or destitute girls of all sorts, or by men among like classes of boys, is inspired by the same feeling, it would be hard to say; but it must be a very considerable proportion. I think myself that the best philanthropic work just because it is the most personal, the most loving, and the least merely formal and self-righteous, has a strong fibre of the Uranian heart running through it; and if it should be said that work of this very personal kind is more liable to dangers and difficulties on that account, it is only what is true of the best in almost all departments.

Eros is a great leveler. Perhaps the true democracy rests, more firmly than anywhere else, on a sentiment which easily passes the bounds of class and caste, and unites in the closest affection the most estranged ranks of society. It is noticeable how often Uranians of good position and breeding are drawn to rougher types, as of manual workers, and frequently very permanent alliances grow up in this way, which although not publicly acknowledged have a decided influence on social institutions, customs and political tendencies. These would have a good deal more influence could they be given a little more scope and recognition. There are cases that I have known (although the ordinary commercial world might hardly believe it) of employers who have managed to attach their workmen, or many of them, very personally to themselves, and whose object in running their businesses was at least as much to provide their employees with a living as themselves; while the latter, feeling this, have responded with their best output. It is possible that something like the guilds and fraternities of the middle ages might thus be reconstructed, but on a more intimate and personal basis than in those days; and indeed there are not wanting signs that such a reconstruction is actually taking place.

The *Letters of Love and Labor* written by Samuel M. Jones of Toledo, Ohio, to his workmen in the engineering firm of which he was master, are very interesting in this connection. They breathe a spirit of extraordinary personal affection towards, and confidence in, the employees, which was heartily responded to by the latter; and the business was carried on, with considerable success, on the principle of a close and friendly co-operation all round.

These things indeed suggest to one that it is possible that the Uranian spirit may lead to something like a general enthusiasm of humanity, and that the Uranian people may be destined to form the advance guard of that great movement which will one day transform the common life by substituting the bond of personal affection and compassion for the monetary, legal and other external ties which now control and confine society. Such a part of course we cannot expect the Uranians to play unless the capacity for their kind of attachment also exists, though in a germinal and undeveloped state, in the breast of mankind at large. And modern thought and investigation are clearly tending that way, to confirm that it does so exist.

Dr. E. Bertz in his late study of Whitman as a person of strongly homogenic temperament brings forward the objection

that Whitman's gospel of comradeship as a means of social re-
generation is founded on a false basis, because (so Dr. Bertz
says) the gospel derives from an abnormality in himself, and
therefore cannot possibly have a universal application or create
a general enthusiasm. But this is rather a case of assuming the
point which has to be proved. Whitman constantly maintains
that his own disposition at any rate is normal, and that he
represents the average man. And it may be true, even as far as
his Uranian temperament is concerned, that while this was specially developed in him the germs of it are almost, if not quite,
universal. If so, then the comradeship on which Whitman
founds a large portion of his message may in course of time
become a general enthusiasm, and the nobler Uranians of today
may be destined, as suggested, to be its pioneers and advance
guard. As one of them himself has sung:

> These things shall be! A loftier race,
>   Than e'er the world hath known, shall rise
> With flame of freedom in their souls,
>   And light of science in their eyes.
> Nation with nation, land with land,
>   In-armed shall live as comrades free;
> In every heart and brain shall throb
>   The pulse of one fraternity.

To proceed. The Uranian, though generally high strung and
sensitive, is by no means always dreamy. He is sometimes
extraordinarily and unexpectedly practical; and such a man
may, and often does, command a positive enthusiasm among
his subordinates in a business organisation. The same is true of
military organisation. As a rule, the Uranian temperament (in
the male) is not militant. War with its horrors and savagery is
somewhat alien to the type. But here again, there are exceptions; and in all times there have been great generals (like
Alexander, Cæsar, Charles XII of Sweden, or Frederick II of
Prussia, not to speak of more modern examples) with a powerful strain in them of the homogenic nature, and a wonderful

capacity for organisation and command, which combined with their personal interest in, or attachment to, their troops, and the answering enthusiasm so elicited, have made their armies well-nigh invincible.

The existence of this great practical ability in some Uranians cannot be denied; and it points to the important work they may some day have to do in social reconstruction. At the same time I think it is noticeable that politics (at any rate in the modern sense of the word, as concerned mainly with party questions and party government) is not as a rule congenial to them. The personal and affectional element is perhaps too remote or absent. Mere "views" and "questions" and party strife are alien to the Uranian man, as they are on the whole to the ordinary woman.

However, if politics are not particularly congenial, it is yet remarkable how many royal personages have been decidedly homogenic in temperament. Taking the kings of England from the Norman Conquest to the present day, we may count about thirty. And three of these, namely, William Rufus, Edward II and James I were homosexual in a marked degree, might fairly be classed as Urnings, while some others like William III had a strong admixture of the same temperament. Three out of thirty yields a high ratio, ten per cent, and considering that sovereigns do not generally choose themselves, but come into their position by accident of birth, the ratio is certainly remarkable. Does it suggest that the general percentage in the world at large is equally high, but that it remains unnoticed, except in the fierce light that beats upon thrones? or is there some other explanation with regard to the special liability of royalty to inversion? Hereditary degeneracy has sometimes been suggested. But it is difficult to explain the matter even on this theory; for though the epithet "degenerate" might possibly apply to James I, it would certainly not be applicable to William Rufus and William III, who, in their different ways, were both men of great courage and personal force, while Edward II was by no means wanting in ability.

But while the Uranian temperament has, in cases, specially fitted its possessors to become distinguished in art or education or war or administration, and enabled them to do valuable work in these fields; it remains perhaps true that above all it has fitted them, and fits them for distinction and service in affairs of the heart.

It is hard to imagine human beings more skilled in these matters than are the intermediates. For indeed no one else can possibly respond to and understand, as they do, all the fluctuations and interactions of the masculine and feminine in human life. The pretensive coyness and passivity of women, the rude invasiveness of men; lust, brutality, secret tears, the bleeding heart; renunciation, motherhood, finesse, romance, angelic devotion, all these things lie slumbering in the Uranian soul, ready on occasion for expression; and if they are not always expressed are always there for purposes of divination or interpretation. There are few situations, in fact, in courtship or marriage which the Uranian does not instinctively understand; and it is strange to see how even an unlettered person of this type will often read love's manuscript easily in cases where the normal man or woman is groping over it like a child in the dark. [Not of course that this means to imply any superiority of character in the former; but merely that with his double outlook he necessarily discerns things which the other misses.]

That the Uranians do stand out as helpers and guides, not only in matters of education, but in affairs of love and marriage, is tolerably patent to all who know them. It is a common experience for them to be consulted now by the man, now by the woman, whose matrimonial conditions are uncongenial or disastrous, not generally because the consultants in the least perceive the Uranian nature, but because they instinctively feel that here is a strong sympathy with and understanding of their side of the question. In this way, it is often the fate of the

Uranian, himself unrecognised, to bring about happier times and a better comprehension of each other among those with whom he may have to deal. Also he often becomes the confidant of young things of either sex, who are caught in the tangles of love or passion, and know not where to turn for assistance.

I say that I think perhaps of all the services the Uranian may render to society it will be found some day that in this direction of solving the problems of affection and of the heart he will do the greatest service. If the day is coming as we have suggested, when love is at last to take its rightful place as the binding and directing force of society (instead of the cash-nexus), and society is to be transmuted in consequence to a higher form, then undoubtedly the superior types of Uranians, prepared for this service by long experience and devotion, as well as by much suffering, will have an important part to play in the transformation. For that the Urnings in their own lives put love before everything else, postponing to it the other motives like money making, business success, fame, which occupy so much space in most people's careers, is a fact which is patent to everyone who knows them. This may be saying little or nothing in favor of those of this class whose conception of love is only of a poor and frivolous sort; but in the case of those others who see the god in his true light, the fact that they serve him in singleness of heart and so unremittingly raises them at once into the position of the natural leaders of mankind.

From this fact, i.e., that the folk think so much of affairs of the heart, and from the fact that their alliances and friendships are formed and carried on beneath the surface of society, as it were, and therefore to some extent beyond the inquisitions and supervisions of Mrs. Grundy, some interesting conclusions flow.

For one thing, the question is constantly arising as to how society would shape itself if free: what form, in matters of love and marriage, it would take, if the present restrictions and sanctions were removed or greatly altered. At present, in these matters, the law, the church, and a strong pressure of public opinion interfere, compelling the observance of certain forms; and it becomes difficult to say how much of the existing order is caused by the spontaneous instinct and common sense of human nature, and how much to mere outside compulsion and interference: how far, for instance, monogamy is natural or artificial; to what degree marriages would be permanent if the law did not make them so; what is the rational view of divorce; whether jealousy is a necessary accompaniment of love; and so forth. These are questions which are being constantly discussed, without finality; or not infrequently with quite pessimistic conclusions.

Now in the Urning societies, a certain freedom (though not complete, of course) exists. Underneath the surface of general society, and consequently unaffected to any great degree by its laws and customs, alliances are formed and maintained, or modified or broken, more in accord with inner need than with outer pressure. Thus, it happens that in these societies there are such opportunities to note and observe human grouping under conditions of freedom, as do not occur in the ordinary world. And the results are both interesting and encouraging. As a rule, I think it may be said that the alliances are remarkably permanent. Instead of the wild "general post" which so many good people seem to expect in the event of law being relaxed, one finds (except of course in a few individual cases) that common sense and fidelity and a strong tendency to permanence prevail. In the ordinary world so far has doubt gone that many today disbelieve in a lifelong free marriage. Yet among the Uranians, such a thing is common and well known; and there are certainly few among them who do not believe in its possibility.

Great have been the debates, in all times and places, concerning jealousy; and as to how far jealousy is natural and instinctive and universal, and how far it is the product of social opinion and the property sense, etc.

In ordinary marriage, what may be called social and proprietary jealousy, is undoubtedly a very great factor. But this kind of jealousy hardly appears or operates in the Urning societies. Thus we have an opportunity in these latter of observing conditions where only the natural and instinctive jealousy exists. This, of course, is present among the Urnings, sometimes rampant and violent, sometimes quiescent, and vanishing almost to nil. It seems to depend almost entirely upon the individual; and we certainly learn that jealousy though frequent and widespread, is not an absolutely necessary accompaniment of love. There are cases of Uranians both men and women who, though permanently allied, do not object to lesser friendships on either side, and there are cases of very decided objection. And we may conclude that something the same is true of the ordinary marriage, the property considerations and the property jealousy being once removed. The tendency anyhow to establish a dual relation more or less fixed, is seen to be very strong among the intermediates, and may be concluded to be equally strong among the more normal folk.

Again with regard to prostitution. That there are a few natural born prostitutes is seen in the Urning society; but prostitution in that world does not take the important place which it does in the normal world, partly because the lawbound compulsory marriage does not exist there, and partly because prostitution naturally has little chance and cannot compete in a world where alliances are free and there is an open field for friendship. Hence, we may see that freedom of alliance and of marriage in the ordinary world will probably lead to the great diminution or even disappearance of prostitution.

In these and other ways, the experience of the Uranian world forming itself freely and not subject to outside laws and institutions comes as a guide, and really a hopeful guide, towards the future. However, I would say that in making these remarks about certain conclusions which we are able to gather from some spontaneous and comparatively unrestricted associations, I do not at all mean to argue against institutions and forms. I think that the Uranian love undoubtedly suffers from want of a recognition and a standard. And thought it may at present be better off than if subject to a foolish and meddlesome regulation; yet in the future it will have its more or less fixed standards and ideals, like the normal love. If one considers for a moment how the ordinary relations of the sexes would suffer were there no generally acknowledged codes of honor and conduct with regard to them, one then indeed sees that reasonable forms and institutions are a help, and one may almost wonder that the Urning circles are so well conducted on the whole as they are.

I have said that the Urning men in their own lives put love before money making, business success, fame, and other motives which rule the normal man. I am sure that it is also true of them as a whole that they put love before lust. I do not feel sure that this can be said of the normal man, at any rate in the present stage of evolution. It is doubtful whether on the whole the merely physical attraction is not the stronger motive with the latter type. Unwilling as the world at large is to credit what I am about to say, and great as are the current misunderstandings on the subject, I believe it is true that the Uranian men are superior to the normal men in this respect, in respect of their love-feeling, which is gentler, more sympathetic, more considerate, more a matter of the heart and less one of mere physical satisfaction than that of ordinary men. All this flows naturally from the presence of the feminine element in them, and its blending with the rest of their nature. It should be expected *a priori,* and it can be noticed at once by those who have any acquaintance with the Urning world. Much of the current misunderstanding with regard to the character and habits of the Urning arises from his confusion with the ordinary *roué* who, though of normal temperament, contracts homosexual habits out of curiosity, etc., but this is a point which I have touched on before, and which ought now to be sufficiently clear. If it be once allowed that the love nature of the Uranian is of a sincere and essentially humane and kindly type then the importance of the Uranian's place in society, and of the social work he may be able to do, must certainly also be acknowledged.

[EDITOR'S NOTES]

In the entire literature dealing with homosexuality, Edward Carpenter's writings are among the most interesting, the most remarkable, yet from the viewpoint of present-day thinking, the least valid.

In addition to the book reprinted in this volume, he devoted one section of his influential *Love's Coming of Age* to this theme, compiled an anthology "of friendship" known as *Iolaus,* authored *Intermediate Types Among Primitive Folk,* and devoted much of his life to proselytizing, organizing, and lecturing. A product of mid-Victorian morals, Carpenter never rebelled against that morality, but carried its ethics and its code directly into the world of the homosexual. His was the effort to be puritan and deviant, both at one time, and to urge a puritanical world to accept the deviant because that world, too, abhorred the body and its sensual manifestations.

Carpenter was the Mrs. Grundy of homosexuality. This entire book is an exaltation of love that is lifelong and eternal, that (he hopes and implies) does not have its grosser aspects, that is at least as deep and as "pure" as any love between man and woman. When the physical element which, he apologetically admits, is "sometimes present in the love of which we are speaking" it is "a difficulty and a stumbling-block." His entire picture is not only at variance with the facts as they exist today, but also with the facts as they were in his time.

Like many other writers of his period, Carpenter assumed that sexual inversion was congenital; and in such congenital cases, he asserts, "there is a mixture of male and female elements in the same person."

Glorifier of continence which he equates with "purity," he condemns the *roué* and then goes on to justify his attitude by putting such a person outside the realm of true inversion, defining the man who seeks pleasure frequently with other men as being one who, "though of normal temperament, contracts homosexual habits out of curiosity and so forth."

Today, there is little need to dispute the views of Carpenter; they are completely self-defeating. It is interesting that there is a great internal contradiction in his writings, because when he deals with prostitution—a very naughty word, in the Carpenter vocabulary—he insists that this phenomenon is little found in the homosexual world. Why? Because it "has little chance and cannot compete in a world where alliances are free and there is an open field for friendship." The meaning of Carpenter's friendship here becomes apparent; for no puritan before or since has contended that anyone visits a prostitute (male or female) to seek friendship.

Let us not be too harsh with Carpenter. It is true that, if widely read today, he might be a nefarious influence, not because he could "corrupt" the minds of youths and influence them to turn toward homosexuality, but because he could instill within a youth, so inclined, a deep guilt because his life does not coincide with the ideal portrait Carpenter paints. The homosexual today who reads Carpenter, if he does not ridicule the man entirely, will only feel that he is the roué so severely condemned.

But Carpenter does make a positive contribution, albeit not the one he intended. More than any other writer in the English language, he shows that homosexuality is culture-bound and culture-rebound. In an era of puritanism, he was a puritan, and within the homosexual world he sought, no matter how difficult, to construct an ethic that would fit into the puritan society. The values he set are false for the present-day reader, not only because they were based upon distortion, contradiction, and misunderstanding, but because they were a mirror-image of a world whose values have been discarded.

D. W. C.

TERMINAL ESSAY

The Book of the Thousand Nights and a Night

Richard Burton

LIMITED EDITION PUBLISHED FOR THE BURTON CLUB, PRIVATE
SUBSCRIBERS ONLY, LONDON, 1886.

PEDERASTY

The *"execrabilis familia pathicorum"* first came before me
by a chance of earlier life. In 1845, when Sir Charles Napier
had conquered and annexed Sind, despite a fraction (mostly
venal) which sought favour with the now defunct "Court of
Directors to the Honourable East India Company," the veteran
began to consider his conquest with a curious eye. It was reported to him that Karachi, a townlet of some two thousand
souls and distant not more than a mile from camp, supported
no less than three lupanars or bordels, in which not women but
boys and eunuchs, the former demanding nearly a double
price, lay for hire. Being then the only British officer who could
speak Sindi, I was asked indirectly to make enquiries and to
report upon the subject; and I undertook the task on express
condition that my report should not be forwarded to the Bombay Government, from whom supporters of the Conqueror's

207

policy could expect scant favour, mercy or justice. Accompanied by a *Munshi,* Mirza Mohammed Hosayn of Shiraz, and habited as a merchant, Mirza Abdullah the Bushiri passed many an evening in the townlet, visited all the porneia and obtained the fullest details which were duly despatched to Government House. But the "Devil's Brother" presently quitted Sind leaving in his office my unfortunate official: this found its way with sundry other reports to Bombay and produced the expected result. A friend in the Secretariat informed me that my summary dismissal from the service had been formally proposed by one of Sir Charles Napier's successors, whose decease compels me *parcere sepulto.* But this excess of outraged modesty was not allowed.

Subsequent enquiries in many and distant countries enabled me to arrive at the following conclusions:

1. There exists what I shall call a "Sotadic Zone," bounded westwards by the northern shore of the Mediterranean (N. Lat. 43°) and by the southern (N. Lat. 30°). Thus, the depth would be 780 to 800 miles including meridional France, the Iberian Peninsula, Italy and Greece, with the coast regions of Africa from Morocco to Egypt.

2. Running eastward the Sotadic Zone narrows, embracing Asia Minor, Mesopotamia and Chaldea, Afghanistan, Sind, the Punjab and Kashmir.

3. In Indo-China, the belt begins to broaden, enfolding China, Japan and Turkistan.

4. It then embraces the South Sea Islands and the New World where, at the time of its discovery, Sotadic love was, with some exceptions, an established racial institution.

5. Within the Sotadic Zone, the vice is popular and endemic, held at the worst to be a mere peccadillo, whilst the races to the North and South of the limits here defined, practise it only sporadically amid the opprobium of their fellows who, as a rule, are physically incapable of performing the operation and look upon it with the liveliest disgust.

Before entering into topographical details concerning peder-asty, which I hold to be geographical and climatic, not racial, I must offer a few considerations of its cause and origin. We must not forget that the love of boys has its noble, sentimental side. The Platonists and pupils of the academy, followed by the Sufis or Moslem Gnostics, held such affection, pure and ardent, to be the *beau idéal* which united in man's soul the creature with the Creator. Professing to regard youths as the most cleanly and beautiful objects in this phenomenal world, they declared that by loving and extolling the *chef-d'œuvre,* cor-poreal and intellectual, of the Demiurgus, disinterestedly and without any admixture of carnal sensuality, they are paying the most fervent adoration to the *Causa causans.* They add that such affection, passing as it does the love of women, is far less selfish than fondness for and admiration of the other sex which, however innocent, always suggest sexuality; and Easterns add that the devotion of the moth to the taper is purer and more fervent than the Bulbul's love for the rose. Amongst the Greeks of the best ages the system of boy favourites was advocated on considerations of morals and politics. The lover undertook the education of the beloved through precept and example, while the two were conjoined by a tie stricter than the fraternal. Hieronymus, the Peripatetic, strongly advocated it because the vigorous disposition of youth and the confidence engendered by their association often led to the overthrow of tyrannies. Socrates declared that "a most valiant army might be com-posed of boys and their lovers; for that of all men they would be most ashamed to desert one another." And even Virgil, despite the foul flavour of Formosum pastor Corydon, could write:

Nisus amore pio pueri.

The only physical cause for the practice which suggests itself to me (that must be owned to be purely conjectural) is that within the Sotadic Zone there is a blending of the masculine and feminine temperaments, a crasis which elsewhere occur only sporadically. Hence the male *féminisme* whereby the man becomes *patiens* as well as *agens,* and the woman a tribade, a votary of mascula Sappho, Queen of Frictrices or Rubbers. Prof. Mantegazza claims to have discovered the cause of this pathologic love, this perversion of the erotic sense, one of the marvellous list of amorous vagaries which deserve, not prosecution but the pitiful care of the physician and the study of the psychologist. According to him, the nerves of the rectum and the genitalia, in all cases closely connected, are abnormally so in the pathic who obtains, by intromission, the venereal orgasm which is usually sought through the sexual organs. So amongst women, there are tribads who can procure no pleasure except by foreign objects introduced *a posteriori.* Hence his threefold distribution of sodomy; 1 Peripheric or anatomical, caused by an unusual distribution of the nerves and their hyperesthesia; 2 luxurious, when love *a tergo* is preferred on account of the narrowness of the passage; and 3 the psychical. But this is evidently superficial: the question is what causes this neuropathy, this abnormal distribution and condition of the nerves?

As Prince Bismarck finds a moral difference between the male and female races of history, so I suspect a mixed physical temperament effected by the manifold subtle influences massed together in the word climate. Something of the kind is necessary to explain the fact of this pathological love extending over the greater portion of the habitable world, without any apparent connection of race or media, from the polished Greek to the cannibal Tupi of the Brazil. Walt Whitman speaks of the ashen grey faces of onanists: the faded colours, the puffy features and the unwholesome complexion of the professed pederast with his peculiar cachetic expression, indescribable but once seen never forgotten which stamps the breed, and Dr. G. Adolph is justified in declaring *"Alle Gewohnneits-paederasten erkennen sich einander schnell, oft met einen Blick."* This has nothing in common with the *féminisme* which betrays itself in the pathic by womanly gait, regard and gesture:

it is a something *sui generis;* and the same may be said of the colour and look of the young priest who honestly refrains from women and their substitutes. Dr. Tardieu, in his well known work *"Étude medico-légale sur les attentats aux mœurs,"* and Dr. Adolph note a peculiar infundibuliform disposition of the "after" and a smoothness and want of folds even before any abuse has taken place, together with special forms of the male organs in confirmed pederasts. But these observations have been rejected by Caspar, Hoffman, Brouardel and Dr. J. H. Henry Coutagne ("Notes sur la sodomie," Lyon 1880), and it is a medical question whose discussion would here be out of place.

The origin of pederasty is lost in the night of ages; but its historique has been carefully traced by many writers, especially Virey, Rosenbaum and M. H. E. Meir. The Ancient Greeks who, like the modern Germans, invented nothing but were great improvers of what other races invented, attributed the formal apostolate of Sotadism to Orpheus, whose stigmata were worn by the Thracian women;

> —*Omnemque refugerat Orpheus*
> *Fœmineam venerem;—*
> *Ille etiam Thracum populis fuit auctor, amorem*
> *In teneres transferre mares: citraque juventam*
> *Ætatis breve ver, et primos carpere flores.*
>
> *Ovid Met. x:79-85.*

Euripides proposed Laius, father of Oedipus, as the inaugurator, whereas Timeus declared that the fashion of making favourites of boys was introduced into Greece from Crete, for Malthusian reasons said Aristotle attributing it to Minos. However, Herodotus knew far better, having discovered that the Orphic and Bacchic rites were originally Egyptian. But the father of history was a traveller and an annalist rather than an archeologist and he tripped in the following passage.

"As soon as they (the Persians) hear of any luxury, they instantly make it their own, and hence, among other matters, they have learned from the Hellenes a passion for boys" ("un-natural lust" says modest Rawlinson). Plutarch asserts, with much more probability, that the Persians used eunuch boys according to the *Mos Greciæ,* long before they had seen the Grecian main.

In the Holy Books of the Hellenes, Homer and Hesiod, dealing with the heroic ages, there is no trace of pederasty, although, in a long subsequent generation, Lucian suspected Achilles and Patroclus as he did Orestes and Pylades, Theseus and Pirithous. Homer's praises of beauty are reserved for the feminines, especially his favourite Helen. But the Dorians of Crete seem to have commended the abuse to Athens and Sparta and subsequently imported it into Tarentum, Agrigentum and other colonies. Ephorous in Strabo gives a curious account of the violent abduction of beloved boys by the lover; of the obligations of the ravisher to the favourite and of the "mar-riage-ceremonies" which lasted two months. Servius (Ad Eneid. x. 325) informs us *"De Cretensibus accepimus, quod in amore puerorum intemperantes fuerunt, quod postea in Laconas et in totam Greciam translatum est."* The Cretans and afterwards their apt pupils the Chalcidians held it disreputable for a beau-tiful boy to lack a lover. Hence Zeus the national Doric god of Crete loved Ganymede; Apollo, another Dorian deity, loved Hyacinth, and Hercules, a Doric hero who grew to be a sun god, loved Hylas and a host of others: thus Crete sanctified the practice by the examples of the gods and demigods. But when legislation came, the subject had qualified itself for legal limi-tation and as such was undertaken by Lycurgus and Solon, according to Xenophon, who draws a broad distinction be-tween the honest love of boys and dishonest lust. They both approved of pure *pederastia,* like that of Harmodius and Aris-togiton; but forbade it with serviles because degrading to a free man. Hence the love of boys was spoken of like that of women, *e.g.,* "There was once a boy, or rather a youth, of ex-ceeding beauty and he had many lovers"—this is the language of Hafiz and Sa'adi. Eschylus, Sophocles and Euripides were allowed to introduce it upon the stage, for "many men were as fond of having boys for their favourites as women for their mistresses; and this was a frequent fashion in many well-regulated cities of Greece." Poets like Alceus, Anacreon, Agathon and Pindar affected it and Theognis sang of a "beautiful boy in the flower of his youth." The statesmen Aristides and Themistocles quarrelled over Stesileus of Teos; and Pisistratus loved Charmus who first built an altar to Puerile Eros, while Charmus loved Hippias son of Pisistratus. Demosthenes, the orator, took into keeping a youth called Cnosion greatly to the indignation of his wife. Xenophon loved Clinias and Autolycus; Aristotle, Hermeas, Theodectes and others; Empedocles, Pausanias; Epicurus, Pytocles; Aristippus, Eutichydes and Zeno with his Stoics had a philosophic disregard for women, affecting only *pederastia*. A man in Atheneus left in his will that certain youths he had loved should fight like gladiators at his funeral; and Charicles in Lucian abuses Callicratidas for his love of "sterile pleasures." Lastly, there was the notable affair of Alcibiades and Socrates, the "sanctus pederasts" being *violemment soupçonné* when under the mantle: *non semper sine plagâ ab eo surrexit.* Atheneus declares that Plato represents Socrates as absolutely intoxicated with his passion for Alcibiades. The ancients seem to have held the connection impure, or Juvenal would not have written.

Inter Socraticos notissima fossa cinedos,

followed by Firmicus who speaks of "Socratici pedicones." It is the modern fashion to doubt the pederasty of the master of Hellenic Sophrosyne, the "Christian before Christianity;" but such a world-wide term as Socratic love can hardly be explained by the *lucus-a-non-lucendo* theory. We are overapt to apply our ninetenth century prejudices and prepossessions to the morality of the ancient Greeks who would have specimen'd such squeamishness in Attic salt.

The Spartans, according to Agnon the Academic (confirmed by Plato, Plutarch and Cicero), treated boys and girls in the same way before marriage: hence Juvenal uses "Lacedemonius" for a pathic and other writers apply it to a tribade. After the Peloponnesian War, which ended in B.C. 404, the use became merged in the abuse. Yet some purity must have survived, even amongst the Bœotians who produced the famous Narcissus, described by Ovid:

> *Multi illum juvenes, multæ cupiere puellæ;*
> *Nulli illum juvenes, nulle tetigere puellæ:*

for Epaminondas, whose name is mentioned with three beloveds, established the Holy Regiment composed of mutual lovers, testifying the majesty of Eros and preferring to a discreditable life a glorious death. Philip's reflections on the fatal field of Chaeroneia form their fittest epitaph. At last the Athenians, according to Eschines, officially punished Sodomy with death; but the threat did not abolish bordels of boys, like those of Karáchi; the Porneia and Pornoboskeia, where slaves and *pueri venales* "stood," as the term was, near the Pnyx, the city walls and a certain tower, also about Lycabettus; and paid a fixed tax to the state. The pleasures of society in civilised Greece seem to have been sought chiefly in the heresies of love —Hetairesis and Sotadism.

It is calculated that the French of the sixteenth century had four hundred names for the parts genital and three hundred for their use in coition. The Greek vocabulary is not less copious and some of its pederastic terms, of which Meier gives nearly a hundred, and its nomenclature of pathologic love are curious and picturesque enough to merit quotation.

To live the life of Abron (the Argive) *i.e.,* that of pathic or passive lover.

The Agathonian song.

Aischrourgía = dishonest love, also called Akolasía, Akrasía, Arrenokoitía, etc.

Alcinoan youths, or "non-conformists,"

In cute curandâ plus æquo operata Juventus.

Alegomenos, the "unspeakable," as the pederast was termed by the Council of Ancyra: also the Agrios, Apolaustus and Akolastos.

Androgyne, of whom Ansonius wrote:

Ecce ego sum factus femina de puero.

Badas and badízein = *clunes torquens*: also Bátalos = a catamite.

Catapygos, Katapygosyne = *puerarius and catadactylium from* Dactylion, the ring, used in the sense of Nerissa's, but applied to the corollarium puerile.

Cinedus (Kínaidos), the active lover derived either from his kinetics or quasi = dog-modest. Also Spatalocinedus (*lasviciâ fluens*) = a fair Ganymede.

Chalcidissare (Khalkidizein), from Chalcis in Eubœa, a city famed for love *à posteriori;* mostly applied to *le léchement des testicules* by children.

Clazomenæ = the buttocks, also a sotadic disease, so called from the Ionian city devoted to Aversa Venus; also used of a pathic,

—et tergo femina pube vir est.

Embasicoetas, prop. a link boy at marriages, also a "night-cap" drunk before bed and lastly an effeminate; one who *perambulavit omnium cubilia* (Catullus). See Encolpius' pun upon the Embasicete in Satyricon, cap. iv.

Epipedesis, the carnal assault.

Geiton lit. "neighbour" the beloved of Encolpius, which has produced the Fr. Giton = Bardache, Ital. bardascia from the Arab. Baradaj, a captive, a slave; the augm. form is Polygeiton.

Hippias (tyranny of) when the patient (woman or boy) mounts the agent. So also Kelitizein = *peccare superne* or *equum agitare supernum of* Horace.

Mokhthería, depravity with boys.

Paidika, whence pedicare (act) and pedicari (pass): so in the Latin poet:—

> *Penelopes primam DIdonis prima sequatur,*
> *Et primam CAni, syllaba prima Remi.*

Pathikos, Pathicus, a passive, like Malakos malacus, mollis, facilis), Malchio, Trimalchio (Petronius), Malta, Maltha and in Hor. (Sat. ii. 25)

> *Malthinus tunicis demissis ambulat.*

Praxis = the malpractice.

Pygisma = buttockry, because most actives end within the nates, being too much excited for further intromission.

Phonicissare = *cunnilingere in tempore menstruum, quia hoc vitium in Phœnicia generata solebat* (Thes. Erot. Ling. Latinæ); also *irrumer en miel.*

Phicidissare, denotat actum per canes commissum quando lambunt cunnos vel testiculous (Suetonius): also applied to pollution of childhood.

Samorium flores (Erasmus, Prov. xxiii.) alluding to the androgynic prostitutions of Samos.

Siphniassare (from Siphnos, *hod.* Sifanto Island)=*digito podicem fodere ad pruriginem restinguendam,* says Erasmus (see Mirebau's Erotika Biblion, Anoscopie).

Thrypsis = the rubbing.

Pederastia had in Greece, I have shown, its noble and ideal side: Rome, however, borrowed her malpractices, like her religion and polity, from those ultramaterial Etruscans and debauched with a brazen face. Even under the Republic Plautus makes one of his characters exclaim, in the utmost sang-froid, *"Ultro te, amator, apage te a dorso meo!"* With increased luxury the evil grew and Livy notices, at the Bacchanalia, *plura virorum inter sese quam feminarum stupra.* There were individual protests; for instance, S. Q. Fabius Maximus Servilianus punished his son for *dubia castitas;* and a private soldier, C. Plotius, killed his military Tribune, Q. Luscius, for unchaste proposals. The Lex Scantinia (Scatinia?), popularly derived from Scantinius the Tribune and of doubtful date (B.C. 226?), attempted to abate the scandal by fine and the Lex Julia by death; but they were trifling obstacles to the flood of infamy which surged in with the Empire. No class seems then to have disdained these "sterile pleasures:" *l'on n'attachoit point alors à cette espèce d'amour une note d'infamie, comme en païs de chrétienté,* says Bayle under *"Anacreon."* The great Cæsar, the *Cinædus calvus* of Catullus, was the husband of all the wives and the wife of all the husbands in Rome; and his soldiers sang in his praise Gallias Cæsar subegit, Nicomedes Cæsarem (Suet. cics. xlix.); whenece his sobriquet "Fornix Birthynicus." Of Augustus the people chaunted

> *Videsne ut Cincædus orbem digito temperet?*

Tiberius, with his *pisciculi* and *greges exoletorum,* invented the Symplegma or nexus of Sellarii, *agentes et patientes,* in which the *sprinthriæ* (lit. women's bracelets) were connected in a chain by the bond of flesh. Of this refinement, which in the earlier part of the nineteenth century was renewed by sundry Englishmen at Naples, Ausonius wrote:

> *Tres uno in lecto: stupram duo perpetiuntur;*

And Martial had said:

> *Quo symplegmate quinque copulentur;*
> *Qua plures teneantur a catena; etc.*

Ausonius recounts of Caligula he so lost patience that he forcibly entered the priest M. Lepidus, before the sacrifice was completed. The beautiful Nero was formally married to Pythagoras (or Doryphoros) and afterwards took to wife Sporus who was first subjected to castration of a peculiar fashion; he was then named Sabina after the deceased spouse and claimed queenly honours. The *"Othonis et Trajand pathici"* were famed; the great Hadrian openly loved Antinoüs and the wild debaucheries of Heliogabalus seem only to have amused, instead of disgusting, the Romans.

Uranopolis allowed public lupanaria where adults and meritorii pueri, who began their career as early as seven years, stood for hire: the inmates of these cauponæ wore sleeved tunics and dalmatics like women. As in modern Egypt pathic boys, we learn from Catullus, haunted the public baths. Debauchees had signals like freemasons whereby they recognised one another. The Greek Skematízein was made by closing the hand to represent the scrotum and raising the middle finger as if to feel whether a hen had eggs, *tâter si les poulettes ont l'œuf*: hence the Athenians called it Catapugon or sodomite and the Romans *digitus impudicus* or *infamis,* the "medical finger" of Rabelais and the Chiromantists. Another sign was to scratch the head with the minimus—*digitulo caput scabere.* The prostitution of boys was first forbidden by Domitian; but Saint Paul, a Greek, had formally expressed his abomination of *le vice;* and we may agree with Grotius that early Christianity did much to suppress it. At last the Emperor Theodosius punished it with fire as a profanation, because *sacro-sanctum esse debetur hospitium virilis animæ.*

In the pagan days of imperial Rome her literature makes no difference between boy and girl. Horace naïvely says:

Ancilla aut verna est præsto puer;

and with Hamlet, but in a dishonest sense:

—Man delights me not
Nor woman neither.

Similarly the Spaniard Martial, who is a mine of such pederastic allusions:—

Sive puer arrisit, sive puella tibi.

That marvellous Satyricon which unites the wit of Molière with the debaucheries of Piron, whilst the writer has been

described, like Rabelais, as *purissimus in impuritate,* is a kind
of triumph of pederasty. Geiton the hero, a handsome curly-
pated hobbledehoy of seventeen, with his *câlinerie* and wheed-
ling tongue, is courted like one of the *sequor sexus*: his lovers
are inordinately jealous of him and his desertion leaves deep
scars upon the heart. But no dialogue between man and wife
in extremis could be more pathetic than that in the scene
where shipwreck is imminent. Elsewhere everyone seems to
attempt his neighbour: a man *alte succinctus* assails Ascyltos;
Lycus, the Tarentine skipper, would force Encolpius, and so
forth: yet we have the neat and finished touch: "The lamentation was very fine (the dying man having manumitted his
slaves) albeit his wife wept not as though she loved him. *How
were it had he not behaved to her so well?"*

Erotic Latin glossaries give some ninety words connected
with pederasty and some, which "speak with Roman simplic-
ity," are peculiarly expressive. *"Aversa Venus"* alludes to
women being treated as boys: hence Martial, translated by
Piron, addresses Mistress Martial:

> *Teque puta, cunnos, uxor, habere duos.*

The *capillatus* or *comatus* is also called *calamistratus,* the
darling curled with crisping-irons; and he is an *Effeminatus*
i.e., *qui muliebria patitur;* or a *Delicatus,* slave or eunuch for
the use of the Draucus, Puerarius (boy lover) or Dominus. The
Divisor is so called from his practice *Hillas dividere or cædere,*
something like Martial's *cacare mentulam* or Juvenal's *Hester-
næ occurrere cænæ. Facere vicibus, incestare se invicem* or
mutuum facere, is described as "a puerile vice," in which the
two take turns to be active and passive: they are also called
Gemelli and Fratres = compares *in pædicatione. Illicita libido*
is = *præpostera seu postica Venus,* and is expressed by the picturesque phrase *indicare (seu incurvare) aliquem. Depilatus,
divellere pilos, glaber, lævis and nates pervellere* are allusions
to the Sotadic toilette. The fine distinction between *demittere*

and *dejicere caput* are worthy of a glossary, while *Pathica puella, puera, putus, pullipremo, pusio, pygiaca sacra, quadrupes, scarabæus* and *smerdalius* explain themselves.

From Rome the practice extended far and wide to her colonies, especially the Provincia now called Provence. Athenæus charges the people of Massilia with "acting like women out of luxury"; and he cites the saying "May you sail to Massilia!" as if it were another Corinth. Indeed the whole Keltic race is charged with *le vice* by Aristotle and Diodorus Siculus. Roman civilisation carried pederasty also to Northern Africa, where it took firm root, while the Negro and Negroid races to the South ignore the erotic perversion, except where imported by foreigners into such kingdoms as Bornu and Haussa. In old Mauritania, now Morocco, the Moors proper are notable sodomites; Moslems, even of saintly houses, are permitted openly to keep catamites, nor do their disciples think worse of their sanctity for such license: in one case the English wife failed to banish from the home "that horrid boy."

Yet pederasty is forbidden by the Koran. In chapter iv, 20 we read: "And if two (men) among you commit the crime, then punish them both," the penalty being some hurt or damage by public reproach, insult or scourging. There are four distinct references to Lot and the Sodomites in chapters vii, 78; xi 77-84; xvi 160-174 and xxix 28-35. In the first the prophet commissioned to the people says, "Proceed ye to a fullsome act wherein no creature hath foregone ye? Verily ye come to men in lieu of women lustfully." We have then an account of the rain which made an end of the wicked and this judgment on the Cities of the Plain is repeated with more detail in the second reference. Here the angels, generally supposed to be three, Gabriel, Michael and Raphael, appeared to Lot as beautiful youths, a sore temptation to the sinners and the godly man's arm was straitened concerning his visitors because he felt unable to protect them from the erotic vagaries of his fellow townsmen. Therefore, he shut his doors and from behind them argued the matter: presently the riotous assembly attempted to climb the wall when Gabriel, seeing the distress of his host, smote them on the face with one of his wings and blinded them so that all moved off crying for aid and saying that Lot had magicians in his house. Hereupon the "cities" which, if they ever existed, must have been Fellah villages, were uplifted: Gabriel thrust his wing under them and raised them so high that the inhabitants of the lower heaven (the lunar sphere) could hear the dogs barking and the cocks crowing. Then came the rain of stones: these were clay pellets baked in hell fire, streaked white and red, or having some mark to distinguish them from the ordinary and each bearing the name of its destination like the missiles which destroyed the host of Abrahat al-Ashram. Lastly the "Cities" were turned upside down and cast upon earth. These circumstantial unfacts are repeated at full length in the other two chapters; but rather as an instance of Allah's power than as a warning against pederasty, which Mohammed seems to have regarded with philosophic indifference. The general opinion of his followers is that it should be punished like fornication unless the offenders made a public act of penitence. But here, as in adultery, the law is somewhat too clement and will not convict unless four credible witnesses swear to have seen *rem in re*. I have noticed the vicious opinion that the Ghilmán or Wuldán, the beautiful boys of Paradise, the counterparts of the Houris, will be lawful catamites to the True Believers in a future state of happiness: the idea is nowhere countenanced in Al-Islam; and, although I have often heard debauchees refer to it, the learned look upon the assertion as scandalous.

As in Morocco so the vice prevails throughout the old regencies of Algiers, Tunis and Tripoli and all the cities of the South Mediterranean seaboard, whilst it is unknown to the Nubians, the Berbers and the wilder tribes dwelling inland. Proceeding Eastward we reach Egypt, that classical region of all abominations which, marvellous to relate, flourished in closest contact with men leading the purest of lives, models of moderation and morality, of religion and virtue. Amongst the ancient Copts *le vice* was part and portion of the ritual and was represented by two male partridges alternately copulating. The evil would have gained strength by the invasion of Cambyses (B.C. 524), whose armies, after the victory over Psammenitus, settled in the Nile-Valley, and held it, despite sundry revolts, for some hundred and ninety years. During these six generations, the Iranians left their mark upon Lower Egypt and especially, as the late Rogers Bey proved, upon the Fayyum the most ancient Delta of the Nile. Nor would the evil be diminished by the Hellenes who, under Alexander the Great, "liberator and saviour of Egypt" (B.C. 332), extinguished the native dynasties: the love of the Macedonian for Bagoas the Eunuch being a matter of history. From that time and under the rule of the Ptolemies the morality gradually decayed; the Canopic orgies extended into private life and the debauchery of the men was equalled only by the depravity of the women. Neither Christianity nor Al-Islam could effect a change for the better; and social morality seems to have been at its worst during the past century when Sonnini travelled (A.D. 1717). The French officer, who is thoroughly trustworthy, draws the darkest picture of the widely-spread criminality especially of the bestiality and the sodomy which formed the "delight of the Egyptians." During the Napoleonic conquest Jaubert in his letter to General Bruix says, *"Les Arabes et les Mamelouks ont traité quelque-uns de nos prisonniers comme Socrate traitait, dit-on, Alcibiade. Il fallait périr ou y passer."* Old Anglo-Egyptians still chuckle over the tale of St'id Pasha and M. de Ruyssenaer, the high-dried and highly respectable Consul-General for the Netherlands, who was solemnly advised to make the experiment, active and passive, before offering his opinion upon the subject.

In the present age extensive intercourse with Europeans has produced not a reformation but a certain reticence amongst the upper classes: they are as vicious as ever, but they do not care for displaying their vices to the eyes of mocking strangers.

Syria and Palestine, another ancient focus of abominations, borrowed from Egypt and exaggerated the worship of Androgynic and hermaphroditic deities. Plutarch notes that the old Nilotes held the moon to be of "male-female sex," the men sacrificing to Luna and the women to Lunus. Isis also was a hermaphrodite, the idea being that Æther or Air (the lower heavens) was the menstruum of generative nature; and Damascius explained the tenet by the all-fruitful and prolific powers of the atmosphere. Hence the fragment attributed to Orpheus, the song of Jupiter:

> *All things from Jove descend*
> *Jove was a male, Jove was a deathless bride;*
> *For men call Air, of two-fold sex, the Jove.*

Julius Firmicus relates that "The Assyrians and part of the Africans" (along the Mediterranean seaboard?) "hold Air to be the chief element and adore its fanciful figure (*imaginata figura*), consecrated under the name of Juno or the Virgin Venus. . . . Their companies of priests cannot duly serve her unless they effeminate their faces, smooth their skins and disgrace their masculine sex by feminine ornaments. You may see men in their very temples amid general groans enduring miserable dalliance and becoming passives like women (*viros muliebria pati*) and they expose, with boasting and ostentation, the pollution of the impure and immodest body." Here we find the religious significance of eunuchry. It was practised as a religious rite by the Tympanotribas or Gallus, the castrated votary of Rhea or Bona Mater, in Phrygia called Cybele, self-mutilated but not in memory of Atys; and by a host of other creeds: even Christianity, as sundry texts show, could not altogether cast out the old possession. Here too we have an explanation of Sotadic love in its second stage, when it became, like cannibalism, a matter of superstition. Assuming a nature-implanted tendency, we see that like human sacrifice it was

held to be the most acceptable offering to the God-goddesses in
the Orgia or sacred ceremonies, a something set apart for
peculiar worship. Hence in Rome as in Egypt the temples of
Isis (*Inachidos limina, Isiacæ sacraria Lunæ*) were centres of
sodomy and the religious practice was adopted by the grand
priestly castes from Mesopotamia to Mexico and Peru.

We find the earliest written notices of the vice in the myth-
ical destruction of the Pentapolis, Sodom, Gomorrah (= 'Ámi-
rah, the cultivated country), Adama, Zeboïm and Zoar or Bela.
The legend has been amply embroidered by the Rabbis who
make the Sodomites do everything *à l'envers*: e.g., if a man
were wounded he was fined for bloodshed and was compelled
to fee the offender; and if one cut off the ear of a neighbor's ass
he was condemned to keep the animal till the ear grew again.

The Jewish doctors declare the people to have been a race of
sharpers with rogues for magistrates, and thus they justify the
judgment which they read literally. But the traveller cannot
accept it. I have carefully examined the lands at the North and
at the South of that most beautiful lake, the so called Dead Sea,
whose tranquil loveliness, backed by the grand plateau of
Moab, is an object of admiration to all save patients suffering
from the strange disease "Holy Land on the Brain." But I
found no trace of craters in the neighborhood, no signs of vul-
canism, no remains of "meteoric stones": the asphalt which
named the water is a mineralised vegetable washed out of the
limestones, and the sulphur and salt are brought down by the
Jordan into a lake without issue. I must therefore look upon
the history as a myth which may have served a double purpose.
The first would be to deter the Jew from the Malthusian practices of his pagan predecessors, upon whom obloquy was thus
cast, so far resembling the scandalous and absurd legend which
explained the names of the children of Lot by Pheiné and
Thamma as "Moab" (Mu-ab) the water or semen of the father,
and "Ammon" as mother's son, that is, bastard. The fable
would also account for the abnormal fissure containing the

lower Jordan and the Dead Sea, which the late Sir R. I. Murchison used wrong headedly to call a "Volcano of Depression": this geological feature, that cuts off the river basin from its natural outlet the Gulf of Eloth (Akabah), must date from myriads of years before there were "Cities of the Plains." But the main object of the ancient lawgiver, Osarsiph, Moses or the Moseidæ, was doubtless to discountenance a perversion prejudicial to the increase of population. And he speaks with no uncertain voice, "Whoso lieth with a beast shall surely be put to death." If a man lie with mankind as he lieth with a woman, both of them have committed an abomination: they shall surely be put to death; their blood shall be upon them. Again, "there shall be no whore of the daughters of Israel nor a sodomite of the sons of Israel."

The old commentators on the Sodom-myth are most unsatisfactory, e.g., Parkhurst, Kadesh. "From hence we may observe the peculiar propriety of this punishment of Sodom and of the neighbouring cities. By their sodomitical impurities they meant to acknowledge the Heavens as the cause of fruitfulness independently upon, and in opposition to Jehovah; therefore Jehovah, by raining upon them not genial showers but brimstone from heaven, not only destroyed the inhabitants, but also changed all that country, which was before as the garden of God, into brimstone and salt that is not sown nor beareth, neither any grass groweth therein."

It must be owned that to this Pentapolis was dealt very hard measure for religiously and diligently practising a popular rite which a host of cities even in the present day, as Naples and Shiraz, to mention no others, affect for simple luxury and affect with impunity. The myth may probably reduce itself to very small proportions, a few Fellah villages destroyed by a storm, like that which drove Brennus from Delphi.

The Hebrews entering Syria found it religionised by Assyria and Babylonia, whence Accadian Ishtar had passed west and had become Ashtoreth, Ashtaroth or Ashirab, the Anaitis of

Armenia, the Phœnician Astarte and the Greek Aphrodite, the great Moon-goddess, who is queen of Heaven and Love. In another phase she was Venus Mylitta = the Procreatrix, in Chaldaic Mauludatá and in Arabic Moawallidah, she who bringeth forth. She was worshipped by men habited as women and vice versa; for which reason in the Torah the sexes are forbidden to change dress. The male prostitutes were called Kadesh the holy, the women being Kadeshah, and doubtless gave themselves up to great excesses. Eusebius describes a school of impurity at Aphac, where women and "men who were not men" practised all manner of abominations in honour of the Demon (Venus). Here the Phrygian symbolism of Kybele and Attis (Atys) had become the Syrian Ba'al Tammuz and Astarte, and the Grecian Dioniæ and Adonis, the anthropomorphic forms of the two greater lights. The site, Apheca, now Wady al-Afik on the route from Bayrut to the Cedars, is a glen of wild and wondrous beauty, fitting frame-work for the loves of goddess and demigod: and the ruins of the temple destroyed by Constantine contrast with Nature's work, the glorious fountain, splendidior vitro, which feeds the River Ibrahim and still at times Adonis runs purple to the sea.

The Phœnicians spread this androgynic worship over Greece. We find the consecrated servants and votaries of Corinthian Aphrodite called Hierodouli, who aided the ten thousand courtesans in gracing the Venus temple: from this excessive luxury arose the proverb popularized by Horace. One of the headquarters of the cult was Cyprus where, as Servius relates, stood the simulacre of a bearded Aphrodite with feminine body and costume, sceptered and mitred like a man. The sexes, when worshipping it, exchanged habits and here the virginity was offered in sacrifice: Herodotus describes this defloration at Babylon but sees only the shameful part of the custom which was a mere consecration of a tribal rite. Everywhere, girls before marriage belong either to the father or to the clan and thus the maiden paid the debt due to the public before becoming private property as a wife. The same usage prevailed in ancient Armenia and in parts of Ethiopia; and Herodotus tells us that a practice very much like the Babylonian "is found also in certain parts of the Island of Cyprus:" it is noticed by Justin and probably it explains the "Succoth Benoth" or Damsels' booths which the Babylonians transplanted to the cities of Samaria. The Jews seem very successfully to have copied the abominations of their pagan neighbours, even in the matter of the "dog." In the reign of wicked Rehoboam (B.C. 975) "There were also sodomites in the land and they did according to all the abominations of the nations which the Lord cast out before the children of Israel." The scandal was abated by zealous King Asa (B.C. 958) whose grandmother was high-priestess of Priapus (princeps in sacris Priapi): he "took away the sodomites out of the land. Yet the prophets were loud in their complaints, especially the so called Isaiah, "except the Lord of Hosts had left to us a very small remnant, we should have been as Sodom"; and strong measures were required from good King Josiah (B.C. 641) who amongst other things, "brake down the houses of the sodomites that were by the house of the Lord, where the women wove hangings for the grove." The bordels of boys (*pueris alienis adhæseverunt*) appear to have been near the Temple.

Syria has not forgotten her old "praxis." At Damascus, I found some noteworthy cases amongst the religious of the great Amawl Mosque. As for the Druses we have Burckhardt's authority: "unnatural propensities are very common amongst them."

The Sotadic Zone covers the whole of Asia Minor and Meso-potamia now occupied by the "unspeakable Turk," a race of born pederasts; and in the former region we first notice a peculiarity of the feminine figure, the *mammæ inclinatæ, jacentes et pannosæ,* which prevails over all this part of the belt. Whilst the women to the North and South have, with local exceptions, the *mammæ stantes* of the European virgin,

those of Turkey, Persia, Afghanistan and Kashmir lose all the
fine curves of the bosom, sometimes even before the first child;
and after it the hemispheres take the form of bags. This cannot
result from climate only; the women of Marathá-land, inhabiting a damper and hotter region than Kashmir, are noted for
fine firm breasts even after parturition. *Le vice* of course prevails more in the cities and towns of Asiatic Turkey than in
the villages; yet even these are infected; while the nomad Tur-
comans contrast badly in this point with the gypsies, those
Bedouin of India. The Kurd population is of Iranian origin,
which means that the evil is deeply rooted: I have noted in
The Nights that the great and glorious Saladin was a habitual
pederast. The Armenians, as their national character is, will
prostitute themselves for gain but prefer women to boys: Geor-
gia supplied Turkey with catamites, while Circassia sent concubines. In Mesopotamia, the barbarous invader has almost
obliterated the ancient civilisation which is antedated only by
the Nilotic: the mysteries of old Babylon nowhere survive save
in certain obscure tribes like the Mandæans, the Devil-wor-
shippers and the Alí-iláhi. Entering Persia we find the reverse
of Armenia; and, despite Herodotus, I believe that Iran borrowed her pathologic love from the peoples of the Tigris-
Euphrates Valley and not from the then insignificant Greeks.
But whatever may be its origin, the corruption is now bred in
the bone. It begins in boyhood and many Persians account for
it by paternal severity. Youths arriving at puberty find none of
the facilities with which Europe supplies fornication. Onanism
is, to a certain extent, discouraged by circumcision, and med-
dling with the father's slave-girls and concubines would be
risking cruel punishment, if not death. Hence, they use each
other by turns, a "puerile practice" known as Alish-Takish,
the Latin *facere vicibus* or *mutuum facere*. Temperament,
media, and atavism recommend the custom to the general; and
after marrying and begetting heirs, Paterfamilias returns to
the Ganymede. Hence all the odes of Hafiz are addressed to

youth, as proved by such Arabic exclamations as *'Afaka 'llah* =
Allah assain thee (masculine): the object is often fanciful but
it would be held coarse and immodest to address an imaginary
girl. An illustration of the penchant is told at Shiraz concerning a certain Mujtahid, the head of the Shilah creed, corresponding with a prince-archbishop in Europe. A friend once
said to him:

"There is a question I would fain address to your Eminence
but I lack the daring to do so." "Ask and fear not," replied the
Divine. "It is this, O Mujtahid! Figure thee in a garden of
roses and hyacinths with the evening breeze waving the cypress
heads, a fair youth of twenty sitting by thy side and the assurance of perfect privacy. What, prithee, would be the result?"
The holy man bowed the chin of doubt upon the collar of
meditation; and, too honest to lie, presently whispered, "Allah
defend me from such temptation of Satan!"

Yet even in Persia men have not been wanting who have
done their utmost to uproot the vice: in the same Shiraz they
speak of a father who, finding his son in flagrant delict, put
him to death like Brutus or Lynch of Galway. However, such
isolated cases can effect nothing. Chardin tells us that houses
of male prostitution were common in Persia whilst those of
women were unknown: the same is the case in the present day,
and the boys are prepared with extreme care by diet, baths,
depilation, unguents and a host of artists in cosmetics. *Le vice*
is looked upon at most as a peccadillo and its mention crops
up in every jest book. When the Isfahan man mocked Shaykh
Sa'adi by comparing the bald pates of Shirazian elders to the
bottom of a lotá, a brass cup with a wide necked opening used
in the Hammam, the witty poet turned its aperture upwards
and thereto likened the well abused podex of an Isfahani
youth. Another favourite piece of Shirazian "chaff" is to declare that when an Isfahan father would set up his son in
business he provides him with a pound of rice, meaning that
he can sell the result as compost for the kitchen garden, and

with the price buy another meal: hence the saying *Khakh-i-pái-káhú* = the soil at the lettuce root. The Isfahanis retort with the name of a station or halting place between the two cities where, under pretence of making travellers stow away their riding-gear, many a Shirári had been raped: hence *"Zin o takaltú tú bi-bar"* = carry within saddle and saddle-cloth! A favourite Persian punishment for strangers caught in the Harem or Gynæceum is to strip and throw them and expose them to the embraces of the grooms and negro slaves. I once asked a Shirazi, how penetration was possible if the patient resisted with all the force of the sphincter muscle: he smiled and said, "Ah, we Persians know a trick to get over that; we apply a sharpened tent-peg to the crupper-bone (os coccygis) and knock till he opens." A well known missionary to the East during the last generation was subjected to this gross insult by one of the Persian Prince-governors, whom he had infuriated by his conversion mania: in his memoirs he alludes to it by mentioning his "dishonoured person;" but English readers cannot comprehend the full significance of the confession. About the same time, Shaykh Nasr, Governor of Bushire, a man famed for facetious blackguardism, used to invite European youngsters serving in the Bombay Marine and ply them with liquor till they were insensible. Next morning the middies mostly complained that the champagne had caused a curious irritation and soreness in la parte-poste. The same Eastern "Scrogin" would ask his guests if they had ever seen a man-cannon (Adami-top); and, on their replying in the negative, a grey-beard slave was dragged in blaspheming and struggling with all his strength. He was presently placed on all fours and firmly held by the extremities; his bag-trousers were let down and a dozen peppercorns were inserted *ano suo*: the target was a sheet of paper held at a reasonable distance; the match was applied by a pinch of cayenne in the victim's nostrils; the sneeze started the grapeshot and the number of hits on the butt decided the bets. We can hardly wonder at the loose conduct of Persian women perpetually mortified by marital pederasty. During the unhappy campaign of 1856-57 in which, with the exception of a few brilliant skirmishes, we gained no glory, Sir James Outram and the Bombay army showing how badly they could work, there was a formal outburst of the harems; and even women of princely birth could not be kept out of the officers' quarters.

The cities of Afghanistan and Sind are thoroughly saturated with Persian vice, and the people sing

Kadr-i-kus Aughán dánad, kadr-i- kunrá Kábuli:
The worth of coynte the Afghan knows: Cabul prefers the other chose!

The Afghans are commercial travellers on a large scale and each caravan is accompanied by a number of boys and lads almost in woman's attire with kohl'd eyes and rouged cheeks, long tresses and henna'd fingers and toes, riding luxuriously in Kajáwas or camel-panniers: they are called Kúchi-safari, or travelling wives, and the husbands trudge patiently by their sides. In Afghanistan also a frantic debauchery broke out amongst the women when they found incubi who were not pederasts; and the scandal was not the most insignificant cause of the general rising at Cabul (Nov. 1841), and the slaughter of Macnaghten, Burnes and other British officers.

Resuming our way Eastward we find the Sikhs and the Moslems of the Panjab much addicted to *Le Vice,* although the Himalayan tribes to the north and those lying south, the Rájputs and Marathás, ignore it. The same may be said of the Kashmirians who add another Kappa to the tria Kakista, Kappadocians, Kretans, and Kilicians: the proverb says,

Agar kaht-i-mardum uftad, az in sih jins kam giri;
Eki Afghán, dovvuin Sindi, siyyum badjins-i-Kashmiri:
Though of men there be famine yet shun these three—
Afghan, Sindi and rascally Kashmiri.

M. Louis Daville describes the infamies of Lahore and Lakhnau where he found men dressed as women, with flowing locks under crowns of flowers, imitating the feminine walk and gestures, voice and fashion of speech, and ogling their admirers with all the coquetry of bayadères.

Victor Jacquemont's Journal de Voyage describes the pederasty of Ranjít Singh, the "Lion of the Panjáb," and his pathic Guláb Singh whom the English inflicted upon Cashmir as ruler by way of paying for his treason. Yet the Hindus, I repeat, hold pederasty in abhorrence and are as much scandalised by being called *Gánd-márá* (anus-beater) or *Gándú* (anuser) as Englishmen would be. During the years 1843-44, my regiment, almost all Hindu Sepoys of the Bombay Presidency, was stationed at a purgatory called Bandar Chárrá, a sandy flat with a scatter of verdigris-green milk-bush some forty miles north of Karáchi the headquarters. The dirty heap of mud and mat hovels, which represented the adjacent native village, could not supply a single woman; yet only one case of pederasty came to light and that after a tragic fashion some years afterwards. A young Brahman had connection with a soldier comrade of low caste and this had continued till, in an unhappy hour, the Pariah patient ventured to become the agent. The latter, in Arab, *Al-Fá'il* = the "doer," is not an object of contempt like Al-Mafúl = the "done"; and the high-caste sepoy, stung by remorse and revenge, loaded his musket and deliberately shot his paramour. He was hanged by court martial at Hyderabad and, when his last wishes were asked, he begged in vain to be suspended by the feet; the idea being that his soul, polluted by exiting "below the waist," would be doomed to endless transmigrations through the lowest forms of life.

Beyond India, I have stated, the Sotadic Zone begins to broaden out embracing all China, Turkistan and Japan. The Chinese, as far as we know them in the great cities, are omnivorous and omnifutuentes: they are the chosen people of debauchery and their systematic bestiality with ducks, goats, and other animals is equalled only by their pederasty. Kæmpfer and Orlof Torée (Voyage en Chine) notice the public

houses for boys and youths in China and Japan. Mirabeau
⟨L'Anandryne⟩ describes the tribadism of their women in
hammocks. When Pekin was plundered the Harems contained
a number of balls a little larger than the old musket-bullet,
made of thin silver with a loose pellet of brass inside somewhat
like a grelot: these articles were placed by the women between
the labia and an up-and-down movement on the bed gave a
pleasant titillation when nothing better was to be procured.
They have every artifice of luxury, aphrodisiacs, erotic per-
fumes and singular applications. Such are the pills which, dis-
solved in water and applied to the glans penis, cause it to
throb and swell: so according to Amerigo Vespucci American
women could artificially increase the size of their husbands'
parts. The Chinese bracelet of caoutchouc studded with points
now takes the place of the Herisson, or Annulus hirsutus,
which was bound between the glans and prepuce. Of the penis
succedaneus, that imitation of the Arbor vitæ or Soter Kos-
mou, which the Latins called *phallus* and *fascinum,* the French
godemiché and the Italians *passatempo* and *diletto* (whence
our "dildo"), every kind abounds, varying from a stuffed
"French letter" to a cone of ribbed horn which looks like an
instrument of torture. For the use of men they have the "mer-
kin," a heart shaped article of thin skin stuffed with cotton and
slit with an artificial vagina: two tapes at the top and one
below lash it to the back of a chair. The erotic literature of the
Chinese and Japanese is highly developed and their illustra-
tions are often facetious, as well as obscene. All are familiar
with that of the strong man who by a blow with his enormous
phallus shivers a copper pot; and the ludicrous contrast of the
huge membered wights who land in the Isle of Women and
presently escape from it, wrinkled and shrivelled, true Domine
Dolittles. Of Turkistan we know little, but what we know confirms my statement. Mr. Schuyler in his Turkistan offers an
illustration of a "Batchah" (Pers. *bachcheh* = catamite), "or
singing-boy surrounded by his admirers." Of the Tartars Mas-

ter Purchas laconically says, "They are addicted to Sodomie or Buggerie." The learned casuist, Thomas Sanchez, the Spaniard had (says Mirabeau in Kadhésh) to decide a difficult question concerning the sinfulness of a peculiar erotic perversion. The Jesuits brought home from Manila a tailed man whose movable prolongation of the os coccygis measured from 7 to 10 inches: he had placed himself between two women, enjoying one naturally while the other used his tail as a penis succedaneous. The verdict was incomplete sodomy and simple fornication. For the islands north of Japan, the "Sodomitical Sea," and the "nayle of tynne" thrust through the prepuce to prevent sodomy.

Passing over to America, we find that the Sotadic Zone contains the whole hemisphere from Behring's Strait to Magellan's Strait. This prevalence of "mollities" astonishes the anthropologist, who is apt to consider pederasty the growth of luxury and the especial product of great and civilised cities, unnecessary and therefore unknown to simple savagery where the births of both sexes are about equal and female infanticide is not practised. In many parts of the New World, this perversion was accompanied by another depravity of taste, confirmed cannibalism. The forests and campos abounded in game from the deer to the pheasant-like penelope, and the seas and rivers produced an unfailing supply of excellent fish and shell-fish; yet the Brazilian Tupis preferred the meat of man to every other food.

A glance at Mr. Bancroft proves the abnormal development of sodomy amongst the savages and barbarians of the New World. Even his half-frozen Hyperboreans "possess all the passions which are supposed to develop most freely under a milder temperature." The voluptuousness and polygamy of the North American Indians, under a temperature of almost perpetual winter is far greater than that of the most sensual tropical nations." I can quote only a few of the most remarkable instances. Of the Koniagas of Kadiak Island and the Thinkleets we read, "The most repugnant of all their practices is that of male concubinage. A Kadiak mother will select her handsomest and most promising boy, and dress and rear him as a girl, teaching him only domestic duties, keeping him at women's work, associating him with women and girls, in order to render his effeminacy complete. Arriving at the age of ten or fifteen years, he is married to some wealthy man who regards such a companion as a great acquisition. These male concubines are called *Achnutschik* or *Schopans*" (the authorities quoted being Holmberg, Langsdorff, Billing, Choris, Lisiansky and Marchand). The same is the case in Nutka Sound and the Aleutian Islands, where "male concubinage obtains throughout, but not to the same extent as amongst the Koniagas." The objects of "unnatural" affection have their beards carefully plucked out as soon as the face-hair begins to grow, and their chins are tattooed like those of the women. In California, the first missionaries found the same practice, the youths being called Joya (Bancroft, 415 and authorities Palon, Crespi, Boscana, Mofras, Torquemada, Duflot and Fages). The Comanches unite incest with sodomy.

"In New Mexico according to Arlegui, Ribas, and other authors, male concubinage prevails to a great extent, these loathsome semblances of humanity, whom to call beastly were a slander upon beasts, dress themselves in the clothes and perform the functions of women, the use of weapons being denied them." Pederasty was systematically practised by the peoples of Cueba, Careta, and other parts of Central America. The Caciques and some of the headmen kept harems of youths who, as soon as destined for the unclean office, were dressed as women. They went by the name of Camayoas, and were hated and detested by the goodwives. Of the Nahua nations Father Pierre de Gand (alias Oe Musa) writes, "*Un certain nombre de prêtres n'avaient point de femmes, sed eorum loco pueros quibus abutebantur. Ce péché était si commun dans ce pays que, jeunes ou vieux, tous étaient infectés; ils y étaient si adon-*

nés que mêmes les enfants de six ans s'y livraient." Among the
Mayas of Yucatan, Las Casas declares that the great prevalence
of "unnatural" lust made parents anxious to see their progeny
wedded as soon as possible. In Vera Paz a god, called by some
Chin and by others Cavial and Maran, taught it by committing
the act with another god. Some fathers gave their sons a boy to
use as a woman, and if any other approached this pathic he
was treated as an adulterer. In Yucatan images were found by
Bernal Diaz proving the sodomitical propensities of the people. De Pauw has much to say about the subject in Mexico
generally: in the northern provinces men married youths who,
dressed like women, were forbidden to carry arms. According
to Gomara, there were at Tamalipas houses of male prostitution; and from Diaz and others we gather that the *pecado
nefando* was the rule. Both in Mexico and in Peru it might
have caused, if it did not justify, the cruelties of the Conquistadores. Pederasty was also general throughout Nicaragua, and
the early explorers found it amongst the indigenes of Panama.

We have authentic details concerning *le vice* in Peru and its
adjacent lands, beginning with Cieza de Leon, who must be
read in the original or in the translated extracts of Purchas,
not in the cruelly castrated form preferred by the Council of
the Hakluyt Society. Speaking of the New Granada Indians
he tells us that "at Old Port (Porto Viejo) and Puna, the
*Deuill so farre prevayled in their beastly Deuotions that there
were Boyes consecrated to serue in the Temple; and at the
times of their Sacrifices and Solemme Feasts, the Lords and
principall men abused them to that detestable filthinesse;*" i.e.
performed their peculiar worship.

Generally in the hill countries the Devil, under the show
of holiness, had introduced the practice; for every temple or
chief house of adoration kept one or two men or more which
were attired like women, even from the time of their childhood, and spoke like them, imitating them in everything; with
these, under pretext of holiness and religion, their principal

men on principal days had commerce. Speaking of the arrival
of the Giants at Point Santa Elena, Cieza says, they were detested by the natives, because in using their women they killed
them and their men also in another way. All the natives declare
that God brought upon them a punishment proportioned to
the enormity of their offence. When they were engaged together in their accursed intercourse, a fearful and terrible fire
came down from Heaven with a great noise, out of the midst
of which there issued a shining angel with a glittering sword,
wherewith at one blow they were all killed and the fire consumed them. There remained a few bones and skulls which
God allowed to bide unconsumed by the fire, as a memorial
of this punishment. In the Hakluyt Society's bowdlerisation,
we read of the Tumbez Islanders being "very vicious, many of
them committing the abominable offence"; also,

"If by the advice of the Devil any Indian commit the abominable crime, it is thought little of and they call him a woman."
In chapters 52 and 53 we find exceptions. The Indians of
Huancabamba, "although so near the peoples of Puerto Viejo
and Guayaquil, do not commit the abominable sin;" and the
Serranos, or island mountaineers, as sorcerers and magicians
inferior to the coast peoples, were not so much addicted to
sodomy.

The royal commentaries of the Yncas shows that the evil was
of a comparatively modern growth. In the early period of
Peruvian history, the people considered the crime "unspeakable:" if a Cuzco Indian, not of Yncarial blood, angrily addressed the term pederast to another, he was held infamous
for many days. One of the generals having reported to the
Ynca Ccapacc Yupanqui that there were some sodomites, not
in all the valleys, but one here and one there, "nor was it a
habit of all the inhabitants but only of certain persons who
practised it privately," the ruler ordered that the criminals
should be publicly burnt alive and their houses, crops and
trees destroyed: moreover, to show his abomination, he com-

manded that the whole village should so be treated if one man fell into this habit. Elsewhere we learn,

"There were sodomites in some provinces, though not openly nor universally, but some particular men and in secret. In some parts, they had them in their temples, because the Devil persuaded them that the Gods took great delight in such people, and thus the Devil acted as a traitor to remove the veil of shame that the Gentiles felt for this crime and to accustom them to commit it in public and in common."

During the times of the Conquistadores, male concubinage had become the rule throughout Peru. At Cuzco, we are told by Nuno de Guzman in 1530;

"*The last which was taken, and which fought most couragiously, was a man in the habite of a woman, which confessed that from a childe he had gotten his liuing by that filthinesse, for which I caused him to be burned.*" V. F. Lopez draws a frightful picture of pathologic love in Peru. Under the reigns which followed that of IntiKapak (Ccapacc) Amauri, the country was attacked by invaders of a giant race coming from the sea: they practised pederasty after a fashion so shameless that the conquered tribes were compelled to fly. Under the pre-Yncarial Amauta, or priestly dynasty, Peru had lapsed into savagery and the kings of Cuzco preserved only the name. *Toutes ces hontes et toutes ces misères provenaient de deux vices infâmes, la bestialité et la sodomie. Les femmes surtout étaient offensées de voir la nature frustrée de tous ses droits. Elles pleuraient ensemble en leurs réunions sur le misérable état dans lequel elles étaient tombées, sur le mépris avec lequel elles étaient traitées. * * * * Le monde était renversé, les hommes s'aimaient et étaient jaloux les uns des autres. * * * Elles cherchaient, mais en vain, les moyens de remédier au mal; elles employaient des herbes et des recettes diaboliques qui leur ramenaient bien quelques individus, mais ne pouvaient arrêter les progrès incessants du vice. Cet état de choses con-*

stitua un véritable moyen âge, qui dura jusqu'à l'établisse-ment du gouvernement des Incas."

When Sinchi Roko (the nineteenth of Montesinos and the twentieth of Garcilazo) became Ynca, he found morals at the lowest ebb. *"Ni la prudence de l'Inca, ni les lois sévères qu'il avait promulguées n'avaient pu extirper entièrement le péché contre nature. Il reprit avec une nouvelle violence, et les femmes en furent si jalouses qu'un grand nombre d'elles tuèrent leurs maris. Les devins et les sorciers passaient leurs journées à fab-riquer, avec certaines herbes, des compositions magiques qui rendaient fous ceux qui en mangaient, et les femmes en faisaient prendre, soit dans les aliments, soit dans la chicha, à ceux dont elles étaient jalouses."*

I have remarked that the Tupi races of the Brazil were in-famous for cannibalism and sodomy; nor could the latter be only racial as proved by the fact that colonists of pure Lusi-tanian blood followed in the path of the savages. Sr. Antonio Augusto da Costa Aguiar is outspoken upon this point. "A crime which in England leads to the gallows, and which is the very measure of abject depravity, passes with impunity amongst us by the participating in it of almost all or of many (*de quasi todos, ou de muitos*). Ah! if the wrath of Heaven were to fall by way of punishing such crimes (*delictos*), more than one city of this Empire, more than a dozen, would pass into the cate-gory of the Sodoms and Gomorrahs." Till late years pederasty in the Brazil was looked upon as a peccadillo; the European immigrants following the practice of the wild men who were naked but not, as Columbus said, "clothed in innocence." One of Her Majesty's Consuls used to tell a tale of the hilarity pro-voked in a "fashionable" assembly by the open declaration of a young gentleman that his mulatto "patient" had suddenly turned upon him, insisting upon becoming agent. Now, how-ever, under the influences of improved education and respect for the public opinion of Europe, pathologic love amongst the Luso-Brazilians has been reduced to the normal limits.

Outside the Sotadic Zone, I have said, *le vice* is sporadic, not endemic: yet the physical and moral effect of great cities where puberty, they say, is induced earlier than in country sites, has been the same in most lands, causing modesty to decay and pederasty to flourish. The Badawi Arab is wholly pure of *le vice*; yet San'á the capital of Al-Yaman and other centres of population have long been and still are thoroughly infected. History tells us of Zú Shanátir, tyrant of "Arabia Felix," in A.D. 478, who used to entice young men into his palace and cause them after use to be cast out of the windows: this unkindly ruler was at last poinarded by the youth Zerash, known from his long ringlets as "Zú Nowás." The Negro race is mostly untainted by sodomy and tribadism. Yet Joan dos Sanctos found in Cacango of West Africa certain "*Chibudi, which are men attyred like women and behaue themselves womanly, ashamed to be called men; are also married to men, and esteem that vnnaturale damnation an honor.*"

Madagascar also delighted in dancing and singing boys dressed as girls. In the Empire of Dahomey I noted a corps of prostitutes kept for the use of the Amazon-soldieresses.

North of the Sotadic Zone, we find local, but notable instances. Master Christoper Burrough describes on the western side of the Volga "a very fine stone castle, called by the name Oueak, and adioyning to the same a Towne called by the *Russes, Sodom,* * * * which was swallowed into the earth by the justice of God, for the wickednesse of the people." Again: although as a rule Christianity has steadily opposed pathologic love both in writing and preaching, there have been remarkable exceptions. Perhaps the most curious idea was that of certain medical writers in the middle ages: "*Usus et amplexus pueri, bene temperatus, salutaris medicina*" (Tardieu). Bayle notices (under "Vayer") the infamous book of Giovanni della Casa, Archbishop of Benevento, *De laudibus Sodomiæ,* vulgarly known as *Capitolo del Forno.* The same writer refers to the report that the Dominican Order, which systematically decried *le vice,* had presented a request to the Cardinal di Santa Lucia that sodomy might be lawful during three months per annum, June to August; and that the Cardinal had underwritten the petition "Be it done as they demand." Hence the Fæda Venus of Bassista Mantovano. Bayle rejects the history for a curious reason, venery being colder in summer than in winter, and quotes the proverb *"Aux mois qui n'ont pas d'R, peu embrasser et bien boire."* But in the case of a celibate priesthood, such scandals are inevitable: witness the famous Jesuit epitaph Ci-git un Jésuite, etc.

In our modern capitals, London, Berlin and Paris, for instance, the vice seems subject to periodical outbreaks. For many years, also, England sent her pederasts to Italy, and especially to Naples whence originated the term *"Il vizio Inglese."* It would be invidious to detail the scandals which of late years have startled the public in London and Dublin: for these the curious will consult the police reports. Berlin, despite her strong flavour of Phariseeism, Puritanism and Chauvinism in religion, manners and morals, is not a whit better than her neighbours. Dr. Gaspar, a well known authority on the subject, adduces many interesting cases especially an old Count Cajus and his six accomplices. Amongst his many correspondents one suggested to him that not only Plato and Julius Cæsar but also Winckelmann and Platen belonged to the society; and he had found it flourishing in Palermo, the Louvre, the Scottish Highlands and St. Petersburg, to name only a few places. Frederick the Great is said to have addressed these words to his nephew, *"Je puis vous assurer, par mon expérience personelle, que ce plaisir est peu agréable à cultiver."* This suggests the popular anecdote of Voltaire and the Englishman who agreed upon an "experience" and found it far from satisfactory. A few days afterwards the latter informed the Sage of Ferney that he had tried it again and provoked the exclamation, "Once a philosopher: twice a sodomite!" The last revival of the kind in Germany is a society at Frankfort and its neighbourhood, self-stlyed *Les Cravates Noires* in opposition, I suppose, to *Les Cravates Blanches* of A. Belot.

Paris is by no means more depraved than Berlin and London; but, whilst the latter hushes up the scandal, Frenchmen do not: hence we see a more copious account of it submitted to the public. For France of the seventeenth century consult the *Histoire de la Prostitution chez tous les Peuples du Monde,* and *La France devenue Italienne,* a treatise which generally follows *L'Histoire Amoureuse des Gaules* by Bussy, Comte de Rabutin. The headquarters of male prostitution were then in the Champ Flory, i.e., Champ de Flore, the privileged rendezvous of low courtesans. In the seventeenth century, "*quand le Francais a tête folle,*" as Voltaire sings, invented the term *péché philosophique,* there was a temporary recrudescence; and, after the death of Pidauzet de Mairobert (March, 1779), his *Apologie de la Secte Anandryne* was published in *L'Espion Anglais.* In those days the Allée des Veuves in the Champs Elysees had a "*fief reservé des Ebugors*"— "veuve" in the language of Sodom being the *maîtresse en titre,* the favorite youth.

At the decisive moment of monarchial decomposition Mirabeau declares that pederasty was *reglementée* and adds, *Le goût des pédérastes, quoique moins en vogue que du temps de Henri III* (the French Heliogabalus), *sous le règne desquel les hommes se provoquaient mutuellement sous les portiques du Louvre, fait des progrès considérables. On sait que cette ville* (Paris) *est un chef-d'œuvre de police; en conséquence, il y a des lieux publics autorisés à cet effet. Les jeunes gens qui se destinent à la profession, sont soigneusement enclassés; car les systèmes réglementaires s'étendent jusques-là. On les examine; ceux qui peuvent être agents et patients, qui sont beaux, vermeils, bien faits, potelés, sont réservés pour les grands seigneurs, ou se font payer très-cher par les évêques et les financiers. Ceux qui sont privés de leurs testicules, ou en termes de l'art (car notre langue est plus chaste qui nos mœurs), qui n'ont pas*

*le poids du tisserand, mais qui donnent et reçoivent, forment
la seconde classe; ils sont encore chers, parceque les femmes en
usent tandis qu'ils servent aux hommes. Ceux qui ne sont plus
susceptibles d'érection tant ils sont usés, quoiqu'ils aient tous
ces organes nécessaires au plaisir, s'inscrivent comme patiens
purs, et composent la troisième classe: mais celle qui préside
à ces plaisirs, vérifie leur impuissance. Pour cet effet, on les
place tout nus sur un matelas ouvert par la moitié inférieure;
deux filles les caressent de leur mieux, pendant qu'une troisième frappe doucement avec des orties naissantes le siège des
désirs vénériens. Après un quart d'heure de cet essai, on leur
introduit dans l'anus un poivre long rouge qui cause une irritation considérable; on pose sur les échauboulures produites
par les orties, de la moutarde fine de Caudebec, et l'on passe
le gland au camphre. Ceux qui résistent à ces épreuves et ne
donnent aucun signe d'érection, servent comme patients à un
tiers de paie seulement.*

The Restoration and the Empire made the police more
vigilant in matters of politics than of morals. The favourite
club, which had its *mot de passe,* was in the Rue Doyenne, old
quarter St. Thomas des Louvre; and the house was a hotel of
the seventeenth century. Two street-doors, on the right for the
male gynæceum and the left for the female, opened at 4 p.m.
in winter and 8 p.m. in summer. A decoy-lad, charmingly
dressed in women's clothes, with big haunches and small waist,
promenaded outside; and this continued till 1826 when the
police put down the house.

Under Louis Philippe, the conquest of Algiers had evil results, according to the Marquis de Boissy. He complained
without *ambages* of *mœurs Arabes* in French regiments, and
declared that the result of the African wars was an *éffrayable
débordement pédérastique,* even as the *vérole* resulted from
the Italian campaigns of that age of passion, the sixteenth
century. From the military the *fléau* spread to civilian society
and the vice took such expansion and intensity, that it may be

said to have been democratised in cities and large towns; at least so we gather from the *Dossier des Agissements des Pédérastes*. A general gathering of *La Sainte Congrégation des glorieux Pédérastes* was held in the old Petite Rue des Marais where, after the theatre, many resorted under pretext of making water. They ranged themselves along the walls of a vast garden and exposed their podices: bourgeois, richards and nobles came with full purses, touched the part which most attracted them and were duly followed by it. At the Allée des Veuves, the crowd was dangerous from 7 to 8 p.m.: no policeman or *ronde de nuit* dared venture in it; cords were stretched from tree to tree and armed guards drove away strangers amongst whom, they say, was once Victor Hugo. This nuisance was at length suppressed by the municipal administration.

The Empire did not improve morals. Balls of sodomites were held at No. 8 Place de la Madeleine where, on Jan. 2, 1864, some one hundred and fifty men met, all so well dressed as women that even the landlord did not recognise them. There was also a club for sotadic debauchery called the Cent Gardes and the Dragons de l'Impératrice. They copied the imperial toilette and kept it in the general wardrobe: hence *faire l'Impératrice* meant to be used carnally. The site, a splendid hotel in the Alleé des Veuves, was discovered by the Procureur-Général who registered all the names; but, as these belonged to not a few senators and dignitaries, the Emperor wisely quashed proceedings. The club was broken up on July 16, 1864. During the same year, *La Petite Revue,* edited by M. Loredan Larchy, son of the General, printed an article, "*Les échappés de Sodome*": it discusses the letter of M. Castagnary to the Progrès de Lyons and declares that the vice had been adopted by *plusieurs corps de troupes*. For its latest developments as regards the *chantage* of the *tantes* (pathics), the reader will consult the last issues of Dr. Tardieu's well-known *Études*. He declares that the servant-class is most infected;

and that the vice is commonest between the ages of fifteen and twenty-five.

The pederasty of *The Nights* may briefly be distributed into three categories.

The first is the funny form, as the unseemly practical joke of masterful Queen Budúr and the not less hardy jest of the slave-princess Zumurrud.

The second is in the grimmest and most earnest phase of the perversion, for instance where Abu Nowas debauches the three youths.

In the third form, it is wisely and learnedly discussed, to be severely blamed, by the Shaykhah or Reverend Woman.

To conclude this part of my subject, the *éclaircissement des obscénités*. Many readers will regret the absence from *The Nights* of that modesty which distinguishes "Amadis de Gaul;" whose author, when leaving a man and a maid together says:

"And nothing shall be here related; for these and suchlike things which are conformable neither to good conscience nor nature, man ought in reason lightly to pass over, holding them in slight esteem as they deserve." Nor have we less respect for Palmerin of England who after a risqué scene declares, "Herein is no offence offered to the wise by wanton speeches, or encouragement to the loose by lascivious matter."

But these are not oriental ideas and we must e'en take the Eastern as we find him. He still holds *Naturalia non sunt turpia,* together with *Mundis omnia munda*; and, as Bacon assures us the mixture of a lie doth add to pleasure, so the Arab enjoys the startling and lively contrast of extreme virtue and horrible vice placed in juxtaposition.

Those who have read through these ten volumes will agree with me that the proportion of offensive matter bears a very small ratio to the mass of the work. In an age saturated with cant and hypocrisy, here and there a venal pen will mourn over the "pornography" of *The Nights*, dwell upon the "Ethics of Dirt" and the "Garbage of the Brothel;" and will lament the

"wanton dissemination (!) of ancient and filthy fiction." This
self-constituted *Censor morum* reads Aristophanes and Plato,
Horace and Virgil, perhaps even Martial and Petronius, because "veiled in the decent obscurity of a learned language;"
he allows men *Latinè loqui*; but he is scandalised at stumbling
blocks much less important in plain English. To be consistent,
he must begin by bowdlerising not only the classics, with
which boys' and youths' minds and memories are soaked and
saturated at schools and colleges, but also Boccaccio and
Chaucer, Shakespeare and Rabelais; Burton, Sterne, Swift
and a long list of works which are yearly reprinted and re-
published without a word of protest. Lastly, why does not this
inconsistent Puritan purge the Old Testament of its allusions
to human ordure and the pudenda, to carnal copulation and
impudent whoredom, to adultery and fornication, to onanism,
sodomy and bestiality? But this he will not do, the whited
sepulchre! To the interested critic of the *Edinburgh Review*
(No. 335 of July, 1886), I return my warmest thanks for his
direct and deliberate falsehoods: lies are one-legged and short-
lived, and venom evaporates. It appears to be that when I
show to such men, so "respectable" and so impure, a landscape
of magnificent prospects whose vistas are adorned with every
charm of nature and art, they point their unclean noses at a
little heap of muck here and there lying in a field corner.

[EDITOR'S NOTES]

This remarkable study of homosexuality among the Arabs, which appeared as an essay in Burton's *"Arabian Nights,"* seems to have reflected a special interest of the author. For it is not in *The Nights* that there is such a great content of stories on this theme that he should have found it necessary to make a special study of the subject.

Burton's essay is frequently quoted (although seldom read) because of its approach to homosexuality as thriving in certain climates—particularly, as he termed it, the Sotadic Zone. The vice, he says, is "geographical and climatic, not racial" he contends. Nevertheless, in elucidation of this thesis, he actually repudiates it. On the one hand, this repudiation takes the form of such expressions as "a race of born pederasts." And, on the other, he shows the existence of "vice" in many areas outside of the so-called zone.

One should not read this piece without pondering over the eloquent plea against censorship and expurgation with which this essay ends. Certainly these words should be reread and reprinted widely in an era in which freedom of thought is again being challenged.

D. W. C.

THE
PERVERSIONS OF LOVE

Paolo Mantegazza

FIRST ENGLISH TRANSLATION PUBLISHED IN 1932 BY THE
ANTHROPOLOGICAL PRESS, NEW YORK

The naturalistic psychologist must not hesitate to set foot in the human mire; it is, rather, his duty to study it, inasmuch as all that is human falls within his province, the lofty and the base, the sublime and the revolting. It is not possible to ameliorate man's condition until after all the possibilities in the case have been studied. It is not by means of declamatory phillipics, nor by casting over it a hypocritic veil, that human abjectness may be done away with; this last may only be accomplished through an indulgent and dispassionate study of the causes of that abjectness.

It is impossible to erect the boundaries between love's physiology and its pathology. The highest rungs of eroticism may be the first steps on the ladder of perversion; and amid that hurricane of the senses, compounded of passion and imagination, in which a man and a woman who possess each other with desire are wrapped, it is only the sophist's casuistry which can distinguish that which is good from that which is evil. And even where this good and this evil are concerned, there is room for difference of opinion, according as one considers the hygienic or the moral aspect of the problem. It is true that with a more reasonable and scientific morality, such as that which is to come, hygiene and ethics ought to go perfectly in accord; but up to the present time, the two are very frequently at daggers' points and in contradiction to each other, a certain proof either that hygiene is ignorant or that morality is false.

However, putting to one side those dimly distinguishable forms which serve as a connecting link between ideal love and the most perverted lust, we have some very well known forms of sensual aberration, which have special names and quite distinct characteristics. It is our duty to study these as rapidly and delicately as possible, touching them as lightly as we should a painful open wound.

The abstruse and shameful aberrations of physical love all come from one of two sources: from the difficulty or impossibility of satisfying, in a physiological manner, the need for the sexual embrace; or from the desire to provide new pleasures, differing from those already known. This, in plain but strictly scientific language, is the psychology of all the sexual perversions from Sodom to Lesbos, and from Babylon to the Isle of Capri.

Masturbation is a thing so natural and spontaneous in the man who is without a woman, and the woman who is without a man, that it tends to spring up at all times and in all countries. It is, nonetheless, a perversion that is more common among highly civilized peoples, inasmuch as with them there are many causes, moral, economic, and religious, which impede or render supremely difficult the coming together of the two sexes. Where bodies are nude and love is free or very easy, masturbation is almost wholly unknown; I have been able to verify this circumstance by contrasting, close up, in America and in India, the adjacent native and European societies. Colleges, monasteries, schools, all institutions which bring young men together, are the breeding places and seminaries of masturbation.

With the possible exception of those countries where polygamy prevails, masturbation is everywhere a good deal more common in the man than in the woman, for many reasons, but chiefly this one, that in the male the secretion of spermatozoa renders pollution constantly necessary; and where the individual is not sufficiently virtuous to be satisfied with spontaneous nocturnal emissions, his hand comes to supply the lack of a woman. To this are to be added the constant and formidable erections in the male who is past the age of puberty and the numerous occasions for rubbing against the penis. It is only in polygamous countries that the woman, in the course of her long periods of idleness and the prolonged abstinences imposed upon her in the harem or the zenana, at once learns to masturbate.

Ethnically speaking, masturbation is a true physical and moral disease, which tends to leave a mark of abjectness and decadence with a people or with a race. It debases the man in what should be his poetic and his ardent years, by substituting for the gloriously violent combats of love the easy and secret pleasures of the hand or of an implement yet more vile; as the result of this comes vileness, hypocrisy, brutalisation, and the prostitution of character. A hundred, a thousand times better is the lust which lies in a love that is at least shared, which, even in its extremes, encounters a certain restraint in the complete satisfaction of a natural need naturally shared between two beings.

The sexual embrace very rarely slays with its excesses; whereas masturbation is often suicide, and when the organism does not die, the character and dignity do, the light of amorous idealism is extinguished, and every fibre of manly resolution is obliterated. If an inhabitant from another planet were to come down from above, and if he could contemplate with eagle's eye, upon the psychologic chart of our planet, the varying characteristics of the human race, he would certainly jot down in his note book, among the moral characteristics of Europeans and their overseas colonists, this stigma: *race of masturbators*. And it may be, that winged contemplator would become aware of an odor of moral decay, of a moldy, sexual smell on all sides, with thousands of young men and girls spilling in the sheets or in dark passage-ways mankind's sovereign life-giving fluid. Until such time as this convulsed and scrofulous civilization of ours shall learn to give to every man born of woman a loaf of bread and a woman, the nauseous stench of solitary vice will continue to contaminate every vein of our body social, transforming love's joyous grape-cluster into a handful of musty corn, devoured by cryptogamia.

It appears that the Moabites were accustomed to masturbating obscenely in chorus, as they danced about the incandescent statue of Moloch, after the seven bronze mouths of the god had devoured the offerings of the faithful, offerings which consisted of flour, turtle-doves, lambkins, rams, calves, bulls, and young lads. Any one who has read the Bible must remember the terrible curses hurled by Moses at those Hebrews who fornicated with Moloch. Baal-Phegor, too, or Belphegor, who was the favorite divinity of the Madianites, was received with a fanatic enthusiasm by the Jews, and his cult was not less obscene than the rites of Moloch.

Solitary lust tends to approach the embrace, when it seeks a lustful ally. Man may masturbate man, and woman may do the same to woman. In the former instance, there is merely an exchange of manual labor; but in the latter, the situation is more complicated and there is room for refinements to enter; owing to the special structure of the female genitals and the wayward character of the feminine imagination, lust is readily turned into a proteiform and special vice. Thus, woman may simply reciprocate, by giving to her companion the pleasure which she herself has received; but more often, she employs her tongue, and then we have *cunnilingus* and *Lesbian* love, so named from the Isle of Lesbos, to which historic tradition assigns the origin of a perversion which, in all truth, must have been born along with womankind. Another form of reciprocal masturbation in women occurs when a woman possessing an exceptionally long clitoris is thereby enabled to simulate the sexual embrace with another woman. It is this form of vice which may more accurately be termed Tribadism, the practitioners of which were known to the Latins as *frictrices* or *subigatrices*. Today, however, tribadism is synonymous with physical love between two women, whether such love finds satisfaction in one or another mode.

The most surprising circumstance in connection with modern tribadism is one cited by Duhousset.—Two women friends had been satisfying themselves in this manner for a long while, when one of them married, without however breaking off voluptuous relations with the other woman. It happened, then, that the one who had remained unmarried became pregnant, possibly for the reason that her companion, without being aware of it, had spilled into her vagina the husband's semen. This singular occurrence, the credibility of which must remain a matter that concerns M. Duhousset, was reported on the 15th of February, 1877, to the Anthropologic Society of Paris. I, myself, have known two Lesbian friends who had relations from time to time, one of them possessing a clitoris that was something like five or six centimeters long.

Dr. Paul Eram, who for long years practised medicine in the Far East, states that tribadism *"est une condition extrêment commune chez les jeunes filles en Orient"* ("is a condition extremely rare among young women of the Orient"). And elsewhere:

"In order to form a general idea of its frequency among young girls of the Orient, one has but to reflect upon their lack of exercise, their idle and sedentary lives, their boredom, and above all, the over confidence and credulity of their

mothers, who fail to provide any kind of supervision whatsoever over their daughter's occupations in her hours of solitude."

Among the Khoikhoins (Nama Hottentots), masturbation
among the youngest girl-infants is so common it may almost be looked upon as a natural vice. No secret is made of it,
and there is allusion to it in the folk stories and fables of the
country.

Tegg relates various cases of matrimony between women.
He sees in them only cases of fraud, but it is more likely that
they are instances of Lesbian passion. On the 5th of July,
1777, there was brought before the courts of London a woman
who, wearing male attire, had been three times married to
other women. She was exposed in the pillory, to the scornful
gaze of all the other members of her sex, so that they might
recognize her in the future, and was thereafter condemned to
six months in prison. In 1773, another woman disguised as a
man paid court to a lady, aspiring to the latter's hand; but the
daring imposture did not succeed.

The most extraordinary case cited by Tegg is that of two
women who lived together as husband and wife for the course
of thirty-six years. The wife revealed the secret, but only on
her death bed, to relatives.

Occasionally, in tribadism, there is question merely of physical pleasure, pure and simple, the woman enjoying the voluptuous caress of another woman's tongue, just as she does in
the case of a man. But more often, there is associated with
lustful desire, a true and ardent passion, one which makes all
the demands that true love does, and which is capable of all
the latter's jealousies. Parent-Duchâtelet speaks at length of
the love letters written by such a pair, and describes the
jealous scenes and criminal consequences of such a feminine
attachment. For my part, I knew two young and beautiful
girls, one of them blonde, the other brunette, who were ardently
in love with each other, while being exceedingly cold and

utterly without volition where the embraces of men were concerned.

Tribadism, which is common in the Orient among women of the harem, is very frequent among European prostitutes, who often have a lover of the same sex as themselves, the only one to give them a real sexual thrill. Among those who market their love, this other passion is strengthened by the absolute indifference which they feel toward the men to whom they abandon themselves; their erotic sensitivity would appear to be restricted to that narrow province of pleasure afforded by the clitoris.

Even among our own women folk, this vice is by no means rare. I have known a number of women, married and with children, who seek pleasure only of a woman friend or a female lover, whom they passionately adore, and of whom they are very, very jealous. More often than once, Lesbianism brings with it domestic unhappiness; and it behooves the married man to keep a sharp eye out for those strange and hidden manifestations of lasciviousness, which, taken in the beginning, may be dominated and overcome by physiologic love. Where the vice is of long standing, a cure is all but impossible; for the reason that the clitoris, with prolonged exercise of its nerves, becomes unduly sensitive and overdeveloped, and all normal pleasure is thereafter a pale and colorless thing, compared to the Lesbian's convulsive spasms. The husband then may find himself in a cruel dilemma, having to choose between loathing and condemning the companion of his loves, or himself acquiring a vice, which alone can satisfy and make her happy. A wholesome, honest upbringing may, however, almost always forestall such an aberration, the fruit of that unhealthy hypocrisy with which we are used to surrounding the mysteries of love.

Love's most shameful phase, shameful above all, is sodomy, which a man may practice either upon a woman, or upon a person of his own sex. Sodomy with a woman is sufficiently common, and is born of a curious desire for new experience, or is resorted to with a Malthusian objective in view, that of limiting the progeny. It is impossible to draw up even approximate statistics as to this vice, for the reason that it remains hidden among the mysteries of the marriage bed, and, where it is indulged in with the consent of both parties, never comes before a court of justice, which would be highly embarrassed at having to deal with such a case. The woman, in this variety of sodomy, is passive, the act is a painful one to her, and she yields to the shameful proceeding only out of weakness or a passion for sacrifice. Not rarely, however, she actually enjoys and even invites it, being unable to achieve a venereal orgasm in any other fashion. I know a young prostitute who was in the habit of selling her body daily, but without ever experiencing any pleasure in the act; when she happened to meet a man she liked and for whom she felt the vague stirrings of desire, she would ask him to alter his approach, that they might share the chalice of lustful pleasure. This circumstance, rare it is true, but which does occur, will serve to cast a light upon the lurid mystery of masculine sodomy.

Love between males is one of the most terrifying facts to be met with in human psychology; it has always been, and still is, in all countries, a vice that is a good deal more common than it is thought to be. Let us look first at the facts, and make our comments afterwards.

Carthage was famous for vice contrary to nature, and the Carthaginians applauded in the male his prowess in the practice of such vices. Salvianus, a preacher of that time, has this to say: *"et illi se magis virilis fortitudinis esse crederent, qui maximi viros foemini usus probrositate fregissent"* ("and they believed themselves to be displaying the greater masculine valor, the more they lent themselves to these disgracful practices characteristic of the female").

According to mythologic tradition, pederasty goes back to the time of Orpheus and the Thracians.

"Ille etiam Thracum populis fuisse auctor amorem
In teneros transferee mares, citraque juventam
Breve ver aetatis et primos carpere flores."

Ovid.

Aristotle tells us that this vice was authorized by law in the Island of Crete, in order to prevent an excessive increase in population. Athenaeus speaks of the sodomy of the Cretans, but attributes the vice as well to the Chalcidians of Eubœa. Lycophron accuses Achilles of having assassinated upon the altar of Apollo the young Troilus, who had refused to consent to his immodest behests. Sodomy was, of a certainty, a Greek vice; for that people carried it even into Olympus, making guilty of it Jove and Ganymede, Apollo and Hyacinth, Hercules and Hylas. Sophocles and Aeschylus went so far as to speak of it in their tragedies, and Anacreon hymned Baihyllus. Even the godlike Socrates was a lover of young boys.

Rome is not at all unworthy of her great teacher in this field. Caesar sold the first fruits of his youth to Nicomedes, King of Bithynia; Horace sung of his masculine loves, Ligurinus, Gyges, Lyciscus, etc. Virgil made immortal, under the name of Alexis, his love for the young Alexander. The Roman populace thought of Augustus, when it heard spoken upon the stage the famous line

"Videsne ut Cinaedus orbem digito temperet?"

A Roman emperor reared statues and temples to his paramour; and of Tiberius, the immortal historian wrote: "he would take infants not yet weaned and put them to his private parts as to a teat, holding that, by reason of their tender years, they were the better adapted to his variety of lust . . . and at the sacrifice, smitten by the face of the officiating priest, he scarcely could wait until the divine service was over, but must, at once and on the spot, seduce and defile him with his penis; and he took care to do the same to the priest's brother, a flute-player, that the two of them might have the same sin with which to reproach each other."

Of Caligula, what Ausonius has to tell us is enough:

> *"Tres uno in lecto; stuprum duo perpetiuntur*
> *Et duo committunt; quatuor esse reor.*
> *Falleris, extremis ad singula crimina, et illum*
> *Bis numeres medium qui facit, et patitur."*

Heliogabalus is portrayed for us by Lampridius in a single phrase: *"quis enim ferre possit principem, per cuncta cava corporis libidinem recipientem?"* ("For who could endure a prince, all of the cavities of whose body are receptacles for lust?")

Nero had himself wed to Doryphorus, amid nude women and lubricious dances: "Where licit or illicit depravity was concerned, he left no vice untried that afforded an opportunity for corruption. . . . He would invade the private parts of men and women bound to the stake, and then at the proper point would finish off with the freedman, Doryphorus."

Vice readily became a passion; for, indeed, Heliogabalus *"sic amavit* (the eunuch Hierocles) *ut eidem inquina osculuretur, floralia sacra se asserens celebrare"* ("so loved the eunuch Hierocles that he was in the habit of kissing his privates and of decreeing floral festivals in his honor").

The entire Roman world was then but one great orgy; and we find Juvenal describing in this manner the aphrodisiac dances which were given in the theatre, and which were designed to spur the erotic chord to its highest degree of vibration:

> *"Forsitan expectes ut Gaditana canoro*
> *Incipiat prurire choro, plausuque probatae*
> *Ad terram tremulo descendant clune puellae:*
> *Irritamentum Veneris languentis et acres*
> *Divitis urticae: major tamen ista voluptas*
> *Alterius sexus, magis ille extenditur et mox*
> *Auribus atque oculis concepta urina movetur."*

If we pass from Greco-Roman antiquity to the Gauls, to America, or to those savage tribes which are living today, we shall not find sodomy any the less widespread.

The Gauls indulged in libidinous orgies, in which sodomy played a part.

In certain northern parts of Mexico, marriages were performed between men who, clad like women, were forbidden to bear arms. At Tamaulitas, according to Gomara, cases of prostitution occurred in which men took the part of women. Diaz tells us that along the coast of old Mexico, pederasty was a common vice, but that it was looked upon as a crime and severely punished by law.

Duflot found vice against nature to be very common among the aborigines of California. Pederasty was also general in Nicaragua. Among the natives of Panama, the first discoverers found pederasty common, but looked upon as an abominable vice. And similarly, along the shores of ancient Peru, in the region which is now Guayaquil, it appears that unnatural vice was very prevalent.

Many travelers speak of such vice among the aborigines of North America, where men were to be seen dressed as women and remaining at home to do woman's work, this indicating all too plainly to what use these abject creatures were put. From Alaska to Darien were to be seen young men brought up and dressed as women and living in concubinage with lords and princes.

The Aleutians and the Codiaks were also pederasts, and the same would seem to have been true of the inhabitants of Nutka. The old time travellers frequently mention unnatural vice among the Caribs of the *tierra firme;* but at Cumanea, it would seem that sodomy was abhorred. In Madagascar, also, unnatural vice was not lacking, as is evidenced by native male dancers and singers clad as women.

In the Orient, and for that matter in civilized Europe as well, women or boys are offered for purposes of pleasure according to the taste of the pleasure seeker; and in certain Italian cities, the sodomists have a sign language, with which in the public highway they express their desires, indicating whether the verb love with them is to be actively or passively conjugated (*cinaedi* or *pathici*). Nor is this shameful, infamous, practice restricted to the most depraved classes of society; it extends upward into the spheres of wealth and intelligence. In the brief course of my own experience, among sodomists who were more or less scandalous in their conduct, I have known a French journalist, a German poet, an Italian politician, and a Spanish jurisconsult, all men of exquisite taste and the highest culture!

How in the name of heaven does it come that this form of lust is so frequently to be met with? In order that I might be able to give a proper answer to this question, which one must blush in putting to himself, I have made a thorough-going study of this problem over a period of years, and I believe that I have solved it.

Anatomicians are acquainted with the spinal nervous structure which has to do with lustful desire, and they know how intimate a relationship there is between those nerves distributed in the intestinal and rectal tract and those which run down to the genital organs. I, personally, believe, it is by an anatomic anomaly that the sensual nerve branches are deflected to the rectum; this explains how it is their excitation produces in the *patici* a venereal orgasm, which in ordinary cases may only come through the love organs. This would seem to be established by the finding of women who are *cinaedae,* and others who, in lesbianism, love to have the rectum excited with the finger; there are also all those cases in which an erection in a man can only be produced by the introduction of foreign bodies into the anus. I very well recall a great writer, who confessed to me that it was impossible for him to say whether he derived a greater pleasure from the sexual embrace or from the act of defecation.

It is easier to explain the voluptuous inclination of the *cinaedi,* who derive from the act a true erotic pleasure but only by a filthy path, one selected for the greater narrowness of diameter it affords. This explains why it is that in many countries sodomy is practiced only upon boys, which has led to giving the name of pederasty to the practice; it at the same time goes to account for the fact that this vice is a good deal more common in warm countries, where the woman is often dishearteningly large in her organ, and where nudity is ever visible and women are easy to be had, all of which circumstances are but spurs to lust.

Many times, however, sodomy is not of peripheral origin, but has its seat in the nervous centers; and so, I think we should distinguish a peripheral or anatomic sodomy (the latter due to an abnormal distribution of nerves), a lustful sodomy (due to a desire for womb-narrowness), and finally, a psychic sodomy. I have often had occasion to study this last form, which is especially common among intelligent, cultivated and often neurasthenic men.

A young man who was as chaste as could be desired, and of high social rank, once consulted me. It was with an unspeakable horror that, upon reaching the age of puberty, he became aware of the fact that he amorously desired persons of his own sex, while remaining wholly insensible to the seductions of a woman. He would at once experience an erection and violent desires, whenever he embraced another lad; but when taken to houses of prostitution that he might there admire and possess women, he remained like ice under the most ardent of provocations. This poor lad, who had never once yielded to his perverse inclinations, but had combatted them with all the strength of a vigorous will power and a noble mind, confessed to me that he meant to kill himself, unless he could succeed in bringing his erotic instincts back into the proper physiologic paths. As to whether or not he achieved his purpose, I cannot say, for I never saw him again.

Psychic sodomy is not a vice, but a passion. A blame-worthy one, if you like, unclean and revolting, but a passion none the less. A number of sodomists have written me letters over which I have wept, telling me of their ardent loves and jealousy. They were accustomed to keeping amorous rendezvous with their lovers, and they wrote them letters brimming with a pure affection, making use in these epistles of expressions that had been inspired by the loftiest poetry. I happen to know that, in one Italian city, there are certain darker places in the public parks where inverts go of an evening to exchange kisses and to fondle each other's genitals, with a sensual ardor and a passion which they are quite unable to resist.

Just as in malacia and pica, the patient eats coal, gravel and earth with an infinite relish, so in psychic pederasty does man love the male! Sodomy, studied with the pitying and forgiving eye of the physician and psychologist, is accordingly a disease which ought to be curable, and which many times is cured.

I shall not leave this unpleasant subject until I have set forth a singular case which I, myself, observed in America, and which affords an example of the strangest sort of perversion of the erotic sense, one which for me is to be set beside that of sodomy. If the unfortunate one ever reads these pages, I trust he will pardon me for having published his confession in the interest of science:

"I am a young man of good family, about twenty-two years of age, and of a good constitution physically and morally. However, from the moment the sense of sex was awakened in me and I came to know under what form it manifests itself in other men (with the rarest of exceptions), I began to understand that I was widely different from the rule, and that my own case was a very strange exception. The truth is, whereas generally in a man the symptoms surrounding fecundation make their appearance upon a physical or moral contact with the feminine sexual organs, for me those organs hold no attraction whatsoever, but the same effects, that is, erection and ejaculation, are produced in me by other circumstances; while I am altogether indifferent to, and experience no emotion whatsoever for, the woman's natural parts, I am as excited as can be by their lower extremities, that is to say, by women's feet, and to be more precise, by their shoes; for while a foot that is nude or covered only with a stocking produces no effect on me whatsoever, one covered with a shoe, or even the shoe alone, without a real woman, excites me very greatly (producing ejaculation, etc.) and brings about the identical effect which in others is produced by the real 'altar of Venus.' It is necessary, however, that these shoes be of black leather, buttoned down the side and with a heel as high as possible, in a word, they must be as fashionable as possible. Shoes of another form or material have a much less effect upon me. I then experience a desire to handle them, to kiss them, to put them on myself and walk in them, etc.; and it is to be noted that my sexual organ all the while is not subjected to any mechanical action, either with my hands or otherwise; the ejaculation is quite spontaneous. The height of pleasure, it seems to me, would be literally to prostrate myself before a pair of pretty little feet so shod, let myself be trod on by them. It is none the less a fact, that if the shoes happen to be on the feet of an ugly woman, my fancy is at once dispersed and no consequences ensue; yet when I have before me merely the shoes, my imagination pictures as being near me a woman of beautiful appearance, and then the ejaculation comes. If I have occasion to be near a woman, it is not her sexual organ, but rather her feet, or better her shoes, which hold me fascinated; this for reasons which have been set forth previously. In my erotic dreams, asleep at night, whenever I see beautiful women, the center of attraction for me is their *boots* and nothing else.

"As I have already said, the *sine qua non* of ejaculation for me are a female's shoes and not the female herself. Hence it is, gazing into a shoemaker's window, where fashionable ladies'

boots are on display, impresses me as being a highly immoral
act, just as it does to speak of boots. Whereas, speaking of a
woman's private parts is for me an innocent and insipid thing.

"Well, then, if this mode of ejaculation amounts to masturbation (since it is not necessary nor desirable for me that
it take place within the feminine vagina), then I must face
the dilemma of resigning myself to perpetual chastity or continuing to live in a state of masturbation. The former of these
alternatives almost terrifies me, especially after the encouragement I have received from the reading of your excellent book,
The Hygiene of Love. I would have you understand, my dear
sir, that man is very often weak, and especially in such cases
as this.

"Many times, I have attempted to perform coitus in the
usual fashion, but without any success whatsover, not being
even able to produce an ejaculation.

"When I seek and find pleasure, by putting on a lady's
boots to walk in them, I find that the pain they give me by
their tightness is not enough, but I must previously have put
into them a number of little tacks or big-headed nails with the
points upward, and thus at every step that I force myself to
take, those nails pierce the flesh of my foot, which naturally
causes me quite a good deal of pain, but which is nevertheless
accompanied by a real pleasure occasioned by pollutions. It
is really my imagination at work, which makes me fancy that
I am sacrificing myself body and soul at the feet of Venus,
enduring tortures for the sake of giving her pleasure."

The shameful list of amorous perversions is not, however,
finished as yet. Man also makes love with animals.

In the Bible, you will find mentioned many times the sin
of bestiality while the obscene paintings of India depict monstrous intertwinings of men and animals.

David Forbes, who lived for a long time in Peru, where he
was engaged in studying geology, states that in that country
the belief is current that syphilis is a malady peculiar to the

alpaca and that from this animal it has been passed on to man as the result of vice against nature. There was formerly in force in Peru a law prohibiting bachelors from keeping female alpacas in their homes. In Peruvian guano have been found human figures carved out of wood, bearing about their necks a rope or a serpent in the act of devouring the virile member. Forbes and W. Frank suppose that it is meant to represent the introduction of syphilis through convicts.

It is quite possible that man has made love with all the domestic animals whose size would permit of such relations. Ewes, nannygoats, hens are the preferred ones; but man has also defiled mares, geese, ducks, etc., etc. The Chinese are famous for their love affairs with geese, the necks of which they are in the habit of cruelly wringing off at the moment of ejaculation, in order that they may get the pleasurable benefit of the anal sphincter's last spasms in the victim.

At Rimini, more than one young Apennine shepherd, suffering from nervous dyspepsia, confessed to me having abused she-goats in an extraordinary manner. It appears that they are also very fond of sows!

Woman, too, is not spared the shame of bestiality. Plutarch tells us that from the most remote times women had to subject themselves to the libidinous caprices of the sacred goat at Mendes. Today, after so many centuries, the dog is often an agent of voluptuousness for women deprived of love, for those who are prisoners in their homes, or who are oversexed. Quite often, ladies who are in every way adorable, whom we look upon with envy and desire, and who move in the highest realms of civilized European society, secretly adore their poodle for reasons which they would not confess to a living soul. More rarely, the dog is not a poodle; and then, perversion takes a still lower form, and in place of animal tribadism, we have a case of the sexual embrace with an animal, of connubial sacrilege, of a union of the loveliest of creatures with the most odious and unclean of domestic animals!

[EDITOR'S NOTES]

Ninteenth-century Europe saw the emergence of a new group of scientific investigators, men concerned with the sexual relations of mankind (to borrow a phrase from the title of the book written by Paolo Mantegazza). Many of these writers are being read today; sometimes for historical reasons; at other times, because the modern reader is unaware of the out-of-date character of the material. The works of Krafft-Ebing, Forel, and Mantegazza continue to be published in many languages, quoted by some as if their century-old finds are still gospel truth; disputed seriously by others as if their findings are worthy of debate; ignored by a few as if they had made no contribution to the development of man's knowledge.

Yet, upon rereading, is it not obvious that the significance of these writings (of which this is but one of the best examples) is to be found in the fact of their existence, rather than in the concepts brought forth. Take Mantegazza, for example. Before his time, there was hardly a reference in a scientific volume to the existence of homosexuality; only in belles lettres, legal, or ecclesiastical documents could it be found. After Mantegazza, homosexuality became a subject for scientific investigation.

Viewed as a pioneer and explorer, Mantegazza is erudite and advanced. Viewed as a forerunner of modern scientific thought, these pages are punctuated by remarkable clarity.

A modern scientist would write more dispassionately; he would not characterize a subject under study as unpleasant, unclean, revolting, blameworthy, to use but a few of many adjectives that adorn these pages. Yet, this method of writing may have been a reflection of nineteenth-century culture upon a scientist who had broken at least with the traditions of silence; or it may have been the author's method of making it possible for himself to speak of what was, at the time, literally unspeakable.

It is not in the theories of Mantegazza (nor Krafft-Ebing, Forel, and others) that one must search today for an understanding of this subject; it is rather to their writings that one must go in order to discover the first halting efforts to arrive at understanding through open investigation, in an age ruled by taboos.

D. W. C.

MALE HOMOSEXUALITY
IN
ANCIENT GREECE

Hans Licht

FROM SEXUAL LIFE IN ANCIENT GREECE, ROUTLEDGE & KEGAN
PAUL, LTD., LONDON, 1932, TRANSLATED BY J. H. FREESE.

GENERAL AND INTRODUCTORY

Henry Beyle (Stendhal) writes in his book *De l'Amour:* "There
is nothing more comical than our usual views of the ancients
and ancient art. As we read only superficial translations, we do
not recognize that they devoted a special cult to the Naked,
which repels us moderns. In France only the feminine is called
'beautiful' by the masses. Gallantry did not exist among the
ancient Greeks, but on the other hand, only a love which appears perverted to us to-day. . . . They cultivated, we may say,
a feeling rejected by the modern world."

From this feeling the fact is no doubt to be explained that
the generally known and in other respects excellent handbooks
pass over this subject in almost complete silence. To give an
example: In Holm-Deecke-Soltau's book of almost 600 pages
(*Kulturgeschichte des Klassischen Altertums*, Leipzig, 1897),

homosexuality is not determined at all; in L. Schmidt's profound work in two volumes (*Die Ethik der alten Griechen,* Berlin, 1882) the subject is limited to something less than three pages; in the four gigantic volumes of Burckhardt's *Griechische Kulturgeschichte* one finds next to nothing, and indeed in the new and revised edition of Pauly's well-known *Realenzyklopädie der klassischen Altertumswissenschaft* (increased to ten volumes each of at least 1300 pages) the catch-word *Päderastie* contains four pages by the distinguished Breslau university Professor W. Kroll, in which certainly much that is correct is stated, yet so incompletely, that though it might perhaps suffice as a summary, it is unworthy of monumental work which professes to treat exhaustively the whole culture of classical antiquity. The article "Hetairen" in the same encyclopedia fills twenty pages.

The result of this treatment, which is to be found throughout present-day literature, is to give the reader, who is himself unable to consult the authorities, the idea that in the case of Greek homosexuality it was a merely subsidiary phenomenon, something which happened in isolated instances, rarely, and only here and there.

Without anticipating the argument, listen first to the great philosopher Plato, who wrote:

"Since then Eros is acknowledged to be the oldest god, we owe to him the greatest blessings. For I cannot say what greater benefit can fall to the lot of a young man than a virtuous lover and to the lover than a beloved youth. For what those who intend to live a noble life ought to regard as their whole life, this neither kinship nor wealth nor honours nor anything else can afford us so well as love. And what is this? I mean modesty in regard to shameful things, in good things ambition; for without these it is impossible for any city or private individual to perform great and noble deeds. Therefore, I assert that a man who loves, if he is found doing or suffering anything disgraceful at anyone's hands, without defending himself through cowardice, would not be so pained if he were seen by his father or his companions or anyone as he would were it by his favourite. Similarly, we see that a young man who is loved is specially ashamed when his lover sees him committing an offence. If then, there were any means whereby a state or army could be formed of lovers and favourites, they would administer affairs better than all others, provided they abstain from all disgraceful deeds and compete with one another in honest rivalry. And such men together with others like them, though few in number, so to speak would conquer the world. For the man who loves would be ashamed to abandon his post or throw aside his arms in the presence of his favourite more than in the presence of anyone, and would often prefer to die in his place. For no one is so base as to leave his beloved in the lurch and not to help him when in danger, for Eros himself inspires him with valour, so that he behaves like a man of the greatest courage. For, as Homer says, this courage is breathed into the souls of some of the heroes by the god, but this love of itself inspires it in those who love" (*Symposium*).

In order to be able to face the problem, the solution of which at the same time indicates the key to the understanding of the whole of Greek culture, it is necessary first of all to become acquainted with the facts that are accredited and undisputed.

TERMINOLOGY

The word most frequently used, "pederasty" (*pederastia*), comes from *pez* (boy) and *eros* to love), and consequently denotes the spiritual and sensual affection for a boy, though it should be noted, as will later be more fully shown, that the word "boy" is not to be understood offhand in the modern colloquial sense. In the Greek language the word "pederasty" had not this ugly sound it has for us today, since it was regarded simply as an expression for one variety of love, and had no sort of defamatory meaning attached to it.

The word "paderos" is only once found in the sense of "pæderast," but the verb "paderastin" frequently. Lucian once has the expression *nta pederastika* for "pederasty." Frenzied, uncontrolled passion for boys was called *pedomnia*, and a man filled with such passion *pedomans*, both words being derived from "mahria" (passion, frenzy). The word *pedopiphs* (one who stares at or spies after boys) had a harmlessly jesting additional note which again represents a different shade of meaning, i.e. one who gapes after, or ogles boys with fair hair.

The words *paidotribes* and *paidotribein*, harmless in themselves and originally meaning a teacher of boys in the art of wrestling, are also used obscenely, and the secondary sense is easy to understand, since the words are connected with the verb *tribein*.

Later authors, especially the Fathers of the Church, prefer to use, in an obscene sense, the words *paidophthoria, paidophthoros, paidophthorein* (seduction of boys, seducer of boys, to seduce boys).

In addition to these expressions *paidon epois* and *paidikos* (love of boys, boyish love) were in common use.

The word *ephebophilia* is not ancient, but a new formation; it means the love for an ephebos, by which was understood a young man who had passed the age of puberty; certainly, however, the adjective *philephebos* (fond of young men) existed. So far as I know, the noun *paidophilia* (love of boys) does not occur in any Greek author; but the verb *paidophilein* (to love boys) and *paidophiles* (lover of boys) are fairly frequent.

A boy's lover had different names in the several Greek dialects; as, for example, on the island of Crete, where the love of boys flourished from the earliest times, he was called *erastes*, and after the alliance was completed, *philetor*, a word difficult to translate—perhaps "wooer and friend;" the boy who was the object of affection was called *eromenos* (loved), as long as he was still courted, but if he became the friend of a great personage he was called *kleinos* (the famous, the celebrated).

The word *philoboupais* stands by itself, and is used of one who is fond of over-matured boys. The word *boupais* denoted what we call "a big young man." The word *philomeiraz* also rarely occurs; it is derived from *meiraz*, by which a boy in his best prime was meant, and consequently signifies one who especially loves beautiful boys. In Athens it was the title of honour given to Sophocles.

The expression which meets us most frequently in the Greek writings to denote the beloved boy or young man is *ta kaidika* (boyish things, things connected with boys), and the explanation is that a man loved in the object of his love just "what was boyish," that is, the qualities of mind and body that distinguish the boy; that he held him dear, since he beheld in him the embodiments of boyhood. I do not know a translation that completely reproduces the idea of this word and am unable to coin one.

In the Doric dialect the usual word for the lover was *evspelas* literally "the inspirer," which contains the hint that the lover, who indeed, as we shall see later, was also responsible for the boy in every sort of connection, inspired the young receptive soul with all that was good and noble. Therefore the Dorians used the word *eiapnein* in the sense of "to love," if it was a question of a boy. That this "blowing in" is to be understood in the above-mentioned ethical sense is expressly stated by Ælian. Even more definitely and indisputably Xenophon expresses himself: "By the very fact that we breathe our love into beautiful boys, we keep them away from avarice, increase their enjoyment in work, trouble, and dangers, and strengthen their modesty and self-control."

With this, the Dorian name for the loved boy—*aitas*, the "listening, the intellectually receptive"—agrees.

By the side of these highly serious terms there grew up in course of time a number of others, which owed their origin to joking or derisive caprice. These will be discussed later; but it may be mentioned in passing that, by a secondary meaning easy to understand, the lover was sometimes called the "wolf," while the loved boy would be the "lamb" or "kid." The wolf was to the ancient Greeks the symbol of greediness and audacious fierceness. Thus we read in an epigram of Straton: "Going out in revel after supper, I, the wolf, found a lamb standing at the door, the son of my neighbour Aristodicus, and throwing my arms round him I kissed him to my heart's content, promising on my oath, many gifts."

Plato has an epigram: "As wolves love lambs, so do lovers love their loves."

Occasionally the lover was also called a "raven," while "Sathon" and "Posthon" were tolerably frequent names for the boy favourite. Both these words were also serious family names, the Greeks being in all sexual matters astonishingly naïve.

BOYHOOD AND THE GREEK IDEAL OF BEAUTY

When discussing the Greek love of boys, one thing especially must not be forgotten: that it is never a question of boys (as we mostly use the word), that is, of children of tender age, but always of boys who are sexually matured, that is, who have reached the age of puberty. This age alone is meant by the *pais* in by far the greater number of passages of the Greek authors, so far as we are here concerned with them; indeed, in not a few an age which we should never consider a boy's age but rather that of a youth, corresponding sometimes to what we should call " a young man," is indicated. We must also bear in mind that in Greece, as in all countries of the so called Sotadic zone, puberty sets in earlier than in the north, so that we can well keep to the word "boy," if we do not forget that all these boys have reached the age puberty. Sexual intercourse with boys in our sense of the word, that is, sexually immature youths, was of course punished, and sometimes very severely, in ancient Greece.

On the different ages of boys and youths who were loved

by the Greeks, a treatise might be written, with a motto from Goethe, who, in regard to this problem, so unintelligible to most of the men of the present day, showed himself to be the universal intellect that knew and understood all; for in the *Achilleïs* we read: "Now to the son of Cronos came Ganymede, with the seriousness of the first look of youth in his childlike eye, and the god rejoiced."

We should also recall a passage in Homer's *Odyssey* (x, 277), where we hear how Odysseus, in order to explore the island of Circe, went into the interior of the country. On the way he is met by Hermes (of course unknown to him) "in the form of a youth with the first down of his beard upon his chin, in whom the charm of youth is fairest."

The Greek poet Aristophanes (*Clouds*, 978) also praises his Greek boys in the same manner, except that the down he speaks of is not the down of their cheeks and lips.

The beginning of the *Protagoras* of Plato refers to the passage from Homer quoted above: "Whence come you, Socrates? And yet I need hardly ask the question, for I know that you have been in chase of the fair Alcibiades. I saw him the day before yesterday, and he had got a beard like a man—and he is a man, as I may tell you in your ear. But I thought that he was still very charming.

"*Socrates.* What of his beard? Are you not of Homer's opinion, who says that 'Youth is most charming, when first the beard appears?' And that is now the charm of Alcibiades."

On the different degrees of age Straton (Anth. Pal., xii, 4) says: "The youthful bloom of the twelve-year-old boy gives me joy, but much more desirable is the boy of thirteen. He whose years are fourteen, is a still sweeter flower of the Loves, and even more charming is he who is beginning his fifteenth year. The sixteenth year is that of the gods, and to desire the seventeenth does not fall to my lot, but only to Zeus. But if one longs for one still older, he no longer plays, but already demands the Homeric 'but to him replied.' "

To facilitate the understanding of the Hellenic love of boys, it will be as well to say something about the Greek ideal of beauty. The most fundamental difference between ancient and modern culture is that the ancient is throughout male and that the woman only comes into the scheme of the Greek man as mother of his children and as manager of household matters. Antiquity treated the man, and the man only, as the focus of all intellectual life. This explains why the bringing up and development of girls was neglected in a way we can hardly understand; but the boys, on the other hand, were supposed to continue their education much later than is usual with us. The most peculiar custom, according to our ideas, was that every man attracted to him some boy or youth and, in the intimacy of daily life, acted as his counsellor, guardian, and friend, and prompted him in all manly virtues. It was especially in the Doric states that this custom prevailed, and it was recognized so much as a matter of course by the State that it was considered a violation of duty by the man, if he did not draw one younger to him, and a disgrace to the boy if he was not honoured by the friendship of a man. The senior was responsible for the manner of life of his young comrade, and shared with him blame and praise. When a boy on one occasion uttered a cry of pain at gymnastic exercises, his older friend, as Plutarch relates (*Lycurgus,* 18), was punished for it.

If this originally Doric custom was not also spread throughout Greece, yet the daily intercourse of the male youth with men, the close community of life from early morning till late evening, was a matter of course in all Greece. Thereby in the man was developed that understanding of the soul of the boy and the young man, and an almost unexampled zeal to scatter the seed of everything good and noble in the young, receptive hearts and to bring them as near as possible to the ideal of an excellent citizen. For the ideal of male perfection the Greek has coined the formula *kalos kagathos,* good and beautiful, or "beautiful in body and soul." Thus, then, a value was placed upon the bodily development of boys, the importance of which it would be difficult to overestimate. We may affirm without exaggeration that Greek boys spent three-quarters of the day in the palæstræ and gymnasia, which, in contrast to the German—though not to the English—sense of the word, served essentially for bodily development. In all these bodily exercises boys and youths were naked, to which the derivation of the word (from *gumnos,* naked) points.

BOYISH BEAUTY IN GREEK LITERATURE

From the immense number of passages available, some few may be selected as especially characteristic. As early as the *Iliad* youthful beauty is glorified, when the poet speaks of Nireus, who outshone all the other Greek youths in beauty. Indeed, the beauty of Nireus afterwards became proverbial and is mentioned constantly (*Il.,* ii, 671).

The esthetic pleasure of the Greek eye in beautiful youth is prominent in the *Iliad* in another exquisite passage, where Hector's father, the aged King Priam, standing in great distress before Achilles and begging for the dead body of his beloved son, can yet find it in his heart to glance with admiration upon the beauty of the youth who had slain his Hector (*Iliad,* xxiv, 629). On this passage Gerlach (*Philologus,* xxx, 57) finely observes: "We must accordingly form a higher idea of the beauty of Achilles than of the charms of Helen; for Priam, on whom the most unspeakable sorrow has been inflicted by the former, admires it and is able to be surprised at it, at the very moment, when he is begging for the dead body of his son."

In a fragment of his poetry, the wise Solon (frag. 44) compares the beauty of boys with the flowers of spring. We may quote the verses from the poems of Theognis (1365 and 1319): "O most beautiful and charming of boys, stand before me and listen to a few words from me;" and "O boy, since the goddess Cypris has given you charming grace and your beauty of form is the admiration of all, listen to these words and place my gratitude in your heart, knowing how hard it is for men to bear love."

Ibycus (frag. 5), known to everyone from Schiller's ballad, does homage to the beauty of his favourite with the words: "Euryalus, offshoot of charming Graces, object of the fair-haired maidens' care, Cypris and mild-eyed Persuasion have reared you in the midst of rosy flowers."

Pindar (*Nemea*, viii, 1) sings the praise of boyish beauty with the words: "Queen of youthful prime, harbinger of the divine desires of Aphrodite, thou that, resting on the eyes of maidens and of boys, bearest one in the hands of gentle destiny, but handlest another far otherwise—'tis sweet for one who hath not swerved from due measure in aught that he doeth, to be able to win the nobler prize of love."

Licymnius (frag. 3 in Ath., xiii, 564c), the lyric poet born in the island of Chios, had related in one of his poems the love of Hypnos, the god of sleep, for Endymion: "He was so fond of looking at the eyes of Endymion, that he did not allow him to shut them when he put him to sleep, but made him keep them open, that he might enjoy the charm of looking at them."

Straton (Anth. Pal., *a*, xii, 195, *b*, 181) is above all a eulogist of the beauty of boys: (*a*) "The meads that love the Zephyr are not abloom with so many flowers, the crowded splendour of the spring-tide, as are the high-born boys thou shalt see, Dionysius, all moulded by Cypris and the Graces. And chief among them, look, flowers Milesius, like a rose shining with its sweet-scented petals. But perchance he knows not, that as a lovely flower is killed by the heat, so is beauty by a hair." (*b*) "It is a lying fable, Theocles, that the Graces are good and that there are three of them in Orchomenus; for five times ten dance round thy face, all archers, ravishers of other men's souls."

The verses of Meleager (Anth. Pal., xii, 256) describe the beauties of various boys: "Love hath wrought for thee, Cypris, gathering with his own hands the boy-flowers, a wreath of every blossom to cozen the heart. Into it he wove Diodorus the sweet lily, and Asclepiades the scented white violet. Yea, and thereupon he planted Heracleitus when, like a rose, he grew from the thorns, and Dion, when he bloomed like the blossom of the vine. He tied on Theron, too, the golden-tressed saffron, and put in Uliades, a sprig of thyme, and soft-haired Myiscus the evergreen olive shoot, and despoiled for it the lovely boughs of Aretas. Most blessed of islands art thou, holy Tyre, which hast the perfumed grove where the boy-blossoms of Cypris grow."

Nor is the great poet Callimachus (Anth. Pal., xii, 73) ashamed to sing the praises of the beauty of boys: "It is but the half of my soul that still breathes, and for the other half I know not if it be Love or Death that hath seized on it, only it is gone. Is it off again to one of the lads? And yet I told them often. 'Receive not, ye young men, the runaway.' Seek for it at . . . ; for I know that it is somewhere there that the gallows-bird, the love-lorn, is loitering."

It is a matter of course for Greek thought and feeling, that even the lofty pathos of serious tragedy is not ashamed to pay homage to boyish beauty on every possible occasion.

Sophocles (frag. 757: *oto d'erotos degma paidikon prosen;* cf. also Pindar, frag. 123: "wound from the bite of youthful beauty"), in one of the fragments that we still possess, praises the beauty of the youthful Pelops with words given elsewhere (frag. 433). Even Euripides (frag. 652: *opaidez, oion philtron anthropois phrenos),* the great negationist, gives expression to his enthusiasm in the words: "O what a magic comfort are boys to men!"

Comedy also often finds occasion to speak of the beauty of boys. Thus in 421 B.C. Eupolis had brought on the stage his comedy *Autolycus.* The hero of the piece, Autolycus, was a youth of such beauty, that Xenophon (*Sympos.,* i, 9) says of him admiringly: "As when a light flashes up in the night and draws the eyes of all upon it, so the shining beauty of the youthful Autolycus guided all eyes towards it."

The following verses are preserved from an unknown comedy of Damoxenos (Ath., i, 15b [*CAF.*, III, 353]), in which the beauty of a boy from the island of Cos is described: "A youth about seventeen years old was throwing a ball. He came from Cos, the island that produces seeming gods, and whenever he looked at those who were seated, or took or gave the ball, we all raised a shout, for symmetry and character and order were seen in everything he did. It was the perfection of beauty; I had never seen or heard of such grace before. I should have fared worse, if I had remained longer; and now I do not think that I am well."

An unknown poet (*CAF.*, III, 451, in Plutarch, *Moralia*, 169b) of Greek comedy has left us the lines: "And beholding his comeliness, I made a slip. . . . A beardless, tender, and beautiful youth . . . would that I could die embracing him and gain an epitaph."

Anyone who, after reading the above passages, should be of the opinion that for such glorification of the beauty of boys we are indebted only to the poetically idealized caprice of the poet, would be greatly mistaken. Greek prose also is full of inspired praises of beauty, indeed of enthusiastic hymns on the beauty of boys. A whole volume could be put together, from the letters of Philostratus alone, of which the following are instances:—

1. *To a boy*—These roses desire with longing to come to you and their leaves as wings carry them to you. Receive them kindly as a memorial of Adonis, or as the purple blood of Aphrodite, or as the choicest fruits of the earth. The crown of olives adorns the athlete, the towering tiara a great kind, the helmet a warrior; but the rose is the ornament of a beautiful boy, since it resembles him in fragrance and in colour.

It is not you who will adorn yourself with roses, but the roses themselves with you.

2. *To the same*—I have sent you a crown of roses, not (or at least not exclusively) to give you pleasure, but out of affection for the roses themselves, that they may not fade.

3. *To the same*—The Spartans clad themselves in purple-coloured garments, either to frighten their enemies by the obtrusive hue, or in order that they might not see when they were wounded, owing to the resemblance of the colour to blood. So must you beautiful boys arm yourselves only with roses, and let that be the equipment that your lovers will present to you. Now the hyacinth suits a fair-haired boy well, the narcissus a dark-haired one, but the rose suits all, since once it was itself a boy. It infatuated Anchises, deprived Ares of his weapons, enticed Adonis; it is the hair of spring, the brightness of the earth, the torch of love.

4. *To the same*—You reproach me for not having sent you any roses. I omitted to do so, not from forgetfulness, not from want of affection, but I said to myself, you are fair and beautiful, and on your cheeks your own roses bloom, so that you need no others besides. Even Homer does not set a garland on the head of the fair-haired Meleager—that would have been adding fire to fire—nor on that of Achilles, nor of Menelaus, nor of any other who is famous in his poems for the beauty of his hair. Also this flower is of a sorry kind, for its appointed time is only brief, and it soon fades away, and, as we are told, the first beginning of its existence is melancholy. For the thorn of a rose pricked Aphrodite as she passed by, as the people of Cyprus and Phœnicia tell. Yet why should we not crown ourselves with the flower, which spares not even Aphrodite?

5. *To the same*—How did it happen that the roses, which, before they came to you, were beautiful and smelt delight-

fully—else I would never have sent them to you—withered and died away so quickly when they reached you? I cannot tell you the real reason, for they would disclose nothing to me, but probably they did not want to be overcome in comparison with you and were afraid to enter into competition with you, so that they died at once, when they came in contact with the more charming fragrance of your skin. Thus the light of the lamp is darkened, conquered by a blazing flame, and the stars became extinct, since they cannot endure the sight of the sun.

6. *To the same*—The nests afford shelter for the birds, the rocks for the fishes, and the eyes for beauty. Birds and fishes roam around, change places, wander hither and thither wherever chance leads them; but if beauty is once fixed firmly in the eyes, then it never again abandons this shelter. So you dwell in me, and I carry you in the nets of the eyes everywhere. If I go oversea, you rise up from it, like Aphrodite in the story; if I cross the meadow, you shine from the flowers to meet me. What grows there that is like you? The flowers also are beautiful and charming, yet they bloom only for a day. If I look up to heaven, I think the sun has set, and that you are shining in its place. But when the dusk of night surrounds us, I see only two stars, Hesperus and you.

The vast number of passages from prose literature, in which the beauty of boys is praised, makes it impossible to enumerate them all, yet at least a small selection may be given from Lucian.

In the first *Dialogue of the Dead* (Diogenes and Polydeuces) "fair hair, black flashing eyes, ruddy complexion, tight sinews and broad shoulders" are named as marks of manly beauty.

Lucian's *Charidemus* is entirely devoted to the nature of beauty: "The occasion for our conversation, which you would like to know, was the beautiful Cleonymus himself, who sat between me and his uncle. Most of the guests who, as has been mentioned, were ignorant persons, could not keep their eyes from him, they saw nothing but him, and forgetting nearly everything else, vied with one another in praising this youth's beauty. We learned people could not help fully appreciating their good taste, but we were obliged to consider it unpardonable negligence to let ourselves be overcome by laymen in what we regarded as our own speciality; so we naturally hit upon the idea of making little impromptu speeches, which we were to deliver one after the other. For, for the sake of decency and to avoid increasing his self-conceit, it did not appear suitable for us to enter into a special praise of the young man."

Then Philo began his panegyric on beauty: "All men desire to have beauty, although only few have been thought worthy of it. The few who have obtained this boon are always supposed to have been the happiest of men, being honoured as they deserved by gods and men alike. And here is a proof of this. Among all the mortals who have ever been thought worthy of associating with the gods there is not a single one who has not had to thank his beauty for being thus preferred. It was simply thanks to his beauty that Pelops shared the ambrosia of the gods at their table, and Ganymede, the son of Dardanus, had such power over the chief of the gods, that Zeus would not allow any of the other gods to accompany him when he flew down to the heights of Ida to fetch this his favourite to heaven, where he now remains with him for all time. When Zeus approaches beautiful youths he becomes so gentle and mild and just to all, that he always seems to put off the character of Zeus, and for fear of not being pleasant enough to his favourites in his own form, he assumes the form of someone else, always one so beautiful that he can be certain of attracting all who look at him. Such is the honour and respect paid to beauty!"

Zeus, however, is not the only one among the gods over whom beauty exercises such power, and anyone who looks into the history of the gods will find that in this matter they all have the same taste—Poseidon, for example, fell a victim to the beautiful Pelops, Apollo to Hyacinthus, Hermes to Cadmus. If then beauty is something so noble and divine and in the eyes of the gods themselves is so highly valued, should it not be our duty to imitate the gods in this and to contribute to its glorification by doing all we can to assist, both in words and actions?

Lastly, Philon expresses the pleasure which one has in the national games where he can feast his eyes upon the courage and steadfastness of the competitors, their beautiful bodily forms, the vigorous structure of their limbs, their inconceivable cleverness and skill, their invincible strength, boldness, condition, patience, and perseverance, and their inextinguishable desire to be victorious.

Further, we read in Lucian's *Scytha* of a youth who "will capture your heart at the first glance by his manly comeliness and noble stature, but as soon as he begins to speak he will lead you away fettered by the ears. As often as he speaks in public our feelings are such as the Athenians experienced towards Alcibiades. The whole city listens to him with such eager attention, that it seems desirous of swallowing with mouth and eyes everything he says. The only difference is that the Athenians soon repented of their enthusiastic love for Alcibiades, whereas here, on the contrary, the whole State not only loves the athlete, but finds him, in spite of his youth, worthy of respect."

BOYISH BEAUTY IN GREEK ART

To how great an extent the boyish ideal appeared to the Greeks the embodiment of all earthly beauty may be further appreciated from the fact that in plastic art specifically female beauty is represented as approximating to the type of the boy or youth; and the truth of this assertion can be proved by rapidly turning over the pages of any illustrated history of Greek art. Indeed, even the prototypes of female charm and female seductiveness, the Sirens, were often enough represented as boyish. In Greek art, and especially in vase-paintings, boys and youths are portrayed far more frequently and with much greater attention to detail than are girls, as must strike everyone who even casually examines one of the great works on vases; a favourite subject above all is the youthful Eros, together with Hyacinthus, Hylas, and other boy-favourites, of whom Greek mythology tells us.

Further, it must be remembered that in mythological handbooks whole chapters were filled with a list of beautiful boys, as in Hyginus's book of myths for schools (*Fabularum Liber*, 271); and here also may be mentioned the *Erotes* of Phanocles, to be afterwards discussed—a poetical list of many beautiful boys and their lovers.

A further proof that the Hellenes saw the ideal of beauty in the boy and the youth, is the very remarkable fact that the inscription *kalos* (beautiful boy) occurs on an enormous number of vases, while the inscription *kale* (beautiful girl) is comparatively rare. In regard to these so-called inscriptions on favourites the following account may be given.

It was (and is, in certain sections of the community) a common custom everywhere to write down, carve, or scrawl hurriedly the names of specially beloved friends, wherever opportunity offers or the material to hand permits. It was the same in ancient Greece, and we have a very large number of passages from which it is clear that it was customary to write the name of a favourite boy or girl on the walls, the doors, or wherever there was room—especially in the Ceramicus at Athens (of which we spoke when discussing Lucian's *Dialogues of Courtesans*) or to cut them on the bark of trees. Indeed, the great artist Pheidias was not ashamed to do homage to his favourite by inscribing "beautiful Pantarkes" (*Pausanias*, v, ii, 3; vi, 10, 6; 15, 2; Clem. Alex., *Protrepticon*, 35c) on the finger of his mighty statue of Zeus at Olympia. A brick has been preserved on which a workman named Aristomedes has scratched the words: "Hippeus is beautiful! *'Ippeus kalos Aristomedei*

dokei, CIGr., 541), so it seems to Aristomedes." Indeed, sentimental lovers write the name of the dead loved one (female)
with the addition of the "beautiful" with their own blood
(Iamblichus in Photius, *Bibliotheca,* 94—p. 77, Becker) on
the grave.

The names of favourite boys were also written on graves, as
is shown by an epigram of Aratus (Anth. Pal., xii, 129): "Phil-
ocles the Argive is beautiful; this the pillars of Corinth and
the tombstones of Megara announce. It is written that he is
fair as far as the baths of Amphiaraus. But what need is there
of the testimony of the stones? Everyone who knows him will
admit it."

It was only a step to the inscribing of these love-tokens also
on vases. The word "beautiful" is sometimes found alone,
more frequently in the form "The boy is beautiful," or combined with a name as an inscription on Greek vessels; also on
columns, shields, basins, footstools, pillars, altars, chests, bags,
discus rims, and a large number of other objects. Indeed,
many vases exhibit regular dialogues—such as one at Munich
where between the ornamentation stands the inscription
written in wavy letters:—

A. Beautiful is Dorotheus, O Nicolas, beautiful!

B. To me also he appears to be beautiful, indeed; but so
also the other boy, Memnon, is beautiful.

A. To me also he is beautiful and dear.

It may also be mentioned that the epithet *kalos* for the
favourite is found even on vases where scenes from the school-
room are represented: e.g. on a red-figured bowl of Duris
which has often been copied and is now kept in the Antiquarium of the old Berlin Museum.

Although for these inscriptions on favourites a comprehensive literature already exists, the nature and purpose of them
have not even yet been adequately explained; but the results
of the investigations hitherto carried out can be fairly summarized in the following propositions:

1. Essentially the names of favourites were only usual on vase paintings in Attica and only during a period of about 70 years of the fifth century B.C.

2. The inscription *kalos* (beautiful) has different meanings. Sometimes the artist wanted to praise himself; at other times the inscription had to do with individuals of the figures represented by him, whereby he meant to express the naïve joy which he felt because this or that form had been especially successful.

3. But more frequently the vase painter wanted to offer homage to the boy who was his favourite.

4. Many also, who ordered vases from the artist, caused the addition "the beautiful Hippias" or whatever the name happened to be, to be put upon the vessels, in order to delight the boy to whom they intended to present the vase, by praising his bodily charms, especially as at that time every boy was proud of his beauty, and did not think it a disgrace but a high distinction when he found anyone to admire his mental and bodily excellencies.

5. Lastly, the vase painters also wrote on their vessels the names of those boys and youths, about whose beauty and daring tricks the whole city was enthusiastic. It may be assumed that many a manufacturer could dispose of his wares more readily, if they were ornamented with the name of a boy who at the time was idolized by everybody.

ANALYSIS OF THE GREEK IDEAL OF BOYS

After having thus considered the Greek ideal of beauty in its main features and made the attempt to render the understanding of it easier to the modern point of view, we have to go more closely into the details of the Hellenic ideal of boys. Of all the bodily charms of a boy, there is none by which the Greek was more enchanted than by the eyes, which accordingly enjoy their greatest triumphs in poetry. Sophocles has perhaps found the most beautiful words, when in the fragment (certainly difficult to translate) he says of the eyes of the youthful Pelops: "His eyes are the infatuating magic charm of love (frag. 433 in Ath., xiii, 564*b*); they are flames, with the fire of which he warms himself and scorches me." And in the drama the *Lovers of Achilles* (frag. 161), Sophocles had spoken of the "longing inflamed by the flash of the eyes," of the eyes "which hurl the darts of love." Hesychius (iii, 203: *omma teios póthos dià tò en tò oràn haliskesthai eroti ek gar tou esoran ginetai anthropois eran. Kai en Achilleos erastais ommaton apo logchas iesiñ*), who quotes these words, reminds us that the eyes of the one to be loved are the entrance-gates of love, for, according to a Greek proverb, "love arises in men by beholding."

We have already mentioned how Licymnius spoke of the beautiful eyes of his favourite. Sappho begs (frag. 29 in Ath., xiii, 564*d*): "Stand in front, my friend, and shed thy grace over the eyes."

From Anacreon we have the verses (frag. 4): "O boy, with a maiden's look, I seek thee, but thou dost not hear, not knowing that thou ridest thy chariot over my heart."

The mighty-voiced Pindar (frag. 123) begins a skolion not preserved with the words: "Right it were, fond heart, to cull the flower of love in due season, in life's prime; but whoever, when once he hath seen the rays flashing from the eyes of Theoxenus, does not swell with desire, his black heart with its frozen flame is forged of adamant or iron."

The great philosopher Aristotle (frag. 81R, Ath., xiii, 564*b*), the mightiest and most universal thinker of antiquity confesses: "Lovers look at none of the bodily charms of their favourites more than at their eyes, wherein dwells the secret of boyish virtues."

Of course, the lyric poets are not behindhand in eulogizing boys' eyes. Thus Ibycus celebrates them in a poem (frag. 2 and 3) beginning: "Eros again, gazing languishingly at me from beneath his dark eyelids with the greatest possible charm, flings me into the inextricable nets of Cypris."

At another time he compares the eyes of a boy with the stars, which sparkle in the sky when dark with night.

With especial frequency the praise of boy's eyes is sung by the poets of the Palatine Anthology. Thus Straton (Anth. Pal., 196) says of a boy: "Thy eyes are sparks, Lycinus, divinely fair; or rather, master mine, they are rays that shoot forth flame. Even for a little season I cannot look at thee face to face, so bright is the lightning from both."

And in another passage (ibid., 5): "Nor do I dismiss brown eyes; but above all I love sparkling black eyes."

These few quotations in which beautiful eyes are praised give an idea of the homage paid by the Greeks to the bodily charms of their boys; and although it is a fact that other parts of a boy's body were lauded quite as much as the eyes, there is no need to weary the modern reader by considering each bodily charm and systematically supplying appropriate quotations from the Greek writers concerning each, and it will suffice to mention briefly the other physical attractions that evoked special attention.

At the sight of a boy on whose cheeks the charming blush of bashful confusion had flamed up Sophocles quoted the verse of the tragic poet Phrynichus (frag. 13; *TGF.*, p. 723, in Ath., xiii, 604*a*): "There shines on his ruddy cheeks the fire of love;" and Sophocles (*Antigone,* 783) himself had said that "tender cheeks are where Eros keeps vigil."

To the Greeks one of the chief beauties of boys was the hair. Horace (*Odes,* i, 32, 19) certifies of the great poet Alcæus: "He sang of Bacchus and the Muses and Venus and the boy who always clung to her side, and of Lycus, distinguished by his black eyes and black hair."

If we may believe Cicero (*Nat. Deor.,* i, 28, 79) Alcæus for a while took special pleasure in a mole on the finger of this boy, Lycus.

The comic writer Pherecrates (frag. 189; *CAF.*, I, 201) had praised a boy who was adorned with fair curly hair with the words: "O thou, who shinest in curly golden hair."

When Anacreon stayed at the court of Polycrates, ruler of Samos, he had fallen in love with the beautiful Smerdis (Ælian, *Var. hist.*, ix, 4) amongst other royal pages, and was never tired of gazing at the lad's splendid curly hair or of celebrating the dark abundance of these locks in his poems. In boyish vanity, Smerdis was highly pleased at the praise so bountifully lavished upon him. But Polycrates, in tyrannical caprice and a fit of jealousy had his hair cut off, to annoy the boy and the poet. The latter, however, showed no annoyance, but behaved as if the boy of his own free will had deprived himself of the ornament of his hair, and reproached him for his folly in a new poem, which thereby became an act of homage. From it only the words are preserved: that "he cut off the irreproachable bloom of his soft hair, whereas before he was wont to throw it back so saucily." Of the boyish ideal of Anacreon (frag. 48, 49) we can even today form a living idea.

Another favourite of his was Bathyllus (cf. Maximus of Tyre, xxvii, 439; Horace, *Epod.*, 14, 9), who enchanted the poet not only by his beauty, but also by the skill with which he played the flute and cithara. Polycrates had had a statue of the youth set up in the temple of Hera at Samos, described by Apuleius (Apuleius, *Florilegium,* ii, 15), who had seen it.

According to the ancient conception, love is nothing but the longing for the beautiful, and so, after all we have described, it is by no means surprising if the sensual love of the Greeks was also directed towards their boys and that they sought and found in intercourse with them community of soul. There was added to the ideal of beauty the richer and more highly developed intellectual talents of the boys, which made rational conversation possible, where with girls a man could only have jested. Thus the Greeks took refuge in their trusted sexual companions not only in a social sense but also intellectually.

The old Greek love of boys (*paidophilia*) appears to us modern men as an insoluble riddle, but it can be proved, from the history of the Greek love of boys and its expression in literature, that it was just the most important and influential supporters of Greek culture who held the most decidedly homosexual opinions.

Theodor Däubler, in his book on Sparta (Leipzig, 1923) has expressed this as follows: "Anyone who is unable to regard the love of the Hellene for boys, or Sappho's inclination for her own sex, as something elevated and sacred, denies it in the face of Greece. We are more indebted to their heroic lovers than to mankind's most glorious art for Europe's freedom and the complete destruction of the Persian despotism in face of the diversity of the natural impulses in man. . . . Any attack on the love of boys in Sparta's prime would have acted with destructive effect, would have been considered unwholesome, and as a betrayal of the people." (Cf. Lucka, *Die drei Stufen der Erotik*, p. 30; M. Hirschfeld, *Die Homosexualität des Mannes und der Weibes*, 1914).

FURTHER PHASES OF THE GREEK LOVE OF BOYS

If the qualities sketched in the preceding pages are existent, then the boy is worthy to become an object of consideration.

In the twelfth book of the Palatine Anthology, a hymn of the love of boys is preserved to us. In the literary and historical survey we must return to this, but we may content ourselves at present with describing individual phases of pædophilia from poetical passages contained in this collection, and with occasional quotations from the poems themselves.

If Straton (Anth. Pal., xii, 198) once confesses that "everything boyish" enchants him, he thereby reveals not only his own soul but that of most of the Greeks and has therewith spoken from the heart to many Hellenes.

Another time (Anth. Pal., xii, 192) he confesses: "I am not charmed by long hair or by needless ringlets taught rather in the school of Art than of Nature, but by the dusty grime of a boy fresh from the playground, and by the colour given to his limbs by the gloss of oil. My love is sweet when unadorned, but an artificial beauty has in it the work of a female Cypris."

Wherever drinking-bouts are represented in ancient literature and art, we also find boys who present wine to the guests, joke with them, or even offer their luxuriant hair as a towel, as Petronius informs us (27, 31, 41) to mention only one example. He relates how "boys from Alexandria pour water cooled with snow over the hands of the guests, while others wash their feet and pare their nails with the utmost care." In another passage of the same author it is said: "After we had thus conversed, a very beautiful boy came, crowned with vine-leaves and ivy, carrying round a little basket of bunches of grapes, and singing at the same time with a voice as clear as a bell. And we kissed the beautiful boy, as he flitted about, to our heart's content."

How intimately the boyish ideal was connected by the Greeks with their drinking-bouts is quite clear from the story told by Philostratus (i, 105, 13), that in the palace of a mighty Indian king there were four costly tripods which were carried by bronze automatons in the form of boys "who were as beautiful as the Greeks imagine their Ganymede or Pelops to be." Often enough boys may also have taken part in the carousal, as appears from a fragment of the comic writer Philyllios (Ath., xi, 485b [CAF., I, 783]).

MALE PROSTITUTION

Love has at all times and among all peoples been purchasable for money, and always will be, however much it may be regretted for very various reasons. Male prostitution also is as old as love itself. We have already said often enough that among the temple prostitutes beautiful boys as well as women were to be found. How widespread male prostitution was at Athens in Solon's time is clear from the fact that this great statesman, poet, and philosopher, not only forbade pederasty to slaves by legislation, since this freest manifestation of man's self-determination was only permitted to free men, but laid under a penalty those who made a trade of their beauty. "It is to be feared," says the orator Eschines (*Tim.*, 13, 138, 137), to whom we are largely indebted for our knowledge of these laws of Solon—of which, certainly, some details as transmitted are vague—"that anyone who sells his own body for money will also lightly sacrifice the common interests of the State."

However much the Greeks at all times approved of the relation between man and youth that rested upon mutual liking, they in the same manner rejected it if the boy sold himself for money. This is not only clearly attested by Æschines in his famous speech against Timarchus, but it is clear from many passages in other authors. Professional male love was called *hetairesis* or *hetaireia,* and to sell oneself for money *hetaipein.*

It remains to quote the numerous passages from Greek authors, which prove that boys and youths were to be had everywhere for money or presents or for both. By way of proof, we may be reminded of the lines of Aristophanes (*Plutus*, 153): "And they say that the boys do this very thing, not for their lovers', but for money's sake. Not the better sort, but the sodomites; for the better sort do not ask for money."

Hence, we must not pass by in silence the complaints of the poets upon the greediness of boys, especially as they know how to conceal this avarice by all the arts of coquetry. Thus Straton (Anth. Pal., xii, 212) complains: "Woe is me! Why in tears again and so woe-begone, my lad? Tell me plainly; I want to know; what is the matter? You hold out the hollow of your hand to me. I am done for! You are begging perhaps for payment; and where did you learn that? You no longer love slices of seed cake and sweet sesame and nuts to play at shots with, but already your mind is set on gain. May he who taught you perish! What a boy of mine he has spoilt!"

With slight changes this unpleasant subject recurs very

frequently in the motifs inspired by the Muse of boys, but we
may be satisfied with this single representative specimen.

Especially prominent or handsome men could hardly resist
all the boys who offered themselves. Thus Carystius (Ath., xii,
542f—FHG., iv, 358), in his *Recollections,* relates: "All the
boys of Athens were so jealous of Diognis, the special favourite of Demetrius, whose acquaintance they were anxious to
make, that the most beautiful boys in the city, when he went
for a walk in the afternoon, all came where he was in order to
be seen by him."

Boys were not merely to be bought for money; they could
even be hired by contract for a longer or a shorter time. Besides other evidence, we have a particularly interesting testimony in the speech written by Lysias in 393 B.C. for an
Athenian who loved a boy from Platææ, named Theodotus,
and was accused by a certain Simon, who was also in love with
the boy, of intentional violation of his body, which at that
time was an offence punishable by banishment and confisca-
tion of property. In this memorable legal document it is
related, with the greatest detail and frankness, and quite as a
matter of course, that a man hired a youth by contract for the
purpose of using him in this way. By the terms of settlement,
Theodotus is said to have received 300 drachmæ (about thirty-
six dollars).

Yet more. We have several written authorities, from which
it appears to be tolerably certain that in Greece, at least in
Athens and other harbour towns, there were brothels or
houses of accommodation, in which boys and youths were to
be had alone or with girls for money. Thus Eschines says:
"Look also at those who are acknowledged as carrying on the
trade, if they sit in the 'public' houses. They also draw a kind
of curtain to hide their shame and shut the doors" (*Tim.*, 30).

Often enough the inmates of such houses may have been
young people who had been taken as prisoners of war and
afterwards sold. The best known example of this is Phædo of

Elis (Diog. Laërtes, ii, 105), with whom Socrates on the day of his death held the famous dialogue on the immortality of the soul. Phædo belonged to a distinguished family and, at the time of the war between Elis and Sparta, and while still very young, had fallen into the hands of the enemy who sold him to Athens, where he was purchased by the possessor of a "public" house. There Socrates made his acquaintance, and induced one of his well-to-do adherents to buy him off. It is surely a remarkable fact, that the much-admired dialogue *Phædo,* perhaps the most touching that Plato ever wrote, is named after a young man, and is carried on for the most part with one who, although under compulsion, only a short time before was at the disposal in a brothel of anyone who cared to pay for him.

But free youths also voluntarily roamed about in such houses, to earn money by the sale of their bodies. Eschines thus reproaches Timarchus (*Tim.,* 40): "As soon as he had left his boyish years behind him, he stayed in the Piræus in the bathing-place of Euthydicus, on pretence of learning this trade, but in fact with the purpose of selling himself, as the event has shown."

From what Eschines says further it is clear that boy-prostitutes were not only visited by their lovers in the "public" houses (brothels with male inmates are also mentioned by Timæus in Polyb., xii, 13—*FHG.,* I, 227—*tõn epi tegous apo ton somatos eirgasmenon),* but also went to them to their own homes, to be at the disposal of the master of the house alone or, at festivities, of the guests.

"There is, O Athenæus," says Eschines, "a certain Misgolas, otherwise a man of honour and beyond reproach, who is excessively devoted to the love of the boys and cannot live unless he always has some singers and players on the cithara about him. As soon as he observed why Timarchus stayed in the bathing-place, he took him away from there after paying something on account and kept him with him, since he grew up wanton,

young, voluptuous, and thoroughly adapted for the things
which he had resolved to do himself, and Timarchus had
decided to tolerate. Timarchus had no scruples about doing
this, but submitted to him, although he would have had no
lack of anything provided his claims had been moderate." One
of the Athenian boys' brothels appears to have been on the
rocky cone of mount Lycabettus that rises some 900 feet above
the city of Athens, as may be concluded from a passage in the
comic poet Theopompus (in Schol. Pind., *Pyth.*, 2, 75—*CAF.*,
I, 740), where mount Lycabettus personified says: "On my
rocky height boys willingly give themselves up to those of the
same age and to others."

THE ETHICS OF GREEK LOVE OF BOYS

In spite of these facts, it would be entirely wrong to assume
that sensuality denoted the only (or at least the most important) element of the Hellenic love of boys. Quite the contrary
is the case: everything that made Greece great, everything that
created for the Greeks a civilization which will be admired
as long as the world exists, has its root in the unexampled
ethical valuation of the masculine character in public and
private life. Allusion has already been made to Plato's high
opinion of the love of boys (see Lagerborg, *Die platonische
Liebe,* Leipzig, 1926), and it is now time to describe in greater
detail the ethical tendencies of Greek pedophilia.

Eros is the principle not only of the sensual, but also of the
ideal side of Greek pædophilia. A beautiful vase painting in
the Berlin Antiquarium represents this ideal side symbolically
and has hence been called "the ecstasy of Love." We see a
winged Eros flying away towards the heights of heaven with
enraptured look and carrying up with him a boy, who appears
to be struggling, but at the same time lovingly regards Eros.
Hartwig says rightly (*Meisterschalen,* p. 659): "Perhaps what is
here intended is that generic Eros, who brings to boys sometimes a flower, a lyre, or a hoop, who addresses them with

lively gesture or impetuously hurls himself down upon them:
an ideal representation of the wooing of men in love, which
the pictures on the cups of this period so often realistically
present."

Pædophilia was to the Greeks at first the most important way
of bringing up the male youth. As the good mother and house-
wife was to them the ideal of the girl, so *kalokagathia,* the sym-
metrically harmonic development of body and soul, was that
of the boy. For the Greeks the most excellent way of approaching this ideal was the love of boys; and while, especially among
the Dorians, the State expected that every man should choose
a youth as his favorite, and, further, while a boy was blamed if
he failed to find an older friend and lover—a lapse that
appeared to be intelligible only if he had some moral taint—
both man and boy exerted themselves as far as possible to
develop manly virtues. As the older was responsible for the
behaviour of the younger, the love of boys was not persecuted,
but fostered, to become the power that maintained the State
and upheld the foundation of Greek ethics. These ethical tendencies we find proved in numerous passages of Greek literature, best of all in the words of Plato already quoted.

That Plato, however, does not indulge in optimistic dreams
is shown by historical facts. This was why at Chalcis (Plut.,
Amat., 761) in the island of Eubœa songs were sung in praise
of good fellowship; this was why the Spartans before the battle
sacrificed to Eros (Ath., xiii, 561*e*); this was why the Theban
army, named the sacred band (*ieros lochos*), was the pride of
the nation and the object of the admiration of Alexander the
Great; and this was why, before they went into battle, friends
at the tomb of Iolaus in Thebes took the last oaths of fidelity.

When the Chalcidians were at war with the Eretrians, Cleomachus came to their assistance at the head of an imposing
squadron of cavalry; but he loved a youth. The battle was
furious, for the enemy's cavalry was well equipped. Cleomachus asked his favourite, whether he would like to see the

battle with him. He said yes, kissed his friend, and set his helmet on his head. Then high spirit filled the elder man's heart and in contempt of death he sprang into the enemy's ranks. He gained the victory but only at the price of his own heroic death. The Chalcidians buried him with all honours and erected on his grave a column, an eternal remembrance for coming generations.

According to Atheneus, the reason why before the battle the Spartans offered sacrifice to Eros was that "they were convinced that in the comradeship of a pair of friends fighting side by side lay safety and victory."

The "sacred band" of the Thebans also has given for all time the best evidence of the lofty ethics of the Greek love of boys. This band of men of noble blood, 300 in number, who had exchanged the oath of love and friendship, was formed, it is said, by Gorgidas. A witticism used to be quoted which Pammenes (Plutarch, *Pelop.*, 18; also Philip's exclamation), the friend of Epameinondas, had coined. He blamed Homer, since in the *Iliad,* (ii, 363) Nestor once makes the people draw themselves up for battle "arranged according to clans and tribes," and thinks that he ought to have formed the order of battle of pairs and friends, since it would then have been indissoluble and unbreakable. The sacred band proved itself brilliantly in the battle of Mantinea, in which Epaminondas fell with Cephisodorus, and the traditions of the gallant band maintained themselves unconquered until the defeat of Cheronea, in which the flower of Greek freedom was broken. When the victor, King Philip of Macedon, surveyed the field of battle after the engagement and saw that all the bodies of the 300 had fatal wounds in their breasts, he could not suppress his tears, and said: "Woe to them who think evil of such men."

It is easy to quote parallels to the Theban sacred band. The words with which Plato attests the greater excellence in war and the lofty joy of sacrifice of these hosts have already been quoted, although Socrates indeed in Xenophon's *Symposium*

(8, 32) does not declare his agreement with them unreservedly. But let one read the story in Xenophon's *Anabasis* (vii, iv, 7) of the emulation of Episthenes and a boy, how each is ready to suffer death for the other. It was that same Episthenes of Olynthus, who later "formed a whole company of beautiful youths and proved himself a hero amongst them." In the *Cyropedia* (vii, 30) it is said once that "it has been shown many times on other occasions that there can be no stronger order of battle than one composed of comrades who are close friends," which is confirmed in the battle between Cyrus and Crœsus, no less than in the battle of Cunaxa (Anab., i, 8, 25; i, 9, 31), in which together with the younger Cyrus his "friends and messmates" also suffer the death of heroes. All this is confirmed by Ælian (*Var. hist.*, iii, 9), who explains the joy of sacrifice by saying that one who loves is animated by two gods, Ares and Eros, while the warrior who does not love is only inspired by Ares. Even in the *Eroticus* of Plutarch, which does not approve of the love of boys, the power of love in war is shown by many examples. Wölfflin (*Philologus*, xxxiv, 413) has drawn attention to the company of friends in the army of Scipio and Cæsar speaks of a league of youth in the land of the Sontiates, a Gallic tribe (*Bell. Gall.*, iii, 22).

After these parallels, which could easily be increased, one will no longer find what is reported of the Theban "sacred band" to be exaggerated. Certainly the life of this phenomenon, like that of the whole of Hellenism itself, was only of short duration. We hear of it first at the battle of Leuctra (371 B.C.) and after the unhappy battle of Chæronea (338 B.C.) its end had come; thus it existed only 33 years.

The story told by Plutarch (*Lycurgus*, 18) also deserves mention. When a youth uttered a painful scream in battle, his lover was afterwards punished by the State.

Consequently, one who loves will, with the assistance of Eros who inspires him "go through fire, water, and raging storm" (Plut., *Amat.*, 760d) for the loved one (as a line from

the unknown tragedian runs), and the courage of the lover
even defies the divine wrath. When the sons of Niobe (Soph.,
frag. 410—*TGF.*, 229) were shot by Apollo for their mother's
sin, the friend endeavours to protect the tender body of the
youngest daughter, and when this is in vain, he carefully
wraps the body in the sheltering garment. Even of the ideal of
Greek heroic might, of Heracles, it is related that his mighty
deeds became easier, when he carried them out before the eyes
of his beloved Iolaus, a gymnasium and shrine in honour of
whom existed until comparatively late times before the gate
of the Prœtidæ in Thebes (Pausan. ix, xxiii, 1; cf. also Plut.,
Pelop., 8). In memory of the love between Heracles and Iolaus
there was celebrated in Thebes the Iolæia (Pind., *Olymp.*, vii,
84, and Schol.) consisting of gymnastic and equestrian games,
in which arms and brazen vessels were given as prizes to the
victor.

In Pausanias we read that an Athenian named Timagoras
loved a certain Meles (i, 30, 1) or Meletus, but had been scorn-
fully treated by the boy. Once, when he found himself on a
steep mountain slope with Timagoras, Meles requested him to
hurl himself down, and he did so, since he valued his life less
highly than the absolute fulfillment of any wish expressed by
his favourite. In despair at the death of his friend Meles then
threw himself also down from the rock.

If we are to draw conclusions from what has been said as to
the ethics of Greek love of boys, the following emerges as an
undeniable fact: The Greek love of boys is a peculiarity of
character, based upon an esthetic and religious foundation.
Its object is, with the assistance of the State, to arrive at the
power to maintain the same and at the fountain-head of civic
and personal virtue. It is not hostile to marriage, but supple-
ments it as an important factor in education. We can also
speak of a decided bi-sexuality among the Greeks.

That passion yields to the seriousness of death and makes
room for the clarified happiness that revels rather in recollec-

tion—that friendship lasts beyond the grave, is shown to us by many epitaphs which, in tenderness of language, dignity of subject, and beauty of form belong to the noblest remains of Greek poetry.

The seventh book of the Palatine Anthology, with its 748 epitaphs, some of them quite excellent, show with what choice taste and tactful feeling the Greeks adorned the grave of their dead heroes and erected tokens of honour of them. I have already collected those devoted to the love of boys in an earlier work, so that it may be sufficient to give only the most beautiful of them here. This epigram was written by the poet Crinagoras (Anth. Pal., vii, 628) to his boy, whom he named Eros; the boy died early on an island and was buried there, and so the poet wishes that this and the neighbouring islands may henceforth be called the Islands of Love. "Other islands ere this have rejected their inglorious names and named themselves after men. Be called Erotides (Love islands), ye Oxeiai (sharp islands) ; it is no shame for you to change; for Eros himself gave both his name and his beauty to the boy whom Dies laid here beneath a heap of clods. O earth, crowded with tombs, do thou lie light on the boy, and do thou lie hushed for his sake."

NEGATIVE AND AFFIRMATIVE OPINIONS

In Greek antiquity there were also of course not wanting opinions which, either generally or under definite assumptions, repudiated the idea of the love of boys. Thus the epigram of Meleager (Anth. Pal., v, 208), which contains the thought that "one who gives this love cannot at the same time also receive it," is negative. Certainly, Meleager did not always hold the same opinion, since we possess numerous epigrams of his, in which love of youths is extolled.

In the romance of Xenophon of Ephesus (ii, 1) the pair of lovers, Habrocomes and Antheia, fall into the hands of pirates, the leader of whom conceives a violent passion for Habrocomes. But the latter says "Oh, the unhappy gift of beauty! So long kept I myself chaste, only now to yield in shameful lust to the love of a pirate! What then is left to me to live for, if from a man I must become a harlot? But I will not submit to his desires, I would rather be dead and save my chastity!"

The seduction of boys was in any case unreservedly repudiated. Thus it is said in a comedy of Anaxandrides (frag. 33, 12, in Ath., vi, 227b—CAF., II, 147) "and a little boy in the bloom of youth, by what kind of charms or by what seductive words could anyone succeed in catching him, if one did not also make use of the art of the fisherman?" In a comedy of Baton (frag. 5 in Ath., iii, 103c and vii, 279a—CAF., III, 238) an indignant father complains of a philosopher who has corrupted his son by his false doctrines.

Further, it was quite generally made the subject of reproach if a boy gave himself up for money or any other kind of payment. I have already proved this by a quotation from the *Plutus* of Aristophanes (153 ff.), and poets are never weary of recalling the good old times when a boy, as a reward for favours granted, was satisfied with a little bird, a tomtit, a missel-thrush, a robin, a quail, or even a ball to play with and such-like trifles.

Here it may be mentioned that women, as was to be expected, on the whole objected to everything that had to with this love of boys, and thus, in a comedy by an unknown author, a woman says: "I do not care for a man who himself wants one" (frag. in Lucian, *pseud.*, 28—CAF., iii, 497).

That hetairæ also were jealous of the homosexual intrigues of their customers was a matter of course, but is also confirmed by the conversation of the two hetairæ Drosis (the dewy) and Chelidonion (the little swallow) in Lucian (*Dial. meretr.*, 10). Drosis has received a letter from the pupil Cleinias in which he writes that he cannot visit her any more, since the teacher Aristænetus watches every step. She complains of her trouble to her friend Chelidonion:—

"*Drosis*: Meanwhile, I am dying for love. Now Dromon tells me that Aristænetus is a pederast and only uses his knowledge as an excuse to attract the most beautiful young men; he talks much and often secretly with Cleinias and makes him great promises, as if he would make him equal to the gods. He also reads to him certain erotic dialogues of the old philosophers with their pupils, and, in a word, he is always about with him, but Dromon has threatened to tell the young man's father.

"*Chelidonion*: You ought to have greased his palm properly!

"*Drosis*: I have done that, but he is mine without that, for he is violently in love with that maid of mine, Nebris.

"*Chelid.*: If that is so, be of good courage: everything will turn out as you wish. I think I will also write on a wall of the Ceramicus, where his father is in the habit of walking, in large letters: 'Aristænetus is corrupting Cleinias,' so that I may support Dromon's accusation."

(Perhaps the writer might attain her object, to separate the lover from his rival; but it would at the same time terribly compromise the loved one. In ancient Greece there was no idea of this kind. It is, of course, not so much the reproach of pederasty as such, with which she hopes to injure Aristænetus, as the fact that he misuses his influence as teacher. While the father hopes that the son is being brought up by his teacher to become a famous man, he is only regarded by him as a favourite.)

"*Drosis*: But how will you write that without anyone seeing you?

"*Chelid.*: By night, Drosis, with a lump of coal.

"*Drosis*: Good luck to you! If you help me to fight, I still hope to get the better of that windbag Aristænetus."

HISTORY OF GREEK LOVE OF BOYS

Naturally, it cannot belong to our task in the present book to examine more closely the different theories, especially of medical men, as to how the problem generally is to be explained. It would also be superfluous, since not only have these different attempts at explanation been clearly and conveniently collected in Hirschfeld's standard work, but also that Greek love of boys at least, of which alone we are speaking here, in general needs no explanation at all as a phenomenon difficult to understand. Some space may be given, however, to a description of its historical development.

Goethe's assertion that "the love of boys is as old as humanity" is confirmed by modern science. The oldest literary testimony hitherto known dates back more than 4500 years, and is to be found in an Egyptian papyrus which proves not only that pederasty was at that time widespread in Egypt, but also that it was presumed to exist amongst the gods as a matter of course.

The first beginnings of the Greek love of boys are lost in prehistoric times, even in the darkness of Greek mythology, which is completely saturated with stories of pædophilia. The Greeks themselves transfer the beginnings to the oldest times of their legendary history. The assertion, often naïvely made, that in the Homeric poems there is as yet no trace of the love of boys to be met with, and that it was a phenomenon which first appeared during the so-called decadence is, in my opinion, false, for I have already shown in an earlier work (in *Anthropophyteia*, ix, pp. 291 ff.) that the bond of friendship between Achilles and Patroclus (the most important passages are *Iliad*, 84; ix, 186, 663; xviii, 22 ff., 65, 315, 334; xix, 209, 315), however ideal it was, yet contains a high percentage of homoerotic sentiment and action; that the Homeric epos also abounds in undoubted traces of ephebophilia, and that no one in the ancient times of Greece ever supposed otherwise.

The *Iliad*, the greatest old epos of the Greeks that has come down to us, represents a hymn to friendship. From the third book onwards the love of the two youths, Achilles and Patroclus, runs through the whole poem until the conclusion, and is represented in such detail that one can no longer speak of mere friendship. This shows itself still more when Achilles learns that Patroclus has fallen in battle. Terrible is the sorrow of the unhappy youth, who stands, a prey to gloomy forebodings, on the seashore, tormented by uncertainty; words die on his lips, while his soul is torn by sorrow; he strews dust upon the crown of his head; then, quite overcome, he throws himself upon the ground, pulling out his hair. After the first rage of his sorrow has gradually calmed down, when the elementary burst of passion is followed by a slow bleeding to death of the soul, then his only thought is to take vengeance on him who has robbed him of what he loved best. He desires neither food nor drink, and his soul thirsts only for revenge.

He vows to his dead friend that he will not celebrate his obsequies "until he has brought him the weapons of Hector, the murderer. He will also slay twelve noble youths before the funeral pyre, Troy's noble sons, in anger at thy murder." But before he can carry out his revenge, he relieves his heart by a touching lament for the dead. Among other things he says: "O never could anything more bitter come upon me, no, not even if I should hear of my father's death."

All this is language of love, not of friendship, and so the ancients have nearly always regarded the bond. To give only one piece of evidence, one of the poems of the Anthology (Anth. Pal., vii, 143; cf. Pindar, *Olymp.*, x, 19; Xen., Sympos., 8, 31; Lucian, *Toxaris,* 10; Ovid. *Tristia,* i, 9, 29) says: "Two men most distinguished by friendship and in arms, farewell, son of Æacus, and thou, son of Menœtius."

It is clear from the Odyssey (xxiv, 78; cf. iii, 109; xi, 467; xxiv, 15) that, after the death of Patroclus, Antolochus took his place with Achilles, meaning, of course, that Homer is unable to imagine the chief hero of his poem without a favourite. From this passage we further learn that Achilles, Patroclus, and Antilochus were buried in a common grave, as the three were often named together in life.

The bond of friendship between Achilles and Patroclus was referred to by the great tragic writer Eschylus as based on

sensuality, and this author was still near enough to the age
of the Homeric epos to understand its underlying spirit perfectly. A drama of Eschylus that is not preserved was called the
Myrmidons (frag. in *TGF.*, 42 ff.; cf. Ath., xiii, 601a, 602e)
and its subject was as follows: Achilles, grievously offended
by Agamemnon, in his animosity abstains from fighting, and
consoles himself in his tent with the joys of love. The Chorus
consisted of the Myrmidons, the vassals of Achilles, who finally
persuade him to let them take part in the battle under the
leadership of Patroclus. The piece ends with the death of the
latter and the wild sorrow of Achilles.

This is confirmed by Lucian (*Amores*, 54; cf. Plut., *Amat.*,
5, *De adul. et amico*, 19; Xen., *Sympos.*, 8, 31; Eschines, i, 142;
Martial, xi, 44, 9), who says: "Patroclus also, the favourite of
Achilles, did not merely sit opposite to him listening to his
lyre, but the driving-power of this friendship also was lust."

It may be mentioned that Phedrus (Plato, *Sympos.*, 179e ff.),
in his speech on Eros, reverses the situation, making Patroclus
the lover, and Achilles, as the younger and handsomer, the
loved one.

But still further proofs could be brought to show that it is
false to assert that the Homeric epos knows nothing of homosexuality. Homer already speaks not only of the rape of the
Phrygian royal boy Ganymede (*Il.*, xx, 231), and expressly
declared that he was carried off because of his beautiful figure,
but also of an extensive trade in boys, who were chiefly bought
by Phœnician shipmasters, or more frequently carried off, to
fill the harems of wealthy pashas (*Od.*, xiv, 297, xv, 449; cf.
Movers, *Phönizien* ii, 3, 80). When Agamemnon and Achilles
are finally reconciled, Agamemnon offers the latter a number
of gifts of honor, amongst them several noble youths (*Il.*, xix,
193). If the war-chariot of Achilles is called "sacred" (*Il.*, xvii,
464), Nägelsbach has already recognized that the "sacred fellowship of the warrior and his charioteer is thereby meant to
be indicated" (*Homerische Theologie*, p. 50).

Thus, homosexuality meets us from the oldest times when we have any certain information concerning the Greeks. How the exercise of its sensual functions was handed down to posterity by formal documents is sufficiently shown in the rock inscriptions of the island of Thera—the modern Santorin—in the Cyclades. So it remains to the end of the ancient world, and in this historical summary only individual phases of development need be mentioned.

An important turning-point is indicated by the name of Solon (Eschines, *Tim.*, 138; *Charicles,* ii, 262 ff.), who, himself a homosexual, issues important laws for the regulation of pederasty, providing in the first place, especially, that a slave might not have connection with a free-born boy. This shows two things: first, that pædophilia was recognized in Athens by the legislator, and secondly that the legislator did not consider the feeling of superiority of the free born to be diminished by intimate relations with slaves. Further, laws were issued (Eschines, *Tim.,* 13-15) which were intended to protect free-born youths from abuse during their minority. Another law deprived those of their civic rights who incited free boys to offer their charms for sale professionally; for prostitution has nothing to do with pædophilia, of which we are speaking here, and in which we must rather think always only of a voluntary relationship that is based upon mutual affection.

Further, these laws of Solon only affected Athenian full citizens, while the great mass of *Xenio,* that is, non-Athenian immigrants, had complete freedom in this matter. Thereby the efficiency of these laws early became questionable; even the severity of the punishments cannot have acted too much as a deterrent, since the *prophasis philias* always was a way out, that is, the protestation that it was done "out of affection"; and of course youths certainly often chose the momentary advantage, without troubling about the loss of civic privileges that eventually threatened them in the distant future. But that these laws were not meant to strike at pæderastia itself, indeed not even at its organization and use as a profession, is shown by the fact that the State itself levied a tax on those who put boys and youths at the disposal of lovers, as well as on the public women's houses (Eschines, *Tim.*, 119).

Diogenes Laërtius (Xen., *Mem.*, ii, 6, 28) says that Socrates, when a boy, had been the favorite of his teacher Archelaus, which is confirmed by Porphyrius, (ib., 201) who says that Socrates when a youth of seventeen years was not averse from the love of Archelaus, for at that time he was much given to sensuality, which was later supplanted by zealous intellectual work.

Further, Xenophon makes Socrates say: "And perhaps I may be able to help you in the search for good and noble boys, since I am given to love; for whenever I terribly love men I strive with my whole heart that, while loving them, I may in my turn be loved; and desiring them, may in my turn be desired; and that, when desiring to be with them, my society may be sought in return."

In the *Symposion* of Plato (177d, 198d) Socrates says: "I profess to understand nothing but love affairs" and "I affirm that I am capable in matters of love," with which several passages in Xenophon's *Symposion* (i, 9; iii, 27) agree: e.g. "I can mention no time, when I was not madly in love with someone," or when Socrates describes the impression which the young Autolycus makes upon him: "As a fire flaming up in the night draws all men's eyes to him, so the beauty of Autolycus at first captivates all men's looks, none who looked upon him remaining unmoved in heart."

The effect produced when Critobulus sat next him is thus described (Xen., *Mem.*, i, 3, 12): "That was a bad thing. I have been obliged to rub my shoulder for five days, as if an animal had stung me, and into my very marrow I thought I could trace the pain such as an animal inflicts."

Are these the words of a man who has renounced the sensuality of love? It is also clear from the Platonic *Alcibiades,* i, and *Symposion* that the beauty of Alcibiades made a violent and lasting impression on Socrates.

Certainly there are several passages in which Socrates not only did not do homage to sensual love of youth, but even tried to dissuade his friends from it. One such passage is contained in a conversation held by Socrates with Xenophon, in which a warning is given even against kissing a youth: "Do not beautiful boys with their kisses inspire you with something fearful, even though you cannot see it? Do you not know that that animal called Beautiful and Blooming, is much more dangerous than poisonous spiders? These can only hurt by contact, but the other animal, without any contact, pours in its poison that clouds the understanding, even from a great distance, if one only looks at it. Therefore, my dear Xenophon, I advise you, when you see a beautiful boy, to take flight as rapidly as possible." Further expressions of the same kind may be found in Kiefer.

On the other hand, it must not be concealed that Greek antiquity itself did not believe so readily in the pædophilia of Socrates as being only of an intellectual kind; and that is the decisive point so far as we are concerned, for men living in— or so near to—the relevant time were in a very advantageous position for passing an essentially better judgment than is possible for us with our still very fragmentary knowledge. In the *Clouds*, certainly, the humorous comedy of Aristophanes, in which Socrates is made fun of in every conceivable way, there is no single word from which one might conclude that the master was addicted to coarsely sensual pædophilia.

To sum up: Socrates, as a Hellene, certainly always had an open eye for boyish and youthful beauty; intimate companionship with the ephebi was also indispensable for him; but he himself as far as possible abstained from giving any practical bodily proof of his affection. He was even capable of renouncing the sensual, since his incomparable art of regulating the souls of youths and of leading them towards the greatest possible perfection, offered sufficient compensation. This power of abstinence he also sought to place before others as an ideal; that he would have required it from all was nowhere suggested nor would it have been held to be consonant with the wisdom of "the wisest of all the Greeks."

LOCAL DETAILS

To begin with the Cretans, since these, according to Timeus (Ath., xiii, 602*f*) were the first Greeks who were fond of boys, we must first remember that, according to the incontestable testimony of Aristotle (*De Republica,* ii, 10, 1272), the love of boys in Crete was not only tolerated but was also regulated by the State in order to prevent over-population. The extent to which the love of boys was a national practice there, is clear from the fact that the Cretans ascribed the rape of Ganymede which, according to an elsewhere unanimous tradition, was carried out by Zeus to their ancient King Minos, as could be read in the *Cretan History* of Achemenes (Ath., xiii, 601*e*). Whether it was Zeus or Minos who carried off Ganymede, certainly in Crete as in many other Greek states the rape of boys had long been an established custom. The Cretan rape is attested by many writers: it is described most fully by Ephorus of Cyme (Strabo, x, 483*f*; also Plutarch, *De lib. educ,* ii *F*; Plato, Laws, viii, 836), who composed a grandly planned *History of the Greeks* from the earliest times to the year 340 B.C.

"Three or four days beforehand, the *erastes* (lover) announces to his friends that he intends to carry out the rape. To conceal the boy anywhere or to forbid him to go to the street agreed upon, would indicate the greatest disgrace, since it would only mean that the boy does not deserve such a lover. If they have met, and the lover in rank and the like is equal to the boy or is even superior to him, for the sake of the traditional custom they pretend to pursue the lover, but in reality gladly let him go on his way. But if the lover is not his equal, then they snatch the boy from him with violence. But they only pursue him until the lover has brought the boy into his house. But the one who is distinguished for beauty is considered less worth desiring than one renowned for bravery and modesty.

After that the boy is presented by his friend with a present, who takes him where he pleases. But the witnesses of the rape accompany them; then a solemn meal takes place, after which they return to the city. After two months the boy is dismissed with rich presents. His legally established presents are a military equipment, an ox and a goblet, besides a number of valuable gifts, so that his friends contribute towards the expenses. He offers the ox to Zeus and gives his friends a meal from it. But if a beautiful boy of good family finds no lover, this is considered a disgrace, since the reason for it must be in his character. The boys who are given preference by the rape are specially honoured.

Thus they receive the best place in the dances and racing competitions, are allowed to wear the dress with which the lover has presented him, and that distinguishes them from the others, and not only this, but even when they are grown up they wear a special garment, by which everyone, who has become *kleinos* can be immediately recognized; the loved one is called *kleinos* (the famous, the celebrated), the lover *philetor*."

The rape of boys also existed in very ancient times in Corinth, as to which Plutarch (*Amat. narr.*, 2, 772f) has left us an instructive story: "The son of Melissus was Actæon, the most beautiful and the most modest of those of his own age, so that very many desired him, but chiefly Archias, whose family went back to the Heracleidæ and who was prominent among the Corinthians for his wealth and power. Since the boy refused to be persuaded, he resolved to rape him with violence. He consequently rode at the head of a number of friends and slaves before the house of Melissus and attempted to carry off the boy. But the father and his friends offered a bitter resistance, the neighbours also assisted, and during the struggle between the two parties the lad was dragged hither and thither, was fatally injured, and died. But the father lifted up the boy's dead body, carried it into the market-place, and showed it to the Corinthians, while he demanded from them that they should punish those who had been guilty of his death.

They sympathized with him, but otherwise did nothing. The unhappy father afterwards repaired to the Isthmus and threw himself down from a rock, after he had summoned the gods to take vengeance. Soon afterwards a bad harvest and famine visited the state. The oracle declared that it was the wrath of Poseidon, who would not be appeased, until the death of Actæon was expiated. When Archias, who was one of those sent to consult the oracle, heard of this, he did not return to Corinth, but sailed to Sicily and founded the city of Syracuse. There, after he had had two daughters, Ortygia and Syracusa, he was murdered by his favourite Telephus."

Such is the story. Its meaning is clear. The rape of boys must remain a seeming one. To employ violence, if the father is not agreed, becomes a crime, the sin of which the gods themselves avenge, and (herein lies the tragic irony) by the hand of the boy; this follows the *Dikē* of Hybris and agrees with the "Laws of Gortyn," which avenge the offering of violence to a boy by severe punishment.

In Thebes, the rape of boys was referred to the ancient King Laïus who, according to the Theban version, had inaugurated pederasty by carrying off Chrysippus the son of Pelops and making him his favourite (Ath., xiii, 602; Elian, *Hist. an.*, vi, 15; *Var. hist.*, xiii, 5; Apollodorus, iii, 44).

As in Thebes (Xen., *Symp.*, viii, 32f; Plato, *Symp.*, 182b), so also in Elis the love of boys had a sensual element, although the religious feeling was not wanting. Plutarch also attests the combination of sensuality and a sacrificing heroic spirit in Chalcis (Plut., *Amat.*, 17; there also the song) on the island of Eubœa and its colonies. A song that became popular there has been preserved and also a similar one of Seleucus (Ath., xv, 697d) by whom the love of boys is called more valuable than marriage on account of the knightly fellowship of which it is the cause. The song of the people of Chalcis, the author of which is unknown, is as follows: "O ye boys of brave fathers, shining in the grace of your charms, never grudge the companionship of your beauty to honourable men, for in the cities of Chalcis, in union with manly virtue still ever blooms your gracious, heart-infatuating sweet youth."

According to Aristotle (Plutarch, *Amat.*, 761), this song went back to the bond of love between the heroic Cleomachus and his young friend; or it may, perhaps, have arisen out of the belief that Cleomachus's victory was due to his enthusiasm having been encouraged and sustained by the presence of his friend as a witness of his bravery. What taste the Chalcidians had for beautiful boys is also proved by the notice of Hesychius, that *chalkdizein* is synonymous with *paiderastein*. This is confirmed by Athenæus, who adds that the Chalcidians, like others, made claim to the honour that Ganymede was carried off from a myrtle grove near their city, and they proudly showed this place, which they called *Harpagion* (the place of the rape) to strangers.

According to Xenophon (*Rep. Lac.*, 2, 13) the love between a man and a youth was considered entirely as a conjugal union.

Throughout Greece there were festivals which served for the glorification of boyish and youthful beauty, or at which it at least appeared conscious of its aim. Thus at Megara the spring-festival *Diocleia* (Theocr., xii, 30) was celebrated, at which contests of boys and youths in kissing took place; at Thespiæ (Plut., *Amat.*, 1; Pausan., ix, 31, 3; Ath., xiii, 601a) the festival of Eros, at which prize songs on the love of boys were sung; at Sparta the festival of the naked boys, the *Gymnopædia*, also the *Hyacinthia*; and the island of Delos

(Lucian, *De Saltat.*, 16) is said to have specially rejoiced in the round dances of boys (see pp. 109, 115, etc., and 164).

When Plutarch (*Prov. Al.*, i, 44), speaking of the boys of the Peloponnesian city of Argos, says that "those who have kept their youthful bloom pure and uncorrupted, as an honourable distinction lead the procession at a festival with a shield, according to old custom," he does not mean that these boys have not been the favourites of men of standing, but only that, so long as they were still boys, they had abstained from female intimacy.

The question of the love of boys in Sparta (Xen., *Rep. Lac.*, 2, 13; *Sympos.*, 8, 35; Plut., *Lyc.*, 17f; *Ages.*, 20; *Cleom.*, 3; *Institut. Lac.*, 7; Elian, *Var. hist.*, iii, 10) is very difficult to decide, since on this point the reports of ancient times are actually contradictory. Xenophon and Plutarch assert that the Spartan love of boys certainly depended upon the sensual pleasure in corporeal beauty, but did not arouse sensual desires also. To have designs upon a boy sensually was put on the same level as a father seeking his son or a brother his brother, and whoever did so was throughout his life "without honour," that is, he was deprived of his rights as a citizen.

Maximus of Tyre (*Diss.*, xxvi, 8), a rhetorician who lived in the time of the Antonines and Commodus and so wrote very late, says that in Sparta the man only loved a boy as a beautiful statue, many men one boy and one boy many men.

This is not only improbable according to the Greek idea of the nature of the love of boys that has been sufficiently described, and above all from physiological reasons, but has also been abundantly proved incredible by the following considerations. Xenophon (*Rep. Lac.*, 2, 14) himself is obliged to admit that it never occurred to any Greek to believe in this ideal side of the Spartan love of boys and no more; the Attic comic poets also have in constant outbursts thrown light upon just that sensual character of the Spartan love of boys, which is still further strengthened by the terms collected by Hesychius and Suïdas (sn. *Kusolakon, lakomzein, lakonikon, tropon*), with which the language of daily life indicated the Spartan peculiarity. But that which turns the scale is that the man who was best acquainted with such matters, namely Plato (*Laws,* i, 636, viii, 836; cf. also Cicero, *Rep.,* iv, 4), decidedly rejects the idea that the Dorian love of boys dispensed with sensuality.

EPIC POETRY

The Mythical Pre-Historic Period

Pamphos (Pausan., 27, 2) had already written hymns to Eros, so that it may be justly affirmed that Eros stands at the beginning of Hellenic culture.

Part of the story of Orpheus, whose existence is denied by Aristotle (Cic., *De nat. deor.,* i, 38, 107), and who is taken by Erwin Rohde to be a symbol of the union of the religions of Appollo and Dionysus, has been already told previously, but after the final disappearance of Eurydice, his wife, into Hades, there comes a singular sequel. Orpheus, in his loneliness, returns to his Thracian mountain home, where the famous singer is surrounded by enthusiastic crowds of women and girls because of his touching love for his wife. But he "rejects all female love," whether it be that he has had unfortunate experience of it before, or whether he was unwilling to be unfaithful to his wife. But he certainly taught the Thracians to turn their affection to the love of tender boys, and, "so long as youth laughs, to enjoy the brief spring of life and its flowers." So says Ovid. An extremely important passage, since it shows that the solitary husband compensates himself with the love of boys, and, what is even more important, that according to the ancient idea of homosexual intercourse this was not regarded as an offence against wedded faithfulness, "since he was unwilling to be unfaithful to his wife." And henceforth he is so devoted to this Greek form of love, that not only does marriage become for him merely an episode but the songs now sung by him contain nothing but the glorification of the love of boys. Thus the paradox becomes a fact; Orpheus, who even at the present day is most widely known as a model of conjugal fidelity, is for antiquity the man who introduced the love of boys in his home in Thrace and was so devoted to it that girls and women, who felt themselves spurned, finally attacked him, cruelly mutilated and killed him. Further, the legend informs us that his head was thrown into the sea and finally cast up on the shore of the island of Lesbos. Of Lesbos? That is, of course, not accidental, for there later Sappho arose, who was for Greeks the greatest advocate of homosexual love.

The Epic Cycle

In the *Œdipodeia* it was told how Laïus the father of Œdipus, fell desperately in love with the beautiful Chrysippus, the son of Pelops, and finally carried him off by violence. Pelops uttered a fearful curse against the robber.

The *Little Iliad* (*Ilias Parva* (see Kinkel, *Epicorum Græcorum Fragmenta*, Leipzig, 1877, p. 41, frag. 6)) of Lesches treated as an episode the rape of Ganymede (*Il.*, xx, 231; v, 266), the young son of the Trojan King Laomedon, upon whom Zeus bestowed as a recompense a vine fashioned of gold by the art of Hephæstus, while in Homer Ganymede is a son of King Tros, who receives a pair of thoroughbred horses as a recompense.

The rape of Ganymede is described in the fifth of the so-called Homeric Hymns (v, 202 ff.) in still greater detail.

Hesiod

In his *Shield of Heracles* (57) the poet Hesiod has told of the struggle with Cycnus which Heracles had to endure. He summons his favorite and brother-in-arms Iolaus, who was "by far the dearest of all men to him." The length of the conversations between them prevents their being given here; their tender language and their whole tone prove that already Hesiod, as all later writers, considered Iolaus to be, not only the companion-in-arms, but also the favourite of the hero.

From a fragment we learn that Hesiod himself loved a youth named Batrachus (Suïdas, in Kinkel), on whose early death he had written an elegy.

Phanocles

At a time which cannot be accurately defined, Phanocles had composed a garland of elegies entitled *Love Stories, or Beautiful Boys*. These elegies represented what may be called a history of the love of boys in poetic form with abundant examples from stories of the gods and heroes. Among the fragments a longer one of 28 lines (longer frag. in Stobæus, *Flor.*, 64, 14) in which the love of Orpheus for the boy Calaïs and the fearful murder of the singer by the Thracian women are described, is prominent. It is interesting to find that the Christian Fathers of the Church—such as Clement of Alexandria, Lactantius, and Orosius—used the poems of Phanocles to prove the immorality of paganism, while Friedrich Schlegel (*Werke*, iv, 52) translated fragments from him.

Diotimus and Apollonius

Diotimus (Ath., xiii, 603*d*; Schol., *Iliad*, xv, 639; Clem. Rom., *Homil.*, v, 15; Suïdas, s.v. *enrubatos*) of Adramyttium in Mysia in the third century B.C. wrote an epos—the *Struggles of Heracles,* in which he endeavoured to prove the rather silly idea that the mighty deeds of Heracles are to be ascribed to his love for Eurystheus.

Apollonius of Rhodes (Apol. Rhod., I, 1207; III, 114 ff.), the most important of the Alexandrine epic writers, lived in the third century B.C. Only the most famous of his poems is preserved, namely, *Argonautica,* that is, the adventure of the Argonauts, in four books. The poem, abounding in charming details, contains the story of the love of Heracles for Hylas, his carrying off by the nymphs of the spring, and the boundless sorrow of the hero at the loss of the boy.

I here quote the episode of Eros and Ganymede: "They were playing for golden dice, as like minded boys are wont to do. And already greedy Eros was holding the palm of his left hand quite full of them under his breast, standing upright and on the bloom of his cheeks a sweet blush was glowing. But the other sat crouching hard by, silent and downcast, and he had two dice left which he threw one after the other, and was angered by the loud laughter of Eros. And lo, losing them straightway with the former, he went off empty-handed."

Nonnus

Nonnus, a Greek of Panopolis in the Egyptian Thebaid, who lived in the fourth or fifth century A.D., is the author of a bulky poem in no fewer than 48 cantos called *Dionysiaca,* that is, the life and deeds of Dionysus. The vast epos describes in bewildering superabundance the victorious expedition of Dionysus to India, interwoven with so many episodes and separate myths, that the whole represents a work that is certainly extremely valuable and interesting, but by no means a unity. The singular thing is that the author was a Christian, but he has created an enthusiastic hymn of Bacchantic, and consequently heathen ecstasy, such as might stand alone in the whole of literature. Hence, there occur in the work so large a number of homosexual episodes that what is most important can only be mentioned here, not given in detail.

The beauty of the youthful Hermes (iii, 412 ff.) is eloquently described, while the beauty of Cadmus (iv, 105) takes as many as fifty-six lines. The Erotes are represented dancing at the wedding of Cadmus and Harmonia (v, 96); with obvious satisfaction the poet tells of the games that Dionysus shared and enjoyed with boys (ix, 160 ff.), and describes in detail how he bathes in company with the wanton and lascivious satyrs (x, 139).

The idyll with the boy Ampelos occupies considerable space (x, 175 to xii), and his beauty is painted in glowing colours; Dionysus sees the boy and the description of the love with which he is inflamed for him runs, with various episodes, through two cantos. Like a second Eros, only without wings and quiver, Ampelos appeared to the god as he formerly revealed himself in a forest of Phrygia, and he is excessively happy because of the love which Dionysus shows towards him. There ensues a love idyll, which is painted by the poet in detail and with great beauty. Dionysus has only the one fear, that Zeus may see the boy and carry him off, since he is even more beautiful than Ganymede. Zeus, however, does not begrudge him his happiness, and that in spite of the Greek idea that everything that is beautiful in the world is destined to find a speedy end. In youthful desire for adventure, Ampelos betakes himself to the hunt, laughing at Dionysus with boyish insolence as the god warns him against the wild animals of the wood. Terrified by an evil omen, Dionysus goes after the boy, finds him safe and clasps him in in his arms enchanted. But destiny does not slumber; an evil spirit prompts Ampelos to ride against an apparently harmless bull, but the bull suddenly turns on him and throws him off his horse, so that he is fatally hurt and dies.

Dionysus is inconsolable, covers the body of the boy, still beautiful in death, with flowers, and strikes up a touching lament. Afterwards he prays to his father Zeus to recall the loved one to life only for a short hour that he may hear once more from his lips words of love; indeed, he curses his immortality, since he cannot now be together with the boy for the whole length of eternity in Hades.

Eros himself takes compassion upon the despair of the

mourner's boundless grief; he appears to him in the form of
a satyr, speaks to him affectionately and advises him to end his
sorrow by taking a fresh love, "for," he says, "the only remedy
for an old love is a new one; look about therefore for a more
excellent boy, even as did Zephyrus who, after the death of
Hyacinthus, became enamoured of Cyparissus;" and, further
to console the bereaved deity and to encourage him to take
a fresh love, Eros then gives him a detailed account of the
story of Calamus and his favourite Carpus.

"Calamus (Kalamos), a son of the river-god Mæander, was
united in tenderest love with Carpus (Karpos), the son of
Zephyrus and one of the Horæ, a youth of surpassing beauty.
When both were bathing in the Mæander and swimming for
a wager, Carpus was drowned. In his grief, Calamus is changed
into a reed, and when it rustled in the wind the ancients heard
in the sound a song of lamentation; but Carpus becomes the
produce of the fields, which returns every year."

A gap in the text does not allow us to know what effect this
had on Dionysus. Probably very little, for now with glowing
sensuality a wanton round dance of the Horæ is described,
which can be introduced here only with intent to bring the
god, who is consumed by longing, to other thoughts. With
this "orgy of the legs, which in the furious whirlwind of the
dance are seen through their transparent robes," the eleventh
book of the story of Dionysus closes.

In the twelfth it is related how the gods, out of compassion
for the sorrow of Dionysus, change the boy Ampelos into a
vine. The god, enchanted, accepts the glorious plant, which is
henceforth sacred to him, and so invents the precious gift of
wine, which he praises in an enthusiastic address. Then the
first gathering and pressing of the newly created wine takes
place, after which a Bacchic orgy concludes the feast that has
developed into a riotous merry-making after a time of deepest
sadness.

Between Rome and Florence a beautiful marble group of

Dionysus and Ampelos was found (cf. Himerius, *Orat.*, 9, 560; Pliny, viii, 31, 74) which is today one of the most valued treasures of the British Museum. The boy is represented just in the act of being changed, offering a bunch of grapes to Dionysus who is tenderly embracing him.

All our extracts from Nonnus, the last epic offshoot of Hellenic beauty and sensual enjoyment, have been taken from the first twelve books, a quarter of the vast poem; the remaining thirty-six cantos contain numerous other homosexual episodes and many descriptions of boyish beauty.

LYRIC POETRY

As lyric poetry is the most direct expression of personal states of mind and feelings, it is only to be expected that in that of the Greeks homosexual love should occupy a large space; and it is, indeed, quite correct to say that lyric poetry generally had its origin in homosexual love. But unfortunately only a lamentably small fragment of Greek lyric has come down to us.

Theognis

Under the name of Theognis, who lived, chiefly in Megara, in the middle of the sixth century B.C., a collection of maxims and rules of life in 1388 lines has come down to us. The last 158 lines are entirely devoted to the love of youths, especially to the poet's favourite Cyrnus. The latter, the son of Polypais, was a noble and beautiful youth, to whom the poet was attached by paternal, but also by sensual love. He desires to teach him worldly wisdom and to bring him up as a true aristocrat. The collection is therefore rich in intrinsic ethical value, which caused it to be used in ancient times as a school book, and at the same time contains a number of love terms of strong, sometimes ardent sensuality.

The poet hesitates between love and indifference, he cannot do without Cyrnus, and yet it is hard to love the modest boy. Indeed, he even threatens to put an end to his life, so that the boy may realize what he has lost. Another time he complained of offended love; that he was sympathetic to Cyrnus, but not Cyrnus to him. The loved one will be famous through him; at all festivals he will be sung of, and even after death he will never be forgotten.

Plato

Under the name of Plato (*PLG.*, frag. 1, 7, 14, 15; cf. Apuleius, *De magia,* 10), the great philosopher and pupil of Socrates, several homosexual epigrams have come down to us. A tender epigram is: "When I kissed you, Agathon, I felt your soul on my lips: as if it would penetrate into my heart with quivering longing." Another epigram is an epitaph on the favourite Dion, "who filled the heart with the madness of love." Two epigrams owe their origin to the beautiful Aster (star). The poet envies the sky, which looks down on his Aster with many eyes, when he, himself a star, looks up at the stars.

Archilochus and Alcæus

Even among the fragments of Archilochus of Paros, who is known for his passionate love for Neobulē, the beautiful little daughter of Lycambes, there is one (frag. 85) containing the admission that "yearning for the boy relaxes his limbs and overpowers him."

Of Alcæus of Mitylene, who was both a poet and hero, mention has already been made. The Lycus there referred to (if Bergk's reading be correct) occurs in a fragment (58) in which the poet, in an attack of ill-humour, says that he will no longer celebrate him in his songs. In another of the few existing fragments (466) he begs someone "to send for the charming Menon, else he would have no enjoyments at the feast."

Ibycus

Only a few of those who enjoy Schiller's beautiful ballad of the *Cranes of Ibycus,* are aware that the hero of the poem, whose death at the hands of a wicked murderer is certain to awaken general sympathy, was called in ancient times the most frenzied lover of boys (Suïdas, sub *Ibycus*). That he did homage to boys all his life, is attested by Cicero (*Tusc.*, iv, 33, 71); even in old age this passion blazed in him to such an extent that Plato expressly drew attention to it (*Parmen.*, 137a); an anonymous epigrammatist in the Palatine Anthology refers to him (vii, 714) as a "lover of boys," and in the same collection he is mentioned in a short list of lyric writers (ix, 184) as one who, during his life, did "cull the sweet bloom of Persuasion and of the love of lads." All this is confirmed by his poetry, of which only a few fragments are preserved. Besides those mentioned above the following (frag. 1) may be quoted: "In spring the quinces, watered by the river streams, bloom in the unspoiled garden of the maidens; and the first shoots of the vine, guarded beneath shady leaves, grow and blossom; but for me love—that, like the Thracian north wind, blasting beneath the lightning and rushing, dark and fearless, from Cypris with scorching madness—is never at rest, and holds possession of my mind throughout my life."

Anacreon and the Anacreontea

Anacreon of Teos, the always cheerful and amiable poet, was born about 560 B.C.; according to Lucian, he lived to the ripe old age of eighty-five, and even in his latter years happiness for him seems to have consisted largely in love and wine. Of his works, the Alexandrians still possessed various poems in five books altogether, most of which have been lost by the unkindness of time. All his poetry is dedicated to love, says Cicero (*Tusc.*, iv, 33, 71; cf. Ovid, *Tristia*, ii, 363). Although he did not disdain female love—and for the sake of example he once complains half jestingly (frag. 14) that a pretty Lesbian girl refuses to play with him, yet during his life it was the ephebus who had just reached his prime to whom his heart and song were devoted, and an imposing list of names is known to us, the bearers of which had inflamed his heart. After a stay at Abdera in Thrace we find him together with Ibycus at the court of Polycrates, the well-known and refined lover of art and magnificence, and ruler of Samos, who had surrounded himself with a court-household of carefully selected pages (Ælian, *Var. Hist.*, ix, 14). Maximus of Tyre says: "Anacreon loves all who are beautiful and extols them all; his songs are full of praise of the curly hair of Smerdis, the eyes of Cleobulus, the youthful bloom of Bathyllus" (xxiv, 9, 247—frag. 44). Again he says that everything that is good is beautiful to love. "I should like to sport with you, O boy, for thou hast the love charm of the Graces" (ibid., 120), and "For the sake of my verses boys would love me; for I sing graceful songs, and I know how to say graceful things" (ibid., 45).

Several epigrams (esp. Anth. Pal., vii, 25, 27, 29, and 31; see also ibid., 23, 23*b*, 24, 26, 28, 30, 32, and 33; and vi, 346) also attest the poet's love for his Smerdis; in the first mentioned, for instance, Simonides in an epitaph says: "Alone in Acheron he grieves not that he has left the sun and dwelleth there in the House of Lethe, but that he has left Megistheus, graceful above all the youth, and his passion for Thracian Smerdis." Of Anacreon's extant fragments at least four are addressed to Smerdis. Thus we read of a stormy wooing, in which he confesses to him that Eros had dashed him down again as powerfully as the smith wields his hammer.

His love for Cleobulus was inflamed in the poet by avenging Nemesis herself, as Maximus of Tyre insists in an anecdote (frag. 3). This love filled the poet with fervent ardour; he entreats Dionysus (frag. 2) to incline the heart of the boy towards him and confesses that he loves Cleobulus, raves after him, looks out only for him.

There is a fragment, in which it is said that no one, if Bathyllus plays the flute, may dance to it, since he cannot turn his gaze away from the charming form of the player (frag. 30). Another fragment is addressed to Megistes (frag. 41;

and see Bergk, *Der Ausgabe des Anakreon*, p. 151, Leipzig, 1834), who takes part in the feast, crowned with a wreath of *agnus castus*, or "tree of chastity," a plant concerning which the ancients gave profound and curious accounts (see esp. Pliny, *Nat. hist.*, xxiv, 38).

Other fragments treat of his love for Leukaspis and Simalos (frags. 18, 22), while others again have come down to us without the name of the favourite. The boy at the mixing-jug is to bring wine and garlands, "that I may not succumb in a boxing-match with Eros." Of a song to Eros, "to whom gods like men are subject," five lines are preserved. The poet also has to complain of rejected love, and at another time he threatens that he will fly up to Olympus, and complain to the Loves, that "my boy will not pass the time of youth with me." He complains that Eros, when, already grown so gray, at last he saw him, waving his gold-glittering wings, flew heedless by. He comically threatens Eros, that he will no longer sing a beautiful hymn in his praise, since he will not wound the ephebus he longs for with his arrow.

Among the imitations of Anacreon—the "Anacreontea"—which are of later date, and in which mention is frequently made of the love of boys, may be specially noticed the little song in which the poet complains that a swallow by its early twittering has awakened him from his dreams of the beautiful Bathyllus. Another cleverly combines the matter of the love song with the manner of the song of war: "You sing of the deeds of the Thebans, of the war shouts of the Phrygians, but I will tell of my conquests; it is neither horse, nor ship, nor foot soldier that hath destroyed me, but another new army launched from the eyes against me."

Pindar

From Pindar, the greatest and most powerful of all Greek lyric poets, who lived from 522 to 442 B.C. we still possess, in addition to an imposing number of fragments, forty-five odes in nearly perfect condition—the songs of victory, which were composed for those who had won the crown in the great national games. The writer's piety made him recast in more respectful form some of the legends that had gathered irreverent accretions. Such a one was that which relates how Tantalus, having invited Zeus to dine, killed the All-Father's son, Pelops, and served him up as a meal as a test of the divine omniscience. But the gods saw through the horrible deception, put the pieces together again and restored the boy to life, and punished Tantalus severely. Such horrors are unendurable to the pious poet; according to his presentation of the legend Pelops has not fallen a victim to the shameful crime of his father, rather had his beauty so inflamed the heart of Poseidon, that he was carried off by him, as later Ganymede was seized by Zeus (*Olym.*, i, 37 ff.).

Pindar thought much the same as his contemporaries about friendship with the ephebi, and we owe to him what is unfortunately only a fragment of one of the most glorious poems ever written (frag. 123). The gods also rejoiced at his friendship for his favourite, Theoxenus. It was related that Pindar had prayed the gods to give him the most beautiful thing there was in the world; Theoxenus was the gift, and when, afterwards, the poet was present at a gymnastic contest in Argos he, during an attack of faintness, leaned on this boy's bosom and died in his arms.

Pindar's ashes were carried to Thebes, where as Pausanias tells us (ix, 23, 2), they were buried in a tomb in the Hippodrome before the Proetidian gate.

Theocritus

Of the thirty idylls preserved under the name of Theocritus, who lived about 310-245 B.C., no fewer than eight are exclusively devoted to the love of youths, and also in the others boys and love for them are frequently spoken of.

One, perhaps, the most beautiful of the poems of Theocritus about youths, inscribed ("the Favourites") contains a conversation of the no longer youthful poet with his own heart. Certainly, his reason advised him to renounce all idea of love, but his heart teaches him that the battle with Eros is a useless enterprise. "For irresistible the life of the boy rushes in like the swift foot of the hind, and in the morning thou already seest him striving further after the fickle kiss of another love. Not lasting, however, was the most delightful enjoyment of youthful bloom. Yet thou consumest thy vigour in the torments of longing, and his charming picture is all that thy dream will paint for thee."

In another poem, which can hardly be Theocritus's own, we read the last complaints of an unhappy lover, who puts an end to his torments by suicide, and the revenge taken by the insulted Eros on the prudish boy who, while he is bathing in the gymnasium, is struck down by a falling marble statue of Eros.

A third poem, also inscribed *paidika,* is a complaint against the inconstancy of the loved one, an exhortation to remain faithful, and a reminder, while still in his tender youthful bloom, of the old age that threatens. He should therefore requite his love, so that their bond may be one day spoken of like the love of Achilles and Patroclus.

Tender and affectionate is a poem which gives expression to the joy of seeing the favourite again after three days of separation, and to the wish that their love may always be like that which flourished in Megara, where Diocles introduced the boys' kissing contest (p. 109), "about whose grave, so surely as spring cometh round, your children vie in a kissing-match, and whosoever presseth lip sweetliest upon lip, cometh away to's mother loaden with garlands." "How blessed are both in the joy of love! Their picture shines to us from ancient time —how he devotes his love to the boy!"

The charming poem entitled the "Harvest Festival," al-

ready called by old Heinsius the "queen" of the poems of
Theocritus, is dedicated to the memory of a day joyfully spent
on the island of Cos, and the poet relates how he wanders
from the city into the country with two friends. On the way
they meet a goatherd by name Lycidas, to whom the poet,
after a brief conversation, proposes that he should rest and try
his skill against him in a country singing-match. Lycidas gladly
consents, and then sings a *propemptikon* (farewell song), in
which he wishes his beloved Ageanax a happy journey over
the sea:

> Ageanax late though he be for Mitylene bound
> Heav'n bring him blest wi' the season's best to have safe and sound;
> And that day I'll make merry, and bind about my brow
> The anise sweet or snowflake neat or rosebuds all a-row,
> And there by the hearth I'll lay me down beside the cheerful cup,
> And hot roast beans shall make my bite and elmy wine my sup;
> And soft I'll lie, for elbow-high my bed strown thick and well
> Shall be of crinkled parsley, mullet, and asphodel;
> And so t'Ageanax I'll drink, drink wi' my dear in mind,
> Drink wine and wine-cup at a draught and leave no lees behind.
> My pipers shall be two shepherds, a man of Acharnæ he,
> And he a man of Lycópè; singer shall Tityrus be,
> And sing beside me of Xénea and neatherd Daphnis' love.

After that Theocritus declares to his friend how much the
song has pleased him, and answers with another, in which he
contrasts his own happiness in love with the ill-luck of his
friend Aratus, a famous physician and poet of Miletus, who
had fallen in love with the beautiful but coy Philinus: "Yet
you, winged host of the Loves, with cheeks red as peaches, now
hit Philinus with curly hair, awake in him desire for my
friend. After all, he is not so young now, already the girls
chaff the fool—'Ay, ay, Philinus, you see your beauty is already gone!' So now take my heartfelt advice. Let the foolish
boy run and let some other pretty ones, my dear friend Aratus,
feel this deep sorrow."

To console his friend Aratus, whose art as a physician could

not help him against the wounds inflicted on him by Eros,
Theocritus wrote a longer epic poem, in which the passionate
love of Heracles for Hylas, his rape by the nymphs of the
spring, and the despair of the lonely hero are fully described.
(Theocritus, 30, 23, 29, 12, 7, 13. Further paidophil passages
in Theocritus are 15, 124; 20, 41; 6, 42; 3, 3: *to Kalon
Kekhilēmene*—a form of address so sweet that (according to
Gellius, ix, 9) it is impossible to translate it; 2, 77-80, 44, 150,
115; epigram 4.)

TRIFLES FROM OTHER LYRIC POETS

Praxilla, the amiable poetess of healthy merriment and
sensual practical wisdom, had told in one of her poems of the
rape of Chrysippus by Laïus, in another of the love of Apollo
for Carnos (frags. 6 and 7).

According to Athenæus Stesichorus, "Who was to no small
extent a sexualist," also wrote this kind of poem, which was
already named in antiquity "a 'song about boys,'" (Ath., xiii,
601a). But none of them is preserved.

Bacchylides (frag. 13) mentions among the works of peace
the occupations of youths in the gymnasia, feasts, and the
bursting forth of songs about boys.

"Skolia" was the name given to the drinking-songs, which
were sung after the meal, when wine loosened men's tongues,
chiefly by the guests in order, and composed *ex tempore*. Such
an improvization runs as follows: "I would that I could become a lyre of ivory; then the boys would carry me to the
Dionysian dance" (Skolion, 19).

The poetical remains of Bion of Smyrna, a younger contemporary of Theocritus, are trifling. From his poem on
Lycidas I mention the lines: "I have sung of another than
Lycidas, but my song then sounded like a lamentable stam-
mer; I sang of the marvels of Eros and Lycidas, the beautiful,
and now my love-song would resound loftily and glorious."

In another poem (ix) he addresses Hesperus, the evening

star: "Evening Star, which art the golden light of the lovely Child o' the Foam, dear Evening Star, which art the holy jewel of the blue blue night, even so much dimmer than the moon as brighter than any other star that shines, hail, gentle friend, and while I go a-serenading my shepherd love show me a light instead of the moon, for that she, being new but yesterday, is all too quickly set. I be no thief nor highwayman, 'tis not for that I'm abroad tonight—but a lover; and lovers deserve all aid."

Lastly, the eighth poem is a list of famous pairs of friends, praising those who found the happiness of mutual love, Theseus and Peirithous, Orestes and Pylades, Achilles and Patroclus.

THE POEMS OF THE ANTHOLOGY

We have already so often had to quote passages by way of testimony from among the thousands of epigrams contained in the Codex Palatinus, that in this summary of homosexual literature only those supplementary ones need be given which furnish anything specially characteristic. Thus Antistius (Anth. Pal., xi, 40): "Cleodemus, Eumenes' boy, is still small, but tiny as he is, he dances nimbly with the boys. Look! he has even girt on his hips the skin of a dappled fawn and a crown of ivy adorns his yellow hair. Make him big, O kindly Bacchus, so that thy little servant may soon lead holy dances of young men." The epigram of Lucilius (xi, 217) strikes us as almost modern: "To avoid suspicion, Apollophanes married and walked as a bridegroom through the middle of the market, saying: 'To-morrow at once I will have a child.' Then when to-morrow came he appeared carrying the suspicion instead of a child."

The twelfth book of the Palatine Anthology, which is quite exclusively devoted to the love of youths (258 epigrams of nearly 1300 lines altogether) bears in the MS. the title "The boyish Muse of Straton." Besides Straton, whose poems stand at the beginning and end of the collection, nineteen other

poets are represented, amongst them good, indeed high-sound-
ing names; we have besides thirty-five epigrams without the
name of the composer. The book may be called a hymn of
Eros; the same subject over and over again, but in as many
forms and endless variations as nature itself.

Straton of Sardis. (Anth. Pal., xii, 1, 2, 5, 244, 198, 201,
227, 180, 195)

This poet, who lived in the time of the emperor Hadrian,
arranged a collection of epigrams on beautiful boys, and the
twelfth book of the Anthology contains ninety-four poems
under his name.

The collection does not begin with an invocation of the
Muses, as the poems of antiquity usually do, but of Zeus, who
in very ancient times had himself set the example to men by
the carrying off of Ganymede and since then was regarded as
the patron of the love of boys. The subject of which the poet
intends to treat differs considerably from that which had
hitherto been usual: "Look not in my pages for Priam by the
altar, nor for the woes of Medea and Niobe, nor for Itys in
his chamber and the nightingales amid the leaves; for earlier
poets wrote of all these things in profusion. But look for sweet
love mingled with the jolly Graces, and for Bacchus. No grave
face suits them."

Straton's Muse also had to do with boys, but as there is no
difference and no choice, he loves all who are beautiful. Nothing can resist this love, it is stronger than the poet, who no
doubt would many times like to shake off the yoke, but time
after time perceives that it is beyond him. If the boy is beautiful and above all his looks so charming that one can see that
the Graces have stood by his cradle, then the poet cannot
rejoice enough; certainly, the greater the beauty, the more
speedy the complaint that it is only transitory and immediately
disappears.

The great passion finds its expression also in poetry, and the twelfth book of the anthology accordingly also contains a number of strongly erotic epigrams, many of them, indeed, highly obscene according to modern feeling.

Meleager. (Anth. Pal., xii, 86, 117, 47, 92, 132, 54, 122, 52, (cf. 53), 125, 137, 84, 164, 256, 154, 59, 106, 159, 110, 23, 101, 65, 133, 60, 127, 126)

Meleager of Gadara in Cœlo-Syria, of whose erotic poems to girls we have already spoken before, lived during his youth at Tyre. There he would have nothing to do with girls, and for that reason was the more susceptible to the beauty of boys, and although the number of those with love of whom he is consumed is very considerable it is a youth Myiscus whom he loves best, and whose name meets us most frequently in the epigrams.

Of the sixty poems of Meleager in the twelfth book of the Anthology, thirty-seven are addressed to boys whose names are given, and we find no fewer than eighteen to whom special poems are devoted; but in addition there are so many others mentioned, that one is astounded at the easy susceptibility of the poet, whether we conceive many of the poems to be exercises in poetry without any real background, or if we assume that the same boy perhaps appears several times, but under different names. In any case, Meleager is firmly convinced that preference is due to the love of boys, and he knows how to offer confirmation of his answer to the question by a new and unexpected argument: "It is Cypris, a woman, who casts at us the fire of passion for women, but Love himself rules over desire for males. Whither shall I incline, to the boy or to his mother? I tell you for sure that even Cypris herself will say 'The bold brat wins.' "

When the marvel of Eros blazes up, then reason is done for and passion prevails. This is intelligible, for Eros has already played with the poet's soul in his tenderest age as with dice. But in everything it is the eyes of the poet, which eagerly drink in the beauty of boys so that Eros gains power over the soul, that are to blame.

Nothing is of avail any longer; the soul is captured and endeavours to escape, as a bird strives to flee from its cage. Eros himself has bound the wings of the soul, kindled a fire in it, and given the thirsty one nothing but hot tears to drink. All lamentation is in vain, as it has allowed Eros to grow up in its inmost parts.

But all that, thinks the poet, is quite natural, for the boy is so beautiful that even Aphrodite would prefer him to Eros as a son. He has obtained his beauty from the Graces themselves, who once met the boy and embraced him; this explains the charming grace of his youthful body, his sweet chatter, and the mute but yet eloquent language of his eyes. Longing for him takes the place of love, when he stays away afar, even when he has been obliged to set out on a journey by sea. Then the poet envies the ship, the waves, and the wind, which may enjoy the presence of the only loved one; and he would become a dolphin, that he might bear him on his back gently towards the longed-for destination.

(a) "Love brought to me under my mantle at night the sweet dream of a soft-laughing boy of eighteen, still wearing the chlamys; and I, pressing the tender flesh to my breast, culled empty hopes. Still does the desire of the memory heat me, and in my eyes still abideth asleep that caught for me in the chase that winged phantom. O soul, ill-starred in love, cease at last even in dreams to be warmed all in vain by beauty's images."

(b) "The South Wind, blowing fair for sailors, O ye who are sick for love, has carried off Andragathus, my soul's half. Thrice happy the ships, thrice fortunate the waves of the sea, and four times blessed the wind that bears the boy. Would I

were a dolphin that, carried on my shoulders, he could cross
the seas to look on Rhodes, the home of sweet lads."

It annoys the poet to be awakened prematurely from such
dreams. The silly crowing of a cock, who puts an end to his
life of dreams, sets him cursing the rude creature in a manner
which because of its bathos has a comic effect.

On another occasion the poet has undertaken a sea-voyage.
Already all the dangers of the sea are happily overcome, joyfully he leaves the rocking ship and sets foot on the mainland;
then again Fate meets him in the form of a slender boy: new
love—new life.

Another time he says: "Sweet it is to mingle the sweet honey
of the bees with unmixed wine, but it is also sweet to be beautiful, if one desires boys. As Alexis loves the curly-headed
Cleobulus such love is sweet, Cyprian honey-drink."

On Myiscus (little mouse): "Sweet is the boy, and even the
name of Myiscus is sweet to me and full of charm. What excuse have I for not loving? For he is beautiful, by Cypris,
entirely beautiful; and if he gives me pain, why it is the way
of love to mix bitterness with honey;" and again, "One thing
only appears to me beautiful, only one thing my eyes yearn-
ingly desire—to look upon Myiscus, for everything else I am
blind."

It is especially the eyes of Myiscus, whose beauty the poet
rapturously praises: (a) "Delicate children, so help me Love,
doth Tyre nurture, but Myiscus is the sun that, when his
light bursts forth, quenches the stars." (b) "My life's cable,
Myiscus, is made fast to thee, in thee is all the breath that is
left to my soul. For by thine eyes, dear boy, that speak even
to the deaf, and by thy bright brow I swear it, if ever thou
lookest at me with a clouded eye I see the winter, but if thy
glance be blithe, the sweet spring bursts into bloom." (c) "It
lightened sweet beauty: see how he flasheth flame from his
eyes." (d) "Shining grace beams; like lightning thine eyes hurl

sparks; has then Eros given thee lightning, O boy, as a weapon? Hail, Myiscus, thou bringest to men the flames of love, beam thou on mortals, on me as an enchanting star."

Earlier, the poet has made himself merry over the fools who have easily fallen in love, yet Eros does not jest with him: "I am caught, I who once laughed often at the serenades of young men crossed in love. And at thy gate, Myiscus, love has fixed me, inscribing on me 'Spoils won from Chastity.' "

Yet not only does Eros rejoice in his triumph, Myiscus himself also with glee congratulates himself, because he has succeeded in subjecting the stubborn one: "Myiscus, shooting me, whom the Loves could not wound, under the breast with his eyes, shouted out thus: 'It is I who have struck him down, the overbold, and see how I tread underfoot the arrogance of sceptered wisdom that sat on his brow?' But I, just gathering breath enough, said to him, 'Dear boy, why art thou astonished? Love brought down Zeus himself from Olympus.' " But he soon allows himself to be converted, and now, since he is sure of the love of his Myiscus, his happiness is only disturbed by the fear that Zeus may be able to carry off the boy from him.

Of the numerous poems which are devoted to other stars, a small selection may here be given: "When thirsty I kissed the tender-fleshed boy and said, when I was free of my parching thirst: 'Father Zeus, dost thou drink the nectareous kiss of Ganymede, and is this the wine he tenders to thy lips? For now that I have kissed Antiochus, fairest of our youths, I have drunk the sweet honey of the soul.' " "If I see Thero, I see everything, but if I see everything and no Thero, I again see nothing."

"I saw Alexis walking in the road at noontide, at the season when the summer was just being shorn of the tresses of her fruits; and double rays burnt me, the rays of love from the boy's eyes and others from the sun. The sun's night laid to rest again, but love's were kindled more in my dreams by the phantom of beauty. So night, who releases others from toil, brought pain to me, imaging in my soul a loveliness which is living fire."

"Pain has begun to touch my heart, for hot Love as he strayed, scratched it with the tip of his nails, and, smiling, said: 'Again, O unhappy lover, thou shalt have the sweet wound, burnt by biting honey.' Since when, seeing among the youths the fresh sapling Diophantus, I can neither fly nor abide."

Asclepiades. (Anth. Pal., xii, 135, 162, 163)

Asclepiades of Samos was regarded as the teacher of Theocritus, by whom he was highly praised as a man and a poet. The epigrams handed down under his name are distinguished by graceful form and tender feeling; eleven of them are preserved in the "boyish Muse" of the Anthology, of which the following is a specimen: "Wine is the proof of love. Nicagoras denied to us that he was in love, but those many toasts convicted him.

"Yes! he shed tears and bent his head, and had a certain downcast look, and the wreath bound tight round his head kept not its place."

In another epigram the poet imagines how the little Love is introduced by his mother into the secrets of reading and writing. But the result of her efforts as a teacher are essentially different from what is expected; instead of a text the docile pupil only reads over and over again the names of two beautiful boys, who are devoted to each other in hearty friendship —a tender glorification of boy-friendship, such as is also described in epigram 163 by the same author.

Callimachus. (Anth. Pal., xii, 102)

Callimachus of Cyrene in North Africa lived about 310-240 B.C. He is by far the most important epigrammatist of the

Alexandrian period. After having studied in Athens together with the poet Aratus, already known to us, we find him in Alexandria, first as a celebrated teacher and grammarian, and then at the luxurious court of Ptolemy Philadelphus as one of the most important collaborators in the business of the world-famed library with its many branches. His literary activity was mainly directed to the department of learning, but he was not disinclined to poetry. In the epigrams left by him, the erotic note is generally heard, and in the twelfth book of the Anthology, no fewer than twelve of them are preserved, which sing the praises of beautiful boys and are devoted to the mysteries of Eros. He knows how to vary the inexhaustible subject with a pleasantly surprising new point:

"The huntsman on the hills, Epicydes, tracks every hare and the slot of every hind through the frost and snow. But if one say to him, 'Look, here is a beast lying wounded,' he will not take it. And even so is my love; it is wont to pursue the fleeing game, but flies past what lies in its path."

The Other Poets

Besides the great poets hitherto mentioned, in the twelfth book of the Anthology, twenty-four poets of the lower class are represented by epigrams on the love of boys.

From Dioscorides (second century B.C.) we have, among a number of other epigrams:—

"Zephyr, gentlest of the winds, bring back to me the lovely pilgrim Euphragoras, even as thou didst receive him, not extending his absence beyond a few month's space; for to a lover's mind a short time is as a thousand years" (171).

Rhianus of Crete (flourished third century B.C.), a slave by birth, had originally been the inspector of a boy's wrestling school. His preference for youths is also to be recognized in his poetry: thus we know that he referred Apollo's service with King Admetus to erotic reasons (cf. Callimachus, *Hymn,* ii, 49). Of the eleven epigrams preserved, six are upon boys, somewhat frivolous, but clever and full of grace. He was successful in the domain of philology, prepared worthy editions of the *Iliad* and *Odyssey* and became known as an epic poet, especially of the second Messenian war.

We have already quoted his poem on the "Labyrinth of Boys from which there is no escape," but here is a further specimen: "Dexionicus, having caught a blackbird with lime under a green plane-tree, held it by the wings, and it, the holy bird, screamed complaining. But I, dear Love, and ye blooming Graces, would fain be even a thrush or a blackbird, so that in his hand I might pour forth my voice and sweet tears" (xii, 142).

An epigram of Alceus of Messene (A. P., xii, 64) is tender and full of fine feeling: "Zeus, Lord of Pisa, crown under the steep hill of Cronus Peithenor, the second son of Cypris. And lord, I pray thee, beckon no eagle on high to seize him for thy cup bearer in place of the fair Trojan boy. If ever I have brought thee a gift from the Muses that was dear to thee, grant that the godlike boy may be of one mind with me."

Alpheus of Mitylene (ibid., 18) makes a fresh point, when in the course of a six-line epigram he says: "Unhappy they whose life is loveless; for without love it is not easy to do aught or to say aught. I, for example, am now all too slow, but were I to catch sight of Xenophilus I would fly swifter than lightning. Therefore I bid all men not to shun but to pursue sweet desire; love is the whetstone of the soul."

Automedon (ibid., 34) strikes a humorously bantering note: "Yesterday I supped with the boys' trainer, Demetrius, the most blessed of all men. One lay on his lap, one stooped over his shoulder, one brought him the dishes, and another served him with drink—an admirable quartette. I said to him in fun, do you, my dear friend, train the boys at night too?"

Evenus (Anth. Pal., xii, 172; cf. Catullus, 85), finds a new formula for the inimitable *Odi et amo* of Catullus: "If to hate is pain and to love is pain, of the two evils I choose the smart of kind pain."

Julius Leonidas (Anth. Pal., xii, 20) employs an idea of his own: "Zeus must be again rejoicing in the banquets of the Ethiopians, or, turned to gold, is stealing to Danaë's chamber; for it is a marvel that, seeing Periander, he did not carry off from earth the lovely youth; or is the god no longer a lover of boys?"

Lastly, we will select three of the thirty-five anonymous epigrams that are preserved in this twelfth book of the Anthology.

"Persistent love, thou ever whirlest at me no desire for woman, but the lightning of burning longing for my own sex. Now burnt by Damon, now looking on Ismenus, I ever suffer pain that will not be appeased. And not only on these have I looked, but, my eye, ever madly roving, is dragged into the nets of all alike" (ibid., 87).

Another time, longing leads the poet safely after a regular carousal: "I will go to serenade him, for I am, all of me, mighty drunk. 'Boy, take this wreath that my tears have bathed.' The way is long, but I shall not go in vain; it is the dead of night and dark, but for me Themison is a great torch" (ibid., 116).

The author of the following is also unknown: "When Menecharmus, Anticles' son, won the boxing match, I crowned him with ten soft fillets, and thrice I kissed him, all dabbled with blood as he was, but the blood was sweeter to me than myrrh" (ibid., 123).

Having thus culled but a few of the flowers that bloom so profusely in the twelfth book of the Anthology, the "Musa puerilis" of Straton, we come now to the so called "cinædic" poetry, whose most important representative, Sotades, has already been discussed.

The earliest meaning of cinædus was "a lover of boys," with an obscene significance; then the name was given to the professional dancers of certain indecent ballets, as they are known to us from Plautus and Petronius and from the wall-paintings of the Villa Doria Pamphili in Rome, which were accompanied with very free, or even according to our ideas highly indecent songs. Only quite unimportant fragments of them have been preserved. The boxer Cleomachus of Magnesia had fallen in love with such a cinædus-actor and a girl kept by him and was thereby induced to take up similar dialogue character parts. (Cinædic Poetry: Plautus, *Mil. glor.*, 668 (iii, 1, 73); Petronius, 23; O. Jahn, *Wandgemälde des Columbariums in der Villa Pamphili* (Philol. Abhandl. der Münchener Akademie, viii, 254 ff.); for the story of Cleomachus see Strabo, xiv, 648a).

According to Atheneus (xv, 697d) "everyone sang a song glorifying the love of boys" by Seleucus (beginning of the second century B.C.) of which two verses are preserved: "I also love boys; this is more beautiful than languishing in the yoke of marriage; for in murderous battle your friend still stays as a protector at your side."

Prose

It is superfluous to give a complete summary of the passages treating of pederasty in Greek prose, since the Greek prose-writers have already been sufficiently discussed. Hence it will be enough to name some writings which were more especially occupied with the subject.

Under the name of Demosthenes, a treatise called *Erotikos* has survived, which, obviously influenced by Plato's *Phedrus*, represents an enthusiastic eulogy in letter-form, of a boy named Epicrates. However agreeable and worth reading this little work may be, it is, nevertheless, as philological criticism has shown, not the work of the great orator. The most important homosexual prose work in ancient Greek literature is, of course, the *Symposion* ('Banquet') of Plato, written several

years after the festive meal which the tragic writer Agathon
had given to his friends Socrates, Phedrus, Pausanis, Eryxi-
machus, and Aristophanes, on the occasion of his dramatic
victory in 416 B.C. After the eatables had been removed and
the drinking begins, on the proposal of Phedrus the importance and power of Eros is chosen as a subject of conversation.
Thus this most beautiful writing of Plato, which is so rich in
colouring and so stimulatingly illustrated and profoundly
treated from so many different standpoints, assumes the form
of a hymn of Eros unique in the literature of the world. By
means of an ingeniously invented myth, Aristophanes defines
love as the search of the one half of the once uniform original
man (separated in two parts by the god) for its other part. The
culminating point is the speech of Socrates, who defines love
as the urge for immortality, which fructifies the body of
women with the seed of children and the soul of boys and
youths with wisdom and virtue. In the definition of Socrates,
Eros attains the highest imaginable ideal: the sensual and
spiritual melt in a wonderful harmony, from which with
logical accuracy the demand results, that the really good
teacher must also be a good pedophil (lover of boys), that is,
that teacher and pupil must do their best by mutual love and
common effort to reach the greatest perfection possible. No
sooner has Socrates finished his speech, perhaps the most beautiful ever written in the Greek or any other language, than
Alcibiades, coming slightly intoxicated from another banquet
into the festive room, delivers the famous panegyric on Socrates, which overflows just as much with an enthusiasm glowing with passion for the beloved creature, as it lifts him up to
the height of supersensuous intellectuality and almost super-
human self-control.

By comparison with the *Symposion,* the Platonic dialogue
Alcibiades seems colourless. It is connected with the love of
Socrates for Alcibiades, the spoilt and idolized favourite of
all, and develops the idea that a future counsellor of the people

has first to decide with himself what is fitting and to their advantage.

The subject of the love of boys is also treated of in the *Phedrus* of Plato, named after the favourite of his youth. Under the towering plane-tree on the bank of the stream Ilissus, at midday, with the grasshoppers chirping around them, the dialogue takes place, which, gradually mounting higher and higher, leads at last to the Socratic definition of Eros, that pedophilia represents the demand for the originally beautiful and the world of ideas.

Whether the *Erastæ* ("The Lovers") is rightly attributed to Plato is not yet with certainty decided. It is named after the favourite one of two boys, with whom Socrates holds a conversation on the thesis that a smattering of various knowledge is by no means synonymous with true philosophical education.

A very favourite subject in philosophical literature is the examination of the question, whether the love of a man for a woman should always be preferred to the love of a man for a boy. Of the numerous passages devoted to this problem the treatise that has come down to us under Lucian's name, no doubt inaccurately, is to be mentioned in the first place, the *Erotes;* that is, the two kinds of love.

In a very charming framework the contest between two friends is brought forward, the Corinthian Charicles, who commends the love between a man and a woman, and the Athenian Callicratidas, who praises that between men and boys.

Lycinus, who acts as arbitrator, finally puts his judgment into the following words, which best characterize the Greek conception of love: "Marriage is for men a life-pressing necessity and a precious thing, if it is a happy one; but the love of boys, so far as it courts the sacred rights of affection, is in my opinion a result of practical wisdom. Therefore let marriage be for all, but let the love of boys remain alone the privilege of the wise, for a perfect virtue is absolutely unthinkable in women. But do not be angry, my dear Charicles, if the crown belongs to Athens, and not to Corinth."

That the *Erotes* enjoyed great popularity in antiquity, is clear from the fact that the little work found several imitators, the best known of whom is Achilles Tatius. In the concluding chapters of the second book of his romance the problem which is the foundation of the *Erotes* is treated of in the same manner in the form of two opposing speeches.

In the romance of Xenophon of Ephesus, which contains the loves of Habrocomes and Antheia, there occurs a homosexual episode, in which Hippothoüs tells how, in his native place, Perinthus, he was passionately in love with a boy named Hyperanthus. But when the boy is bought by Aristomachus, a rich merchant of Byzantium, Hippothoüs follows him thither, kills Aristomachus, and flees with his favourite. Near Lesbos their ship is overtaken by a heavy storm, in which Hyperanthus is drowned, and there nothing remains for the utterly disconcerted Hippothoüs but to erect a beautiful memorial for his dead favourite, after which in despair he takes to a bandit's life.

The philosopher Maximus of Tyre, who lived in the time of the emperor Commodus (A.D. 180-92), has repeatedly examined the problem of the love of boys in his numerous writings. Thus we have from him *diatribai*, that is, discourses on the Eros of Socrates, a subject which the hermaphrodite Favorinus, the most learned and distinguished philosopher of the period of Hadrian, had already treated.

The Love of Boys in Greek Mythology

After all that up to this point has been said of Greek love of boys on the authority of written documents, the conjecture that it also played an important part in the mythology of the Hellenes is abundantly fulfilled. In fact, the entire body of legend concerning the gods and heroes of the Hellenes is so rich in motifs of pedophilia, that R. Beyer was able to write a monograph on the subject. It would be a welcome task here to record these amours with boys of the Greek gods and heroes, since they in great part belong to the most beautiful flowers of Hellenic poetry, but considerations of space forbid any complete or connected presentation in this place of the pedophil myths of the Greeks, and we have moreover, in Beyer's valuable dissertation, a thoroughly sufficient, if not always complete, compilation of pedophil motifs in Greek mythology. We must therefore refer the reader to this work, and be content merely to mention here that as early as the times of antiquity more or less detailed catalogues of the beautiful boys of legend and their lovers were committed to writing. Traces of these lists have been preserved in several cases, as in Hyginus, Athenæus and others; but the fullest is that of the pious and learned Father of the Church, Clement of Alexandria, who has put together the following "Zeus loved Ganymede; Apollo Cinyras, Zacynthus, Hyacinthus, Phorbas, Hylas, Admetus, Cyparissus, Amyklas, Troilus, Branchus, Tymnius, Parus, Potueius, and Orpheus; Dionysus loved Laonis, Ampelus, Hymenæus, Hermaphroditos, and Achilles; Asclepius loved Hippolytus; Hephæstus Peleus; Pan Daphnis; Hermes Perseus, Chryses, Therses, and Odryses; Heracles Abderus, Dryops, Iokastus, Philokteles, Hylas, Polyphemus, Hæmon, Chonus, and Eurystheus."

From this list, which contains the names of but a few lovers among the gods, one gets a glimpse of the astonishing number of pedophil motifs in the mythology of Greece.

Joke and Jest, Based on Homosexuality

Hitherto we have treated the Greek love of boys from its serious side, but the well-known saying of Horace—that "nothing prevents one from telling the truth with a smile on one's lips," is true of the ephebophilia of the Greeks as well as of other forms of the phenomena of human life. There was also cause for many witticisms, a large number of which have been preserved. Since naturally it is not the spiritual content of love, but in a much higher degree its sensual impulse that is the target of jest and joke, I can here only reproduce a few of the sometimes very ingenious witticisms that have come down to us.

The word *cinedus* (kinaidos), already explained, gradually became the nickname for those half-men, who by their feminine behaviour and gestures, by painting the face and other tricks of the toilet, incurred general contempt. A satire in the Anthology (xi, 272) says of them: "They do not want to be men and yet were not born women; they are no men, since they allow themselves to be used as women; they are men to women, and women to men." The affected behaviour of such people is often ridiculed, as in Aristophanes: "I wish, O youth, to ask you who you are. Of what land, you weakling? What's your country, what means thy garb? Why all this confusion of fashions? What does the harp prattle to the saffron-coloured robe? What the lyre to the headdress? What mean the oil-flask and the girdle? How unsuitable! What connection then between a mirror and a sword? And you yourself, O youth, are you reared as a man? Why, where are the tokens of a man? Where is your cloak? Where are your boots? Or as a woman then? Where then are your breasts? What do you say? Why are you silent? Nay then, I'll judge of you from your song, since you are not willing to tell me yourself" (*Thesm.*, 134 ff.).

Menander describes the behaviour of a cinedus with a sly hint at Ctesippus, the son of Chabrias, of whom it was said that he had sold even the stones from his father's grave, to be able to enjoy his life of pleasure (frag. 363).

In comedy such effeminate persons have women's names. Thus Aristophanes speaks of a female Sostratos, that is, instead of the masculine Sostratos he uses the feminine Sostrate, instead of Cleonymus, Cleonyme (*Clouds,* 678, 680). Cratinus ridicules "pleasure boys," calling them "little girlies"; or the feminine article was sometimes put before the masculine name (*CAF.*, I, 29).

A certain ready, if not always very seemly wit was, of course, required for the invention of actually new and appropriate nicknames, and from the abundant store we may first select the coarse word *katapulón* (from *puln*, bum), which is very common, and is known to every reader of Greek comedy; just as common is the still coarser abusive word *enruproktos* (broad-bummed).

A nickname which needs no explanation *stropilos* ("pirou-ette") occurs only once in Aristophanes, while the name *Batalos* is more frequent. The word is explained by a passage from Eupolis, in which it is used as synonymous with *prōtos* ("bum"). It also existed as a proper name, and Plutarch wrote of an effeminate flute-player "Batalos," ridiculed by Aristoph-anes in a comedy. More harmless are *paidopipēs* ("ogler of boys") and *purropipēs* ("ogler of boys with golden curls"), also frequent in comedy.

A droll nickname for pedophils was *alphērtēs*, the first mean-ing of which is a kind of fish. The satirical transference of the name is thus explained by Athenæus (vii, 281): these fish, which are pale yellow in appearance, and in some places pur-ple-coloured, "were always caught in pairs, one swimming behind the tail of the other." Since then one always follows the other, some old writers have transferred the name of these fishes to those who are immoderate and perverted in sensu-ality. The joke becomes still more effective from the fact that the word, in Homer and later writers, is of frequent occur-rence, and is a distinguished epithet of men. In a clever but untranslatable epigram of Straton, in which terms from the theory of music are used in an obscene sense, the pedophil meaning of the word *alphertēs* is also alluded to (Anth. Pal., xii, 187).

Trifles and Supplementary Remarks

Phanias of Eresus has told the following story: "In Heraclea, a city of lower Italy, a boy named Hipparinus, handsome to look at and of noble family, was loved by Antileon, who in spite of many efforts could not win his favour. In the gymnasia he was always by his side, saying again and again how much he loved him, and protesting that he would undergo any labour and do everything he ordered. The boy, for a joke, ordered him to bring the bell from a fortified place which was strongly guarded by Archelaus, tyrant of the Heracleotes, thinking that he would never be able to accomplish this task. But Antileon secretly entered the fort, ambushed and slew the keeper of the bell, and afterwards, when he had come to the boy—who kept his promise—they became very intimate, and henceforward loved each other greatly. It chanced, however, that the tyrant himself became enamoured of the lad and when he threatened violence Antileon, being angry, exhorted him not to imperil his life by refusing, since the tyrant had power to carry out his wishes and his threat; but he himself attacked and slew the tyrant when leaving his house, and having done this, he ran away and would have escaped had he not got mixed up with some herds of sheep and been captured. Wherefore, the city having been freed by the death of the tyrant, brazen statues were set up by the people of Heraclea to both Antileon and the boy, and a law was passed that in future no one should drive herds of sheep through the streets" (*FHG*, II, 298, 16).

Lastly, appreciating the beauty of boys, it is not to be wondered at that beautiful boys were also employed for paying tribute. As early as Homer, Agamemnon offers to present the insulted Achilles with some youths by way of expiation.

Further, we read in Herodotus (iii, 97) that the Ethiopians every other year were obliged to deliver to the King of the Persians, besides pure gold, 200 chests of ebony and twenty elephants' tusks, also five boys; every four years the Colchians sent 100 boys and 100 girls; and both these instances of tribute actually continued in the time of Herodotus.

These boys served the Persian nobles as pages, cupbearers, and favourites. That even a worse lot threatened such boys, is clear from another passage of Herodotus (iii, 48), in which he relates that Periander, the well-known ruler of Corinth, had sent 300 boys from Kerkyra (Corfu), sons of the most distinguished men of the island, to the court of King Alyattes at Sardes, to be castrated and to perform the services customarily discharged by eunuchs. How the inhabitants of the island of Samos, on whom the duty of transporting them was imposed, saved the boys and in memory thereof instituted a feast which was still observed in the time of Herodotus, may be gathered from the historian himself. From a later passage, very interesting from the point of view of the history of civilization, it is clear that many persons made a profession of the castration of boys. Herodotus tells us (viii, 104 ff.): "Xerxes sent with these boys as a guard a certain Hermotimus, a native of Pedasa, who held the first place among the king's eunuchs. In the town of Pedasa, it is said that the following event happens: whenever all the neighbours living round are threatened by the approach of any serious disaster, the priestess of the temple of Athene grows a long beard. And this had already happened twice. Now Hermotimus was one of the inhabitants of Pedasa, to whom it befell to obtain the greatest vengeance that one can imagine upon a man by whom he had been wronged.

Panionius, a citizen of Chios, who supported himself by most wicked acts, bought him when he had been captured by enemies and was put up for sale. For this Panionius, as often as he got possession of any beautiful boys, used to castrate them, take them to Sardes or Ephesus and sell them for a high price. For among the barbarians eunuchs are more valuable than those who are not castrated, and greater confidence is reposed in them in everything. When he had castrated many others, Panionius, who made his livelihood in this manner, then did the same to Hermotimus—to whom it did not come altogether as a misfortune, for he was sent to Sardes with other gifts for the king and in course of time of all the eunuchs of Xerxes he was held in the greatest honour." Under King Darius also eunuchs were given positions at the Persian court; Babylon and the rest of Asyria were obliged to send him as tribute besides 1000 talents of silver also 500 castrated boys.

The town of Lebadea in Bœotia, unimportant in itself, was famous for the very old, highly sacred dream oracle of Trophonius. Pausanias, who had himself questioned the oracle, tells us in detail (ix, 39, 7) the various preparatory steps, which, after the venerable ceremonial, were prescribed to one who desired information from the oracle. Among other things he was conducted to the stream Hercyna that flows through a valley, "where two boys from the town, about thirteen years of age, who are called "Hermæ," anoint him with oil and bathe and perform all kinds of services for him such as boys perform." The name is perhaps to be explained by the fact that Hermes was the patron god of boys and youths, for which reason no Greek gymnasium was without an altar and statue of the friendly god.

A pretty epigram of Nicias in the Anthology of Planudes describes how boys crown the statue of Hermes in the gymnasium, "who stands there as the patron of the charming gymnasium, with evergreen, hyacinths, and violets."

From the last *Erotika* of Clearchus of Soli in Cyprus the following sentiment is preserved: "No flatterer can be a constant friend, for time detracts from the lie of him who pretends to friendship. But the true lover is a flatterer of love for the sake of the bloom of youth and beauty."

The astonishingly perfect understanding of beauty possessed by the Greeks, of their Dionysiac joy in the glory of the human body, ennobled for them every act of sensuality, if only it was based upon true love, that is, on the yearning after beauty.

Hence, for them, pederasty, instead of a vice was but another form of love which they regarded, not as the enemy of marriage, but as a necessary supplement to marriage recognized by the State; and it was publicly spoken of with just as much unconcern as it was brought into the sphere of their philosophical conversations by great intellects such as Socrates, Plato, and Aristotle. Because the fascinations of the sexual were not made still more alluring by being shrouded in a veil of mystery or branded as sinful and forbidden, and further because the almost unchecked sensuality of the Greeks was always dignified by the desire for beauty, their sexual life developed in overflowing force, but also in enviable healthiness. That this is so may be certainly adduced from the fact that sexual perversions, which play so lamentable a part in modern life, seldom occurred in ancient Greece, and that it is difficult to find even occasional traces of them in the classical writings.

[EDITOR'S NOTES]

While one could analyze and discuss this classic study of classic literature almost endlessly, there is one aspect of it that is worthy of especial note. There is frequent mention of "Greek love" among modern writers on this theme, who speak of the "glory that was Greece" and who state that since homosexuality thrived in one of the great cultures of the past in which it was widely accepted, it could find a place in a great modern culture as well. Without going into this argument, it seems important to point out that the Greek culture was one in which the woman was subservient in every respect. It is difficult to believe that "Greek love" as actually practiced and as reflected in this literature, could find equal status in a culture in which the female has a place of equality, if not of actual glorification.

Certainly, Licht made the definitive study of homosexuality in Greek literature, and as such, this work contains a wealth of detail that is worthy of serious study.

D. W. C.

THE
LOVE CALLED "SOCRATES"

Voltaire

FROM VOLTAIRE'S PHILOSOPHICAL DICTIONARY, TRANSLATED
FOR THIS ANTHOLOGY BY DONALD WEBSTER CORY

How can it be that a vice, one which would destroy the human race if it became general, an infamous assault upon Nature, can nevertheless be so natural? It looks like the last degree of thought-out corruption, and, at the same time, it is the usual possession of those who haven't had the time to be corrupted yet. It has entered hearts still new, that haven't known either ambition, nor fraud, nor the thirst of riches; it is a blind youth that, by a poorly straightened-out instinct, throws itself into the confusion upon leaving childhood.

The attraction of the two sexes for each other is welcomed; but regardless of whatever has been said about the women of Africa and Southern Asia, this attraction is usually much stronger in men than in women; it is a law that nature has established for all animals. It is always the male that attracts the female.

The young males of our species, reared together, feeling this force that nature begins to develop in them and not finding the natural object of their instinct, throw themselves upon that which resembles it. A young boy will often, by the freshness of his complexion, by the intensity of his coloration and by the sweetness of his eyes, resemble a beautiful girl for the space of two or three years; if he is loved, it is because nature is misunderstood: on becoming attached to the one who has these beauties, one renders homage to sex, and when age has made this resemblance vanish, the error ceases.

It is well known that this mistake of nature is much more common in mild climates than among the snows of the North, for the blood runs hotter there and the occasion arises more frequently: also, that which is taken as merely a weakness in young Alcibiade is a disgusting abomination in a Dutch sailor and in a Muscovite soldier. I cannot accept the claim that the Greeks permitted license. Some quote Solon because he said, in two bad verses:

> "You shall cherish a beautiful boy
> As long as he remains beardless"

But really was Solon the legislator when he wrote this? He was still young, and, once the rake had become the sage, he did not include such an infamy in the laws of his republic. This is like accusing Theodore de Bége of having practiced pederasty in his church because, in his youth, he had written poems for young Candide, and that he had said: *"Applecton hunc et illam."*

Some also abuse Plutarch's text, when, reading his chatter in the "Dialogue of Love," he has the protagonist state that women are not worthy of true love; but another character upholds the side of women, as he should.

Montesquieu is quite wrong. It is true that, with whatever certainty history can offer, Socratic love was not an infamous love at all: it is this word *Love* that has confused people. Those who were called *the lovers of a young man* were precisely those who, among us, are the companions of our princes, the elite;

these people attended to the education of a distinguished child, partaking of the same education, the same military life: warring and holy institutions, in which some abuses entered, turning it into nocturnal feasts and orgies. The regiment of lovers instituted by Laïnes was an invincible army of young warriors dedicated by the oath to give their lives for one another; and this is the most beautiful thing that ancient discipline had to offer.

Sextus Empericus and others have said that pederasty was recommended by the laws of Persia. Let them quote the text of the law, let them exhibit the Persian Code, and, if they do exhibit them, I still will not believe it, I shall say that it is not true, because it is impossible. No, it is not human nature to make a law that contradicts and outrages Nature, a law that that would make the human race disappear if it were followed to the letter. How many people have taken shameful but tolerated behavior in a country to be the law of the country! Sextus Empiricus, who doubted everything, should have doubted this jurisprudence. Were he alive today, and were he to see two or three young Jesuits take advantage of a few students, would he have the right to say that this was permitted by the laws of Ignatius Loyola?

Love of boys was so common in Rome that they didn't bother to punish it. Octavius Augustus, this debauched murderer, who dared exile Ovid, was pleased to have Virgil sing to Alexis and for Horace to compose little odes for Ligunius; but the ancient law, which prohibited pederasty, survived all along. Emperor Philip reactivated it and expelled from Rome the little boys who were guilty. In conclusion, I do not believe that there has ever been an organized nation which has made laws against morals.

[EDITOR'S NOTES]

That Voltaire wrote on homosexuality at a time when the subject was unmentionable is more important than what he wrote. Yet, intrinsically, he had an understanding that is remarkably advanced for the 18th Century. He understood sexuality in the male is more imperious than in the female, and as it begins to blossom forth, the male who cannot find heterosexual outlets may be forced to seek an outlet among other males. Today, after Freud and Kinsey, we may topographically understand what was written by Voltaire, and perhaps sense the tragedies inherent in these philosophical observations; but despite this developing awareness, the unfortunate basic social attitudes remain unchanged.

DEFENSIVE HOMOSEXUALITY

Homosexuality as a Defense Against Incest

Gilbert Van Tassel Hamilton, M.D.

FROM ENCYCLOPEDIA SEXUALIS PUBLISHED BY DINGWELL-ROCK, LTD., NEW YORK, 1936.

1.

There will be presented here some research findings which point to fear of incest as a major determinant of human homosexuality. Although this factor is of sufficient importance, in my opinion, to justify its separate consideration in an encyclopædia sexualis, I do not present it as a specific or essential "cause." In fact, no specific etiology can be claimed for any of the known psychopathologic formations, once we exclude the obvious resultants of injury, infection, chemical intoxication, arterial changes, neoplasms and endocrinopathies.

In dealing with the total determinant-resultant sequence that comprises the maladaptive aspects of an individual life the significance of any one factor can be arrived at only in terms of its ontogenetic relationship to all other known factors. A still more fundamental approach to the appraisal of a given factor also calls for an examination of its phylogenetic background. It was this latter consideration which led me to divert a considerable amount of time to studies in comparative psychology during the earlier years of my work as a psychiatrist.

354

From 1908 to 1917, I made systematic observations of the sexual behavior of monkeys under both captive and non-captive conditions in a live oak woods near Santa Barbara, California. Twenty different animals—seven females and thirteen males—were used during this period. Three of these, a male and two females, were born in the laboratory woods and survived to the end of the research. Two females and three uncastrated males were acquired before they had reached sexual maturity. Six of these eight young subjects attained sexual maturity while they were under observation. Three castrated males (one adult and two half-grown ones) were acquired. The other nine subjects were sexually mature when purchased. The one unclassified female was larger than any of the other females. There was also one unclassified male. He so far exceeded all the other monkeys in size that impending contact with him invariably precipitated flight on the part of his fellow males. Eighteen of the twenty monkeys were of the familiar rhesus and cynomolgus types, three of them being crosses between these species.

Methods were developed for experimental arrangement of situations which could be fairly well controlled and repeated at will. The research plant in the woods included a primate building which was partitioned off into eleven large cages. Each cage had a door opening into an enclosed common alley, and this in turn opened into a large terminal room, the top and three sides of which were of wire netting. I was thus able to restrict and arrange the social contacts of all the animals whenever they were called in from the woods for experimental purposes.

The results of these studies have been published in detail elsewhere, hence, only a brief summary of them will be given here:

1. Homosexual plays were of daily occurrence among the noncaptive immature males, regardless of the availability of the females. The smaller of a pair of copulating males would

generally assume the passive (female) position, but at times the larger male would play the female rôle. Heterosexual behavior was also observed among immature males.

2. Any male, mature or immature, was likely to assume the female position for copulation when attacked by a more powerful fellow of either sex if escape by flight was impossible. A typical observation taken from my records will illustrate this:

During one of the studies of defensive homosexuality all of the animals were kept in the cages. The alley made it possible to sort them out into couples and groups for separate imprisonment. By leaving open the alley doors of two or more cages it was possible to determine whether a given animal would seek escape from or contact with particular groups or individuals. In one experiment all doors leading into the alley were opened excepting the one in the cage which confined the very large and powerful male already described. He was, therefore, the only animal who did not have free range of ten cages, the alley and the terminal room.

After the monkeys had fought their way through to some sort of tribal integration the big fellow was admitted to the alley. All of them fled at his approach excepting the largest of the females. One recently weaned little male darted into an empty cage and crouched in a corner on the floor. The giant followed, leering at him as if about to attack. The little fellow squealed in terror and looked about for an avenue of escape. Finding none, he assumed the female position of copulation. His enemy now displayed only friendliness and mild sexual excitement, but the youngster ducked between his legs and escaped.

3. Assumption of the female position by a fellow seemed almost automatically to precipitate a copulative (male) reaction in an aggressively hostile monkey of either sex, regardless of the sex of the submissive one. A monkey dashing to a ferocious attack upon a fellow would promptly cease to manifest hostility if the intended victim assumed the female position.

If the aggressor was a female, she would mount her victim, make a few perfunctory copulative movements, then turn to some new interest.

4. Mature males would sometimes lure weaker males to them by assuming the female position, only to spring at the intended victim as soon as the homosexual bait brought the latter close enough to make escape impossible. Such behavior lacked all appearance of sexual motivation on the part of the luring male, who would move to attack before sexual contact occurred. Mature females were also apt to resort to the same trick in luring weaker or more timid female enemies to them.

5. During all my nine years of research with monkeys I observed only one episode of homosexual behavior between two females in which there was definite evidence of sexual excitement on the part of either participant. This occurred when "Kate," a mature female, was freed after more than a year's imprisonment and consequent separation from her immature, noncaptive daughter, "Gertie." As soon as mother and daughter met, they rushed into a front-to-front embrace, then "Gertie" dropped to all fours, turned her posterior to "Katie" and assumed the female position. The mother promptly mounted her and made male copulative movements. Both animals smacked their lips and displayed sexual excitement. They were never again observed to manifest any sexual interest in each other.

6. No uncastrated, sexually mature male was ever observed to assume the female position unless there was a defensive need of doing so or an obvious intention of luring a timid enemy to nonsexual combat.

7. Nursling monkeys of either sex would assume the female position almost reflexly on the approach of any large monkey, if the mother was not close at hand, but with obvious manifestations of terror and none of sexual excitement.

8. The three castrated males were the most timid members of the tribe, and although one of them was of adult size, he

disclosed the same preference for homosexual behavior that was characteristic of the two smaller ones.

2.

When we turn to the well-established fact of human bisexuality, we are confronted by a question as to what, if any, normally adaptive expressions it can have in consciousness and behavior. The bisexuality of infrahuman primates offers an experimental approach to this problem which deserves far more attention than has been given to it by comparative psychologists, but such findings as are available seem to me to throw a considerable light on human homosexuality. The research discussed previously discloses, in my opinion, certain general adaptive needs which are met by infrahuman bisexuality:

1. During immaturity the balance between homosexual and heterosexual tendencies is so nearly even in the male monkey that his erotic impulses can find satisfying expression in sexual plays with fellow males. This outlet sufficiently reduces the strength of his heterosexual compulsions to insure him against entering into dangerous competitions with adult males for possession of the females.

2. Although the balance tips heavily in the heterosexual direction when sexual maturity is attained, the adult male remains sufficiently bisexual to be capable of assuming the female position whenever there is defensive need of doing so. Tribal integration and, in the end, species survival would be impossible if flight were the only defense against the hostile aggressions of stronger fellows. For this reason it is not only important that the male of any age should be ready to play the female rôle in a defensive emergency, but that the aggressor should respond sexually to the female position, regardless of the sex of the submissive one.

3. Copulation involves no structural injury to the immature male, but such a danger exists for the immature female. The

latter, being under no heterosexual compulsion to compete with the mature female for male sexual favors, has no need, according to my theory, of engaging in homosexual plays before maturity, and she does not, in fact, engage in such plays. On the other hand, she is sufficiently bisexual to be capable of offering herself for copulation to hostile females at any age, whenever there is a defensive need of doing so. The screaming flight of the female nursling to her mother before sexual contact can occur when the female position is assumed as a defense against an approaching male or female gives us valuable evidence on this point.

4. The readiness of the adult female to accept an invitation to play the rôle of copulating male when she has directed a hostile attack against a fellow of either sex again discloses the adaptive value of retained bisexuality, since it is in the interests of both individual and species survival.

5. The tendency to lure a timid enemy of the same sex to combat by feigning readiness to sustain the passive sexual rôle discloses another phase of the adaptive value of bisexuality: the individual's standing in the tribe is always enhanced by victory over another fellow.

3.

If, as can be indubitably established by appropriate methods of experimentation, homosexual behavior is at times resorted to as a purely defensive measure by the infrahuman primate, a question arises as to whether defensiveness is a factor in the determination of human homosexuality. My studies of compulsive alcoholism, certain types of the manic-depressive psychosis and overt human homosexuality have led me to the conclusion that fear of incest is a more important factor in the development of sexual inversion than is generally recognized.

1. As early as 1908, Abraham called attention to the fact that homosexual tendencies which are usually repressed are likely to become evident when a man is drunk. In line with

this observation I have found, in common with almost all other psychiatrists, that the periods of prolonged and excessive drinking of the compulsive alcoholic are precipitated by an unconscious need to ease tensions engendered by repressed homosexual urges. An occasional compulsive alcoholic will be frankly, overtly homosexual during his sprees, but as a rule, these patients do not go beyond socially allowable verbal expressions of their loyalty to and admiration of male friends. Although they are not, as a rule, rated as being anything less than perfectly heterosexual by themselves and their friends, it is easily apparent to the trained observer that only a very thin repressive line separates them from their overtly homosexual brothers.

Two almost unfailing observations led me to study the compulsive drunkard's mother: (a) her overpossessive love of him during his infancy and early childhood, and (b) her underlying hatred of his wife, no matter how wise, devoted and long suffering the latter may be. I found that the typical mother of such a patient is the kind of woman who obviously, albeit unconsciously, turns to her male child for the emotional satisfactions that are normally found in the spousal relationship. In some cases, the early death or defection of the husband, more rarely his impotency or repellant unworthiness as a human being, could be blamed. In the majority of cases, the fault lay with the mother's own repressions, which prevented her from developing an adult love life.

I do not mean to imply that the mother of the future compulsive alcoholic makes conscious overt sexual advances to her male child. She avoids direct genital contact with him and is often quite intolerant of his masturbation, "unclean thoughts" and anything suggestive of erotic advances on his part toward females of his own age. Her eroticism toward him takes the form of much kissing, fondling, verbal endearments and a not oversubtle maternal coquetry. Even after he has reached adolescence and has fallen in love with a girl of his own generation, such a mother will reproach him for his infidelity to her, demand assurance that he loves his maternal "sweetheart" best after all and display a very real jealousy.

Illness in the family, an unexpected guest or any other excuse for juggling the family sleeping arrangements are made occasions for occupying the same bed with her son. One victim of a subtly incestuous mother told me that he and his mother slept together all during the winter he came into puberty. Illness in the family was her excuse. In another case the mother of two future drunkards would playfully crawl into bed with them on Sunday mornings from the time they were little boys until they had reached an age when either of them could have made her pregnant. Examples of this kind could be endlessly multiplied, but in each case the situation described would be essentially the same: a mother's persistent efforts to keep alive and even to augment the incestuous tendencies of her male child.

When we study the victim of the unconsciously incestuous mother, we find that the dynamic sequence is fairly simple in its general outlines. The primary direction of this major sexual impulse is heterosexual—with the mother as love-object. This incites fear and repulsion at a functionally higher (i.e., more nearly conscious) level of response, and there is a sharp deflection of the impulse from mother and femaleness in general toward maleness. Other important factors enter here, such as the castration-anxiety of the Oedipus period, regression to narcissistic choice of love-object and, in certain cases, endocrine setup; but my observations as a comparative psychologist and, later, as a psychoanalyst strongly incline me to the opinion that fear of incest is the most important of the factors involved in the overdevelopment of the homosexual tendency.

In the compulsive alcoholic, homosexuality has a demonstrably defensive motivation, but this in turn is feared and repressed. All that comes into consciousness is an urge to ease an intolerable tension and at the same time to obtain a sense of indubitable masculinity. Alcohol satisfies this need and effects a partial release of primarily heterosexual impulses, thus making it possible for the heavily drinking compulsive to function with prostitutes or other women who are not too easily identifiable with the forbidden mother.

It is an extremely significant fact that the compulsive alcoholic usually becomes sexually impotent for his wife if and when the usual maternal element creeps into their relationship. He will cling to an attractive and devoted young wife and fall into a frenzy of despair when she threatens to leave him, but he will also avoid sexual relations with her. Many of these men are sexually frigid toward all women during their sober intervals. It is only when they are drunk that they seek sexual release in sexual orgies with prostitutes or women of their own class who are merely good play fellows for whom they have no significant affection.

2. Manic depressive cycles present some very intricate psychodynamic problems related to the pregenital stages of libidinal development, hence the observations which directly follow have reference to the incest=homosexuality sequence as merely one component of a far more complex determinant-resultant sequence than can be discussed here.

One type of manic-depressive patient is excessively alcoholic during the excited phase, and either very temperate or wholly abstemious at all other times. During the excited phase, after prolonged, excessive drinking, the ordinarily repressed homosexual tendencies break through, either to direct expression in behavior or as delusions to the effect that enemies are accusing him of homosexuality. When such a patient submits himself to a psychoanalysis during a free interval the naïvely presented first few dreams disclose a high degree of unconscious preoccupation with incestuous fantasies, but the free associations elicited by the usual analytic instructions cluster around homosexual themes.

In another group of manic depressives one finds, instead of

alcoholism, a compulsive need of close and ardent friendships with persons of the same sex. This does not ordinarily involve genital or other overtly sexual expressions of love, but it calls for a pathologic degree of repression. Here, too, we find that the patient's sexual impulses are primarily directed toward incestuous satisfactions, and that their homosexual trends are merely a defense against incest. Either at the fastigium of the excited phase or when the depressed phase reaches a severity which involves serious clouding of consciousness, the deeply repressed incestuous trends find their way to overt verbal expression. The manic patient will either freely express incestuous longings or accuse a parent or a sibling of the opposite sex of such longings. The confused, hallucinated melancholiac will hear voices accusing him (or her) of incestuous behavior.

There is a type of manic depressive patient who never marries, and among these I have found a considerable number of patients who were thrown into a panic by the imminence of marriage or even of a proposal. Whenever it has been possible to make intensive studies of such cases I have found that the prospective spouse was rejected because he (or she) had acutely acquired the reactive value of an incestuously loved parent or sibling.

One young woman who discovered that she could not marry the man she loved because "it would be like going to bed with father," became frantically dependent on the affection of a girl friend directly the engagement was broken. There had been a tranquil, unemotional friendship between the two girls for years, but now my patient demanded that their relationship should move over onto a highly emotional basis.

In another case a girl who had never been conscious of any homosexual longings attributed each of her three broken engagements to her inability to escape a feeling that, because she loved her fiancé (a different man in each case), it would somehow be unnatural to have sexual relations with him. I was summoned to see her during the height of her third depression. I found an extremely agitated patient who would not talk to me until the nurse was sent out for a walk. The patient then told me that she had just discovered to her horror that she had an uncontrollable impulse to make sexual advances to the nurse. After some difficulty, I persuaded her to admit the nurse to a three-cornered conference about the matter. My reassurances not only calmed the patient but, as subsequent events proved, gave the nurse courage to yield to her own consciously but timidly held homosexual inclinations. Without any connivance on my part, the two effected a permanent homosexual union. The patient got well and has remained free of attacks for more than a decade. The fact that she had three manic-depressive cycles during the third decade of her life and none thereafter leads one to suspect that in her case an overt and stable homosexual union was a sufficient prophylaxis. She was predictably in for many subsequent attacks unless a successful analysis could be had, and external circumstances rendered this impossible.

3. Overt homosexuality has a complex and variable determination, but there is one factor which, I have begun to suspect, may be invariably present: I have not yet made an intensive study of an overt homosexual who has failed to tell me, *without leading or other kinds of suggestive questioning,* that he (or she) was conscious of having been erotically loved by a parent or sibling of the opposite sex. Even the manic depressive young woman just alluded to volunteered the information that she had always felt that an element of sexual passion entered into her overdemonstrative father's kissing and fondling, and that her somewhat older brother made definite sexual advances to her when she was approaching puberty.

Another young woman, not a manic depressive, had copulated with an older brother all during childhood. A year or so before her first menstruation he returned home after a six months absence. He had come into puberty and his sex organ had greatly increased in size since their last sexual contact.

Their first and only copulation after his return caused her considerable pain and his emission terrified both of them. Fear of pregnancy, an acutely developed sense of guilt and repulsion, and an antagonistic attitude toward the brother directly followed. During her twenties, she was easily seduced by a homosexual woman and was jealously in love with her when the anamnesis was taken.

I have published elsewhere accounts of sexually maladjusted women for whom heterosexuality had, *per se,* the reactive value of incest, and in a recent publication Fenichel made a similar observation. When such a reactive value is established for heterosexuality in consequence of overtly incestuous behavior during childhood, the defensive need of interposing an overdeveloped homosexual tendency between incestuous longings and consciousness seems to be imperative.

Freud makes the following sweeping statement concerning overt male homosexuals: "In all the cases examined we have ascertained that the later inverts go through in their childhood a phase of very intense but short-lived fixation on the woman (usually the mother) and after overcoming it they identify themselves with the woman and take themselves as the sexual object; that is, proceeding on a narcissistic basis, they look for young men resembling themselves in persons whom they wish to love as their mothers loved them."

My own case records justify me in making an equally sweeping statement as to the invariability of this finding in the histories of male inverts, and in stressing the defensive value of their inversion. To this observation I would add that such fixations are almost without exception demonstrably due to the veiled but unmistakable eroticism of "the woman" in her treatment of the future invert. The incestuous aggressiveness of this kind of mother love leaves her male child no alternative to homosexuality but incest. He must either go on surrendering to his mother as love object or defensively direct his sexual impulses away from femaleness in general.

4.

Psychoanalysis offers the most productive of all research techniques for teasing out the detailed psychodynamic structure of overt homosexuality. Its soundness and adequacy as a theory of mind must be credited with this circumstance, but it is also true that the overdeveloped narcissistic exhibitionism of the invert and the impaired repressive strength of his ego greatly facilitate the exploration of his unconscious processes. For this latter reason, the patient's verbal productions on the analytic couch will usually supply a mass of extremely valuable research material before his unconscious resistances require the analyst to add anything to his initial instructions.

Once the homosexual realizes that he must let his stream of consciousness flow through his mind as an unhindered, undirected, uncriticized response to dream components, and that he must hold nothing back from verbalization on the couch, the analyst can play a purely passive rôle during a prolonged initial period of analysis. For this reason. and because their material is so strikingly uniform, the findings of Freud and his followers can be taken as a collection of scientifically established data.

The male homosexual under analysis unerringly uncloaks that period of infancy which was dominated by incestuously directed impulses. While this is a common denominator of all male infantile experience, it is of abnormal intensity with the homosexual. Its abnormal intensity is due, in my opinion, to a correspondingly intense erotic component in the maternal love to which he is subjected. Freud's already quoted statement as to the future invert's fixation on "the woman" sums up a finding which no homosexual male patient of mine has ever failed to verify.

Fenichel has brought together a series of generalizations which I have found to be very helpful in my efforts to tease out this one important strand in the psychodynamic tangle presented by overt homosexuality:

1. He states that "an inner psychological circumstance" excludes woman as a sex object for the male invert.

2. Homosexuality, in his opinion is "like a screen memory" against a repressed heterosexuality which is primarily incestuous. I am quoting him out of full context here. He duly stresses the other factors that enter into account in addition to fear of incest.

3. Homosexuality is a special outcome of the oedipus-castration anxiety. In other words, the future invert so greatly fears castration as a punishment for his incestuous longings and his consequent death wishes against the father that he eschews heterosexual gratification as his consciously held erotic aim. If he copulates with women at all it is usually for the sake of having children or for his own reassurance; he typically speaks of heterosexual experience as unsatisfying.

Nevertheless, even the male invert who is exclusively homosexual, unconsciously longs for heterosexual relations. To quote Fenichel literally, "It is possible to show in all cases of homosexuality . . . the original heterosexual orientation which was rejected as a result of castration anxiety." Fenichel is unnecessarily cautious, in my opinion, in a further statement: "We may, therefore, state as a provisional formulation that for certain individuals, normal sexuality unconsciously means incest and is perceived as entailing danger of castration." In my experience, this holds true in all cases of overt homosexuality I have studied and is usually found in those cases of pathologically repressed homosexuality to which one attributes certain types of the compulsion neurosis, psychical impotency, compulsive alcoholism and the manic-depressive psychosis.

The limitations of this article forbid an elaboration of the psychoanalytic material which would have to be taken into account if an attempt were made to trace the dynamic relationship of fear of incest to all the other known factors entering into the determination of homosexuality. It is necessary, however, to make at least a brief allusion to the tendency of the libido to regress to earlier stages of its development when fear, frustration or the general tendency of the infant to socialize its impulses interfere with the achievement of heterosexual object love. This regressive tendency is marked in the overt homosexual who, at maturity, is preponderantly narcissistic, incapable of object love, still hobbled in his emotional life by the repression of an unresolved oedipus complex and more or less fixed at the anal level of libidinal development.

5.

In summing up the findings of my own studies in comparative psychology, objective psychopathology and psychoanalysis, and correlating them with the well established findings of Freud and his colleagues, I have arrived at two still tentatively held conclusions:

1. The homosexual tendencies that are a normal component of human bisexuality are apt to be overdeveloped as a defense against incest toward the end of infancy by males who have been too erotically loved by their mothers or mother surrogates. Female homosexuality is likewise a defensive against incest, but it has a more complex determination, and post infantile factors, such as the sexual aggressions of brothers or the too erotically tinged affection of fathers, usually play an important rôle.

2. The character traits of the overt homosexual are due to regressions from the phallic stage of libido development to earlier stages, and this in turn is a flight from incest. In this sense the character traits of the homosexual as well as his actual inversion are defensive against incest.

[EDITOR'S NOTES]

In this brilliant study by Hamilton, who so well understood the nature of homosexuality as a defense against incest, one must be impressed with the fact that the author felt that the suppression of the homosexual desires could be far more deleterious than could the expression of those desires to the man and woman. In this, Hamilton was a scientist and not a moralist. Although one must be surprised to find that, as a therapist, he is actually assisting two young women to become involved in a homosexual union, and although this shocking disclosure is likely to overshadow the more important meaning of the case history, Hamilton actually wished to show that the recognition of homosexuality would be a factor in the therapeutic approach to the manic depressive woman. It will be argued by some that Hamilton, following his own logic, should have continued the therapy toward a reorientation of the woman, so that he might remove the incest-block and permit normal relations with men. That he stopped short of such a step is an indication that, in his opinion, homosexuality was an adjustment and not a maladjustment for this patient, and that he had carried the therapy as far as he could.

Nevertheless, this aspect of the Hamilton work is of less importance than the contribution made in the tradition of Freud, to an understanding of the dynamics of overt homosexual development in cases where the child is overloved by the parent of the opposite sex.

D. W. C.

CRITERIA
FOR A HORMONAL EXPLANATION
OF THE HOMOSEXUAL

Alfred C. Kinsey

REPRINTED FROM THE JOURNAL OF CLINICAL ENDOCRINOLOGY,
VOL. 1: NO. 5, MAY 1941

In a recent article Glass, Deuel and Wright compared androgen and estrogen analyses of urine obtained from so called normal and homosexual males. For the homosexuals they reported androgen-estrogen ratios which they consider "significantly lower than those obtained in 31 normal males."

These conclusions are in line with widespread and long-standing popular opinion that homosexual behavior depends on some inherent abnormality which, since the time of the discovery of the sex hormones, is often supposed to be glandular in origin. This assumption is offered as specific explanation in some of the psychology and sociology texts, and some of the psychiatrists are treating homosexuality as an organic disease which is to be cured, if at all, by endocrinologic adjustments. Since these recently published studies are practically the first to test the validity of the current opinion, they are likely to attract some attention; and it is, therefore, desirable to examine the bases of the conclusions and, in fact, to consider the possibility of any hormonal explanations fitting the picture of homosexual behavior as it actually occurs in the human being.

The Glass-Deuel-Wright studies involved androgen and estrogen determinations of single urine samples from 31 supposedly normal males, and two to four samples from each of "17 clinically diagnosed male homosexuals." The summarized data, with some mathematical errors corrected, are as follows:

Samples	Average androgens	Average estrogens	Average of individual ratios
31 Normals	34.1	4.41	12.01
45 Homosexuals	29.9	6.72	7.87
Differences	4.2	2.31	4.14
	±2.46 (S.E.)	±1.08 (S.E.)	±1.85 (S.E.)

The ratios given here represent averages of the ratios obtained from each individual urine sample. Glass, Deuel and Wright introduce an error into their homosexual tables by computing the averages of the several ratios obtained for each individual, and then using the average of all these averages as the final figure for comparison with the normals.

It will be seen that analysis of the table above shows standard errors of such magnitude that the differences can hardly be taken to be conclusive. The samples are small, there is great variation in the samples from different individuals, and in the successive samples from the same individuals. Determinations of androgen in the homosexual group (e.g. *cases 4S, 7S, 14M, 15S*) showed variations of as much as 250 to 350%. Variation in successive measurements of estrogens for some of the homosexuals was as much as 300 to 2300% (*cases 3S, 5M, 6S, 7S, 8S, 9S, 10S, 14M, 15S, and 16M*). One is not warranted in concluding that the relatively small differences in averages between two such small groups are significant when successive samples from single individuals show 7 to 50 times as much difference.

The published study utilized results obtained by two different methods of collection of the urine. Part of the specimens represented 2-day pooled collections (in the case of the normals) and 5-day pooled collections (for the homosexuals). Part of the samples from each group represented 7 night-and-first-morning specimens. In analyzing their material, the authors pooled the results from both methods of sampling. But if the averages for each type of collection are handled separately, the record is as follows:

Samples	Average androgens	Average estrogens	Average of individual ratios
17 homosexuals: 5-day	36.95	8.37	8.44
20 normals: 2-day	34.50	4.86	10.86
Differences	2.45	3.51	—2.42
	±3.51 (S.E.)	±2.08 (S.E.)	±2.59 (S.E.)
28 homosexuals: 7-night-morning	25.69	5.72	7.47
11 normals: 7-night-morning	33.43	3.61	14.10
Differences	—7.74	2.11	—6.63
	±4.01 (S.E.)	±2.40 (S.E.)	±3.36 (S.E.)

By one method of sampling, the homosexual group seems to show more androgen than the normal group; by the other method of sampling there is less androgen. The methods of sampling may have had something to do with the results. In all these cases, however, the differences involve such large standard errors that little significance can be attached to the results.

FIELD DATA ON HOMOSEXUALITY

More basic than any error brought out in the analysis of the above data is the assumption that homosexuality and heterosexuality are two mutually exclusive phenomena emanating from fundamentally and, at least in some cases, inherently different types of individuals. Any classification of individuals as 'homosexuals' or 'normals' (= heterosexuals) carries that implication. It is the popular assumption and the current psychiatric assumption, and the basis for such attempts as have been made to find hormonal explanations for these divergences in human behavior. But what would a study of the phenomena themselves show? Until we know the nature of the gross behavior itself, no hormonal or other explanation is likely to fit the actuality.

Unfortunately there is a paucity of data on homosexual behavior. Our civilization so strongly condemns the behavior, that scientific examination of it has hardly begun. The best of the published studies are based on the select homosexual population which is found within prisons, and it seems, heretofore, to have been impossible to discover the extent to which the phenomenon occurs in otherwise socially adjusted portions of the population. At this time, therefore, it seems appropriate to publish certain data which we have collected on homosexuality.

These data are drawn from a series of more than 1000 histories which we have accumulated in connection with a general study on human sex behavior. Each history covers a minimum of 255 items, and many of the histories cover something more, up to as many as 495 items. All of the histories have been obtained by personal interview. We need ten thousand or more histories before we can draw definite conclusions on most of the phenomena involved. It is imperative that we have complete histories, covering all phases of each individual's sexual behavior, for our interpretation of any part of the picture is dependent upon our knowledge of its relation to the total experience of the individual. The published studies on particular aspects of human sexual behavior sometimes arrive at erroneous conclusions because they do not recognize that total behavior always involves an adjustment in which each item is affected by all of the others in the complex. Our experimentation with the sort of written questionnaire which has been the basis of most of the published studies shows that it is wholly inadequate for discovering any item against which there are strong social taboos. Over 1300 of the histories were obtained by the present author; 300 of them were collected by

Glenn V. Ramsey, of Peoria, Illinois, whose important studies on sexual behavior at the junior and senior high school level are being coordinated with our own on the older age groups.

Descriptions of the sampling methods and other technics which are being used in this study will be given in detail at another time, in another place; but here it should be indicated that about 58% of these histories have come from college populations, the remainder from a wide variety of social levels. Over 140 American colleges and universities are represented in the series. Special effort has been made to obtain a representative sample of socially average males and females. The adequacy of the series is being tested by a series of whole samples which represent all of the individuals in particular social groups, such as fraternity and rooming houses, professional and social organizations.

Of the first 1058 males in our series, 354 have been involved in homosexual behavior. This figure includes only those cases in which one or both parties in the relation have come to ejaculation as a result of stimulation provided by another male. There is another and highly significant group which responds to homosexual stimulation and which, in many cases, has had a considerable amount of homosexual contact; although it has not led to actual orgasm; but for the sake of the present discussion we shall confine our statements to cases which have come to full climax in the relation. This means that over 35.5% of all of the individuals in the series have had one or more homosexual experiences. The figure is a little over 30% for the college bred portion of the series. Elaborate analyses of these data suggest that they provide a fair basis for estimating the frequency in our American population as a whole, although the validity of this conclusion can only be indicated in the present brief article by citing the figure of 27% obtained from the 329 histories which we have from our whole samples. This last figure is a bit lower than the others, probably because the whole samples are, at present, overloaded with younger ages and with college groups.

At any rate, it seems warranted to believe that something between one-quarter and one-third of all the males in any mixed-aged group has had some homosexual experience.

But, in the course of a lifetime, it is probable that 50% or more of the male population will become involved in homosexuality. In support of this generalization we present the record on the age groups for which we have 50 or more histories per group. The less adequate data which we have for other ages indicate that there may be some further rise in the figures for the older groups. The figures for the younger groups are summarized in table 1. The figures for the "total adolescent population" represent the total number of individuals in

Age group	Entire series		College population		Whole samples	
	Total adolescent population	With homosexual experience	Total adolescent population	With homosexual experience	Total adolescent population	With homosexual experience
		%		%		%
10	22	9.1	—	—	7	14.3
11	132	16.7	80	15.0	52	17.3
12	445	16.6	273	16.1	161	19.3
13	765	19.2	505	16.2	241	22.4
14	909	23.6	675	19.7	236	22.5
15	883	26.4	699	21.9	214	23.3
16	857	29.1	710	24.5	209	24.4
17	836	29.4	712	25.5	208	24.5
18	805	30.7	709	26.9	205	25.8
19	726	32.1	653	28.5	166	28.3
20	627	32.7	565	29.2	111	28.8
21	520	33.1	465	29.2	80	27.5
22	375	33.9	328	29.3		
23	279	38.0	237	32.9		
24	208	40.8	175	35.4		
25	168	45.8	140	41.4		
26	139	46.0	113	41.6		
27	108	45.4	85	41.2		
28	85	49.5	65	46.2		
29	74	48.7	55	43.6		
30	61	49.2				
31	52	50.0				

TABLE 1. 1,058 MALES, PERCENTAGE WITH SOME HOMOSEXUAL EXPERIENCE

our series who were adolescent as they passed through each age group, up to the age at which the history was reported. The columns marked "with homosexual experience" show the percentage in each age group which has made homosexual contact at any time prior to the date of reporting.

The data given above are summarized in figure 1. It will be seen that the whole-sample curve closely coincides with the curve for the college series from which the whole samples were largely derived.

In brief, homosexuality is not the rare phenomenon which it is ordinarily considered to be, but a type of behavior which ultimately may involve as much as half of the whole male population. Any hormonal or other explanation of the phenomenon must take this into account. Any use of so-called normals as controls, in the way in which Glass, Deuel and Wright used them in their measurements, should allow for the possibility that a quarter to a half of these 'normals' may, in actuality, have had homosexual experience at some time in their lives; and, as we shall show further along, it must similarly be recognized that there are very few 'homosexuals' who have not had at least some, and in many cases a great deal of heterosexual experience.

It is true that many of the individuals in these tabulations have had only a very small amount of homosexual experience incidental to their other sexual activities, while others have had thousands of contacts and exclusively homosexual histories for long periods of their lives. The higher figures come, of course, from older, professional homosexuals who are making daily contacts, and who are regularly capable of repeated climax in a single 24-hour period. The literature constantly makes a sharp distinction between incidental and exclusively homosexual experience, between so-called 'acquired, latent and congenital (constitutional) homosexuality,' and between 'true inverts' and 'normals.' But although we have more detailed data on a larger number of cases than are recorded in any of the published studies, we fail to find any basis for recognizing discrete types of homosexual behavior. An analysis on any basis will show every type of intergradation between the extreme cases in our series. There are individuals who have had a lone and more or less accidental experience; there are cases which have had as many as fifteen or twenty thousand

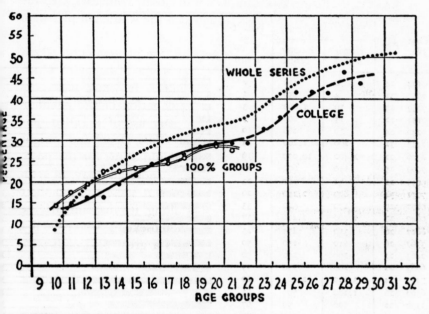

Fig. 1. ACCUMULATIVE CURVE OF INCIDENCE OF HOMOSEXUAL EXPERIENCE.
At successive age groups in 1058 males.

homosexual contacts (*cases 2777, 6341*); but between these individuals there are cases which involve all points between one and twenty thousand. There are cases which have confined their homosexuality to a single male partner; in our series there are cases of single males (e.g. *cases 1439, 2777, 6341, 7434, 7527, 8360*) who have contacted from 1000 to 15,000 other males. There are cases which began in preadolescent sex play, and cases (*0182, 5102, x8661*) which did not begin until after 30 or 40 years of age. We have cases where the homosexuality was confined to a small portion of the life span, a case (*4340*) where it has extended over 60 years of the life span, and other cases which show it extending through periods of every intermediate length. The homosexual may be confined to early or late adolescence, or to the third, or the fourth, or perhaps

Case No.	Age	Estimated frequency		Percentage homosexual	
		Homosexual	Heterosexual		
0104	24	0	450	0	
2697	22	4	550	1	HETEROSEXUAL
7099	19	30	1,000	3	
2153	22	15	200	7	
6246	24	30	266	10	
2433	31	200	1,200	14	
8306	22	2,400	10,000	19	
7009	25	150	600	20	
9053	22	30	100	23	
7031	34	800	2,250	26	
0892	19	150	300	33	
0640	27	1,400	2,400	37	
8817	26	350	475	43	
3367	26	150	150	50	
2463	21	200	200	50	
6983	22	200	150	57	
7434	24	3,000	2,000	60	
6369	26	1,200	700	63	
3599	22	100	50	67	
8153	21	500	150	77	
2777	29	15,000	4,200	78	
8460	21	800	200	80	
7864	31	1,000	200	83	
9924	25	700	100	88	
3687	27	1,250	100	93	
7841	29	2,000	100	95	
8837	41	3,000	100	97	
0168	19	500	4	99	
4047	24	1,600	0	100	HOMOSEXUAL
2432	29	4,000	0	100	

Fig. 2. COMBINATIONS OF HETEROSEXUAL-HOMOSEXUAL EXPERIENCE. Showing every gradation between exclusively heterosexual and exclusively homosexual experience in a selected series of 30 males.

later decade of life. There are cases in which the homosexual activity was continuous throughout a single period of the history, there are cases where it has been discontinuous with breaks of anything up to 34 years between the periods of participation. A popular opinion bases a classification on the technics involved in the physical relation, and makes a sharp distinction between the so called active and passive partners in the relation. Many of the so-called 'passives' regularly show that they can respond to homosexual stimulation by coming to climax in the relation.

There are popular and even clinical concepts of physical stigmata which are attached to the homosexual; and although there are some 'homosexuals' who show what are popularly considered to be 'effeminate' characteristics, there are others that are physically as robust and as athletically active as the most 'masculine' of men. There are, in short, intergradations between all of these types, whatever the items by which they are classified.

In this paper, only a single instance of intergradation can be presented in more detail. This involves the proportion in which the homosexual and the heterosexual fit into the life of a single individual. For while there are individuals who are exclusively heterosexual, or exclusively homosexual, there are many who carry on both types of activity, sometimes successively at different periods in their lives, more often simultaneously in a single period of the life span. This is illustrated by the series of 30 cases shown in figure 2. The chart is based on the percentage frequency of orgasm (actual ejaculation) inspired by human social contacts (in distinction to such autosexual outlets as masturbation and nocturnal emissions). It includes cases in which the homosexual has provided only a small proportion of the outlet, cases in which the homosexual and heterosexual have contributed more or less equally to the picture, cases in which the homosexual has provided the whole of the socialized outlet, and every type of case between the

extremes. It will be seen that one of the most actively homosexual cases in the series (*case 2777*) is a male with some 15,000
male contacts, and a concurrent heterosexual element which
includes intercourse an estimated four or five thousand times.

The curves showing the frequencies in these various types of
the heterosexual-homosexual balance are different for various
age groups in our series. In general, cases in which the heterosexual-homosexual ratio is near 50:50 are more abundant in
the earlier age groups; those in which the homosexual or heterosexual are more nearly exclusive are more frequent in the
older groups. There is evidence that the transformation to the
more frequently exclusive pattern of the older individuals is
partly the result of psychic conditioning, partly the result of
social pressure which fixes the heterosexual by custom and by
law, but which as effectively fixes the homosexual by ostraciz-
ing the individual who departs from the accepted mores. We
are particularly indebted to the Ramsey series of histories for
the interesting material on the younger age groups. The detailed record back of these generalizations must be published
elsewhere.

It should be more generally understood that there are many
cases of individuals who regularly include both the heterosexual and the homosexual among their activities in the course
of any month, week, or day. We have cases (e.g. *2777, 4651,
6341, 8306*) in which both types of contacts were successfully
made in the course of a single hour.

Finally, it must be realized that an exclusively homosexual
or exclusively heterosexual pattern may be replaced at a later
period in the life of a single individual by more or less exclusive activity in the other direction. Of the first 108 individuals
in our series who have had more than 100 homosexual contacts
each, 55 (= 51.%) have made distinctly successful heterosexual
adjustments. There are two cases of males (*cases 3063, 8360*)
who had had 15 and 17 years of almost exclusively homosexual
experience, who at ages 30 and 28 (respectively) began prac-

tically exclusive heterosexual activities which involved intercourse 3 to 7 times per week. On the other hand, we have a few cases (e.g. males *7504, 8425, 9957*, females *0632, 2302, 4541, 6367*) in which exclusively heterosexual activities were abandoned within a brief span of time for more or less exclusively homosexual activities.

Throughout the case histories, the circumstances of the first sexual experience, psychic conditioning, and social pressures are obvious factors in determining the pattern of the behavior. It would appear that no similar correlation has as yet been shown between hormones and homosexual activity. It is, of course, not impossible that endocrines are involved; but in order to demonstrate that, it would be necessary to show a correlative variation in hormones and behavior which includes such gradations, combined patterns, and changes of pattern as have been described here.

SUMMARY

Glass, Deuel and Wright report androgen content and androgen-estrogen ratios in male homosexuals which are lower than those in a 'normal' control group. Their conclusions are invalidated by the small size of their series, by the great variation shown among the individuals in the series and in successive samples from single individuals, and by the contradictory results which were obtained by the two different technics of securing urine samples.

Any hormonal or other explanation of the homosexual must allow for the fact that something between a quarter and a half of all males have demonstrated their capacity to respond to homosexual stimuli; that the picture is one of endless intergradation between every combination of homosexuality and heterosexuality; that it is impossible to distinguish so called acquired, latent, and congenital types; and that there is every gradation between so called actives and passives in a homosexual relation.

Any hormonal or other explanation of the homosexual must allow for the fact that both homosexual and heterosexual activities may occur coincidentally in a single period in the life of a single individual; and that exclusive activities of any one type may be exchanged, in the brief span of a few days or a few weeks, for an exclusive pattern of the other type, or into a combination pattern which embraces the two types.

Any explanation of the homosexual must recognize that a large portion of the younger adolescents demonstrates the capacity to react to both homosexual and heterosexual stimuli; that there is a fair number of adults who show this same capacity; and that there is only a gradual development of the exclusively homosexual or exclusively heterosexual patterns which predominate among older adults.

The Administration and the Dean of the Graduate School of Indiana University are responsible for a part of the financial support of these studies. Glenn V. Ramsey, Boys Health Director in a high school at Peoria, Illinois, secured the very important series of histories which we have on the youngest age groups. Clyde E. Martin is responsible for the intelligent and careful handling of our files and for the extensive computations which have been involved in the analyses of the data. My wife, Clara McMillen Kinsey, has materially contributed to our interpretations of the case histories and their objective treatment in this study.

[EDITOR'S NOTES]

The name of Alfred C. Kinsey is too well known to warrant any discussion. No man in our century has had so profound an effect on the thinking of Americans (and Europeans) on things sexual, as has Kinsey.

The "hormonal" explanation of homosexuality has had its fashions; there is hardly a serious nineteenth century writer, in fact, who did not believe that at least "some cases" of homosexuality were congenital—the forerunner of the "endocrinological" approach.

While most modern thinkers, from Freud on, have abandoned this outlook, it is still referred to, quoted, and to a smaller extent upheld. What Kinsey has done in this important contribution is to place this entire question in its proper perspective by demonstrating what the hormonal approach fails to explain, and what would be necessary in order that the hormonal approach be accepted and proved.

D. W. C.

PASTORAL COUNSELING
FOR HOMOSEXUALS

George W. Henry M.D.†

REPRINTED FROM PASTORAL PSYCHOLOGY, NEW YORK,
NOVEMBER 1951

Society has a way of dealing harshly with minorities. The homosexual is definitely a member of a minority group, and a minority group which has been held in special scorn by the community from time immemorial. Other minority groups have had some rights, but at no time in western civilization has the homosexual ever had any rights, as a homosexual, that the community has felt itself bound to respect. Because acts of homosexual intercourse have been adjudged criminal, for all practical purposes the homosexual can be considered a member of the criminal underworld, or half-world.

Although homosexuals have tried to justify themselves, to themselves, by pointing out great men in history who have been so conditioned, the justification is not too dissimilar to that of the bandit who might derive comfort from the fact that

† Associate Professor of Clinical Psychology, Cornell University Medical College.

384

Stalin is said to have been some sort of bandit in his earlier days.

Twenty years ago, it would have been impossible to discover a clergyman who would be willing to state that he counseled and helped homosexuals. Polite society might be willing to admit that there was such a thing as homosexuality in the world, but its presence was carefully concealed, and if an individual sought ministerial help he came to the pastor's study, in all likelihood, in secrecy. It would be a clergyman of unusual courage who would dare to discuss the problem of homosexuality at a ministerial conference. Two world wars and the publication of the Kinsey report, which forced upon a still suspicious world the fact that the ramifications of homosexuality were much more widespread than anyone cared to admit, have made it possible to discuss homosexuality with a certain degree of freedom. Watered down versions of the commonplaces of academic circles have at last reached the general public. Newspapers now dare to exploit the possibilities of stories affecting homosexuals, and one newspaper has published a series of articles concerning the manners and morals of the group in a section of New York alleged to be given over to loose living.

Under my direction, an experiment was tried in the Magistrates' Court of the City of New York, under which men arrested for homosexual disorderly conduct were placed on probation and advised to obtain psychiatric aid, and in some cases ministerial counseling. A panel of physicians and clergymen made their services available for this type of therapy, and the results of the experiment clearly demonstrated that the position of the homosexual could be improved to a very considerable degree with this help.

The popular conception of the homosexual is that of an extremely flamboyant individual, outlandishly dressed, effeminate in speech and appearance, walking with mincing gait, and given to exaggerated mannerisms which proclaimed his idiosyncrasies to all and sundry. Such is the case with only a minority of the group. The ordinary run of homosexuals are not to be distinguished from their fellow citizens by a casual observer. Only a trained individual, keen to detect nuances of appearance and behavior, can successfully recognize the average homosexual who is sufficiently concerned about the concealment of his interests and activities to adopt the protective coloration he finds necessary for his ordinary day-to-day existence in a world which is not prepared or willing to accept him. To illustrate this, there is presented the case of an individual sent to me for study and treatment by one of the criminal courts in the city of New York.

John came to us following his arrest in a subway toilet where he had been detected in intimacies with a minor. After several interviews sufficient of his story came to light so that his progress, or deterioration, as the case may be, could be traced. John was the only child of well-educated parents. When we first saw him, he was 28 years of age and an English instructor in a local college. He was white, single, nominally Protestant, with a Master's degree from a New England university. He liked to think of himself as detached from the world of ordinary things and people, and living in what he considered a rarefied atmosphere of good music, good art, and good literature. He was careful enough to adopt inconspicuous clothing, and he appeared before us most of the time in well-fitting and expensive grey flannels, buttoned-down Oxford shirt and black knitted necktie—a costume, by the way, very much in vogue among the more conservative and better-to-do homosexuals.

John had been brought up in a home which was indistinguishable from thousands of middle-class homes throughout the country, in a small New England town where his father enjoyed a social position as a minister but very little in the way of money. His father died when John was eight, and his mother, described as a dominating woman, contrived to have the boy sent to one of the better private schools and a conservative New England college. There he acquired a taste for the "better" things of life, but unfortunately lacked the pocket-book to support his expensive tastes. In many senses, John was a fish out of water. Although he lacked the means to move in the circles in which he desired to move, he identified himself with those of superior station. With less than the income of a workingman, his innate refinement prevented him from living within the means of those similarly situated. Yet at no time do we find him becoming involved in financial dishonesty.

John reports that his first interest in men became manifest to him while he was an undergraduate at college. He denies any previous experimentation, although it seems certain that his interest in males must have given him concern much earlier in life than he is prepared to admit. While in college, he was engaged in some immature sex play. He confined himself to mutual masturbation and to some "necking" with younger students. He tells us that he always felt fatherly toward younger boys.

With the advent of the war, John went into the Army, and very quickly he was sent to officer candidate school. He was commissioned, served well overseas, and received one minor decoration. He managed to contain himself for the most part sexually, and indulged himself in sex play only with a younger officer. He was careful to avoid intimacies with enlisted men and civilians. After his discharge, he was confronted with the necessity of making a living, his mother having died without leaving enough to support him. He was able to turn his intellectual interests to account, and he now teaches English quite successfully in a metropolitan college. There he is admired by his students as an individual of respected qualities, and he is the center of a group of hero-worshipping youngsters. With men of his own or similar station, John finds it impossible to become intimate physically. Therefore, he sought hole-and-corner adventure with unprepossessing youths. He frequented the Times Square area, and made himself somewhat conspicuous among the hoodlum male prostitutes who frequent the area to gain donations of cash and gifts. Actually he did try on many occasions to befriend some of the youths with whom he was intimate. Eventually, disaster overtook him in a subway toilet. He had gone from the point of mutual masturbation to acts of sodomy with the boys who struck his fancy. Unfortunately, as was noted in the article on the sex offender, we see again the case of a man whose relations with a youth start on a high plane, and somewhere the object of his benevolence becomes a sex object, with tragic results for all concerned.

Because the man was discovered to have a latent religious sense of considerable depth, it was decided that he should be seen by a minister as well as psychiatrist. Minister and psychiatrist together undertook the patient's readjustment. At the end of a two-year probationary period, he was discharged from court supervision as improved. Considerable maturity had been acquired by the patient during his period of treatment. He had gained more than a little insight into his situation, and he had adopted a much more mature outlook in respect to his sexual activity.

This individual is representative of homosexuals who might seek ministerial counsel, either of their own volition, or through reference by the courts, social agencies, schools, or interested individuals. What has the minister to offer such a person?

Space does not permit us to attempt to canvass what is called the etiology of the homosexual maladjustment. We are confronted with a hard, cold, brutal fact, the man is a homosexual. How he got that way may be of considerable speculative interest. Society is more concerned with relieving his condition than in contemplating its genesis. The task of the minister is not the exploration of a half-remembered history of childhood dereliction. It is highly improbable that many ministers would have sufficient experience to deal with complicated psychiatric case histories. The ministerial function is twofold: first, to put the patient in the way of getting realistic psychotherapy, and, secondly, to rid him of his guilts. It is no more the minister's task to condemn than it is to condone. The minister finds his place as an accepting, unquestioning friend who takes the patient as he is. Despite the fact that the patient may have violated the taboos which seem necessary for the maintenance of church and state, the man is still a human being in need of help. Some form of punishment may be necessary to relieve his guilts. God, acting on the penitent himself, does an infinitely better job of punishing than does any judge, prison keeper, or policeman. Conscience cannot be entirely stilled, all our protestations and rationalizations notwithstanding.

If we bear in mind that the patient is a human being, subject to the frailties of the flesh, then we are more realistic in our dealings with him. Too many ministers find it easier to see extenuating circumstances in the thief and the wife beater than they do in the homosexual—the threat to the ministerial security is less. One elevates an eyebrow at a whoremaster; one becomes empurpled at the homosexual. Why is this so? Society has been conditioned too long to regard the homosexual as a pariah and an outcast lower than the untouchables of India. The homosexual in his turn, again despite such protestations, rationalizations and justifications as he might offer, is equally sure that he has placed himself beyond the pale. And there we unite the tragedy of it all, minister and penitent forced by Anglo-Saxon social attitudes to condemn a person who may in large part be the victim of circumstances. It is no wonder, then, that homosexuals are aware that the minister follows rather than leads the procession. They seek his help, if at all, with the greatest of misgivings. The minister in his anxiety for ethical and social conformity, unconsciously, and sometimes all too consciously, reflects the publicly scornful and condemnatory attitudes in his half-hearted dealings with homosexuals. Nor has maudlin sympathy any place in treatment. Condescension is worse than forthright condemnation.

We have no assurance that the homosexual has committed the unpardonable sin. We have strong scriptural warrant that he has as much right as any other sinner to approach the Throne of Grace for the absolution and remission of his sins. We have no reason to believe that the clergy cannot hold out to him the chance of a socially useful life. The minister's position should be one of understanding and of promise that there is a place for him in the Kingdom of God. The minister is under a moral obligation to be considerate of him as he is of any penitent. To be an effective counselor, the minister must gain enough insight into his own situation to overcome the homosexual's fear of ministerial condemnation. He must help the penitent find respect for himself as a person. It matters not how the penitent has lost his self-esteem: the minister's job is to help him find it. The Kingdom of God is also the kingdom of self-respect. Let the minister beware of counseling homosexuals unless he, himself, is first well assured that he is able to accept the homosexual as a person. This does not involve condonation of offenses; yet no minister can hope to deal effectively with a penitent who is unable to hold his head erect as a free man in a free society. Until the homosexual can feel that he can walk without the finger of contempt and loathing pointed at him, he is still in jeopardy.

Here, then, is the dilemma. The homosexual lives in a society which accounts him an object of public condemnation. At most, a measure of secret tolerance may be afforded him in a charitable moment. Neither psychiatrist, minister, nor social worker can remake social attitudes overnight. The homosexual must be taught to live with himself in a society which punishes his illegal activities and scorns his desires. Somehow he must be helped to make the compromises with his instincts which will enable him to function as a socially useful member of the community. He must be helped to take his place as a worker and as a citizen. At the same time, the counselor must help the homosexual to raise the level of his emotional immaturity.

Fortunately we have a very important clue to the working out of some adequate and acceptable solutions of the adjustment of the homosexual to our social order. Too often the ill-informed public, and again, alas, those who should know better, regard homosexuality as an end in itself. The symptom is mistaken for the disease. Homosexuality is not a disease; it is an indication of a deep-seated personality disorder. Our task with the homosexual is to seek the roots of the insecurity of which one expression is his sexual aberration. As we relieve the patient's insecurity, we are able to bring him to a more adult level of interest and conduct, and, as we heighten his security, the less he finds it necessary to express himself as immaturely as he does in the psychosexual field.

Too often we lose sight of the fact that the patient's psychosexual immaturity is but one manifestation of a general emotional immaturity. We must look below what appears on the surface.

It is too easy for us to view the patient, especially if he comes to us from the courts, as solely a member of the criminal classes. Very quickly the homosexual senses the therapist's attitude, and our dealings with him are colored in the terms of the criminal law. It is easy to emphasize to the patient the pitfalls of his homosexual ways, further arrests, disease, blackmail, a prison term, and so on. Perhaps it is important that the patient be warned of the evil consequences that lie in wait if he continues in his course. The reiteration of these warnings tends to deepen the gulf between the therapist or counselor and the patient. On the one hand we have the righteous man; across the desk sits the sinner. Both the righteous and the sinner will confirm themselves in their attitudes. It is of paramount importance to make the patient aware of what awaits him if he goes his way. Unfortunately, intellectual awareness of the consequences of his acts is not enough. There was a time when thieves were publicly hanged. Yet pickpockets congregated around the gallows at Tyburn to make a good thing of the spectators' carelessness in guarding their pocketbooks as they were absorbed in watching the criminal dangling from the gibbet. Criminals know that the logical consequence of ordinary crime is the prison or the electric chair. Yet thieves and murderers persist in stealing and murdering. It is quite easy to overdo warning.

The minister in his relation with the homosexual must be careful to underplay his own righteousness and the patient's wrong-doing. He must be careful to think with the patient in the terms of tomorrow's possibilities, rather than yesterday's wrong-doing.

All that has been said here can be summed up in the endeavor to restore to the patient his self-respect. Unless the patient is helped to face himself with a certain amount of equanimity, he is already defeated. The minister's duty is to bring the patient into a working relation with himself. With that established, he can face the world with a reasonable amount of optimism. Like everyone else, the homosexual has to live with himself as well as with society. If he can be helped to live on reasonably good terms with himself, we have some right to say that he has been helped to take his place in the social order and to have worked out the beginning of a valid religious experience. Whitehead was everlastingly right when he defined religion as what a man does with his solitariness.

[EDITOR'S NOTES]

Few writers on homosexuality come to their subject so well equipped as does Dr. George W. Henry, not only because he is author of the work, *Sex Variants,* but because of the remarkable social work in this field carried out by a group working under his leadership and direction. This group having recommended pastoral counseling for many homosexuals must have faced the question: what type of counseling can the minister offer to a young person faced with overt homosexuality and its concomitant problems?

The minister, states Dr. Henry, must seek to restore self-respect in the individual, bring him into a working relationship with himself, help him to face the world with optimism. Can this be accomplished when the individual must face a world of hostility? Perhaps, but only if he is convinced that this hostility is unwarranted, unjustified, and to be rejected. Yet he must not combat too vigorously and overtly the viewpoints he rejects, because active struggle against them will bring him into greater conflict with the society in which he is trying to live. This is the dilemma which Dr. Henry has had the courage to face.

HOMOSEXUALITY, SODOMY
AND CRIMES AGAINST NATURE

Morris Ploscowe †

FROM SEX AND THE LAW, PUBLISHED BY PRENTICE-HALL, INC.,
NEW YORK, 1951

When an attendant in the New York City Magistrates Court formally opens the hearing on a charge of overt homosexual behavior with the reading of the complaint in open court, his normally stentorian voice drops to a whisper. He shares a widespread feeling that acts of sexual perversion are not matters for public consumption. Even where sexually deviant behavior comes to the attention of official agencies, it must be handled as quietly and discreetly as possible. It may be the subject of gossip; the derision of the "pansy," "fairy," or "queer" is frequent in private conversation. But public presentation of the problems of perversion, even of its significance to the community, is generally taboo.

Suddenly, however, the homosexual or sex deviant became a matter for headlines. At a Senate Foreign Relations Committee hearing, Secretary of State Acheson was questioned

† Executive Director, Commission on Organized Crime, American Bar Association.

about the number of persons dismissed from his department as poor security risks. One of his deputies, John Peurifoy, then in charge of personnel, volunteered the information that "ninety-one persons, most of them homosexual," had resigned under investigation over a period of three years. The resulting clamor for a "purge of the perverts" in Washington led to the separation from government service of many minor employees who may have had a homosexual episode at some time in their lives.

The action of the State Department in quietly ridding itself of known homosexuals rested on the well-founded opinion that homosexuals are notoriously subject to blackmail, particularly if they are wealthy and hold positions of importance. Threats to reveal their failings have induced many homosexuals to pay unscrupulous persons large sums of money. The same susceptibility to blackmail makes them poor security risks. Agents of foreign powers can trade on homosexuals in key governmental positions to obtain information to which they are not entitled. Apparently this is a technique that Hitler employed, for he is alleged to have had a list of homosexuals in high posts all over the world. This list is supposed to have fallen into the hands of the Russians.

But the political uproar over the State Department revelations and the resulting clamor for a "purge of the perverts," which led to the separation from government service of many employees, rested on another basis. It capitalized on the average man's revulsion to abnormal sexual activity, and on his ignorance of the nature, extent, and causative factors that determine homosexuality as well as other forms of deviant sex behavior.

Homosexuality is the preference by an individual for a person of the same sex, rather than a person of the opposite sex, as a sexual companion. If is an anomaly which afflicts both men and women. It is encountered in persons in all walks of life and in all professions or occupations. It may afflict long-shoremen as well as college professors, barbers or beauticians

as well as ministers or members of Congress, laborers as well as
captains of industry, waiters as well as prize fighters. It is not
recognizable by physical signs alone. Effeminacy sometimes
characterizes the male homosexual and masculinity the female,
but more often male and female homosexuals are indistinguishable in body structure, voice timbre, or general behavior
from ordinary heterosexual individuals. Homosexual activity
may violate penal statutes. Under the designation of sodomy
and crimes against nature, specific kinds of sexual behavior
usually indulged in by homosexuals are prohibited. However,
such behavior as fellatio, sodomy, and cunnilingus is not confined to homosexuals. It may also be indulged in by heterosexual individuals, both married and single.

The law has considered sodomy, crimes against nature, and
homosexual behavior as serious perversions, the free choice
of depraved individuals, the product of vicious desires rather
than anomaly or disease. Moreover, modern judges and legislators, like their predecessors, have labored under the impression that the proscribed forms of sexual behavior are comparatively rare, that they are not indulged in by ordinary individuals, and their very abnormality requires their suppression.

However, modern research has cast doubt upon these prem-
ises. In the first place, acts of sodomy and crimes against nature
occur in widely different social situations, and these social
situations must be understood before there can be any judgment with respect to the offense or the persons involved.

Much of the sexual satisfaction of male and female homosexuals is obtained from behavior that violates sodomy and
crime-against-nature statutes. Mutual masturbation, interfem-
oral masturbation, fellatio, and anal coitus are the normal
methods of male homosexual satisfaction. Mutual masturbation, clitoral and vaginal stimulation, and cunnilingus are the
usual techniques of the female homosexual. But the social
situations in which these types of sexual activities are carried
on vary just as widely as in the case of heterosexual behavior.

Much homosexual activity which violates sodomy and crime-against-nature statutes results from contacts with male prostitutes. Every large city has the type of individual who will engage in any kind of sexual activity for a fee. As one male prostitute put it, "I have had men of all different ages, from twenty to seventy. The majority are extremely wealthy members of clubs. They are people who can't spend their incomes, some of the best people in their worst moments. I have sex with them for a specific sum, from twenty to one hundred dollars a night." Occasionally male prostitutes dress up in female attire. Many a man has been surprised to discover that the "girl" he has hired for the night was masculine.

One sociologist, observing male prostitutes over a period of forty-nine nights, noted 121 actively soliciting in a large city square. He interviewed thirty-six of them. Few of them showed effeminate characteristics; they were pleased when he told them they did not look the type. Many of them, however, adopted feminine mannerisms to attract attention and customers. Few of these male prostitutes admitted any pleasure from homosexual behavior; most of them declared it repulsive. Their basic reason for soliciting was money. The interviewer found that these boys were willing to perform almost any sexual act desired by a customer for a minimum of two dollars up to a maximum of fifty dollars.

At the other end of the scale from the male prostitute is the homosexual couple, either male or female, who live quietly and discreetly together for relatively long periods, establishing a quasimarital relationship. There is a fair degree of fidelity between the partners as long as the liaison lasts. The fact that the physical aspect of the relationship rests upon the violation of penal statutes is accepted as one of the inevitable necessities of the situation.

Normally, there is no real permanence to homosexual relationships. The quality of emotional instability encountered in homosexuals, both male and female, makes them continually dissatisfied with their lot. Many of them are continually on the prowl, looking for new sexual partners and new sexual adventures. New liaisons, when formed, are normally carried on with discretion. But there is a type of exhibitionistic homosexual who finds great satisfaction from sexual acts in the company of others. Thus, if the roofs could be taken from certain rooms in which homosexuals congregate, one might find them engaged in sodomy and crimes against nature. The homosexual term for this type of exhibitionism is the "daisy chain."

Homosexual activity is not restricted to inverts who have a horror of sexual intercourse with persons of the opposite sex. Some is carried on by persons who are bisexual in nature. They enter into normal sexual relations with persons of the opposite sex. Occasionally they even marry and have children. But their preference is for companions of their own sex. While married, they enter into sexual liaisons with persons of their own sex.

Whenever men are isolated from women, or women from men, for any length of time, homosexual relationships and activity inevitably develop. They caused problems in our armed services, which brought together large numbers of men under conditions of emotional stress. Homosexuality is a common problem in ships, schools, camps, prisons, and other institutions in which men or women are segregated. Much of this homosexual activity is what the psychiatrists call "faute de mieux." It is normally sloughed off when contact with the opposite sex again becomes possible.

Some individuals engage in homosexual activity sporadically even though they may not be deprived of contacts with women. Liquor has a tendency to release latent homosexual impulses. Men who normally have their homosexual impulses under control, but who have lost their control as a result of excessive drinking, frequently appear in court on charges of sodomy or homosexual activity in public places.

Much homosexual activity is due to adolescent curiosity and

sex experimentation. It is normally carried on with school-
mates or friends of the same age, and is a problem for board-
ing schools and camps confined to one sex. But occasionally the
introduction to homosexual activity is made by older men.
Ramsey, who studied the sexual development of 291 boys, determined that at least 35 per cent had been involved in one or
more homosexual experiences between the onset of adolescence
and the age of seventeen. The homosexual partners were normally boys of approximately the same age. Thirty-five of the
291 boys studied, however, had been approached by adult
males who desired homosexual relationships, and eight of the
boys had accepted these proposals and had participated in
sexual relationships with older men. Most of the adults making the advances to the boys were strangers. Occasionally, however, the older man occupied a position of trust toward the
boy, such as a teacher, pastor, or camp counselor.

Obviously, the notion of judges and legislators that sodomy
and crimes against nature are loathsome perversions which
occur only in rare instances and must be severely repressed because of their very abnormality is erroneous.

Nor is homosexuality a rarity in our culture. It has been
estimated by such authorities as Hirschfeld and Havelock Ellis
that from 2 to 5 per cent of a particular population are homosexual. Kahn, who studied homosexuals in New York City
Penal Institutions, estimated that there were from 100,000 to
500,000 in that city alone. Professor Kinsey criticized these and
similar estimates. Since a man or woman may be engaging in
both kinds of sexual activity at different times, Kinsey declared
it impossible to answer the question as to how many persons
are homosexual and how many are heterosexual in any given
population.

The Kinsey investigators did find it possible to rate individuals according to the degree of their homosexual and heterosexual experience. On this basis, the Kinsey report notes
that at least 37 per cent of the male population has had some

homosexual experience between the beginning of adolescence and old age. Among males who remained unmarried until they were thirty-five years old, "almost exactly 50 per cent . . . had homosexual experience between the beginning of adolescence and that age." This does not mean that all these individuals are genuine homosexuals, for some of them have but a single experience while others have behind them a lifetime of homosexual activity. But all have had "at least some experience to the point of orgasm."

Female homosexuality has been studied much less intensively than male homosexuality, but it too is far more widespread than is generally realized. Havelock Ellis estimated that there was twice as much female homosexual activity as male. Katherine B. Davis studied twelve hundred unmarried college graduates who averaged thirty-seven years of age. Of this number, half had experienced intense emotional relations with other women and over three hundred, or one-fourth of the total, reported sexual activities with other women. Of one hundred married women studied by Hamilton, one-fourth admitted homosexual physical episodes. Of forty Lesbians studied by Henry, thirty-two admitted bisexual experience, but only eight of these women stated that they obtained any sexual satisfaction from men. The rest found such gratification only with women.

Homosexuality among either men or women is therefore no rare phenomenon. Nor does anyone contend that the homosexual either male or female, is better able to control sexual impulses than the heterosexual. Hirschfeld, in fact, points out that only 5 per cent of the homosexuals he studied were able to curb their sexual impulses or to satisfy them by solitary masturbation. He estimated that 95 per cent of these individuals find their impulses uncontrollable and seek sexual satisfaction at varying intervals. Such sexual satisfaction almost invariably involves a violation of sodomy and crime-against-nature statutes.

Only a minute portion of the homosexual and heterosexual activity that violates sodomy and crimes-against-nature statutes ever comes to the attention of law-enforcement officials. When the number of arrests and convictions are compared with the types of social situations which produce sodomistic acts and crimes against nature, with the estimates of homosexuality, and with reports on the incidence of unconventional methods of sexual satisfaction, it is obvious that legal prohibitions against sodomy, homosexuality, and crimes against nature are practically unenforceable. One study estimated that six million homosexual acts of sodomy, fellatio, and mutual masturbation take place each year for every twenty convictions.

The small number of cases of homosexuality, sodomy, and crimes against nature which comes to the attention of law-enforcement agencies despite the age-old religious and legal denunciation of them and the mounting evidence of their widespread occurrence raises the question of the proper role of the criminal law in the prohibition and suppression of these acts. There can be no answer without a consideration of the nature of the drive that leads men and women to unconventional sexual activity. The law has simply assumed that men and women engage in unnatural methods of sex satisfaction through choice, depravity, and wickedness.

Until late in the last century, the stock explanations for homosexuality and sodomistic practices was excessive masturbation or appetites jaded by normal means of sexual expression. But science today offers an explanation of homosexuality in terms of growth processes and the failure of the sexual impulse to develop normally. The crucial period is adolescence. Then boys and girls crystallize their interest in the opposite sex. Then they begin the experimentations which lead to the eventual choice of a mate. In adolescence, the boy who is homosexually inclined or the girl who has a leaning toward Lesbianism may discover an aversion for the other sex and the strong attraction of his own sex. They may be confirmed in these feelings if, as frequently happens, they become initiated into homosexual practices by experienced adults or even adolescents.

Students of homosexuality disagree as to why the sex impulse fails to develop normally in certain individuals. Some believe that biological and constitutional factors predominate in the development of the homosexual. All persons are said to have within themselves characteristics and qualities of both sexes. In the normal individual, the process of growth and development pushes the characteristics and qualities of his own sex to the fore. But in the homosexual, either through congenital defect, hereditary taint, or endocrinological imbalance, the growth process is arrested and the individual remains with many of the characteristics and qualities of the opposite sex. Thus many an invert or homosexual male has traces of physical as well as psychological effeminacy, the feminine carrying angle of the arm, a feminine body conformation, long legs, narrow hips, deficient hair on face, chest and back, a high pitched voice, a feminine distribution of pubic hair, small penis and testicles, an excess of fat on the shoulders, buttocks and the abdomen. In some cases the physical and mental differences between genuine homosexuals and normal human beings are so marked that some scientists like Hirschfeld regard the homosexual as an intersex, a third sex which is neither altogether masculine nor altogether feminine. Another scientist declared that homosexuality is nature's way of redressing the male-female balance, because he found that while there are normally 106 male births to every 100 female, among the siblings of male homosexuals the ration was 121.1 to 100. Homosexuals themselves frequently express the conviction that they are an intermediate type between man and woman and that they therefore have a biological and inherent right to deviant types of sexual satisfaction.

Psychiatrists and particularly psychoanalysts reject the explanation of homosexuality on any constitutional or biological basis. They are more likely to agree with Bergler that "homosexuality is not due to biological hermaphroditism. . . . Endocrinology has nothing therapeutic to contribute to the problem of homosexuality."

In attempting to determine what psychogenic factors determine the individual's homosexuality psychiatrists stress his early childhood, the oversolicitousness and overprotection of the parent of the opposite sex, and the gross abusiveness or negative role of the parent of the same sex, the marked emotional instability of the parents, the fact that the parents wanted a child of a different sex and showed it in the treatment of the child. Thus the latent homosexual may be foreseen in the boy who is tied to his mother's apron strings, who does not play the usual boyhood games with his own age group, who prefers girls' games and girlish activities. Similarly, Lesbianism may be predicted in the girl who identifies herself with her father rather than her mother, who engages in tomboy activities, who prefers boys to girls as playmates, who would rather play baseball and football than dolls or house. Psychiatrists stress the decisive role of homosexual seduction around puberty and the disastrous influence of contact with experienced older homosexuals. Under the influence of factors like these, psychiatrists feel that homosexuality may develop in anyone regardless of constitutional factors. Additional explanations of the mechanism of homosexuality coming from the psychoanalysts involve such ideas as the Oedipus complex, the castration anxieties and penis pride of boys, the penis envy of young girls, and the unconscious identification on the part of many homosexuals of breast and penis.

Where experts differ, the layman certainly has difficulty in deciding which of the conflicting theories of sexual development best explains the homosexual and the sexually deviant personality. All the theories, however, make it clear that homosexuality is a process of development, not a matter of choice; that while the homosexual's methods of sexual gratification

may be prohibited by law, the latter cannot change his essential nature. The mounting evidence of the widespread existence of homosexuality presented by Kinsey and others, con-
trasted with the meager number of cases brought into court,
is a clear indication of how ineffective the criminal law is in
restricting homosexual practices. Legal provisions do not prevent homosexuals from living according to the dictates of their
nature. The ineffectiveness of the criminal law in dealing with
homosexual behavior would seem to require a change in present legal provisions. Adult homosexual behavior which occurs
privately and which does not give rise to public scandal is
presently not being punished by the law. It might be desirable
to eliminate the legal prohibitions against adult homosexual
behavior in private altogether. Such prohibitions benefit nobody but blackmailers at the present time. The elimination of
prohibitions against adult homosexuality in private would not
imply social approval of homosexual conduct. It has been said
that there are no happy homosexuals and that there can be
none as long as they must live in a heterosexual world. It
would simply mean that realities are being recognized; homosexuals cannot be changed by law. Changes in their patterns of
behavior can only be brought about by the more personal
influences of religion, education, psychiatry, and social work.

For similar reasons, the legal provisions against heterosexual
behavior between adults which violates sodomy and crimes-
against-nature statutes should be eliminated. The law is probably even less effective in repressing unconventional methods
of sexual expression between heterosexual than between homosexual adults.

With the situations which the law is powerless to correct
out of the way, the other legal provisions relating to homosexuality and crimes against nature should be rigidly enforced.

First and foremost, children and minors must be protected
against sexual advances, whether such advances are heterosexual or homosexual in character. Exposure to the sex deviate
may have a decisive and harmful effect upon a child's develop-

ment of a normal sex life as an adult. Despite their differences of opinion, students of homosexuality seem to agree that exposure during adolescence may be the precipitating factor in the adult development of the homosexual. The law must make it possible to take effective action against twisted adults who use children and minors as sexual objects.

Secondly, male prostitution must continue to be suppressed. This is a major source of crime, disorder, and disease in every large city. The promiscuous sex activity of the male homosexual prostitute is just as much a spreader of disease as that of the female prostitute. Police departments are familiar with larceny, extortion, blackmail, and murders arising out of male prostitution.

The apprehension, conviction, and imprisonment of male prostitutes, overt homosexuals, and seducers of children does not solve either their or the public's problems. The ordinary prison has no facilities for modifying the sexual behavior patterns which have brought them into conflict with the law. What is worse, the ordinary penal institution, with its concentration of young men or young women, offers widespread opportunities for the practice of sexually deviant behavior. This is well recognized by prison wardens, who normally segregate homosexuals from the rest of the prison population. Otherwise they find prison discipline disrupted by conflicts and jealousies over homosexual partners. But segregation with similarly afflicted individuals, while it may relieve the strain on the penal institution, is useless as a means of redirecting homosexual behavior. It must be combined with medical and psychiatric treatment which is generally unavailable in penal institutions. The result is that overt homosexuals and male prostitutes continue their activities during confinement and after they are released.

If these types of individuals are to be effectively controlled, new methods of treatment and new types of institutions, as well as new legal provisions for their arrest and custody, will be required.

[EDITOR'S NOTES]

Nowhere has the attitude of the modern jurist toward homosexuality been expressed with such clarity as seen in this piece by Judge Morris Ploscowe. For it is today widely felt, although not too often stated, that the legal restrictions against homosexual relations between adults should be eliminated. Children and minors should be protected against such practices, Judge Ploscowe contends, a thesis with which only a few extremists (as Rene Guyon) would argue; and the author cites the reason for this thinking: "Exposure during adolescence may be the precipitating factor in the adult development of the homosexual." Since this adult development is frequently fraught with anxiety, loneliness, and even tragedy, steps should be taken to prevent such development.

The second restriction against homosexual activities, Judge Ploscowe contends, should be the regulation of prostitution. This would involve a more careful definition of prostitution; for casual homosexual relations between people who had been strangers before and will continue to be strangers after, is usually not accompanied by the payment of funds. It is this casual activity that is responsible for the spread of disease, and for larceny, extortion, blackmail, and even murder.

The need for a reevaluation of all sex laws (or, one might say, anti-sex laws) is a part of this problem; the repeal of antiquated restrictions on sexual activity voluntarily engaged in between adults should seem to be the main orientation. In drawing up new statutes, certain types of sexual activity would continue to be punished, and the fact that such activity might be homosexual would, in fact, be incidental.

D. W. C.

ARE HOMOSEXUALS
NECESSARILY NEUROTIC?

Albert Ellis

REPRINTED FROM ONE MAGAZINE, APRIL 1955 (WITH PERMISSION
OF THE AUTHOR).

In the January 1955 issue of One, The Homosexual Magazine,
there are two articles whose writers contend that homosexuality is not necessarily neurotic, and who imply that homosexuals
can be just as "normal" as, and in some ways perhaps more
"normal" than non-homosexuals. Thus, in "Literature and
Homosexuality," David L. Freeman writes: *"But there is a
way out of the morass of degenerate mediocrity. Ideals of the
original Mattachine, concepts eloquently set forth by Cory,
and principles adopted by One magazine (all indirectly re-
inforced by Kinsey's researches) embraces an altogether new
approach: Homosexuals are not necessarily neurotic and, when
they are, their neuroses generally spring from their homosexuality in a heterosexual world. This approach provides an
entirely new, optimistic rallying point for America's five to
fifteen million homosexuals and should be a clarion call to all
of them aspiring to do creative writing in the interest of their
minority."*

Later in the same issue of One, Chris Rezak, writing from the feminine viewpoint in an article entitled "For Writers: an Appeal," notes that "there are a very, very few excellent novels on the shelf of homosexual literature—they need company. This then is a call to arms—to others, to myself. Let's begin to think in terms of writing a warm, beautiful novel, full of depth and passion, seasoned with humor—a book about people who live proudly and happily with their homosexuality, who are strong and capable and find life great fun—and who never even think of suicide."

Although I, too, have several times gone on record as stating that homosexuals are not necessarily neurotic; although I am the author of the highly approving introduction to Donald Webster Cory's "The Homosexual in America;" although I have been a consistent supporter of Dr. Alfred C. Kinsey's work and have publicly defended the first and second Kinsey reports more, perhaps, than any other psychologist in the United States; and although I have no insignificant reputation as a non-homosexual who staunchly upholds the rights of homosexuals and opposes any persecution of them, I must strongly protest against the expressed and implied sentiments of Freeman, Rezak, and all others who fail to see that although all homosexuals are not *necessarily* neurotic, the great majority of them indubitably are. Moreover, if we mean by "homosexual" an individual whose sex desires are exclusively oriented toward the members of his (or her) own sex, or who is incapable of enjoying sex participation except with a member of his (or her) own sex, then there can be little doubt that *all* such homosexuals are, and *necessarily* are, neurotic. To deny this is folly, and will only do great harm to innumerable homosexuals.

The problem of homosexuality and neurosis can only be clearly understood if we first understand what is neurosis or sexual abnormality, perversion, or deviation. From a psychological or psychiatric standpoint, neurosis or perversion can only be meaningfully defined by using some criterion of illogicality, irrationality, childishness, fixation, fetishism, inflexibility, rigidity, or exclusivity. A neurotic, in other words, is an individual who is theoretically endowed with normal intelligence and education, but who nonetheless acts in a childish, irrational, effectively stupid manner. A pervert or deviant is one who is physiologically or theoretically able to obtain sex satisfaction in several different ways, since man, biologically, is a plurisexual animal who has several available roads to sex stimulation and orgasm but who actually is limited to one or two major forms of sex outlet because he is irrationally, fearfully fixated or fetishistically restricted by certain ideas or behavioral habits which he learned at some earlier time in his life.

A neurotic and a pervert, in other words, are exactly the same, although one of the greatest psychologists of all time, Sigmund Freud, mistakenly thought otherwise. A pervert or sex deviant is actually a sexual neurotic; and a neurotic is nothing but a nonsexual deviant. The definitive characteristic of both the neurotic and the pervert is that they both arbitrarily narrow down a potentially wide field of action into a very limited act which they feel, out of irrational fear, that they must perform if they are to be comfortable or satisfied.

The fact that neurotics and perverts are really the same may, as I point out in my book "The American Sexual Tragedy," clearly be seen if we forget about sex perverts for a moment and talk about individuals whom we may call food perverts. Suppose, for example, an individual who is in good physical health and has no special allergic reactions insists on eating nothing but meat and potatoes; or suppose he only will eat once a day, at three in the morning, and will not touch a bit of food at any other time, even if he is starving; or suppose he will only eat off a particular set of blue plates, and will absolutely refuse to eat if these are not available. Obviously, in the popular parlance, this individual would be crazy; more technically, we would call him a neurotic or a food pervert.

By the same token, sex perverts are just as obviously neurotic—are emotionally disturbed individuals who are fetishistically attached to one particular mode of sex activity, and who usually, though not always, became fetishistically attached to this form of behavior because of peculiarities or fixations which arose during their childhood. Sexual neuroses are essentially the same as other forms of neurosis, except that, in our antisexual society, we emotionalize them and tend to view them in a special light.

Are, then, all individuals who engage in homosexual activity perverted and hence neurotic? By no means so. As Dr. Kinsey most effectively points out, most individuals who engage in homosexual activity do so for only a few years of their lives or do so along with their equally satisfying heterosexual experiences or other sex experiences. If one wishes to call all such individuals "homosexuals," then there is no question that all "homosexuals" are not perverted or neurotic.

If, however, by "homosexual" we mean an individual who exclusively desires homosexual participation, who derives little or no satisfaction from heterosexual activity, and who either avoids heterosexual relations or is heterosexually potent but anesthetic, then we are, almost by definition, describing a sex pervert or neurotic. For such a "true" or "essential" homosexual is quite arbitrarily and illogically, out of some underlying or conscious fear of heterosexual behavior, narrowing down his sex activity and/or desire to inverted behavior. By exactly the same token, any individual who *exclusively* enjoys masturbation, sadistic or masochistic sex practices, sex relations with animals, or *any* one form of sex act, and who under *no* circumstances can truly enjoy and receive orgasm through some other kind of sex acts—that person is indubitably a sex pervert or a neurotic.

How about exclusive heterosexuals, then? Are they necessarily perverted or neurotic? Technically, yes. If by exclusive heterosexual we mean an individual who exclusively desires sex relations with members of the other sex; who *under no circumstances,* even if he were marooned on a desert island with only members of his own sex for a long period of time, could achieve sex satisfaction and orgasm through homosexual or other sex outlets; and who is utterly afraid of trying all non-heterosexual outlets and is compulsively tied to heterosexual ones;—then that individual is indubitably neurotic or perverted. By unequivocally stating this in "The American Sexual Tragedy" and several of my scientific papers on human sexuality, I have drawn upon my head the wrath of numerous professional and lay readers. But I unhesitatingly say so again, and shall continue to say so until someone proves otherwise. What is sauce for the goose should be sauce for the gander. And if exclusive homosexual desire is perverted and neurotic, which it most certainly seems to be, then exclusive heterosexual desire may be just as perverted and just as neurotic.

Otherwise stated: any individual who can *only,* under *all* circumstances, enjoy one specialized form of sexual (or nonsexual) activity; anyone who is compulsively or obsessively fixated on one single mode of sexual (or nonsexual) behavior; anyone who is fearfully and rigidly bound to any *exclusive* form of sexual (or nonsexual) participation;—that individual is unquestionably a pervert and a neurotic. What is more, all such individuals—and I mean *all*—can undoubtedly be cured of their neuroses or perversions, in the sense that they can be helped to find satisfaction in *other* sex acts than the one to which they are fetishistically fixated, if they really want to be cured and will work, in a psychotherapeutic relationship, for such a cure. This I have proven over and over again with homosexual patients (and other sex perverts) who come to see me with a genuine desire to gain heterosexual satisfactions.

To state or imply, then, as Freeman and Rezak distinctly state and imply, that homosexuals, by which they apparently mean exclusive or near-exclusive homosexuals, are neurotic only because "their neuroses generally spring from their homosexuality in a heterosexual world," and that they can easily "live proudly and happily with their homosexuality" is to state dangerous nonsense. It is certainly true that our heterosexual world unfairly persecutes homosexuals and makes them considerably *more* neurotic than they might otherwise be; it is also true that some homosexuals can "adjust" to their homosexuality in the sense of losing their guilt about it, and that they consequently can live more proudly and happily with their homosexuality than if they did not "adjust" to it. But an adjusted neurotic is still a neurotic—and often a much more serious neurotic than an "unadjusted" one: since the unadjusted neurotic at least admits how disturbed he is, and may possibly eventually go for treatment. But an "adjusted" neurotic, as shown by literally millions of our citizens who are much too inhibited truly to enjoy life, but who keep insisting that "nothing is wrong with me" and "only crazy people go to see psychologists," is perhaps the most tragic neurotic of all: for absolutely nothing can be done to help him.

Let you homosexuals face it, therefore: all of you, every mother's son of you who is exclusively desirous of homosexual relations, is indubitably neurotic. Those of you, like Cory himself, incidentally, who are capable of being happily married and having heterosexual satisfactions right along with your homosexual affairs, may not necessarily be emotionally disturbed (though, on some other count, you may be). But those of you who are disgusted by the mere thought of boy-girl relations; who are more or less impotent in heterosexual affairs; who are potent but unsatisfied by heterosexual relations; who are afraid to make any sexual overtures to members of the other sex; who compulsively engage in homosexual acts even though you find little enjoyment in them; who are unable to love virtually any of your sex partners; who are horrified at the thought of masturbation or other nonhomosexual acts; who dogmatically refuse to try any heterosexual participations; —all of you are just about as neurotic as you could possibly be, and you had better run, not walk, to the nearest psychotherapist.

Certainly, if you want to say so, innumerable heterosexuals are neurotic and perverted, too. That is their problem. But if you refuse to admit your own emotional disturbance, and try to ape the ostrich by pretending that your neurosis is solely a result of societal ostracism and persecution, you are sadly fooling only yourselves. And that, too, is what neurosis essentially is—illogically, out of some underlying fears, acting in a certain manner, or adopting what we psychologists call a set of neurotic symptoms, in order *not* to face the facts of the underlying fears or guilts. Those exclusive homosexuals, in other words, who most loudly proclaim that they are not necessarily neurotic are, by their very head-in-the-sand attitudes, conclusively proving how seriously neurotic they actually are.

By all means, then, let us try to see that homosexuals, like all other neurotics, are able to live as happily as possible in this neuroticizing society. By all means let us try to put a halt to the unfair calumny and persecution that now is heaped on them. By all means let us try to change society, and its antisexual attitudes in particular, so that it accepts homosexual acts without encouraging exclusive, obsessive-compulsive homosexuality. But let us not, please, confuse what Dr. Kinsey calls homosexual outlets with what the gay world usually means by homosexuality. The former is a normal biological *part* of human sex activity; the latter is a fetishistic sickness. To say otherwise would be to gratify many homosexuals who are desperately trying to deny their own emotional disturbances; but it would be a scientific untruth. I should indeed be a false friend to my many homosexual correspondents, associates, and patients were I not to make this vitally important point. I can only finally repeat: He who engages sporadically or non-exclusively in homosexual acts is not necessarily a pervert or a neurotic. But he who has exclusively inverted desires, or is truly "gay," necessarily is. This is fact; all else is wishful thinking.

[EDITOR'S NOTES]

In his short and significant article, *Are Homosexuals Necessarily Neurotic?* Albert Ellis states many facts that have become obscured in the modern attitude of benign sympathy that has characterized certain advanced psychological circles. Because homosexuality is so often associated with compulsions, fears, and obsessions, it is a neurosis; this statement, few can deny. This poses the problem: Must homosexuality be tied up with such neurotic fears and obsessions? It is difficult to imagine the homosexual (let alone the *exclusive* homosexual) who is not obsessed with fears and driven by compulsions. Otherwise, he would not be homosexual.

However, Ellis further contends, the heterosexual who can enjoy, under *all* circumstances, only one specialized form of sexual activity, is likewise a pervert and a neurotic. The phrase, "under all circumstances," with the emphasis in the original on the word "all," covers a very wide territory. It would seem necessary, therefore, to clarify this thinking a little further. The individual who can and does choose only heterosexual activities, under the usual conditions of life in modern society, is hardly neurotic. However, what seems to be a perversion is for that individual, no doubt as a defensive action against any latent homosexual desires, to express hatred and fear of homosexuality to the point of starting a holy crusade or a lynching party.

Ellis has posed an important question and has answered it, but let no one distort this forthright reply in order to gain solace therefrom.

D. W. C.

THE INFLUENCE OF
HETEROSEXUAL CULTURE

Albert Ellis

REPRINTED FROM THE INTERNATIONAL JOURNAL OF SEXOLOGY,
NOVEMBER 1951

I have recently had a good deal of first-hand contact with several highly intelligent homosexuals in New York City, and I have had occasion to make a serious study of four recent books on homosexuality, all published by Greenberg Publishers. One of these books is a nonfictional presentation titled, *The Homosexual in America* by Donald Webster Cory, and I am sure that it will have an important influence on many of our ideas of homosexuality which are now mistakenly prevalent. The other three books are novels: *The Divided Path* by Nial Kent; *The Invisible Glass* by Loren Wahl; and *Quatrefoil* by James Barr. All four works are notable in that they have been written by authors who appear to have had intimate personal experience with homosexuality and who are as frankly sympathetic to homosexuals as it is possible for any writer to be.

While I have learned many interesting facts from my recent first-hand and literary contacts with frank defenders of homosexual attitudes and behavior, the one particularly new idea

which I have gained from these contacts is the recognition of
the enormous extent to which homosexuals in our culture are
unconsciously influenced and limited by the heterosexual
ideologies and practices of the culture in which they reside.
For while all the proponents of homosexuality with whom I
have had intercommunication in recent weeks have been quite
understandably critical of the persecutory attitudes of heterosexuals toward homosexuals, and while they consciously have
declared themselves opposed to virtually all heterosexual views
and acts toward members of the "gay" world, they have also,
most ironically, unconsciously espoused and upheld one after
another sexual philosophy which can easily be traced to the
firmly intrenched biases of heterosexual society.

Take, for example, the question of sexual promiscuity. Present-day opposition to nonmonogamous or promiscuous sex relations unquestionably stems from the ancient heterosexual
notions of virginity and chastity which, albeit in somewhat
newly modified forms, we have inherited from our ancient and
medieval forbears. One would expect that present-day homosexuals, who are presumably violently opposed to heterosexual
puritanical sanctions, would take no stock in the antipromis-
cuity creeds which are today almost ubiquitous among middle
class women of our society. But, on the contrary, I find that the
majority of frank homosexuals are, in one degree or another,
consciously or unconsciously disturbed about their own promiscuous desires or actual promiscuity. Thus, in *The Divided
Path,* two homosexuals who are openly living together seriously advise the homosexual hero against living alone because
"It's bad for you mentally and it makes for promiscuity. . . ."
And in *The Invisible Glass* and *Quatrefoil* the homosexual
protagonists are consistently revolted by the thought of their
possibly being promiscuous in their sex relations.

Take, again, the matter of romanticism in sex relations. As
I have shown in my *Folklore of Sex,* and as many other sexo-
logical writers have also pointed out, modern romantic views

of sexual behavior are frequently but toned-down, subtle presentations of the notion that sexual intercourse, in, of, by, and for itself, is a wicked and nasty business, and that therefore it must be "purified" to some extent by an overlay of highly romanticized feeling on the part of the heterosexual lovers. One would expect that homosexuals, who are hardly thought by the general public to be propuritanical, would have little use for this rather hypocritical romantic philosophy. But, on the contrary, one finds homosexual relationships frequently developing on a superromantic basis. Moreover, one finds that when such relations are thoroughly *non*romantic, then the homosexuals themselves tend to feel extremely uncomfortable about them. Thus, the hero of *The Divided Path* gives up one possible homosexual partner after another because he is obsessively-romantically attached to a man he has never even kissed. The hero of *The Invisible Glass* becomes disgusted about the unromantic, pickup aspects of a gay bar. The two homosexual protagonists of *Quatrefoil* become so romantically enamored of each other that they presumably become capable of telepathically reading each other's questions before they are asked, and they both shudder at the thought of nonromantic homosexual attachments.

A third thoroughly heterosexual attitude which homosexuals in our culture tend to take over lock, stock, and barrel is that relating to monogamic fidelity. A heterosexual woman in our society invariably becomes quite disturbed when she discovers that her husband has been sexually unfaithful to her even once. She, at least, has some good socio-economic reasons for her sexual jealousy, since she may lose a dependable provider, helpmate, and father of her children as a result of her husband's infidelity. Similarly, a wife's infidelity may result in a distinct nonsexual, as well as sexual, loss to a modern husband. Homosexuals, who do not normally have the same kind of marital ties as do heterosexuals, would not, one might suppose, be so disturbed by sexual infidelities on the part of their partners. But, actually, they frequently are. In *The Divided Path,* for example, the hero goes through the worst possible tortures when one of his boyfriends is unfaithful to him; and in *Quatrefoil,* when one of the homosexual protagonists tells his partner that he has had a single sex episode with an old buddy of his whom he will presumably not see again for a long time, the other partner strikes him violently across the eyes, and apparently knocks him unconscious.

So it consistently goes. My recent contact with frankly pro-homosexual writers and discussants has thoroughly convinced me that the average homosexual in our society is, quite unconsciously for the most part, deeply enmeshed in beliefs and actions which are unquestionably resultants of our distinctly heterosexual mores and philosophies. While he may consciously aver that he is quite opposed to heterosexual teachings, and that he feels that he is unfairly forced to follow heterosexual customs which he actually does not want to follow, the grimly ironic fact remains that he, in the depths of his unconscious thinking, does want to follow almost all the heterosexually approved patterns of sex behavior, even though he wants to broaden them to the (relatively slight) extent of their sanctioning homosexual participations. Because in the bottom of his heart, and frequently in the top of his unconsciousness as well, this average homosexual seems to want to have a romantic courtship, engagement, and "marriage;" he wants to avoid promiscuity at all costs; he wants to find a lover who will be utterly faithful to him, and to whom he will be sexually faithful himself; and he wants generally to follow the same pattern in his homosexual affairs as the typical middle-class girl and fellow in our society wish to follow in their heterosexual relationships. In many instances, curiously enough, the homosexual in our culture even has the same ambivalent attitude towards virginity as does the heterosexual; in that he would like to lose his own virginity, and yet is mortally ashamed of so doing; or he would like to take the virginity of another homosexual, and yet is fearfully guilty of so doing. And, perhaps greatest irony of all, the average homosexual in our society appears to have basically the same attitude toward fatherhood (and often, even, toward heterosexual marriage) as does the average heterosexual male. That is to say, the homosexual frequently wants to marry a suitable woman and to be a good husband to her; and, especially, he frequently wants to have children of his own, and wants to be pretty much the same kind of a father to these children as the heterosexual father would like to be.

On the whole, therefore, there seems to be little doubt that most homosexuals in our modern world are consciously or (especially) unconsciously enormously influenced by the heterosexual culture in which they are reared. While they may outwardly decry this culture, and even seem to work against it, they are actually doing their best to uphold it, and to carry almost all its (often quite irrational) traditions over to their own sex mores and ideologies. Which goes to prove, no doubt, that the modern individual's chances of thoroughly removing himself from the underlying forces of the particular culture in which he is raised are exceptionally slight indeed.

HOMOSEXUAL ATTITUDES
AND HETEROSEXUAL PREJUDICES

Donald Webster Cory

REPRINTED FROM THE INTERNATIONAL JOURNAL OF SEXOLOGY,
FEBRUARY 1952

In a recent issue of this journal, Dr. Albert Ellis calls attention to the very important phenomenon of the extremely strong influence that heterosexual prejudices, ideologies, and attitudes have had on homosexuals, particularly in America. That this observation had not previously been made is quite surprising, for actually the homosexual minority displays remarkable parallels in its position in modern culture to the minorities of ethnic, racial, and religous origin, and the latter invariably reflect the biases of the dominant groups. However, in dealing with the homosexual, and particularly with his having taken over some of the attitudes which one might have expected that he be the first to abandon, there are several facets of this problem worthy of further investigation.

First, without denying the basic contention of Ellis, one must beware of assigning too much weight to the statements of novelists, and of accepting their contentions as typical of those of homosexuals as a whole. Many (although not all) of these novelists are anxious to write about sex not only because of their knowledge, experience, and sympathy, but because they are deeply troubled by their own predilections; more troubled, perhaps, than homosexuals who never write a word of fiction. For some of the novelists, the act of writing may be necessary in order to create self-justification. Furthermore, the novelist is motivated by a missionary-like attitude; he looks upon himself as a maker of good will where before there has been so much ill will; and he therefore feels obliged to paint a picture which he believes will be acceptable even to the puritanical society. This is not so much a matter of deliberate dishonesty, but of choice of theme and manner of development, judicious omissions, and ultra-moralistic endings, all designed to give a panorama which the novelist believes (and mistakenly so, incidentally) will be favorable to the homosexual in society. A typical example of such a novelist was Radclyffe Hall (*The Well of Loneliness*). The fictional protagonists in the works of Hall and of the authors cited by Ellis show no desire for any sexual gratification except when they are in love, and then the desire is directed toward only one individual. There are long periods of abstinence, extreme sublimation, and those homosexuals in the novels who will not or cannot go along with such absurd notions are denounced by the authors as degenerates.

Now, it is true that this is a reflection of the romantic, monogamous, and antisexual concepts of the heterosexual society, but it is not true that this is a complete and accurate reflection of the attitudes of most homosexuals. The latter, like the heterosexuals (as Ellis demonstrated in *The Folklore of Sex*) frequently feel an obligation to write about sex in one way, although they behave in quite another. The attitudes assumed in the semiautobiographical novels of homosexuals are more often an indication of the disturbances of the authors, rather than of the groups they are presumably depicting.

Secondly, some prejudices that the homosexual takes over

from the dominant group in society may play a significant role in aiding the invert to make a satisfactory adjustment in our culture. Let us take, for example, the question of the monogamous romantic attachment, with its concomitant jealousy, and its deliberate self-denial of opportunities for gratification except with one preferred partner. For the heterosexual, the belief in the propriety of such modes of behavior may be rooted in the economic status of the woman as the property of the male, and the fear of pregnancy, but is it not entirely possible that the homosexual may obtain from the romantic attachment a sense of sexual security? I am convinced that man suffers from anxiety not only when he cannot obtain sexual gratification and must suppress or divert his desires, but there is an anxiety of a cumulative nature based on a fear that a satisfactory sex partner may not be available at any and all required times in the future. The homosexual who creates a dependency upon another individual obtains from such an attachment a feeling of security that he will not be left lonely and frustrated in time to come. Thus, the prejudices of the homosexual against promiscuity, and his effort to conform, may be a reflection of the cultural impact of the heterosexual society, on the one hand, but on the other may serve a specific purpose and have meaning for the homosexual under the conditions in which he lives. In a society which glorifies the physique of the young, and that sets standards of beauty that are synonymous with youth, the homosexual becomes frightened at the prospect that the ephemeral nature of his beauty will leave him unable to find satisfactory sexual partners in the future. He seeks, under these circumstances, a single partner whom he can "put in the bank," so to speak. This is, obviously enough, a vicious circle, for the monogamous concept is made necessary in modern culture by the lack of sexual opportunity for the unattached older man, and the lack of such opportunity is then utilized as a weapon to justify and strengthen the monogamous concept.

The fact that the homosexual takes over the prejudices of the heterosexual society only when some purpose is served thereby, and at other times rejects such attitudes, is illustrated negatively as well as affirmatively. Some heterosexual attitudes are so completely meaningless for the homosexual that he may even be unaware of their existence. For example, the fear of nudity and exposure, which follows American heterosexual lovers, particularly of the lower economic and educational strata, into their very boudoir, is absent among the analogous homosexual groups. In modern culture, males and females are not permitted to see each other in the nude after the age of about two or three. A little later in life, a sibling, or even a parent of the opposite sex, is kept from viewing or being viewed by the child. "Nude coitus is regularly had by only 66 per cent of those who never go beyond high school, and by 43 per cent of those who never go beyond grade school," Kinsey and his associates noted. ". . . Some of the older men and women in this group (the lower level) take pride in the fact that they have never seen their own spouses nude."

The homosexual of comparable economic and educational group, on the other hand, is almost as devoid of such a taboo in his sexual affairs as it is possible to be in this culture. He frequently believes that it is perfectly proper to carry over the prejudices against exposure, so long as they are applied to intersexual relations. But a homosexual would be considered queer by his friends if he could not undress before other men, gaze at them in the nude, expose himself before his sex partner, and frequently keep the light on during the sexual play.

Now, why is it that the homosexual, in matters pertaining to nudity, feels no impact of heterosexual cultural prejudices, although he feels such impact with indubitable strength in the instances cited by Ellis (particularly as related to promiscuity)? The answer seems to be found in the fact that such a prejudice against nudity plays no constructive role either in his relations with society (his effort to adjust and to obtain greater acceptance) or in his struggle with himself (the need for self-justification and the search for greater sexual satisfaction). Furthermore, in the particular instance I have cited, the entire background of the homosexual is generally based on an acceptance of nudity and exposure with the same sex, and he does not relate society's condemnation of nudity in the presence of the opposite sex to the taboo on viewing a desired person. In a sense, then, he takes over the anti-nudity prejudices literally, continuing to apply them only to men and women, and in so doing these prejudices lose their meaning for his own sexual life.

The basic question, however, is the homosexual's failure, on the one hand, to abide by romantic, long-lasting, faithful attachments, and on the other his deep-felt guilt that issues from such failure. In modern society, the homosexual is beset by two conflicting drives. In his search for self-acceptance, he seeks a tenacious retention of the concept of homosexuality as being completely involuntary to him. He is less anxious about being homosexual if he can be relieved of all responsibility for so being, and many homosexuals relieve themselves of such responsibility by deep condemnation of their own homosexual activities and pursuits. Such people want to feel that they are "vile" and "base" and "degenerate" because these terms of opprobrium convince them that they purge themselves of sin by hating their own homosexuality. For the purpose of carrying out such a seemingly self-condemning but actually self-approving attitude, the homosexual often seizes upon the fact that there is a constant pursuit of sexual gratification with a variety of partners as proof of the degeneracy of gay people in general and of himself in particular.

On the other hand, the homosexual is motivated by the very opposite desire, and that is to gain acceptance for himself and his group in society. He reasons (as do members of other minority groups) that to the extent that he can conform to the morals and mores of society, to that extent might he be successful in gaining acceptance within society. Therefore, instead of calling for a re-evaluation of these moral concepts, he seeks strenuously to abide by them, feels deeply frustrated by his failure to do so, and pretends, particularly in communication with the outgroup, that he is as much a conformist as anyone.

The homosexual, in conclusion, is living in an apparently heterosexual but actually an antisexual society. He is attempting to find a *modus vivendi* in a culture which not only bans homosexuality but also disapproves of all other sexual activity that is not romantic in origin and procreative in direction. In such a milieu, the adjustments of the homosexual can only be half-hearted, for his basic problems stem from the prejudices of society. In the cultural situation in which he finds himself, the homosexual discovers that many heterosexual prejudices can and do fit into his attempt to make a satisfactory adjustment, except that new disturbances are created because these prejudices run counter to his basic sexual drive.

The homosexual is thus simultaneously driven toward attempting to conform (or rather pretending to conform) on the one hand, and shaking his fist at the conformists, on the other. It becomes increasingly clear that the homosexual can only make a satisfactory adjustment when he is prepared completely to accept himself and his way of life, without regrets, misgivings, shame, or unconscious defense. Such self-acceptance will become facilitated as puritanical prejudices (other than and in addition to the taboo on homosexuality) are rejected by all groups in society.

The impact of heterosexual culture on the homosexual is not to be disputed as an established fact. The acceptance of the prejudices of such a culture offers temporary advantages to the homosexual who is already in sharp conflict with the society around him, but at the same time compounds his difficulties and retards total self-acceptance.

[EDITOR'S NOTES]

Both this and the previous paper appeared in The Interna‧tional Journal of Sexology, and together they investigate an aspect of homosexuality hitherto largely overlooked: namely; the attitudes of homosexuals toward love in sex experience, monogamy, and other phases of sexual life. While Ellis pointed out that many of the prejudices harbored by heterosexuals were taken over, lock, stock and barrel, by homosexuals, I responded by pointing out that Ellis had based his thinking to a great extent on a few novels depicting homosexual life in America. These novels were, of course, not accurate reflections of life as it really is.

Nevertheless, the fact that the novelist finds a need to depict a highly romanticized, monogamic love relationship which he knows to be atypical and distorted is itself a sign that he has taken over the prejudices of heterosexual society in theory, and is all the more guilt-ridden over his failure to be able to put such prejudices into practice.

I state that the homosexual "compounds his difficulties and retards total self-acceptance" when he takes over the prejudices of a heterosexual culture. However, such prejudices in many instances are inextricably bound with the etiology of exclusive and compulsive homosexuality. This would seem to be the next step in the investigation of this subject.

D. W. C.

CHANGING ATTITUDES
TOWARD HOMOSEXUALS

Donald Webster Cory

AN ADDRESS DELIVERED TO THE INTERNATIONAL COMMITTEE FOR
SEX EQUALITY AT THE UNIVERSITY OF FRANKFORT, SEPTEMBER 1952

The United States of America today occupies a position unique
in Western culture. As a result of the decline of the British
Empire, the rise in influence of the Soviet Union in Eastern
Europe and in Asia, and the resultant division of the world
into two great and perhaps mutually antagonistic forces, the
United States, with its vast reservoirs of raw materials, its in-
dustrial efficiency and wealth, has emerged in international
affairs in a position of influence and affluence such as has been
centered in no single nation since the decline of the Holy
Roman Empire. In every field of human endeavor, the peoples
of the free world are watching America, hopeful that out of
this land will come new vistas of progress, yet skeptical of the
meaning of American democracy and culture in terms of
human values. Thus, despite the very slow and halting steps
forward that emerge from this land, such progress is watched
with greater interest outside the borders of the forty-eight
states than are similar developments in other countries. The

changes now taking place in American attitudes toward sex, as in other fields, therefore have significance far greater than would be apparent if such changes were to be found in another land, be it France or India or England or the Dominican Republic. Yet the new outlook, simultaneously revolutionary and evolutionary as it paradoxically must be, is formulated in an atmosphere so devoid of the free interchange of thought (the very essence of that highly publicized American democracy) that, outside of a professional few, people are for the most part unaware of what is occurring.

More than any other power, the United States was founded on traditions of Puritanism. The concept of sex as a necessary evil, an ugly pursuit, enjoyed by man because of the devil incarnate in the flesh, was taught by the early cultural leaders of this country. The varying and diverse elements that made up the American melting pot vied with one another to appear before the masses as pure and good, one group not to be outdone by another in the antisexual repudiation of physical desire. Thus the struggle of the Protestant Puritans to maintain a rigid and self-avowedly virtuous ban on all things sexual was strengthened by the several minorities that found conformance the road to acceptance and possibly integration into American life: the immigrants so anxious to abandon their European culture which was to them a stigma; the Jews, who found in their Talmudic codes a reinforcement of sexual repudiation; the Negroes, freed from slavery and desirous of appearing "good" and "moral" and "pure" in the sense that these words were being used and misused; and the Catholics who succeeded in wresting the leadership from the Puritan Protestants in the anti-sexual culture.

It was in this milieu that sex became the unmentionable subject in nineteenth century America. Birth control information dared not be disseminated through the mails; and the education of young people in things sexual consisted in the main of long sermons by ignorant hypocrites who warned that masturbation would lead to insanity.

A revolutionary change has taken place in America during the decades since the Frst World War. American thinking has begun to catch up with American practice. The activities which were indulged in so frequently by men and women, never admitted, always frowned upon, seldom discussed or written about, now became topics of open conversation. No longer did people suffer great shock when they learned the elementary facts of life.

Thus, the changing social scene made it possible for leadership to arise that would provide the scientific data, in psychological and sociological areas, to substantiate the amorphous ideas begining to formulate in the minds of the people, and at the same time such leadership could capture the imagination of large segments of the population. For America has been a land where the masses move slowly, seldom more than passingly alert to an issue, and always seeking to designate the responsibility in the hands of a hero, a movement, a leader. As Gunnar Myrdal reported:

> The idea of leadership pervades American thought and collective action. The demand for "intelligent leadership" is raised in all political camps, social and professional groups, and, indeed, in every collective activity centered around any interest or purpose . . . If an ordinary American faces a situation which he recognizes as a "problem" without having any specific views as to how to "solve" it, he tends to resort to two general recommendations: one, traditionally, is "education;" the other is "leadership." The demand for leadership . . . is a result less of a conscious ideological principle than a pragmatic approach to those activities which require the cooperation of many individuals.

Until a few years ago, this need for leadership, so acutely felt by all those striving to break through the morass of misinformation, hypocrisy, and censorship, was left unanswered.

Then the report of Kinsey and his associates was published. This book, bombshell that it was in the complacent scene of puritanical hypocrisy, denounced as it was from all sides, could never have found the light of a printed page in America some two or three decades earlier. Professor Kinsey, still looked on with some skepticism by die-hards who are more intent on retaining preconceived ideologies than on verifying their scientific validity, nevertheless became an acknowledged leader overnight in an area of American thinking. Yet, to understand the full significance of the American scene, let it be emphasized that this scientist would have been stoned and lynched had his findings been proclaimed in the nineteenth century. Thus, the Kinsey report is in the first instance a manifestation, a proof, of the change that was taking place in this country, although more than that, it facilitated and expedited this changing process. It is therefore one—perhaps the most dramatic, certainly the best known—of many dynamic occurrences, which are made possible by the very events that they, in turn make more possible.

It is against this background that the status of the homosexual in America must be studied. It is today generally recognized that the homosexuals constitute a sociological minority, a factor most important in America, a land in which the minority problem, particularly as concerning the rights and the integration of ethnic groups, has admittedly become the most important domestic situation facing this country. The mutual antagonisms between the various ethnic groups have produced several phenomena that must be noted:

1: The intellectual and cultural leadership of this country has almost unanimously endorsed the ultimate aims and the immediate struggles of the ethnic minorities. As a result, novelists, journalists, statesmen, church and lay leaders today proclaim the principles of brotherhood, espouse a philosophy, based on the recognition of the rights of man, state that all men are brothers and that minorities must be given equal rights in all walks of life. Although many of these leaders would be the first to denounce the homosexual, to deny that they favor rights for this maligned group, their propaganda, to the extent that it has any impact at all on American thinking, is one which coincides with the aspirations of all minorities, not excluding the sexual.

2: However, a great gap exists between American leadership and the American people on the ethnic minority problems. The great mass of American people, not only in the South, but even in the North, certainly do not practice equality with Negroes, and continue to a large extent to practice antiSemitism in their social and economic affairs. This cultural gap results from the lesser influence of tradition, superstition, and outworn ideology on the thinking of the more intelligent, the more educated, and the more enlightened. It is a gap that will in due time be closed by the process of education and enlightenment that is in the hands of the leadership, but most important of all, it is a gap which, I maintain, I can already find in existence so far as the homosexual minority is concerned.

3: The segmentation of the populace into mutually antagonistic ethnic groups causes certain divisive influences within the homosexual minority. First, some homosexuals (although the proportion is smaller than among heterosexuals) reflect the antagonistic attitudes toward some ethnic groups, and hence a unified minority is difficult to fuse. Secondly, some members of the Jewish-homosexual and the Negro-homosexual double minorities fear to conduct a struggle on behalf of their sex group because it might, they reason, vitiate their struggle on behalf of their ethnic group. The latter is usually considered by these people to be their first loyalty, their original and their lasting group identification. They are furthermore unconvinced of the propriety of the struggle for sexual rights on the same level and with the same righteous vigor as the struggle for ethnic rights.

4: Nevertheless, most homosexuals do participate in a greater amount of interethnic mingling than do heterosexuals, and this, too, is a double-edged sword. On the one hand, it aids the unity within the homosexual group, but it creates an antagonistic attitude toward homosexuals on the part of many individuals who, still under reactionary influences so far as minorities are concerned, look upon the Negro-white alliances as further proof, not of liberalism and emancipation, but of degeneracy.

The current status of the American homosexual is character-ized by the following main phenomena: 1. increasing aware-ness of the existence of the group, and of the widespread adher-ence to its practices, on the part of the large masses of people; 2. increasing expressions of support of and sympathy for the group by leadership in psychological, sociological, and other areas of American thought; 3. tendency to accept the existence of the group as an unfortunate necessity, a problem that can-not be erased, but a continued unwillingness to accept the individual members who become adherents of it or identified with it; 4. tolerance toward certain group activities so long as they remain anonymous and hide behind a facade of respect-ability, no matter how thin the veil; 5. a tendency within the group to feel that (a) this status is not unbearable, (b) a better one is not deserved, and (c) the struggle for change may bring down the wrath from law-makers and other authorities.

These are characteristics that differ considerably from the situation that prevailed some thirty or forty years back. At that time, the manifestations of homosexuality were carefully hidden, the word unspoken and unknown save in medical circles, the members of the group concealing their activities in the most complete and utter fear. The problem could not be mentioned in newspapers or magazines, and many educated people lived for decades without any awareness of it. His-torians of the American scene have even been deluded into believing that the complete cloak of silence existed because there was no homosexuality at the time, and they denounce those who interpret in this manner the writings of Herman Melville, Walt Whitman, and Henry James, as being inconsistent with the prevailing puritanical codes of nineteenth century America.

This change that has taken place is not so much one of greater acceptance of the homosexual on the part of American society, but rather an acknowledgment of the existence of the minority and of the problem involved therein. Once "homosexual" was the most unmentionable, the most unprintable, of any word, except for the so-called obscenities, in the English language. Today it is mentioned and printed everywhere, but, to use the expression of Menninger, it is today the "most electric" word in our language. From silence to discussion, even without enlightenment, is progress, for enlightenment becomes inevitable through discussion, and impossible without it.

Within the most advanced cultural circles, it is today rare to find outright condemnation of homosexual activities. Whether one looks to Kinsey, who reaches an audience far wider than any other leader in sex thinking in the history of America (and possibly in world history, save for Freud), or whether one looks to psychiatrists, church leaders, and others, it is today not at all uncommon to find the homosexual defended by men of the highest intellectual integrity.

For example, on the question of arrests, Kinsey recently spoke before the National Probation and Parole Association, and stated that there are cities in the United States where more than half of the alleged sex offenses are initiated by police intent on obtaining blackmail. Furthermore, he said "there are cities in which there is no greater blackmail racket than that operated by police against homosexuals." This statement received wide publicity in the newspapers, and it is a statement that is of utmost importance because it is characteristic of a new thinking and a new approach: namely, the homosexual is no longer a pariah without his intellectual defender. Permit me to cite a few other examples. Dr. Robert W. Laidlaw, speaking before the Section on Marriage and Family Counseling of the National Council on Family Relations, stated: *"It happens that I act as psychiatric consultant in a theological seminary, where one finds a very high type of individual—particularly in the music school—who is beset by homosexual conflicts. . . . A few months ago, in a seminar with the faculty of this seminary, we had quite a discussion in regard to whether homosexuality, per se, should disqualify a man from the ministry. I steadfastly upheld the platform that it should not."*

Those who are unable to find a change in American attitudes should ask themselves whether a psychiatrist could have taken this position twenty or thirty years earlier, and whether he could have defended it at a public gathering without eliciting a single word of disagreement.

Finally, in psychiatric and psychological circles, it is becoming increasingly apparent that, despite the emphasis of these professionals on the disturbances of homosexuals, many of the difficulties can be overcome by a correction of the attitude of society. In his brilliant book, *The Folklore of Sex,* Dr. Albert Ellis writes:

The banning of certain sex outlets—e.g., homosexuality— which would be, under normal circumstances, merely peculiar and idiosyncratic modes of behavior serves to make the users of these outlets neurotic—and to make neurotics use these outlets. In this sense, sex "perversion" does not render society sick, but society makes sick people out of "perverts"—and induces individuals to use "perversion" as neurotic symptoms.

This concept, that the ills of society may be the cause of the difficulties of the homosexual, rather than the effect, was expressed by the eminent physician, Dr. Harry Benjamin, in the *American Journal of Psychotherapy,* as follows: *"If adjustment is necessary, it should be made primarily with regard to*

*the position the homosexual occupies in present day society
and society should more often be treated than the invert."*

But if society is sick, what is to be done about it? And if the
homosexual's disturbance is, at least partially, the result of the
hostility of society, how can he be helped?

First, not all homosexuals think that something should be
done, although most are somewhat dissatisfied with the current
situation. There are some people in the group who, recognizing the status quo as being less hostile, more possible to live
with, than one might have expected, fear the consequences of
a struggle, and fear public reaction to a fast-moving change.
They believe that any effort to broaden the rights of these
people would bring forth the wrath of the police and reaction
in public attitudes, and they contend that the current situation is as liberal as the present American culture might permit.
These same people, therefore, go a step further and justify
some of the hostility toward the group, claiming that the
homosexuals themselves, because of promiscuity, instability,
exhibitionism, violence, and other alleged factors, are unworthy of better treatment and responsible for their own
status. That the attitude briefly summarized here has its psychological foundations in the guilt of the individuals, and is
a defensive justification of hostility which they require for
self-condemnation, are too apparent to require elucidation.

Under these circumstances, a few people who believe mili-
tantly in the necessity of struggle have become demoralized.
The situation, they state, is hopeless. Hostility prevents the
emergence of the forces that are necessary to educate the public and the gay group, but without such forces hostility will
continue its indefinite reign. Such pessimistic nihilism is not
infrequently encountered.

Nevertheless, with the diminished hostility in the most advanced circles of American public opinion, with the open
espousal of the rights of homosexuals by many leaders who
have access to America's eyes and ears, with the increasing

attention given to the problem by many of the most prominent and talented writers, a new dynamic process is set in motion that will counteract the vicious circle of do-nothingism that has hitherto strangled the possibilities for effective homosexual action.

The gap that exists between important American thinkers, on the one hand, and large numbers of men and women, on the other, is a sociological phenomenon that cannot remain stagnant. The writers, philosophers, lecturers, jurists, even though they may reach but a few people with their message, impress their thought on teachers, preachers, journalists, and others, whose new outlook, once it has been formulated, is made known to many others. This is a long, a drawn-out, and often a discouraging process, with the difficulties multiplied many times by prejudices and fears, but eventually the masses do catch up to their teachers, and then the lawmakers, politicians, rabble-rousers, begin to reflect this new attitude of the people, no longer finding it profitable to exploit a waning prejudice.

The struggle for social betterment is furthermore impeded by the secondary interest taken therein by the heterosexuals who have spoken out for improvement in status (as Kinsey, Ellis, Benjamin, and others), and by the fear surrounding the homosexuals who might be expected to have the motivation and incentive to give leadership to a more militant movement.

It is unrealistic to expect to find, within the group of sociologists, psychologists, and others, those people who are themselves heterosexual and yet are anxious to devote themselves to a cause with the perseverance, the fervor, the willingness to withstand calumny, that are required if any success is to be attained. These people, in the first instance, have certain reservations, not of a moral but of a psychological nature, and in the second place they are involved only intellectually, not emotionally.

So that the leadership would have to fall on those most

vitally concerned, but a complete anonymity surrounds the individual members of this enormous group. Particularly those most capable of offering leadership, the college professors and university officials, the many authors, philosophers, journalists; the popular heroes in the sports and entertainment world, the prize fighters and baseball players and movie actors; the sociologists already engaged in a struggle for ethnic minority rights—these people have a vested interest in retaining their anonymity. What chance would a politician have, not only for election, but even for appointment to a position for which he was eminently qualified, if he should openly proclaim himself as part of a great movement to struggle for the rights of the homosexuals?

Without leadership, where can a movement originate and how can it gather strength? How can public attitudes be changed if those most capable of facilitating such a change have an interest in remaining silent, on the one hand, or, on the other, can devote themselves to this situation only as a secondary pursuit?

It would seem, on the face of it, that we have here an insolvable contradiction. There can be no change without guidance from the more advanced, and no individuals offering such guidance dare to come forth unless a change is first effected to make it possible to function without martyrdom to oneself and one's immediate associates. As a matter of fact, the situation is even more complex, because any homosexuals who might conceivably acknowledge their drives in order to head a struggle would find themselves cut off from larger numbers of their own followers, who could not afford association with one who had dropped the mask of concealment.

And, after all, what could such a leadership do, if it should arise, and if it were possible to conduct a struggle? It would have little access to the popular books and magazines, and through the channels of newspapers and occasionally even on the radio, to speak up in defense of the victimized deviant. It could not formulate an ethic that would reflect the developed thinking of many intelligent men and women, because there is no medium for the argument and exchange of opinion so necessary in the evolution of a group ideology. Yet, without such a development, a leadership can only reflect its own narrow outlook, which may be far removed from that of the people who are ostensibly the followers. Thus, on such fundamental issues as to whether the movement for recognition should be one of militant protest or quiet accommodation; whether it should be one of struggle to effect changes in the laws or to educate the group to abide by certain laws; whether it should be one of teaching the public to accept the concept of variety in sexual expression or of teaching the group to accept the concept of monogamous fidelity to a single loser; whether the orientation should be to look inward toward an inner group minority and an almost segregated life or toward integration as human beings with those of all temperaments— on all of these questions the leadership could not develop an outlook that would reflect the viewpoint of those millions of Americans who are partisans of this minority.

Nevertheless, a leadership is arising in the sense that hostility is being replaced by friendship, understanding, and sympathy. As the intellectual basis for this new attitude finds expression there is simultaneously a questioning of long-accepted values on the part of heterosexuals and a reduction of the guilt and fear within the homosexual group. As the fright at the specter of self-expression is lessened, the homosexual finds it possible to give a certain limited leadership to the protest, and this very small, frequently anonymous struggle can continue to spread a word of enlightenment, both to other homosexuals, and to heterosexuals, thus setting in motion a new cycle. As the shame is diminished with the increasing acceptance, both by oneself and one's associates, the righteousness of the cause of protest is impressed upon the minds of many homosexuals, and in fact the guilt of being homosexual is replaced by the guilt of not defending one's cause.

This is a new situation, and in recent years it has already begun to manifest itself and to produce some small results. The law in some states has been relaxed, and in others many people have called for a change. Lecture groups of gay people have been initiated in several cities; private clubs and veterans' organizations have been formed; a social-work group, having the open cooperation of numerous ministers, psychiatrists, and other professional men, has been incorporated is now functioning to help those who run afoul of the law or who have other difficulties; a correspondence society is in existence; and in Los Angeles, where police terror is particularly outrageous, a group is functioning openly to raise funds and to conduct a public campaign against entrapment and police brutality.

The next steps forward are not easy to predict. The publishing program, both of fiction and non-fiction, can be better controlled, so that there is a wider influence of the group upon the thinking of those who become spokesmen. A magazine, perhaps quite unlike those published in Europe, may be able to be established in the United States, concentrating on literary and other cultural aspects of the group problem, or perhaps not devoted exclusively to this one group. Efforts must be made to enlist friends among the medical, psychological, legal and other professions to conduct a campaign more vigorous than heretofore in defense of the group and of its individual members. Church leaders can be particularly effective in making representations against newspapers and magazines in protest against their one-sided hostility. An educational program to convince the homosexuals themselves of the propriety of their activities is urgently needed.

These are but meager beginnings. Each of these is amorphous, all of them disconnected, many functioning at cross-purposes to the others. But let us not fail to see the enormous importance of the beginnings. For these are the beginnings of the groups, the movements, the activities, and the struggles that make possible the next step forward, that will spread the friendly word of truth both within and without the group, and this in turn will make it both necessary and possible for more such movements, and stronger ones, to arise, and for the influence to spread far and wide. With the greater influence, it will become less difficult for such activities to take place, and with the increased activity, the influence spreads to new circles with new messages. This is a new cycle and a dynamic one, whose aim and goal of sex equality are not beyond human reach.

[EDITOR'S NOTES]

This article was originally delivered as an address at the International Committee for Sex Equality at Frankfort in September 1952. While, in retrospect, I feel that I properly pointed out those factors influencing a change in the attitude of society and the public toward homosexuality, I did not view this as a dynamic process interrelated with the behavioral attitudes of the homosexuals themselves. One cannot divorce social attitudes from behavior patterns. Today I consider it curious that although I have often striven to be objective within an avowedly subjective approach, I should have overlooked this aspect of the problem.

D. W. C.